A GRAMMAR AND DICTIONARY OF THE LUSHAI LANGUAGE

(DULIEN DIALECT)

BY

J. HERBERT LORRAIN AND FRED. W. SAVIDGE,

PIONEER MISSIONARIES TO THE LUSHAIS, OF THE ARTHINGTON ABORIGINES MISSION.

GYAN

Published by

GYAN

Gyan Publishing House
5, Ansari Road
Daryaganj, New Delhi-110002
Phone: 011-47034999, 9811692060
E-mail: books@gyanbooks.com

Distribution Network
gyanbooks.com
India, USA, Canada, UK, Australia, France

ISBN : 978-81-212-0633-4 (HB)
First Published, 1898

2nd Impression 2021

Printed at: Gyan Press, Delhi.

A Grammar and Dictionary of the Lushai Language
Author: J. Herbert Lorrain and Fred. W. Savidge

A GRAMMAR AND DICTIONARY OF THE LUSHAI LANGUAGE (DULIEN DIALECT).

BY

J. HERBERT LORRAIN AND FRED. W. SAVIDGE,

PIONEER MISSIONARIES TO THE LUSHAIS, OF THE ARTHINGTON ABORIGINES MISSION.

Published by Authority.

SHILLONG:

PRINTED AT THE ASSAM SECRETARIAT PRINTING OFFICE.

1898.

CONTENTS.

A

GRAMMAR AND DICTIONARY

OF THE

LUSHAI LANGUAGE.

PART I.—GRAMMAR.

LUSHAI ALPHABET AND PRONUNCIATION.

The Lushai alphabet consists of the following letters:

Alphabet.		Pronunciation.
A	*a*	like *u* in the English word *sun*.
**Â*	*â*	like *a* in the English word *father*.
Aw	*aw*	like *aw* in the English word *awl*.
B	*b*	as in English.
Ch	*ch*	like *ch* in the English word *chop*.
D	*d*	as in English.
E	*e*	like *e* in the English word *tell*.
**Ê*	*ê*	like the first *e* in the English word *there*.
F	*f*	as in English.
G	*g*	used as an initial letter only in foreign words, when it is pronounced like the *g* in the English word *gun*. In Lushai words it is always preceded by *n*, then *ng* is pronounced like the *ng* in the English word *sing*. *Ng* is often used at the beginning of a word in Lushai.
H	*h*	like *h* in the English word *home*. When *h* is placed at the end of a syllable or word, it denotes that the preceding vowel sound must be abruptly shortened.
I	*i*	like *i* in the English word *sit*.
**Î*	*î*	like *i* in the English word *police*.

* The final vowels of words and syllables being generally long, they are not as a rule accented.

Alphabet.		Pronunciation.
J	*j*	as in English (used only in foreign words).
K	*k*	as in English.
L	*l*	
M	*m*	
N	*n*	
O	*o*	like *o* in the English word *pot.*
**Ô*	*ô*	like *o* in the English word *dome.*
P	*p*	as in English.
R	*r*	like *r* in the English word *rock* (this letter is never mute).
S	*s*	as in English.
T	*t*	pronounced with the tip of the tongue touching the teeth.
Ṭ	*ṭ*	pronounced with the tongue against the bars of the roof of the mouth.
U	*u*	like *u* in the English word *full.*
**Û*	*û*	like *u* in the English word *rule.*
V	*v*	as in English.
Z	*z*	sometimes as in English, and sometimes like the *s* in the English word *pleasure.*

NOTE.—When *ch, k, p, s, t* or *ṭ* are combined with *h* they are pronounced as follow:

chh like *ch* in the English word *church,* but distinctly aspirated.
kh like *kh* in the English word *blockhead.*
ph like *ph* in the English word *uphill.*
th like *th* in the English word *neatherd.*
ṭh like *th* in the English words *fat hen.*

There must, however, be no hiatus between the *k* and *h*, *p* and *h*, *t* and *h*, as in the English words, but both must be pronounced with one breath.

sh like *sh* in the English word *ship.* *Sh* and *s* are often interchangeable.

When the liquids *l, m, n, r* are aspirated they are *preceded* by the letter *h.* When the initial *ng* is aspirated it is *followed* by *h.* As *nghet* = firm.

The numbers are represented by the same figures as in English.

NOTE.—The occurrence of an apostrophe indicates that a consonant has been omitted and it often abruptly shortens the preceding vowel.

NOUNS.

Nouns are declined as follows:

Singular.

Nom:	*Naopang, naopang-in* †	A boy.
Voc:	*Naopang*	O! boy.
Poss:	*Naopang, naopang-a*	A boy's.
Obj:	*Naopang*	A boy.

* The final vowels of words and syllables being gererally long, they are not as a rule accented.

† *See* page 4.

Plural.

Nom:	*Naopang-te, naopang-te-in** ...			...	Boys.
Voc:	*Naopang-te-u*	...	...	...	O! boys.
Poss:	*Naopang-te*	...	...	...	Boys'.
Obj:	*Naopang-te*	...	...	...	Boys.

GENDER.

There are three Genders, *viz.*, masculine, feminine and neuter.

(1) Masculine and feminine are sometimes distinguished by different words, as—

nula, a maid; *tlangvâl*, a youth.

(2) By affixing *pa* for the masculine and *nu* for the feminine to the general word, as—

boih, a slave: *boih-pa*, a male slave; *boih-nu*, a female slave.

(3) In the case of full grown animals *chal* is sometimes used instead of *pa* for the masculine, and *pui* is always used for the feminine, as—

kêl, a goat; *kêl-chal*, a he-goat; *kêl-pui*, a she-goat.

(4) Some words are the same in both the masculine and feminine, as—

u, elder brother or sister.
nao, younger brother or sister.

(5) Proper names of the masculine gender end in *a*, those of the feminine gender in *i*, as—

Nêla, Suaka, Liansailova, Vêli, Lalrûmi, Tungi.

(6) The names of animals unless distinguished by a masculine or feminine prefix, and all inanimate objects, are of the neuter gender.

NUMBER.

There are two numbers, *viz.*, singular and plural.

(1) The plural of nouns is formed by affixing one of the following terminations to the singular:

te	...	...	*te-ho.*
ho	...	...	*zong zong.*
ho-te	...	...	*zong-zong-te.*

as—

thing, a tree; *thing-te*, trees.
ârshi, a star; *ârshi hote*, stars.
ramhuai, an evil spirit; *ramhuai ho*, evil spirits.

* See page 4.

hmeichhia, a woman; *hmeichhia te-ho*, women.
mi, a man; *mi zong zong*, men.

NOTE.—Sometimes when the above are used with *postpositions* the postposition precedes the plural affix, as—

Ārshi hnuai-ho-a te, under the stars.
Thing phêna te, behind the trees.

(2) Nouns are not inflected for the plural number when they are qualified by adjectives denoting plurality, as—

mi, a man; *mi anzain*, all men.
in, a house; *in pathum*, three houses.
puan, a cloth; *puan tam tak*, many cloths.

(3) The Lushais very frequently do not distinguish between the singular and the plural, and then the number of the noun can only be determined either by the number of the pronominal particle used with the verb (*see* page 18), or from the context.

Examples—

Ka farnu an dam lo. My sisters are not well.

In this example the plural particle *an* indicates that *farnu* must be plural.

Keimani lu a na. Our heads ache.

Here the pronominal particle *a* does not determine the number of *lu*, because it may be either singular or plural (*see* note, page 18), but *keimani*, 'our', being plural, *lu* must necessarily be so too.

Lung om lo. There are no stones.

The number in such a sentence as this can only be known from something said previously. It might equally mean, 'there is not a stone.'

CASE.

There are four cases, *viz.*, Nominative, Vocative, Objective, and Possessive.

Nominative Case.

When the subject of a sentence is followed by a transitive verb in the active voice it usually takes the termination *in* to distinguish it from the object. In other instances it generally remains unchanged. Frequently for the sake of euphony the termination *in* becomes *vin*, or is contracted into *'n*.

Examples—

Hmeichhia-in naopang a vêl. The woman beat the child.
Sâp-in 'lo-haw roh' a ti. The sahib says 'come'.
Ka pa'n tangka a ru. My father stole the money.
Lal ho-vin chaw an ei. The chiefs are eating rice.

NOTE.—When an intransitive verb comes between the subject and the transitive verb the affix *in* is generally omitted, as—

Lal ho an lo kal u, chaw an ei, the chiefs came and are eating rice.

Vocative Case.

The vocative singular is the same in form as the nominative. The vocative plural is formed by adding *u* to the nominative plural.

Examples—

Noapang, khoiange i kal?	Boy, where have you been?
Mi-khual-te-u engnge in duh?	Oh! strangers, what do you want?

The vocative case of proper names is usually formed by dropping the final *a* in the masculine and the final *i* in the feminine, as—

Nom: *Thangphunga*; Voc: *Thangphung.*
Nom: *Liankungi*; Voc: *Liankung.*

Names which are too short to admit of this elision retain nominative termination, as—

Nom: *Khûma*; Voc: *Khûma.*
Nom: *Tungi*; Voc: *Tungi.*

Sometimes the noun in the vocative case is used as if it were the name of the person addressed, and takes the termination *a* for the masculine and *i* for the feminine, as—

Nom: *ṭhian*, a friend; Voc: { *ṭhiana*, O! friend, masc. / *ṭhiani*, O! friend, fem. }

Objective Case.

This case has no inflection. The noun in the objective case is generally placed immediately before the transitive verb which governs it.

Examples—

I nao, chi lei-tûr-in Sairang-a a kal.	Your younger brother has gone to Sairang to buy salt.
Mu-in âr a man dawn.	The hawk is about to seize the fowl.

The indirect object is usually placed before the direct object. It has no inflection and is frequently followed by the postposition *hnêna*, 'to,' as—

I u sebawng ka pe ang.	I will give a cow to your elder brother.
He zawhtê hi hmeichhia naopang hnêna pe roh.	Give this cat to the girl.

Possessive Case.

The noun denoting the possessor is generally placed immediately before the noun denoting the thing possessed, and is used adjectively without any inflexion, as—

Suaka in a lian e,	Suaka's house is large.
Naopang kor i la em?	Have you taken the boy's coat.

Occasionally the possessive case is formed by affixing *a* to the nominative, as—

Ka farnu-a puan a moi êm êm.	My sister's cloth is very pretty.
Aisawl-a mi heta an om lo.	The men of Aijal are not here.

When the noun denoting the possessor is of the feminine gender *i* is sometimes substituted for the affix *a*, as—

Ka farnu-i puan a moi êm êm.	My sister's cloth is very pretty.

When the noun signifying the thing possessed is understood, the possessor takes the affix *ta*, as—

Saw kor saw i pu-ta ani.	That coat is your grandfather's.
He kêl hi tu-ta nge? An nu-ta.	Whose goat is this? Their mother's.

ADJECTIVES.

Adjectives are placed after the words they qualify, as—

Mi ṭha.	A good man.
In hlui.	An old house.

When an adjective is used to complete the predicate of a sentence, a pronominal particle (*see* page 18) agreeing with the subject is placed before the adjective.

Examples—

Mi a ṭha e.	The man is good (lit., The man he is good).
Lal zong zong an ṭha e.	The chiefs are good (lit., The chiefs they are good).

When a noun is used as an adjective, it *precedes* the noun it qualifies, as—

Lung in.	A stone house.
Thîr no.	An iron cup.
Mao dawh-kân.	A bamboo table.

COMPARISON OF ADJECTIVES.

Comparative Degree.

This is formed by adding the adverb *zawk*, 'more,' to the positive and inserting the conjunction *aiin, aiia* or *hnêk-in*, 'than,' after the object of comparison.

Examples—

Fapa fanu aiin a shang sawk.	The son is taller than the daughter.
Thîr hnêk-in shuan a rit sawk.	Lead is heavier than iron.

Zawk is sometimes omitted.

When *aiin*, etc., are used with the demonstrative adjectives (*see* page 10), they are combined, thus,—

He hi aiin	becomes	*he ai hian.*
Saw saw aiin	"	*saw ai sawn.*
Kha kha aiin	"	*kha ai khân.*
Khu khu aiin	"	*khu ai khuan.*
Khi khi aiin	"	*khi ai khian.*
Chu chu aiin	"	*chu ai chuan.*

The same changes take place in the plural forms of the demonstrative adjectives:

He hi aia, etc.,	becomes	*he ai hian*, etc.
He hi hnêk-in, etc.,	"	*he hnêk hian*, etc.

Examples—

Saw ai sawn hei hi a ṭha sawk.	This is better than that.
Khi hmeichhia ai khian kha nula kha a shâng e.	That maiden near you is taller than that woman up there.

When the object of comparison is not mentioned, *aiin*, etc., are not used, as—

Nangma fapa a shâng sawk.	Your son is taller.

SUPERLATIVE DEGREE.

This is formed by adding the adverb *ber*, 'most,' to the positive and inserting *aiin*, 'than,' *sînga*, 'among,' or *a*, 'of,' after the object of comparison, as—

He mi hi mi zong zong aiin a ṭha ber.	This man is the best man of all.
Sap-te sînga nang i tê ber.	You are the smallest of the sahibs.
Kha kha, lekha-bu a a ṭha ber.	That near you is the best book.

Ber may sometimes be omitted.

When the object of comparison is not mentioned *aiin*, etc., are not used, as—

He mi hi a ṭha ber.	This man is the best.

NUMERALS.

CARDINAL NUMBERS.

They are as follow:

1, *pa-khat.*	11, *shom leh* pa-khat.*
2, *pa-hnih.*	12, *shom leh pa-hnih.*
3, *pa-thum*	13, *shom leh pa-thum.*
4, *pa-li.*	14, *shom leh pa-li.*
5, *pa-nga.*	15, *shom leh pa-nga.*
6, *pa-ruk.*	16, *shom leh pa-ruk.*
7, *pa-sari.*	17, *shom leh pa-sari.*
8, *pa-riat.*	18, *shom leh pa-riat.*
9, *pa-kua.*	19, *shom leh pa-kua.*
10, *shom.*	

* *leh* = and.

The cardinals, 20, 30, 40, 50, 60, 70, 80, and 90 are formed by adding to *shom* the units *pa-hnih*, *pa-thum*, etc., without their common prefix, *pa*, as—

20, *shom-hnih.*	60, *shom-ruk.*
30, *shom-thum.*	70, *shom-sari.*
40, *shom-li.*	80, *shom-riat.*
50, *shom-nga.*	90, *shom-kua.*

The cardinals 21, 22, etc., 31, 32, etc., are formed by adding *pakhat*, *pahnih*, etc., to *shomhnih*, *shomthum*, etc., and inserting the conjunction *leh*, 'and,' as—

21, *shomhnih leh pakhat.*	100, *za.*
32, *shomthum leh pahnih.*	1,000, *shang.*
43, *shomli leh pathum.*	10,000, *shing.*
54, *shomnga leh pali.*	100,000, *nuai.*

Hundreds, thousands, etc., are formed in the same manner as the multiples of ten, as—

700, *za-sari.*	20,000, *shing hnih.*
6,000, *shang ruk.*	500,000, *nuai nga.*

Leh, 'and,' is also inserted between the thousands, hundreds and tens, as:—

725, *za-sari leh shomhnih leh panga.*
1898, *shang leh za-riat leh shomkua leh pasari.*

When the cardinals from 1 to 9 are used to qualify nouns, the prefix *pa* is often omitted, as—

In nga, five houses.
Ni sari, seven days.

NOTE.—The prefix is generally retained when human beings are spoken of, as—

Mi paruk, six men.
Nula pakua, nine maidens.

When any numeral above ten qualifies a noun, the noun is sometimes repeated after each recurrence of the conjunction *leh*, and the prefix *pa* of the numeral is omitted. With words of two or more syllables this rule does not generally apply.

Examples—

Cheng shom leh cheng kua, 19 rupees.
Mihring za leh shomnga, 150 men.

ORDINAL NUMBERS.

These are formed by affixing *na* to the cardinal numbers, as—

A ni thum-na a thi.	He died on the third day.
Lekha-bu a panga-na la roh.	Bring the fifth book.
A pa thum-na ka duh.	I want the third one.
Thing pakua-na bul a va ding roh.	Go and stand at the foot of the ninth tree.

In speaking of the order of *time* the ordinal numbers may also be expressed by repeating the noun after the cardinal, as—

Ni thum ni.	The third day.
Zân nga zân a ka lo-thleng ang.	I shall arrive on the fifth night.

'Every other day' is expressed by *ni khat dan-a*,
'Every third day' " " *ni hnih dan-a*,
'Every fourth day' " " *ni thum dan-a*,
and so on.

DISTRIBUTIVES.

These are formed (1) by adding *hlîr-in*, *theoh-vin* or *zêl-in* to the cardinal; (2) by doubling the cardinal and adding one of the above affixes; (3) by repeating the cardinal without its prefix *pa* and affixing *in*, as—

Pahnih hlîr-in,
Pahnih pahnih zêl-in, } two at a time.
Pahnih hnih-in,

NUMERAL ADVERBS.

These are formed by prefixing *voi* to the cardinal numbers and in the case of the numbers from 1 to 9, omitting the prefix *pa*, as:

Voi thum, thrice.
Voi shomli, 40 times.

In compound numbers *voi* is repeated after each recurrence of the conjunction *leh*, as—

Voi shomli leh voi thum,	43 times.
Voi za li leh voi shomsari leh voi ruk,	476 times.

DEMONSTRATIVE ADJECTIVES.

The demonstrative adjectives are—

Singular.

He, he hi, *Hei, hei hi,*	} this.
Saw, saw saw,	that (there).
Kha, kha kha,	that, that near you.
Khu, khu khu,	that down there.
Khi, khi khi,	that up there.
Chu, chu chu,	that.

Plural.

Hêng, hêng hi,	these.
Sawng, sawng saw,	those (there).
Khâng, khâng kha,	those, those near you.
Khûng, khûng khu,	those down there.
Khîng, khîng khi,	those up there.
Chûng, chûng chu,	those.

When any of the above compound words are used, the noun they qualify is placed between the two words forming the adjective.

Examples—

He khua hi a zao e.	This village is extensive.
Chu ri chu i hria em?	Did you hear that noise?
Khîng in te khi ka-ta ani.	Those houses up there are mine.
Khu sava khu kâp shu.	Don't shoot that bird down there.

The singular forms of the adjectives may also be used with plural nouns. When a plural adjective is used, the noun it qualifies may either take a plural suffix or not.

Examples—

Saw ui te saw tu-ta-nge?	Whose are those dogs?
Hêng in hi a tê êm.	These houses are very small.

The plural forms hêng, hêng hi, etc., may be used with a singular noun with the meaning of 'this kind of,' 'that kind of,' etc., as—

Hêng saidoiûm hi ka duh ber.	I like this kind of bottle best.

When the above compound adjectives are used to qualify a noun which is the subject of a transitive verb (*see* page 4) or which is governed by a postposition, they become in the singular, *he hian, hei hian, saw sawn, kha khân, khu khuan, khi khian, chu chuan*, and in the plural *hêng hian*, *sawng sawn*, *khâng khan*, *khûng khuan*, *khîng khian*, and *chûng chuan*.

Examples—

Khu vok khuan chaw a ei.	That pig down there is eating food.
He kong a hian dah roh.	Put it on this road.
Khîng in a te khian lût shu.	Don't enter those houses up there.

The latter half of each of the above compound forms of adjectives may be used by itself, and then it follows the noun it qualifies, as:

Huan a khuan min nghâk roh.	Wait for me in the garden down there.
Chem kha tât hriam roh.	Sharpen that knife.

The above demonstrative adjectives are used to supply the place of the English article 'the.'

PRONOUNS.

PERSONAL PRONOUNS.

FIRST PERSON, *keima*, 'I.'

Singular.

Nom:	*keima, kei (ka),*	I.
Poss:	*keima, keia, ka,*	my.
	keimata, keima-ata, kei-ata, kata,	mine.
Obj:	*keima min, kei min, min,*	me, to me, for me.

Plural.

Nom:	*keimani, keini (kan),*	we.
Poss:	*keimani, keini, kan,*	our.
	keimani-ta, keini-ta, kanta,	ours.
Obj:	*keimani min, keini min, min,*	us, to us, for us.

NOTE.—*min* is often contracted into *mi'*.

SECOND PERSON, *nangma*, 'thou.'

Singular.

Nom:	*nangma, nang (i),*	thou.
Poss:	*nangma, nanga, i,*	thy.
	nangma-ta, nangma-ata, ita,	thine.
Obj:	*nangma, nang.*	thee.

Plural.

Nom:	*nangmani, nangni (in),*	you.
Poss:	*nangmani, nangni, in,*	your.
	nangmani-ta, nangni-ta, in-ta,	yours.
Obj:	*nangmani, nangni,*	you.

NOTE.—The objective case is frequently formed by omitting or retaining the pronoun and affixing *che*, *a-che*, or *chi-a* in the singular, and *che-u* or *a-che-u* in the plural, as—

Ka vêl ang che.	I will strike thee.
Nangni ka hmu a-che-u.	I saw you.
Nimina ka pe che-a engatinge i nei lo?	I gave it to you yesterday, why have you not got it?

Che, *a-che*, and *chi-a*. also mean—to thee, for thee, from thee,
Che-u and *a-che-u* „ also mean—to you, for you, from you.

THIRD PERSON, *ama*, 'he,' 'she,' 'it.'

Singular.

Nom:	*ama, ani (a),*	he, she, it.
Poss:	*ama, ani, a,*	his, her, its.
	ama-ta, ama-uta, ani-ta, a-ta,	his, hers, its.
Obj:	*ama, ani,*	him, her, it.

Plural.

Nom:	*anmani, anni (an),*	they.
Poss:	*anmani, anni, an,*	their.
	anmani-ta, anni-ta, an-ta,	theirs.
Obj:	*anmani, anni,*	them.

NOTE.—The pronouns (*ka*), (*kan*), (*i*), (*in*), (*a*), (*an*), placed within the parentheses are used as pronominal particles to verbs (*see* page 18).

When a personal pronoun is the subject of a transitive verb in the active voice, it usually takes the termination *in*, or its contracted form *'n*, to distinguish it from the object (*see* Nouns, page 4).

REFLEXIVE PRONOUNS.

When a reflex action is required to be expressed, the pronouns *keima*, *nangma*, *ama*, etc., are used and the particle *in* is prefixed to the verb, as—

Keima ka in-vêl.	I hit myself.
Nangma i in-shât ang.	You will cut yourself.
Ama a in-dem.	He finds fault with himself.

The pronoun may be omitted, as—

Ka in-vêl.	I hit myself.

In the plural, *theoh*, 'each,' or *ve ve*, 'each of two,' is inserted between the personal pronoun and its nominative ending or placed after the verb to prevent confusion with the reciprocal prefix *in* (page 28).

Examples—

Keimani theoh-vin kan in-shât.	We cut ourselves.
Nangmani-in in in-kâp hlum ve ve ang.	You will each shoot yourself.

Other ways of expressing a reflex action may be seen in the following sentences:

Keima leh keima ka in-kâp. *Keima leh keima-in ka in-kâp.* *Mani leh mani ka in-kâp.* *Mani leh mani-in ka in-kâp.* *Mani mani-in ka in-kâp.* *Mani ka in-kâp.* *Mani-in ka in-kâp.*	I shot myself.

All the other persons, singular and plural, may be expressed by substituting for *keima* and *ka* the corresponding pronouns *nangma* and *i*, *ama* and *a*, etc.

RELATIVE PRONOUNS.

The relative pronouns are:

Kha. *Chu.*	Who, which, what, that.
Apiang. *Apiang kha.* *Apiang chu.*	Whoever, whatever, whichever.

Kha is generally used when the antecedent is known to or has been seen by the speaker, whether it is known to or has been seen by the person addressed or not.

Chu is generally used when the antecedent has only been heard of by the speaker, but is known to or has been seen by the one addressed.

The relative pronoun follows the verb of the relative sentence.

When a relative pronoun is used in the nominative case the pronominal particle (*see* page 18) is omitted from the verb in the relative sentence.

Examples—

Nimina mi lo-kal kha khoiange om?	Where is the man who came yesterday?
Puan naktûka ka lei tûr chu ka pe ang che.	I will give you the cloth which I shall buy tomorrow.
Naktûka mi lo-kal tûr chu a ke a bai.	The man who is coming tomorrow is lame.
Mi i duh apiang ko roh.	Call whichever man you like.

When the antecedent is in the plural, the affix *te* or *ho-te*, when used (*see* page 3), immediately precedes the relative pronouns *kha* and *chu*, instead of being affixed to the noun. The other plural affixes follow the noun in the usual way.

Examples—

Shial ka hmu te kha tulange? Whose are the *gayals* which I saw?

Âr zong zong i lei apiang a ṭha lo. Whatever fowls you bought were bad.

Very frequently the relative pronoun is omitted, and then the verb becomes a participle or adjective qualifying the noun in the ordinary manner:

Examples—

Ka lekha ziak a ṭha e. The letter which I have written is good (lit., my written letter is good).

I in shak a lian luțuk ani. The house which you have built is too large (lit., your built house, etc.)

An puan tah a moi êm êm. The cloth which they have woven is very pretty (lit., their woven cloth, etc.)

In sakei hmu a hlao che-u em? Was the tiger which you saw afraid of you? (lit., was your seen tiger? etc.)

The possessive cases 'whose,' 'of which,' and 'whosever' are expressed by using the above nominatives and prefixing the pronominal particle referring to the antecedent to the thing possessed, as—

Nimina, naopanga pu an ka lâk kha, a lo-kal ang. The boy whose cloth I took yesterday will come.

Kêl, a lu ka tan chu, ui-in a ei. The goat, the head of which I cut off, a dog has eaten.

Mi an in i hâl apiang-te kha an tlân bo ta. The men whosever houses you burnt have run away.

Thing, a pâr ka pêk a-che kha, ka huan-a a om. The tree of which I gave you the flower is in my garden.

Sometimes *a* is placed between the verb and the relative, and when the antecedent is of the feminine gender, *i* is occasionally used instead of *a*, as—

Hmeichhia, a chi ka ruk i kha a ṭap. The woman whose salt I stole is crying.

Mipa, a vaibêl ka lâk-sak a kha, a thin-ur. The man whose pipe I took away is angry.

INTERROGATIVE PRONOUNS.

The interrogative pronouns are—

Tu-nge? tu? tu-maw? 'Who.'

When *tunge* is the subject of a verb, the verb does not take the usual pronominal particle (*see* page 18) as—

Tunge lo-kal?	Who came?

When *tunge* is the subject of a transitive verb in the active voice it becomes *tu-in-nge*, as—

Tu-in-nge vêl che?	Who hit you?

Tunge may be split up by a verb as—

Tu vêl che nge ni?	Who hit you?

Tu and *tumaw* are only used by themselves in the following manner:

A lo-kal lo. Tumaw?	He has not come. Who?
A sakor a hral ta. Tu?	He has sold his horse. Who?

Tu-ta-nge? tu-ta? tu-ta-maw? 'Whose'? (used substantively).

Hei hi tu-ta-nge?	Whose is this?

Tu-ta and *tu-ta-maw* are only used by themselves in the following manner:

A lekha bu i hmu em? Tu-ta? (or *Tu-ta-maw*)?	Have you seen his book? Whose?

Tu...nge? tu? tu...maw? 'Whose'? (used adjectively).

When *tu...nge* is used thus, the noun it qualifies is placed between the two parts which make up the word, as—

Tu âr nge i lei?	Whose fowl did you buy?
Tu in a nge i om?	In whose house are you stopping?

When *tu...nge* qualifies a noun which is the subject of a transitive verb in the active voice, the verb does not take the usual pronominal prefix (*see* page 18) as—

Tu ui-in nge sheh che?	Whose dog bit you?

Tu and *tu....maw* can only be used by themselves in the following manner:

A puan a bo ta. Tu puan? (or *tu-puan-maw?*)	His cloth is lost. Whose cloth?

Tu-nge? tu? tu-maw? 'Whom'?

Tunge i hmu?	Whom did you see?

Tu-nge can be split up by a postposition, as—

Tu hnêna nge i ria'ang?	With whom will you lodge for the night?
Tu tân nge i shiam?	For whom are you making it?

Tu and *tu-maw* can only be used by themselves in the following manner:

Suaka'n mi a tîr. Tu? (or *Tumaw*)?	Suaka has sent men. Whom?

Eng-nge? Zeng-nge? eng? eng-maw? 'What'?

Eng-nge i duh? *Zeng-nge i duh?*	What do you want?

When *eng-nge* or *zeng-nge* is used adjectively, it is split up by the noun it qualifies as—

Eng tui nge ka choi ang?	What water shall I draw?

Eng and *engmaw* are only used by themselves in the following manner:

I hmu em? Eng? (or *Ēngmaw?*)	Have you seen it? What?

Eng-a? is only used by itself in answer to a call, or when the person using it did not understand what was said.

Khoi-i-nge? Which?

Khoi-i lekha-bu nge i duh? *Lekha-bu khoi-i-nge i duh?*	Which book do you want?

When *a* is prefixed to any of the interrogative pronouns it gives it a partitive force, as—

A tu-nge i ko?	Whom of them did you call?
Lekha bu a-zeng-nge i duh?	Which of the books do you want?
A eng te nge i hmu?	Which (plural) of them did you see?

When demonstrative adjectives are used with the interrogative pronouns they are placed as follow:

A tu khi nge i tîr?	Whom of those up there did you send?
In zeng khu nge i sha?	Which house down there did you build?
Khûng in khu a zengnge i sha?	Which of the houses down there did you build?

Tih, this may be used with an interrogative pronoun to give it the force of a relative, as:

Tu-nge-ni tih i hria em?	Do you know who it was?
Eng-nge-ni tih ka hre lo?	I do not know what it was?

POSSESSIVE PRONOUNS.

The possessive pronouns are as follow:

Singular.

Keima, keia, ka.	My.
Keima-ta, keima-ata, kei-ata, ka-ta.	Mine.
Nang, nangma-a, nang-a, i.	Thy.
Nangma-ta, nangma-ata, nang-ata, i-ta.	Thine.
Ama, ani, a.	His, her, its.
Ama-ta, ama-ata, ani-ta, a-ta.	His, hers, its.

Plural.

Keimani, keini, kan.	Our.
Keimani-ta, keini-ta, kanta.	Ours.
Nangmani, nangni, in.	Your.
Nangmani-ta, nangni-ta, in-ta.	Yours.
Anmani, anni, an.	Their.
Anmani-ta, anni-ta, an-ta.	Theirs.

DEMONSTRATIVE PRONOUNS.

The demonstrative pronouns are the same as the double forms of the demonstrative adjectives with the exception of *he hi*, which is not used.

INDEFINITE PRONOUNS.

Some of the indefinite pronouns are as follow:

Engma. *Engma...lo.*	} Nothing.
Engpawh. *Eng-pôh.*	} Anything, any, anyone.
Eng-kim.	Everything, all sorts of things.
Eng-lo.	Something.
Eng-emaw.	Something, something or other.
Tu-ma. *Tu-ma...lo.*	} No one, nobody.

NOTE.—*Engma* and *tuma* are only used in answer to a question, and then the rest of the sentence is understood, as —

Engnge i ti? Engma.	What did you say? Nothing.
Tunge om? Tuma?	Who is there? No one.

In other instances it is always followed by *lo*, 'not,' as —

Engma ka hmu thei lo.	I can see nothing.
Tuma'n buh an duh lo.*	No one wants rice.
In a tuma an om lo.*	There is no one in the house.

* When *tuma...lo* is used, the pronominal prefix of the verb is always in the plural.

Tu-pawh. *Tu-pôh.*	} Anyone.
Tu-emaw.	Some one, a certain one,
A-ṭhen...a ṭhen.	Some, others.
A-dang.	Another, others.
An-zain.	All (of persons).
A-zain.	All (of things).

Examples of the use of indefinite pronouns :

Heta lo-kal roh englo ka pe ang che.	Come here, I will give you something.
Nizâna kan khua a tuemaw a thi.	Last night some one died in our village.
Tunge i duh? Tupawh.	Whom do you want ? Any one.
A-ṭhen ka ei a-ṭhen ka paih.	Some I ate, others I threw away.
Engnge i duh ber? Engpawh.	Which do you want most? Any one.

VERBS.

The conjugation of the verb in Lushai is very simple. It has the same form throughout the tense and it is the pronominal particle which alone determines the person and number.

The pronominal particles are as follow :

Singular.		*Plural.*	
1st person—*ka* I.		1st person—*kan*	We.
2nd person—*i* Thou.		2nd person—*in*	You.
3rd person—*a* He, she, it.		3rd person—*an*	They.

The pronoun proper is generally omitted except when emphasis is required, but the pronominal particle must always be used whether the pronoun proper is present or not.

NOTE.—Neuter nouns when in the plural, and used as the subject of a verb, take the *singular* pronominal prefix *a*.

The conjugation of the verb *ni*, 'to be,' is as follows :

INDICATIVE MOOD.

PRESENT TENSE.

Singular.		*Plural.*	
1. *Keima ka ni.*	I am.	1. *Keimani kan ni.*	We are.
2. *Nangma i ni.*	Thou art.	2. *Nangmani in ni.*	You are.
3. *Ama a ni.*	He is.	3. *Anmani an ni.*	They are.

PAST TENSE.

Singular.		Plural.	
1. *Keima ka ni.*	I was.	1. *Keimani kan ni.*	We were.
2. *Nangma i ni.*	Thou wast.	2. *Nangmani in ni.*	You were.
3. *Ama a ni.*	He was.	3. *Anmani an ni.*	They were.

PERFECT TENSE.

Singular.		Plural.	
1. *Keima ka ni ta.*	I have been.	1. *Keimani kan ni ta.*	We have been.
2. *Nangma i ni ta.*	Thou hast been.	2. *Nangmani in ni ta.*	You have been.
3. *Ama a ni ta.*	He has been.	3. *Anmani an ni ta.*	They have been.

NOTE.—*tawh* may be substituted for *ta* throughout the tense *keima ka ni*, etc., equals also, 'I have been,' etc.

FUTURE TENSE.

Singular.		Plural.	
1. *Keima ka ni ang.*	I shall be.	1. *Keimani kan ni ang.*	We shall be.
2. *Nangma i ni ang.*	Thou wilt be.	2. *Nangmani ni in ang.*	You will be.
3. *Ama a ni ang.*	He will be.	3. *Anmani an ni ang.*	They will be.

PERIPHRASTIC FUTURE TENSE.

Singular.		Plural.	
1. *Keima ka ni dawn.*	I am about to be.	1. *Keimani kan ni dawn.*	We are about to be.
2. *Nangma i ni dawn.*	Thou art about to be.	2. *Nangmani in ni dawn.*	You are about to be.
3. *Ama a ni dawn.*	He is about to be.	3. *Anmani an ni dawn.*	They are about to be.

NOTE.—Throughout the tenses and persons of the indicative mood *e* may be affixed without altering the meaning, as—*keima ka ni e*, etc.

When an adjective is used to form the completion of a predicate, *e* may be used alone, either for the singular or plural, as—*i ṭha e*, you are good.

SUBJUNCTIVE MOOD.

Present and Past Tense.

Singular.

1. *Keima ka ni chuan.*	If I be, or If I were.
2. *Nangma i ni chuan.*	If thou be, or If thou wert.
3. *Ama a ni chuan.*	If he, she, or it be, or If he, she, or it were.

Plural.

1. *Keimani kan ni chuan.*	If we be, or If we were.
2. *Nangmani in ni chuan.*	If you be, or If you were.
3. *Anmani an ni chuan.*	If they be, or If they were.

or

Singular.

1. *Ni ila*, or *ni ilang.*	If I be, or If I were.
2. *Ni la*, or *ni lang.*	If thou be, or If thou wert.
3. *Ni shela*, or *ni shelang.*	If he, she, or it be, or If he, she, or it were.

Plural.

1. *Ni ila*, or *ni ilang.*	If we be, or If we were.
2. *Ni ula*, or *ni ulang.*	If you be, or If you were.
3. *Ni shela*, or *ni shelang.*	If they be, or If they were.

Pluperfect Tense.

Singular.

1. *Ni ta ila*, or *ni ta ilang.*	If I had been.
2. *Ni ta la*, or *ni ta lang.*	If thou had been.
3. *Ni ta shela*, or *ni ta shelang.*	If he, she, or it had been.

Plural.

1. *Ni ta ila*, or *ni ta ilang.*	If we had been.
2. *Ni ta ula*, or *ni ta ulang.*	If you had been.
3. *Ni ta shela*, or *ni ta shelang.*	If they had been.

IMPERATIVE MOOD.

Singular.		*Plural.*	
2. *Ni roh.*	Be thou.	2. *Ni roh-u.*	Be ye.
3. *Ni roh se.*	Let him, her, or it be.	3. *Ni roh se.*	Let them be.

NEGATIVE FORM.

Singular.		*Plural.*	
2. *Ni shu, ni shu ang che.*	Be not thou.	2. *Ni shu u, ni shu ang che u.*	Be ye not.
3. *Ni shu se.*	Let him, her, or it not be.	3. *Ni shu se*	Let them not be.

Om 'to be,' 'to exist,' is conjugated in the same manner as *ni.* The verb 'to have' is represented by using *om* in the following manner:

Ka hnêna a om. I have (lit., It is to me).
I hnêna a om. Thou hast (lit., It is to thee), etc., etc.

CONJUGATION OF THE VERB *SHOI*, 'TO SAY.'

NOTE.—In the following conjugation the first person singular of each tense only will be given, as the verb remains unchanged throughout the tense, and the other persons can easily be formed by substituting for *keima ka* the pronouns and particles *nangma i, ama a,* etc.

INDICATIVE MOOD.

PRESENT TENSES.

Indef:	*Keima ka shoi, keima ka shoi ṭhîn.*	I say, I do say.
Imperf:	*Keima ka shoi, keima ka shoi mêk.*	I am saying.
Perfect:	*Keima ka shoi, keima ka shoi ta, keima ka shoi tawh.*	I have said.

PAST TENSES.

Indef:	*Keima ka shoi, keima ka shoi ṭhîn.*	I said, I used to say.
Imperf:	*Keima ka shoi, keima ka shoi mêk ani.*	I was saying.
Perfect:	*Keima ka shoi ta, keima ka shoi tawh.*	I had said.

FUTURE TENSES.

Indef:	*Keima ka shoi ang.*	I shall say.
Imperf:	*Keima ka shoi mêk ang, keima ka shoi tawh mêk ang.*	I shall be saying.
Perfect:	*Keima ka shoi tawh ang.*	I shall have said.
Periphrastic Future:	*Keima ka shoi dawn.*	I am about to say.

In like manner *dawn*, with the meaning of 'about to,' can be used with any of the above present and past tenses.

NOTE.—Throughout the mood in all persons *e* may be added to the end of the verb, and except in the future tenses *ani* or *ani-e*.

CONDITIONAL MOOD.

PRESENT TENSE.

Keima ka shoi tûr. — I would say, I would have said.

PAST TENSE.

Keima ka shoi tawh tûr. — I would have said.

NOTE.—Throughout the mood in all persons *ani*, or *ani e*, may be added to the verb without changing the meaning.

The above two tenses also mean 'I should or ought to say' and 'I should have' or 'ought to have said' respectively.

In Lushai the future tenses are often used where in English we use the conditional mood.

SUBJUNCTIVE MOOD.

PRESENT AND PAST TENSES.

Singular.

1. *Keima ka shoi chuan.*	If I say, said, have said, or had said.
2. *Nangma i shoi chuan.*	If thou say, said, have said, or had said.
3. *Ama a shoi chuan.*	If he say, said, have said, or had said.

Plural.

1. *Keimani kan shoi chuan.* If we say, said, have said, or had said.
2. *Nangmani in shoi chuan.* If you say, said, have said, or had said.
3. *Anmani an shoi chuan.* If they say, said, have said, or had said.

or

Singular.

1. *Shoi ila, shoi ilang.* If I say or had said.
2. *Shoi la, shoi lang.* If thou say or had said.
3. *Shoi shela, shoi shelang.* If he say or had said.

Plural.

1. *Shoi ila, shoi ilang.* If we say or had said.
2. *Shoi ula, shoi ulang.* If you say or had said.
3. *Shoi shela, shoi shelang.* If they say or had said.

PLUPERFECT TENSE.

Singular.

1. *Shoi ta ila, shoi ta ilang.* If I had said.
2. *Shoi ta la, shoi ta lang.* If thou had said.
3. *Shoi ta shela, shoi ta. shelang.* If he had said.

Plural.

1. *Shoi ta ila, shoi ta ilang.* If we had said.
2. *Shoi ta ula, shoi ta ulang.* If you had said.
3. *Shoi ta shela, shoi ta shelang.* If they had said.

NOTE.—If *ma* be inserted between the verb and the subjunctive ending of any of the persons in the second form of the present and past tenses, or of the pluperfect, the meaning becomes 'although' or 'even if' as—

Shoi ma ila	Although I say, even if I say.
Shoi ta ma ila	Although I had said, even if I had said.

The negative forms of the above are as follow :

Singular.

1. *Shoi shu ila*, or *shoi lo ila*. If I say not, said not, have not said, or had not said.
2. *Shoi shu la*, or *shoi lo la*. If thou, etc.
3. *Shoi shu shela*, or *shoi lo shela*. If he, etc.

Plural.

1. *Shoi shu ila*, or *shoi lo ila*. If we, etc.
2. *Shoi shu ula*, or *shoi lo ula*. If you, etc.
3. *Shoi snu shela*, or *shoi lo shela*. If they, etc.

Singular.

1. *Shoi ta shu ila* or *shoi ta lo ila*. If I had not said.
2. *Shoi ta shu la* or *shoi ta lo la*. If thou, etc.
3. *Shoi ta shu shela* or *shoi ta lo shela*. If he, etc.

Plural.

1. *Shoi ta shu-ila* or *shoi ta lo ila*. If we had not said.
2. *Shoi ta shu ula* or *shoi ta lo ula*. If you, etc.
3. *Shoi ta shu shela* or *shoi ta lo shela*. If they, etc.

NOTE.—The final *la* in all the above negative forms may become *lang*.

If *ma* be inserted between the verb and *shu*, or between *lo* and the termination in any of the above, the meaning becomes 'although,' or 'even if,' as—

Shoi ma shu ila. }
Shoi lo ma ila. } Although I say not, etc.

IMPERATIVE MOOD.

Singular.		*Plural.*	
2. *Shoi roh.*	Say thou	1. *I shoi ang, i shoi ang u.*	Let us say.
3. *Shoi roh se.*	Let him, her, it say.	2. *Shoi roh u.*	Say ye.
		3. *Shoi roh se.*	Let them say.

Other forms of the imperative are—

Singular:	*Shoi ang che, shoi ta che, shoi te, shoi che.*	Say thou!
Plural:	*Shoi ang che u, shoi ta che u, shoi te u, shoi che u.*	Say ye!

NEGATIVE FORMS.

Singular.		*Plural.*	
2. *Shoi shu.*	Do not say	1. *I shoi shu ang, i shoi shu ang u.*	Let us not say.
3. *Shoi shu se.*	Let him, her, it not say.	2. *Shoi shu u.*	Do not say.
		3. *Shoi shu se.*	Let them not say.

Other forms are—

Singular:	*Shoi shu ang che, shoi ma ta che.*	Do not say.
Plural:	*Shoi shu ang che u, shoi ma ta che u.*	Do not say.

In the first person plurals *i shoi ang* and *i shoi shu ang* are used of two persons only, *i shoi ang u* and *i shoi shu ang u* of more than two.

When two or more imperatives follow one another in a sentence, the last only, as a rule, takes the imperative termination, the others take the subjunctive endings, as—

Dawr a kal ulang âr lei roh u.	Go to the bazar and buy some fowls.
Khua a leng ila kan ṭhian i hmu ang.	Let us stroll to the village and see our friend.
In a lût shu ula bengchheng shu u.	Don't enter the house, and don't make a noise.

Infinitive Mood—*Shoi*	'To say.'
Participles—*Shoi-a, shoi-in*	'Saying.'
Gerunds—*Shoi-tûr, shoi-tûr-in, shoi-na-tûr, shoi nân, shoi-an, shoi-in,*	'For saying.'

PASSIVE VOICE.

The passive voice in Lushai is generally formed by altering the pronunciation of the verb, and may be seen in the following examples :

Active.		*Passive.*	
Ka vêl a-che.	I beat you.	*I velh ka ni.*	I am beaten by you.
Ka ngai a-che.	I love you.	*I ngaih ka ni.*	I am loved by you.
Ka hua a-che.	I hate you.	*I huat ka ni.*	I am hated by you.
Ka tîr a-che.	I send you.	*I tir ka ni.*	I am sent by you.
Ka shât a-che.	I cut you.	*I sha' ka ni.*	I am cut by you.
Ka that a-che.	I kill you.	*I tha' ka ni.*	I am killed by you.
Ka kâp a-che.	I shoot you.	*I ka' ka ni.*	I am shot by you.
Ka kai a-che.	I pull you.	*I kaih ka ni.*	I am pulled by you.
Ka hnûk a-che.	I drag you.	*I hnu' ka ni.*	I am dragged by you.
Ka phet a-che.	I trip you up.	*I phe' ka ni.*	I am tripped up by you.

NOTE.—Care must be taken in the pronunciation of the verb in the passive voice, as a slight difference in pronunciation may change the meaning from passive to active, as—

Sâp velh ka ni.	I am hit by the Sahib.	*Sâp vêl ka ni.*	I am the hitter of the Sahib.
Mizo huat ka ni.	I am hated by the Lushais.	*Mizo hua' ka ni.*	I am a hater of the Lushais.
Tual tha' a ni.	He was murdered.	*Tual that a ni.*	He was a murderer.'

INTERROGATIVE PARTICLES OF VERBS.

em—This interrogative particle is placed, as a rule, at the end of the sentence, and cannot be translated into English, as—

I kal ang em? Will you go?
A tha em? Is it good?

Ta em or *tawh em* is sometimes contracted into *tem*, as—

I hmu ta em? becomes *I hmu tem?* Have you seen?

em-ni—This particle is sometimes identical with *em*. It is also used when the question is in the affirmative, and the answer is expected in the affirmative, as :

Thing i phur emni? You are carrying wood, are you?

When the question is in the negative, the answer is expected in the negative, as—

Âr tui min thon lo emni? You didn't send me any fowls' eggs, didn't you?

Emni, with the negative *lo,* sometimes becomes *lo vemni* or *lom-ni*, as—

I chaw i ei lovem-ni?	Have you not eaten your food?
Vok in tal lom-ni?	Have you not killed the pig?

e-lo—This is used in the same manner as *emni* in its second meaning, as—

Ruah a shûr elo?	It is raining, is it?

maw—This is used in the same manner as *elo.* It is also used when the person interrogated repeats part of the question before answering, as—

Q.—I nu a dam em?	Is your mother well?
A.—Ka nu maw? A dam e.	My mother? She is well.

e-maw.—This particle is used as in the following example:

Kal i duh emaw?	Do you want to go?

(Here the interrogator supposes that the person addressed does *not* want to go.)

ne-maw—This is sometimes used as a negative form of *e-maw.*

na-nge—This is a negative interrogative particle similar to *lo-vem-ni.*

When interrogative adverbs are used in asking questions the interrogative particles are omitted, as—

Ka lu-khum khoiange i dah?	Where have you put my hat?

NEGATIVE FORM OF VERBS.

When a verb is used negatively, the adverb, *lo,* 'not,' is placed after the root verb, as—

Ka pa'n shial min pe duh lo.	My father does not wish to give me a *gayal.*

Lo with the termination *e* or *a* becomes *lo-ve, lo-va.*
Lo with the termination *ang* becomes *lo-vang* or *long.*
Nêm is sometimes used with the same meaning as *lo-ve.*
Nâng is sometimes used with the same meaning as *lo-vang.*

Example—

Hei hi tu-in-nge siak? Ka hre nêm.	Who wrote this? I do not know.
Naktûka Khama in a dah ang che. Khama in a ka kal nâng.	Put this in Khama's house tomorrow. I am not going to Khama's house.

Shu-e and *uk-shu-ei* are more emphatic negative particles, and are used only in answering a question. When these are used, the verb cannot be preceded by either a noun or pronoun.

Examples—

Aizawl a kal a duh lo maw?	Does he not wish to go to Aijal?
Duh uk-shu-ei.	(He) does not wish.

VERBAL PREFIXES.

There are several verbal prefixes, of which the principal are as follow:

Zuk—Signifies motion downwards, as—

Zuk kal roh.	Go down.
Zuk pe roh.	Go down and give.

Han—Signifies motion upwards, as—

Han la roh.	Go up and fetch.

Han—Signifies motion towards the speaker, as—

Han la roh.	Bring it here.
Min han pe roh.	Come and give it to me.

Lo—Signifies motion towards the speaker, as—

Lo la roh.	Come and take.

It also signifies that the action of the verb has already taken or begun to take effect, and may frequently be rendered by the English word 'become,' as—

Ka lo thlen' in a in a lo kâng.	When I arrived, his house was burning.
Ka zuk en a, a lo om lo.	I went down and looked and it was not (there).
Khu hmeichhia khu a lo that-chhia êm êm.	That woman down there is very lazy (I thought her to be otherwise).

Ron—Signifies motion towards, as—

Min ron pe roh.	Come and give it to me.
Engatinge sangha i ron man.	Why did you go and catch fish.
A hnêna ron hril shu.	Don't go and tell him.

Va—Signifies motion from, generally on level ground or from one place to another of equal elevation, as—

Va hril roh.	Go and tell.

In—Signifies reciprocity, as—

An in sual.	They are fighting with each other.
In vêl shu-u.	Don't strike each other.

ADVERBS.

Some adverbs of place are—

Chunga	on top.	*Khoi-a-ma*	nowhere.
Chunglama	above.	*Hma-sha* }	
Hnuaia	underneath.	*Hma-in* }	before, in front.
Chhûnga	inside.	*Hma-a* }	
Pawna	outside.	*Hnunga*	behind.
Chhaka	above (higher up).	*Kai* }	across.
Thlanga	below (lower down).	*Tan* }	
Heta	here.	*Vêl*	around, round.
Saw-ta	there.	*Khual*	round about.
Khi-ta	up there.	*Râl-a*	in the distance, on the other side, on the opposite bank.
Khu-ta	down there.		
Kha-ta	there.		
Khoi-a-nge?	where?		
Khoi-a-pawh	anywhere.		

Some adverbs of time are—

Tûna	now.	*Naktipa*	day after tomorrow.
Ani-ta	ago.	*Ni-zâna*	last night.
Ni-tin	daily.	*Zân-ina* }	tonight.
Zing-a	in the early morning.	*Nak-zâna* }	
Nakîna	presently.	*Tuk-tin*	every morning.
Ngai	ever.	*Kum-tin*	yearly.
Ngai lo	never.	*Tûn-thleng in*	yet.
Lo	not.	*Nichina*	a short time ago.
Tûn chin a	henceforth.	*Tûkina*	this morning.
Nimina	yesterday.	*Hmâna*	formerly.
Naktûk-a	tomorrow.	*Fo*	often, always.
Voi-in-a	to-day.	*Kum-ina*	this year.
Nimin-piah	day before yesterday.	*Nikuma*	last year.
Engtika-nge?	when?	*Nak-kum-a*	next year.
Tûna-pawh	already.	*Chang-chang-in*	occasionally.
Tlai	late.	*Hnu-hnung-in*	after, afterwards.
Hma	early.	*Hrih, Rih*	for a short time.
Leh	again.	*Hlim*	just now.

Some adverbs of manner are—

Eng-tin-nge?	how?	*Vak*	with force.
Heti-ang-in	thus.	*Ve*	also, too.
Thuai } *Thuai-thuai* }	quickly.	*Tam* } *Mang* }	much.
Zoi-zoi-in	slowly.	*Vek*	quite, entirely.
Ni-e } *Aw* } *Ani* }	yes.	*Rual*	together.
		Dûn	both together.
		Pawh, pôh } *Bok* }	also.
Nilo	no.		
Aw-le	all right.	*Heti-chen*	so much.
Lo	not.	*Heti-zât*	{ so much. so many.
Ma-thei-lo-vin	certainly.	*Eng-zat-nge?*	how much? how many?
Zawk	more.	*Eng-chen-nge?*	how much? (length).
Ber	most.	*Eng-zia-nge?*	how large?
Ber } *Em* } *Em êm* } *Zet* } *Tak* }	very.	*Pal*	accidentally.
		Lui	purposely.
		Mai *Mai mai*	{ merely. gratuitously. to no purpose.
		Va	how.

NOTE.—*va*, 'how,' is only used in exclamatory sentences, as—

I va â êm!	How foolish you are!
A va mak êm!	How very wonderful!

Many adverbs are placed between the root verb and its inflexion. The following are some of them:

Ngai	ever.	*Leh*	again.
Ngai lo	never.	*Ri, hrih*	for a short time.
Kual	round about.	*Fo*	frequently.
Kai } *Tan* }	across.	*Tlai*	late.
		Hma	early.
Thuai-thuai	quickly.	*Kher*	haply, by chance.
Hmasha	before, in front.	*Hlel lo*	undoubtedly.
Hnu-hnung	behind.	*Ve*	also, too.
Bok	also.	*Dûn*	both together.
Vek	entirely.	*Pal*	accidentally.
Mai } *Mai mai* }	gratuitously, merely, to no purpose.	*Lui*	purposely.
		Hle hle	still (not moving).
Lo	not.	*Vak*	with force.

Examples—

'Thawk thuai roh' ka ti fo a-che.	I am frequently saying to you 'work quickly.'
I din' hle hle lo chuan ka vel vak ang che.	If you do not stand still I will beat you severely.
Nak-kum-a vok heti-zât i lei leh ang em?	Will you buy so many pigs again next year?
Sebawng a lo-thleng hma lutûk, tal, hrih shu.	The cow has arrived too soon, don't kill it for a little time.
He mao hi i thliak pal em-ni?	Did you break this bamboo accidentally?
Tûkina ram a sakei ka tawk kher.	This morning I met by chance a tiger in the jungle.

Adverbs may be made by affixing *tak-in* to an adjective, and many adjectives without any change may be used as adverbs by placing them between the root verb and its inflexion, as—

Adjective.		*Adverb.*	
Tha	good.	*Tha-tak-in*	well.
Dik	correct.	*Dik-tak-in*	correctly.
Nûla'n a shoi-dik ṭhîn		The girl always speaks correctly.	

Engatinge i shiam ṭha lo ve?	Why have you not made it well?

Adverbs ending in *in* or *a* are rarely used between the root verb and its termination.

Sometimes an adverb, which is usually placed between the root verb and its inflexion, may be placed before the verb by affixing *tak-in* and in some cases *in* or *a*, as—

Kal thuai roh, may become, *Thuai tak-in kal roh*, 'go quickly.'

A shoi mai mai ani, may become, *Mai mai in a shoi ani*, 'he merely said it.'

The comparative degree of adverbs is formed by adding *leh*, *zual*, or *deo*, to the positive, and the superlative degree by adding *ber*, as—

Tlân chak leh zual roh.	Run more quickly.
Zoi deo vin kal roh.	Walk slower.
Nang i ṭong rang ber.	You talk the fastest.

There are some hundreds of adverbs in Lushai which have no equivalent meaning in English, but which impart slight differences of meaning to the sentences they modify and at the same time point out whether the subject spoken of is large (in size, number, etc.), medium or small. The following are some of them:

Large.	Medium.	Small.
Buk buk	*bok bok.* *bak bak.*	*bik bek.* *bek bek.*
Bub bub	*bob bob.* *bab bab.*	*bib beb.* *beb beb.*
Rem rum	*rom rom.* *ram ram.*	*rim rem* *rem rem.*
Er ur	*er or.* *ar ar.*	*ir er.* *er er.*
Hleih hluih	*hloih hloih.* *hlaih hlaih.* *hleih hloih.*	*hlih hleih.* *hleih hleih.*
Pem pum	*pom pom.* *pam pam.* *pem pom.*	*pim pem.* *pem pem.*
Hek huk	*hok hok.* *hak hak.* *hek hok.*	*hik hek.* *hek hek.*
Nger ngur	*ngor ngor.* *ngar ngar.* *nger ngor.*	*ngir nger.* *nger nger.*
Fer fur	*for for.* *far far.* *fer for.*	*fir fer.* *fer fer.*
Roh	*raoh.*	*reoh.*
Miao muao		*miu miao.*
Hriao hruao		*hriu hriao.*
Biao buao		*biu biao.*
Ruai ruai		*riai riai.*

Examples—

A kal bek bek.	He is walking (*bek bek* shows that he is small and that he is also going slowly).
A hmel a va ṭha nge rngur.	How handsome she is (*nger ngur* shows that she is big and fat).
Thing hnah a tla kolh fer for.	The leaves of the tree have fallen (the *fer for* indicates that the tree is of medium size).

PREPOSITIONS.

The prepositions in Lushai govern the possessive case and are placed after the noun or pronoun they govern, consequently, they are more accurately denominated "postpositions."

Some of them are as follow:

Hnêna	to, with, from.
Hma-a	before.
Kiang-a	near.
Vêl-a	around, round.
Thu	about.
Nghêng-a	against.
Lam-a	towards.
Kâr-a	between.
Ṭân	for.
Zîng-a	among, amidst.
Lai-a	in the middle of.
Chhûng-a	within.
Pawn-a	outside of.
Lo-chu	except, beside.
Shîr-a	by the side of.
Hnung-a	behind.
Hnu-a	after.
Piah	beyond.
Chhak-a	above (higher up).
Thlang-a	below (lower down).
Hnuai-a	underneath.
In	by, with.
A	from, to, in, at, on, upon.
Ṭang-in	from.
Chin-a	as far as.
Chung-a	on top of.
Lo-vin	without.

Examples—

Mi pahnih ka hnêna lo-va an kal.	Two men went with me to the *jhûm*.
Kong shîra ṭhu shu, a lai-a ding roh.	Don't sit on the side of the path, stand in the middle of it.
Kêl ka in thlang-a a om lo, a chhak-a a om.	The goat is not below my house, it is above it.

Âr thingrem chunga bawma dah roh.	Put the fowl in that basket on the top of the box.
Heta ṭangin i khua ka hmu thei lo.	I cannot see your village from here.

Some words are used with verbs and have the force of prepositions, like the following:

Sak 'from,' 'for.'

Examples—

Ka puam min lâk sak.	He took my cloth from me
Kong min hon' sak roh.	Open the door for me.

Khum 'upon'.

Examples—

Engatinge ka lu tui i leih khum?	Why did you pour water upon my head.

Khûm 'over.'

Example—

Sava-in thing a thlawk khûm.	The bird flew over the tree.

CONJUNCTIONS.

The most usual conjunctions are—

Nimashela	nevertheless, yet, still, but.
Shi	yet, still, but, for, although.
Chutichuan	therefore, then, so, so that.
Chuan	if.
Thleng-in *Hma lo zong* *Hma lo chuan*	} until.
Lo chuan	unless.
Avâng-in	because.
China	since.
Leh	and, if, or.
Nge	or.
Ai-in *Ai-a* *Hnêk-in*	} than.
A-hnu-in	since.
Emaw *Emaw-chu*	} whether.
Tih	that.
Mashela, etc.	although (*see* page 23).

Examples—

I thlen' hma-lo-chuan hong shu	Don't open it until you arrive.
Kalkata i kal tih ka hre lo.	I did not know that you went to Calcutta.
Nimin zinga an hawng emaw-chu ka shoi thei lo.	I cannot say whether they went home yesterday morning.
Chaw i ei ang nge, tui i in ang ?	Will you eat rice, or drink water ?
I thlâm aiin ka thlam a ṭha zawk.	My *jhúm* house is better than yours.
'Kal roh' ka ti a, nimashela i kal lo. *'Kal roh' ka ti a, nimashela i kal shi lo.* *'Kal roh' ka ti a, i kal shi lo.*	I said 'go,' but you did not go.

INTERJECTIONS.

Some of the most common are—

Aw ! as in—

Lo-kal roh, aw !	Ho ! Come here.

Ie ! as in—

Ie ! Thing i lei ḍuh em ?	I say ! Do you want to buy wood.

Khai ! as in—

I chaw ei roh, khai !	Come ! eat your rice.
Heta lo en roh, khai !	Now then ! Come and look here.

Chei chei !—An expression of surprise, disbelief, or disapprobation, as in—

Chei chei ! ka oih lo ve	Pooh ! I don't believe it.
Chei chei ! A va zah thlâk êm !	Fie ! How very shameful!
Chei chei ! kha-ti-ang ti shu.	Come ! come ! Don't do so.

Khai khai ! is similar to *chei chei !*

Oi ka ni ! Oi ka rei !	Expressions of pain or fatigue.

Oi !—An expression of surprise or wonder, as—

Oi ! A va mak êm !	Oh ! How wonderful!
Teh chai êm in ! *Teh lul êm in !*	Expressions of disbelief.

PART II.—USEFUL SENTENCES.

(1)

English.	*Lushai.*
How are you? I am well.	I dam em? ka dam e.
What is the name of this?	He mi hi engnge a hming?
What is this?	Hei hi eng-nge ni?
What is your name?	Tunge i hming? engnge i hming?
Where are you going?	Khoi a nge i kal dawn?
What village man are you?	Tu khua mi nge i ni?
How far is your village?	In khua eng ti-a hla nge?
How many days does it take to get to your village?	In khua ni eng zât-a ban nge?
Two days' journey?	Ni hnih ban.
Who are you?	Tunge i ni?
I am Ngûra.	Ngûra ka ni.
Are you a Lushai or a Poi?	Lushei nge i ni Poi?
What are you going to Aijal for?	Eng ti tûr-in nge Aizawl a i kal dawn?
I am going to pay my tax.	Lei ba ka pe dawn.
Why did you not pay it last month?	Thla hmasha khân enga-nge i pêk lo?
Last month we were getting in our rice.	Thla hmasha khân buh kan lâk?
Are your crops good this year?	Kumina in thlawh-hma a ṭha em?
We have a lot of rice, but not much maize.	Buh kan nghah, amaerawchu vai mîm kan nghah mang lo.
What is your father's name?	Tunge i pa hming?
My father is dead.	Ka pa a thi tawh.
When did he die?	Eng lai-in nge a thi?
Three years ago.	Kum thum ani tawh.
How is your mother?	I nu eng tin nge a om?
Is your mother well? (or alive).	I nu a dam em?
I have no mother.	Nu ka nei lo.
Are you married? Have you a wife?	Nupui i nei tawh em?
How many children have you?	Fa eng zât nge i nei?
Is your village higher than Aijal?	Aizawl aiin i khua a zo zawk em?

English.	*Lushai.*
Is there any water near your village?	I khua kianga tui om em?
How many houses are there in your village?	In khua in eng zât nge ni?
Are there many widows in your village?	In khua hmeithai an tam em?
Why has not your chief come to meet me?	In lal-in engatinge mi' hmua' lo?
Are you a muntri?	Upa i ni em?
Call your muntri, I want to speak to him.	In upa ko roh u, biak châk-a ka duh e.
I want twenty coolies early to-morrow morning.	Naktûk zîng tak a puakphur shom-hnih ka duh.
Ten men will not be enough.	Mi shom-in an daih lo vang.
I will stay in the zawlbuk tonight.	Zânina zawlbûk-a ka riak ang.
We want five houses for the sepoys to stay in.	Sipai om na tûr in nga kan duh.
Your village is very dirty, have the streets well cleaned.	I khua a bol-hlawh êm e, kot-lai thian fai tîr roh.
What is the price of that fowl?	Kha âr kha eng za'man nge ni?
How very dear!	A va to êm!
I will buy it for twelve annas.	Sheki thum-in ka lei ang e.
Have you any vegetables?	Thlai in nei em?
We never eat Lushai pork.	Mi-zo vok sha kan ei ngai lo.
Sweep out the zawlbuk.	Zawlbûk phiat fai roh.
Bring some wood quickly and also some water.	Thing leh tui han la thuai roh u.
Kindle a fire here.	Heta hian mei chhêm roh u.
Put the fire out, there is too much smoke.	Mei ti thi roh, a khu êm e.
What a long time you have been!	In va rei êm!
Have the coolies arrived?	Puak-phur an thleng tawh em?
Why have they not arrived?	Engatinge an lo tlen' lo?
The road was not steep.	Kong a chho shi lo va.
Put your loads down here.	In phur hetahian nghat roh u.
Are your loads too heavy?	In phur a rit lutuk em ni?
Tomorrow we will divide them.	Naktûka kan ṭhen ang.
We will rest awhile.	Kan chawl rih ang.
Take up your loads again now.	Tûna in phur phur leh roh u.
When shall we arrive at the stockade?	Kulh eng-hun-a-nge kan thlen' ang?
The road is very slippery, did it rain last night?	Kong a nâl êm e, nizâna ruah a shûr em ni?

English.	*Lushai.*
Do we cross that stream down there?	Khu mi lui khu kan kân tûr em ni?
Is there a bridge?	Lei-lawn a om em?
Is the water deep?	Tui a thûk em?
You cannot carry me, call a stronger man.	Nang-in min paw zo lo vang, mi chak deo ko roh.
Be careful. Walk slower.	Fîm-khur roh. Zoi deo-vin kal roh.
How did this box get wet?	He thing-rem hi eng ti huh nge?
Call the coolies together.	Puak-phur ko khawm roh.
You have worked well to-day.	Voi-in-a in thawk ṭha e.
I am very pleased with you.	In chunga ka lawm êm êm.
We will rest here all day tomorrow.	Naktûka hetahian kan châm. ang.
Is that sick man better?	Mi dam lo kha, a dam deo vem?
Don't make a noise.	Beng-chheng shu u.
Why have you cut down all these trees?	Hêng thing zong zong hi, eng-a-ti-nge in ki'?
What a pity!	A va poi êm!
Last year I told you not to cut down any tea-trees.	Nikuma 'thing-pui kung kit shu u' ka ti che u kha.
If you do this again, I shall fine you.	Hetia i ti leh chuan, lei ka choi tîr ang che.
Your *jhûms* are very extensive.	In lo a va zao êm.
What a lot of rice you have!	Buh in va nghah êm!
How very fortunate you are!	In va ni-hlawh êm!
The water is muddy.	Tui a nu e.
Bring me some clear water.	Tui fîm min han lâk roh.
Eat your rice.	I chaw ei roh.
Come here.	He-ta lo-haw roh.
Do this quickly.	Hei hi ti thuai roh.
Don't forget.	Theih-nghil shu.
Are you afraid?	I hlao vem?
Do not run away.	Tlân bo shu.
Stand up.	Ding roh.
Fetch me a knife.	Chem tê min va lâk sak roh.
Hold my horse.	Ka sakor chelh roh.
Go out.	Chhuak roh u.
Look! The tree is going to fall.	En roh! thing a tlu dawn.
Can you climb this tree?	He thing a hian i lawn thei ang em?
I don't know.	Ka hre lo.
I cannot say.	Ka shoi thei lo.

English.	*Lushai.*
Why are you crying?	Enga-ti-nge i ṭa'?
Walk carefully, the bridge is rotten.	Kal dîm roh. Lei-lawn a rop e.
Walk behind me.	Ka hnunga kal roh.
Open the door.	Kong hong roh.
Shut the door.	Kong khâr roh.
Take this away.	Hei hi kal-pui roh.
Have you been to Lungleh?	Lunglei-a i kal tawh em?
Where is the road to Serchhip.	Sêrchhîp kong khoi-a-nge?
Don't turn to the right. Turn to the left.	Ding lama pêng shu. Vei lama pêng roh.
When will you go?	Engtikange i kal ang?
What does he say?	Eng-nge a shoi?
What is the matter?	Eng-nge-ni?
Is this a grave?	Hei hi thlân em ni?
Are there any tigers round here?	He mi vêl-a sakei a om em?
Why are you ashamed?	Eng-a-nge i za'?
I am exhausted.	Ka chao ta.
I am very thirsty, have you any water with you?	Ka tui a hâl êm a, tui i shin em?
Who is there?	Tu-nge-ni?
Come in.	Lo lût roh.
Get out of the way.	Dang om roh.
The path is very much overgrown.	Kong a hnim êm.
Where is your chief?	In lal khoi-a-nge?
Be quiet! I wish to go to sleep.	Ngoi roh u. Mut ka duh e.
Listen! what was that noise?	Ngoi roh! Eng-ri-nge ni?
Don't shoot that bird up there.	Khi sava khi kâp shu.
The sun is hot.	Ni a sha êm.
It is going to rain.	Ruah a shûr dawn.
Open your umbrella.	I ni-hliap kap-parh roh.
Why are you laughing?	Eng a nge i nui?
Who lived here formerly?	Heta hian hmâna tunge om?
Is he still alive?	A la dam em?
When are you going to make a new village?	Engtikange khaw thar in kai dawn?
He has migrated to another village.	Khaw dang-a a pêm ta.
Don't kill a *gayal* for me.	Shial min tal shu.
What do you think of my words?	Ka thu eng ang in nge i ngai?
To my thinking he is a bad man.	Ka ngai in mi sual ani.
You exactly resemble your father.	I pa dek i ni.
Don't you want me to have it?	Ka nei-a i duh lo maw?

English.	*Lushai.*
I am sitting at rice.	Chaw ka kîl.
What do you think this is?	Hei hi eng ni in nge in hriat?
You are showing a bad example.	Thil ṭha lo i ti hmu.
How do you spend your time?	Eng ti in nge ni i len?
What! are you still here?	I la om cheo maw?
It will answer the purpose.	A tla ang.
Guess how many there are.	Eng-zât-nge i rin shoi roh.
I have chosen you to go.	Nang kal tûr-in ka ruat a che.
Has the dak runner arrived?	Lekha-tlân-pui a lo thleng em?
What is your object in felling this tree?	He thing hi eng-nge i kit chhan?
Go to every house.	In tin a kal roh.
Count the houses in this village.	He khua a in hi chhiar roh.
Don't make excuses.	Chhuan lam shu.
It is impossible to go.	Kal rual ani lo ve.
Go without waiting to be told.	Hril ngai lo-vin kal roh.
Each take it in turns to carry this.	In phur chhawk ṭheoh vang che u.
It is not worth mentioning.	Shoi tham ani lo.
I am busy.	Ka ṭûl e.
He has gone the wrong way.	Ani lo lama a kal.

(2)

Against whom have you a complaint?	Tu chung-a nge thu-poi i nei?
Speak louder, I cannot hear you.	Tong ring deo roh, I ṭong ka hre thei lo ve.
Why did you quarrel?	Eng-a-nge in in-sual?
Who began it?	Tunge ti hma-sha?
Tell me it from beginning.	A bul-a min hril vek roh.
Have you any witnesses?	Hre tu i nei em? A hre ve an om em?
Who is this man?	He mi hi tu-nge-ni?
Tell me only the truth.	Thu tak hlîr min hril roh.
If you lie, I shall be very angry.	I dawt chuan in, ka thin-ur êm êm ang.
Do not keep anything back.	Eng-ma zêp shu.
Why did you not tell your chief?	In lal eng-a-ti-nge i hril lo?
He could have settled it.	Ani chuan a rem thei ang.
Don't beat about the bush.	Shoi koi shu.
Tell me whatever you know.	I hriat apiang min hril roh.
Speak freely. Do not fear.	Hlao lo vin, fel tak-in shoi roh.

English.	*Lushai.*
Do not fidget.	Nin-hlei shu u.
Is this true? It is false.	He thu hi a dik em? Dawt ani.
I do not believe you.	I thu ka oih lo ve.
Speak only one at a time.	Pakhat chaoh zêl-in shoi roh u.
Wait a short time.	Om rih roh.
I will consider your case later.	Nakina i thu ka ngai-tua ang.
Call the next man.	A dot tu ko roh.
What is your complaint?	Eng-nge i thu-poi?
Did you not come to me yesterday?	Nimina ka hnêna i lo-kal lo vem ni?
Why have you come again?	Eng-a-nge i lo-kal leh?
I settled your case last night.	Nizâna khân i thu-poi ka ti-tlu ta.
Do not say any more.	Thu dang shu shu.
Settle your case between yourselves.	In thu buai nangmani in-rem roh u.
You are guilty.	I thiam lo ve.
You are not guilty.	I thiam e.
I shall not punish you.	Ka hrem lo vang che.
Next time I shall fine you ten rupees.	I ti leh huna, cheng shom ka choi-tîr ang che.
You may make your defence.	I thiam-na thu i shoi thei e.
Answer quickly.	Chhang thuai roh.
I will not allow the giving and receiving of bribes.	In tham ruk ka phal lo vang.
Why did you strike him?	Engatinge i vêl?
Did he hit you first?	A vêl hmasha che em ni?
What did you steal?	Eng-nge i rûk?
Where have you hidden the stolen goods?	I bung-rua rûk khoi-a-nge i thu'ruk?
Does this gun belong to you.	He silai hi i ta em ni?
Have you licensed your gun?	I silai i khen-tîr em?
I shall confiscate this gun.	He silai hi ka lâk sak ang che.
Unless your chief is present I cannot decide your case.	In lal a om lo chuan, in thu-poi ka rem thei lo vang.
Which man is the murderer?	A tu hi nge mi that tu?
With what did you kill him?	Eng in nge i tha'?
Was it in the night or in the day time?	Chhûna nge zana?
Where did he cut you?	Khoi-a-nge a sha'che?
Did you kill him accidentally?	I that pal em ni?
You will be imprisoned for five years.	Kum nga lung in-a i tâng ang.

English.	*Lushai.*
I shall send you down to the plains.	Phaitual a ka kal tîr ang che.
Take care of the prisoner.	Mi tâng ṭha tak-in vêng roh.
I shall not hang you for this.	He mi a vâng hian ka awk hlum tir lo vang che.
You did it in ignorance.	I ât vâng-a i ti ani.
I will pardon you.	Ka ngai-dâm ang che.
Are you sorry?	I in-chhîr em?
Release these two men.	He mi pahnih hi thlah roh.
Call them back.	Ko kîr roh.
Run after them.	Um roh.
Do not be impatient.	Nghâk hlel shu.
I can hear no more cases to-day.	Voi-in-a thu-poi dang ka ngaitua thei lo vang.
Come again tomorrow at noon.	Naktûk chaw-fâk huna lo-kal leh roh u.
Let every one go out.	Chhuak vek roh se.
Put these papers together.	Hêng lekha hi dah khawm roh.
Send them to my house.	Ka in a thon roh.

(3)

How many sick men are there to-day?	Voi-in-a dam lo eng-zât-nge om?
Let them come in one at a time.	Pakhat zêl-in lo lut roh se.
What is the matter with you?	I eng-nge na?
Put your tongue out.	I lei chhua' roh.
Open your mouth.	Âng roh.
Let me feel your pulse.	I mar min de' tîr roh.
Where is the pain?	Khoi lai nge na?
Does your head ache?	I lu a na em?
When do you have fever?	Eng ti hun in nge i khua a shik ṭhin?
Do you have fever every other day.	Ni khat dan-a i khua a shik ṭhin em?
Do you go to stool daily?	Nitin i dai-lêng em?
How many times in a day do you stool?	Ni khat-a voi eng-za'-nge i dai-lên'?
Did you perspire last night?	Nizâna i thlan a sha em?
Don't throw the clothes off even if you perspire.	I thlan sha mashela puan dah shu.
Are you costive?	I êk a khal lu-tuk em?
Do you have ague?	I tlun em?

English.	*Lushai.*
Have you a pain in your stomach?	I pum a na em?
What did you eat this morning?	Tukin zînga eng-nge i ei?
Why did you not come before?	Enga-tinge hmâna i lo-kal lo.
Have you a pain in your chest.	I awm a na em?
Are you short of breath?	I thaw a chham em?
Have you a cough?	I khuh em?
Breathe hard.	Thaw vak roh.
Count one, two, three.	Pakhat, pahnih, pathum ti roh.
Speak louder.	Ṭong ring deo roh.
Lie on your back.	Mu zang-thal roh.
Lie on your left side,	Vei lam delh-in, mu sai-shîr roh.
Lie on your stomach.	Mu bok-khup roh.
Do not sit up.	Ṭhu shu.
Keep your legs out straight.	I ke thluang reng roh.
Can you walk a little?	Tlêm i kal thei em?
Bend your arm. Bend your leg.	I bân tom roh. I ke tom roh.
Stoop down.	Kûn roh.
Hold up your hands.	Chung lam ban roh.
Have you diarrhœa?	I kua a ṭha lo vem ni?
Have you dysentery?	San-ten i vei em ni?
Have you syphilis?	Sai-hri i vei em ni?
Have you ever had syphilis?	Sai-hri i vei ngai em?
Have you had a miscarriage?	I fa a tla sual ngai em?
How long have you been ill?	Engtika na nge i ni?
How was the disease at first?	A-tîr-in eng-tin-nge a nat?
Have you ever taken medicine?	Dam-doi i in ngai em?
How very pale you are!	I va dâng em!
Have you ever had small-pox?	Zawng-hri i vei ngai em?
Have you been vaccinated?	I bân an zai tawh em?
How many years ago?	Kum eng-za'-nge ni tawh?
Who amputated your leg?	I ke tu tan nge?
Are you a little better?	I dam deo vem.
Have you stoppage of urine?	I zun a im em?
Does it pain you to urinate?	I zun' in a na em?
Are you hoarse?	I aw a chhâng em?
Can you sleep at night?	Zâna i mu thei em?
How did you get that sore?	I pân kha eng ti pân nge?
Bathe it with this lotion?	He dam-doi tui hian vaw fai roh.
I will bandage your foot.	I ke phah ka tuam ang.
Don't remove this bandage.	He tuam-na hi phelh shu ang che.

English.	*Lushai.*
Come every morning at this time.	He ti hun lai hian tûk-tin lo-kal roh.
Drink this three times a day.	Hei hi nitin voi thum in roh.
Drink so much, once in the morning, once at noon, and once in the evening.	He ti chen zêl hian zînga leh chaw-ſâk-a tlai lama nên in ang che.
Swallow these two at a time, three times daily.	Hei hi pathum zêl-in nitin voi thum lem roh.
Take this before every meal.	Hei hi chaw ei hma apiang-in in roh.
Take one pill after every meal.	Chaw ei zaw apiang-in mûm pakhat-in lem zêl roh.
Eat only very soft boiled rice.	Buh hawp chaoh ei roh.
Do not eat any meat.	Sha engma ei shu.
Keep lying down.	Mu reng roh.
Have you a cold ?	I hri-tlâng em ?
Were you out in the rain ?	Ruah i do vem ?
You have come too late, I cannot give you medicine.	I lo-kal tlai lu-tuk, dam-doi ka pe thei lo vang che.
Will you stay in the hospital ?	Dam-doi-in a i om ang em ?
I will give you food and medicine.	Ei tûr leh dam-doi ka pe ang che.
You will soon get well.	I dam thuai ang.
You have toothache.	I ha a na e.
Shall I extract your tooth ?	I ha ka thlon ang em ?
Your tooth is very much decayed.	I ha a ngêt êm.
Have you a gumboil.	I ha hni a puam em ?
Your throat is very sore.	I hrok a na êm êm.
Are you deaf ?	I beng a ngong em ?
Have you earache.	I beng kua a na em ?
How did this boil first come ?	He khoi-hli hi atîr-in eng tin nge a om ?
What made this bruise ?	Eng ti thi tlin' nge ?
Did anything fall on you ?	Englo in a delh chem ni ?
Have you rheumatism ?	Ruh-sheh i vei em ?
How long have you been lame ?	Engtika bai nge i ni ?
Can you not bend your leg ?	I ke i tom thei lo vem ni ?
Can you come every day ?	Nitin i lo-kal thei ang em.
Keep your head still.	I lu ti-che shu.
Keep quite still ?	Che lo top-in om roh.
Do not fear. I will not hurt you.	Hlao shu. Ka ti-na lo vang che.

English.	*Lushai.*
Write this man's name down.	He mi hming hi ziak roh.
How are you to-day ?	Voi-in-a eng-tin-nge i om ?
When did he die ?	Engtika thi nge ni ?
He is on the point of dying.	A thi lek lek ani.
Do not give him any more medicine.	Dam-doi dang pe shu.
I will come back soon.	Ka lo-kal leh thuai ang.

(4)

Bring a kodali each.	Bawng tuh-thlawh pakhat ṭheoh vin shin roh u.
We will commence cutting the road tomorrow.	Naktûka kong kan shial ṭan tawh ang.
Let ten men go on in front and ten men stay with me.	Mi shom kal hma-sha shela, shom ka hnêna om roh se.
Clear the jungle quickly.	Sâm fai thuai roh u.
Level this ground.	He lei hi ti rual roh u.
Don't all work in one place.	Hmun khat a thawk vek shu u.
Pitch my tent here.	Ka puan-in heta shiam roh u.
Build huts down there for the workmen.	Khu ta khuan hna-thawk om nân in shiam roh u.
Pound this stone into powder.	He lung hi dêng chip roh u.
We will blast this rock.	He lung pui hi kan hâl puak ang.
Tamp with water, not with earth.	Lei-in hnawh shu u, tui leih khat rohu.
I want pure sand.	Ṭiao vai-vut hlîr ka duh.
Push these stones down the khud.	Hêng lung hi nam lum roh u.
Carry away the earth.	Lei zawn bo roh u.
Don't cut down that tree.	Saw thing saw kit shu u.
Make the road wider.	Kong lai zao deo roh.
Fill in the ruts made by the rain.	Tui hawk luan-na kor chhûng khat roh u.
Sift the earth well.	Lei ṭha tak-in hri roh u.
Rake it together.	Hui khawm roh u.
You must cut six feet of earth each.	Lei hlam khat ṭheoh va lai in tum tûr ani.
Mix the lime and sand together.	Chinai leh ṭiao vai-vut polh roh u.
Can you quarry stone ?	Lung lai i thiam em ?
Make a hole three feet deep.	Tong hnih pil-in cho roh.

English.	*Lushai.*
This is too deep. This is too shallow.	Hei hi a thûk lu-tuk. Hei hi a pawn lutuk.
Fill in the hole (of the post).	Ban kua hnawh roh.
Go to the jungle and fetch posts.	Ban la tûr-in ram a kal roh u.
Set up the posts six feet apart.	Hlam khat kâr dan-a ban phun zêl roh u.
They are too close together.	A zing lu-tuk e.
These are too far apart.	Hêng hi a khât lutuk.
Notch them before setting them up.	Phun hma-in rek vek roh u.
This post is not firm.	He ban hi a nghet lo ve.
Ram the earth in harder.	Hnawh nghet roh u.
This middle post is too short.	He shût hi a toi lu-tuk.
Don't peel off the bark.	A hawng pil-khok shu u.
Cut the ridge pole shorter.	Tlûng tan toi deo roh.
That post is not perpendicular.	Kha ban kha a ding ngîl lo.
Tie with cane, not with bamboo.	Mao hnâng in ṭawn shu u, hrui-hnâng in ṭawn roh u.
Why did you not char the bottom of this post?	He ban lei phûm hi eng-a-tinge in hâl lo ?
It is going to rain, cover this up.	Ruah a shûr dawn, hei hi khuh hul roh u.
Send men for sun grass.	Di phur in mi tîr roh.
Tomorrow, put on the thatch.	Naktûka di chih roh u.
Put it on thicker, it will not be watertight.	Chih chhah deo roh u, a hul lo vang e.
Press it well together.	Muk tak-in beng roh u.
There is only a little cane.	Hrui tlêm tê chaoh a om.
Don't waste it, use it very carefully.	Ti hek shu u, ren hle roh u.
How wide is it?	A vâng eng tia nge ?
How long is it?	Eng chen nge, a dung ?
Who broke this pickaxe?	He lung-râl hi tu-in nge ti tliak.
Don't be lazy.	That-chhe shu u.
Now split bamboos (for matting).	Tûna mao chik roh u.
Let two men weave the wall.	Mi pahnih-in bang tah roh se.
Make the walls of ekra.	Luang, bang-a hmang roh u.
Plaster with mud and cowdung.	Bawng êk leh chirh-diak-in bel roh u.
Why have you not made the floor?	Eng-a-ti-nge chhuat i tah lo ?
When will you cut out the windows?	Tuk-verh engtikange i hon' ang ?

English.	*Lushai.*
Shall you finish the doors to-day?	Voi-in-a kong-khâr i shiam zo vang em?
This door is too low at the top.	He kong-ka chung lam hi a hniam lutuk.
I want two men to make a lattice.	Zawng-dai-kalh kalh tûr in mi pahnih ka duh.
Fence in the garden tomorrow.	Naktûka huan hung roh u.
Do you know how to sharpen a *dao*?	Chem ta' i thiam em?
This knife is very blunt. It will not cut.	He chem-tê hi a bil êm. Engma a duh lo.
Saw this post in half.	He ban hi a lai a zai bung roh.
Make a sliprail gate.	She-kot-rolh shiam roh u.
Close up the doorway.	Kong-ka ping roh.
How many coolies are there?	Hna-thawk eng-zât nge om?
How much wages does each get?	Eng-zât-nge an hlawh ṭheoh?
Have you received your wages?	I hlawh i chang em?
You two, share this rupee.	Nangni pahnih-in he tangka hi in-khing roh u.
I have no more eight-anna pieces.	Duli dang ka nei lo.
If you are late again tomorrow I shall cut your pay.	Naktûka i lo kal tlai leh chuan i hlawh ka ti-kiam ang.
Some of you have worked well and some have not.	Nangni zînga a ṭhen an thawk ṭha, a ṭhen an thawk ṭha lo.
I only want ten men tomorrow.	Naktûka mi shom chaoh ka duh ang.
I will pay you at the end of the month.	Thla ral huna hlawh ka pe ang che u.
If you cannot work, get a substitute.	I thaw' thei lo chuan, thlâk-tu zong roh.

(5)

Bring me some hot water.	Tui lum min han pe roh.
I want to shave.	Bak me' ka duh.
Is the barber there?	Lu-met-tu om em?
Clean the hand basin.	Mai-hûn nawt fai roh.
Throw away the dirty water.	Tui bol-hlawh paih roh.
Where is my towel?	Ka hmai-hrûk-na khoiange om?
Where did you put my shirt?	Ka kro-pum khoiange i dah?

English.	*Lushai.*
I can't find my braces.	Ka ke-kor dâr-bak ka hmu thei lo.
Who made this hole in my coat?	Ka kor hi, tunge ti-pop?
Can you mend it?	I thui ṭha thei ang em?
Give me my hat.	Ka lukhum min pe roh.
It is hanging up on the post.	Ban a a bâng.
Make the bed.	Khum a mut-na shiam roh.
Sweep the place well.	Hmun ṭha tak-in phiat roh.
Dust all the furniture.	Bung rua zong zong nawt fai roh.
Air the clothes in the sun.	Puan pho roh.
Shake the carpet.	Chhuat -a puan phah thing roh.
Polish my boots.	Ka phei-kok nawt tle roh.
Put oil in all the lamps.	Khon-vâr zong zong a tui thun roh.
Turn up the wick.	Khonvar puan herh chhuak roh.
Turn down the wick.	Khonvar puan herh-lût roh.
Light the lamp.	Khon var hâl roh.
Light the fire.	Mei chhêm roh.
Clear up these papers.	Hêng lekha hi dah ṭha roh.
Don't touch these books.	Hêng lekha-bu hi khoih shu.
Make the room tidy.	Pindan chhûng hi thian fai roh.
Spread the cloth on the table.	Dawh-kân a puan phah roh.
Bring a clean plate.	Thlêng thiang-hlim min han pe roh.
This basin is dirty.	He berh-bu hi a bâl e.
Give me a glass of water.	Rial-no vin tui min pe roh.
Put the milk here.	Hnutê tui heta dah roh.
Bring some more sugar.	Chi-thlum dang la roh.
This water does not boil.	He tui hi a sho lo ve.
Boil the water.	Tui chhuang sho roh.
Make the tea with boiling water.	Thing-pui tui sho vin shiam roh.
I want a small spoon.	Fian tê ka duh.
Give the Sahib a knife.	Sâp hnêna chem-tê pe roh.
You have lost two silver forks.	Tangka kut pahnih i hlo.
Look for the bottle tomorrow.	Nakiûka saidoi-ûm zong roh.
Your clothes are very dirty.	I puan a bâl êm.
Always wear your turban.	I diar khim fo roh.

English.	*Lushai.*
Give me my pipe.	Ka vai-bêl min pe roh.
Put the matches on the table.	Naw'-alh dawhkân-a dah roh.
Cut some wood for the fire.	Thing tuah tûr tan roh.
Wash your face.	I hmai phih roh.
Wash your hands.	I kut sil fai roh.
Wash your clothes.	I puan shu-fai roh.
Wait a little.	Om rih roh.
Don't leave the house until I return.	Ka lo thlen' hma lo chuan, in kal shan shu.
If the Babu comes tell him to wait for me.	Bâbu a lo-kal chuan min nghâk roh se.
Eat your rice now.	Tûna i chaw ei roh.
Come again in the afternoon.	Chaw-hnua lo kal leh roh.
Wake me very early tomorrow morning.	Naktûk zîng tak a min kai tho roh.
Is my gun loaded ?	Ka silai hlo thun em ni ?
Give me the gunpowder.	Silai hlo min pe roh.
Water the flowers.	Pang-pâr tui leih roh.
Pull up the weeds.	Hnim pot roh.
Dig up this plant.	He kung hi lai chhuak roh.
Sow these seeds.	Hêng chi hi tuh roh.
Plant these trees.	Hêng thing hi phun roh.
When will this plant flower ?	He kung hi engtikange a pâr ang ?
Is this fruit edible ?	He rah hi thei em ni ?
Where can I buy some plantains?	Balhla khoi a mi nge ka lei thei ang ?
Are there no mangoes.	Thei-hai a om lo vem ni ?
Lushai figs are very nice.	Mizo thei-pui a tui êm êm.
I want some melons.	Hmazil ka duh.
They are very nasty.	A tui lo êm êm.
Are there any cucumbers in your garden ?	I huan a fang-hma a om em ?
How much do you want for this egg fruit ?	Hêng bok bawn hi eng-zât-nge i chhiar ?
You ask too much.	I chhiar tam lu-tuk.
I will give you four annas.	Sheki khat ka pe ang che.
I have never seen any sweet potatoes.	Kawl-ba-hra ka hmu ngai lo.
Your yams are not nice.	In ba-hra a tui lo ve.
Your fowls are very dear.	In âr a to êm.
What is the price of fowls' eggs ?	Âr-tui engzât man nge ?

IDIOMATIC SENTENCES.

Lushai.	*English.*
Thi leh thi ka kal ang.	I will go, even if I die.
A ṭha ti roh.	Don't you think it is good?
Vok-sha ka ngeih lo.	Pork does not agree with me.
A ti ngai na reng ka hre lo.	I am at a loss what to do.
A lian deo deo va, a ṭha lo deo deo.	The bigger he grows the worse he gets.
Ka zungchal-in ka chuai zo der der ang.	I could lift it with my little finger.
Pa-fa in ni em?	Are you father and child.
Nang i lor bîk.	You are taller than the rest.
I fapa eng rual nge?	How big is your son?
Bân in-khaw-kherh-in an kal.	They are walking arm-in-arm.
Tawp in tai om dawn lo ve.	There will be no end to it.
Lal min ron biak roh.	Give my respects to the chief.
Ka om ang, eng pawh ni roh se.	I will stay, happen what may.
I ta lo pawh ka ta a ṭha.	Mine is good as well as yours.
Tu kal ni nge?	Whose turn is it to go?
Nang ata va ni shu.	It is not yours.
An ṭap ngai lo ve.	Good children never cry (spoken to crying children).
Dawt an shoi ngai lo ve.	They never tell lies (*viz.*, it is wrong to lie).
Râl hu-in min zâp.	I had a presentiment that an enemy was near.
A hnuk a chat ta.	He has died.
A hnuk a va fei êm ve!	How tenacious of life he is!
A tu zawk emawchu lo-kal ang, ka hre lo.	I do not know who is most likely to come.
Kalkata a kal emaw min ti em ni?	Did you think that I had gone to Calcutta?
Mi shoi chaoh kahria.	I have only heard it spoken of.
Hmu pawh ka hmu lo.	I have not even seen it.
A ei ei ka vêl ang.	I shall beat any one who eats it.
I hmel a ṭha ang e!	There's a good boy!
A kip a koi in Mizo ṭong i hria em?	Do you know all the ins and outs of the Lushai language?
Ir leh ir an chuk-tuah e.	They fell on each other's neck.
Ka ti ang tak na-ngial-in a thi.	He died just as I said he would.

Lushai.	*English.*
Biak châk-a ka duh a che ?	I want to speak to you.
I poi zengnge ka khoih ?	What harm have I done you ?
Ka lei hmawr-in a hria.	It is on the tip of my tongue.
Ṭhat-in min buak.	Good has befallen me.
Ṭhat-in a vûr a che.	Blessings have been showered upon you.
Hmul chhia tîl lo tak-in om roh.	May you remain in perfect safety.
Eng a teh-lul nge i ti ?	Whatever did you do that for ?
Teh-lul êm in !	The idea !
Châk-khai-a ka duh a che.	I want you for something.
Ni leh thla in-kâr-a om apiang.	Everything in the universe.
Lo-kal ma lek roh.	Never mind about coming.
Thim tham-a ti ani lo.	It was not done in the dark.
A kuang tuk nân hmang roh se.	May he use it to make his coffin ! (spoken of a man who has stolen an axe).
A thlân lai nân hmang roh se.	May he use it to dig his grave with ! (spoken of a man who has stolen a spade).
A ruang tuam-nân hmang roh se.	May he use it for his winding sheet ! (spoken of a man who has stolen a cloth).
A vân kai chaw-a hmang roh se.	May he use it for his last meal on earth ! (spoken of a man who has stolen food).
A thlai-chhiah a hmang roh se.	May he use it for sacrificing at his burial ! (used of a man who has stolen an animal).

PROVERBS AND SAYINGS.

Rih âr tui phur i ang e.	You are like one carrying the eggs of the *rih* fowl (spoken to one walking slowly).
Nun chhiat leh suak sual a shim thei, hmel chiat a shiam ṭhat thei lo.	Bad habits and faults may be abandoned, but an ugly face cannot be made good.
Ṭong khaw lo ni shu she la.	If it is not presumptuous to say so.

Lushai.	*English.*
Shâr pawh zâm mashela ka pal chhat ang c.	Even though the *shâr* is visible I will break through (*i.e.*, nothing shall prevent me).
Ka beng a shing-ship a hrâm.	A *shing-ship* is signing in my ear (*viz.*, I have a buzzing in the ear).
Thing pawh, a kung a ṭhat leh a rah a ṭha, a kung a ṭhat lo leh, a rah a ṭha lo vang.	If the tree is good its fruit is good, if the tree is bad its fruit is bad.
Koi pawh, a kawm a ṭhat leh, a ṭha, a kawm a ṭhat lo leh, a ṭha lo.	If the pod of a *koi* bean is good the bean is good, if the pod is bad the bean is bad (*i.e.*, not fit for playing with).
Lal ngai lo, lal a na.	A man who has never ruled, rules oppressively.
Them-thiam lo vin an hriam an mawh-chhiat.	Bad workmen blame their tools.
Mi fing-in a fin' man a ei sheng lo, mi â-in a ât man a choi sheng lo.	A wise man cannot eat all the fruit of his wisdom, and a fool cannot pay all the price of his folly.
Voi-in-a ti tûr, naktûka ti-an khêk shu.	Don't put off till tomorrow what should be done to-day.
Mâni in-fak leh sa-khi ngal a eng-ma a bet lo.	There is no more in self-praise than on the shin of a stag.
Zawng tuar ai-in ngao-vin a tuar.	The innocent suffer instead of the guilty.
A vua tu-in êk a che ti ang ani.	It is like the oppressor saying he is being oppressed.
Pachuao sual ka ang.	I am like Pachuao was when fighting (P. wanted to stop, but was afraid to).
A let-ling vut tui thlor-bêl ti ang-in.	Its like speaking of a lye funnel upside down (*i.e.*, saying a thing happened which never did happen).
Sha leh sha-in in-chan ang.	Like flesh cutting up flesh (spoken of one who is clumsy in doing anything).
She bo hnu-a she kong khâr ang.	Like shutting the *gayal's* stable when the *gayal* is gone.

Lushai.	*English.*
The hme' ang-in a om.	It is like a *thereng* when squeezed (*i.e.*, very quiet).
Lung pui pawh lung tê-in a kam-ki lo chuan ạ om thei lo.	Even a big rock cannot remain without rolling unless supported by small stones (*i.e.*, the great cannot do without the humble).
Aṭha lam kong a chho, a chhe lam kong a phei.	The good road is steep and the bad road is level (*i.e.*, it is easier to do evil than good).

PART III.—DICTIONARY.

LUSHAI-ENGLISH.

NOTE.—The Lushai letters printed in italics are sometimes omitted.

A

Â, (*s.*) a fool, a foolish person, a mad person.
„ (*a.*) foolish, ignorant, mad.
„ (*v.*) to be foolish, etc.
A, (*prep.*), from, in, on, to, of.
A, (*pro.*) he, his, she, her, it, its.
Â baw-raw, (*s.*) an idiot.
„ „ „ (*a.*) idiotic.
„ „ „ (*v.*) to be idiotic.
A-chin, (*conj.*) since.
A chhûn a zân-in, day and night.
A eng-ber-nge, (*pro.*) which? (of a number).
A eng-nge, (*pro.*) which ?
A hmei a pa, (*s.*) men and women (collectively).
A-hnu-in, (*conj.*) since.
Ai, (*s.*) the power of fascinating, charming, or getting power over.
Ai, (*prep.*) instead of, because of, (*conj.*) than.
Ai, (*s.*) a stack, a pile.
Ai, (*v.*) to warm one's self, to bask.
Ai, (*v.*) to perform a ceremony in order to get the spirit of a wild animal killed in the chase into one's power after death.
Ai, (*s.*) a crab (a contracted form of *chak-ai*).
Ai-a, (*prep.*) instead of, because of, (*conj.*) than.
Ai awh, (*v.*) to become a substitute.
Ai awh tu, (*s.*) a substitute.
Ai awt, (*s.*) a crab trap.
Ai bop, (*s.*) the claw of a crab, the hammer of a gun.
Ai en, (*s.*) an augur.
„ (*v.*) to augur.
Ai eng, (*s.*) turmeric.
Ai-en-thiam, (*s.*) an augur.
Ai-fiar kal, (*v.*) to walk upon the hands and feet with stomach upwards.

Ai hni, (*s.*) a hangnail, the pouch under a crab for its young, (*v.*) to have a hangnail.
Ai-in, (*prep.*) instead of, (*conj.*) than.
Ai kaih, (*v.*) to fascinate, to charm, to draw by some mysterious power.
Ai-khirh, (*v.*) to get stiff with being cramped.
Ai-ruah, (*s.*) the rain which comes at the beginning of autumn after a break in the wet weather (said to be the time when crabs appear).
Ai shân, (*s.*) an augur, (*v.*), to augur.
Ai-shân-thiam, (*s.*) an augur.
Ai-thûr, (*s.*) the name of a plant.
A*k*, (*v.*) to sling across the shoulder (as satchel, etc.), to carry in a satchel.
Al, (*a.*) salt, (*v.*) to salt, to be salt.
A-lang-in, (*adv.*) apparently, outwardly, publicly, openly.
Alh, (*s.*) a flame, (*v.*) to flare, to flame, to blaze, to burn.
Ama, (*pro.*) he, his, she, her, it, its, him.
Ama-ata, (*pro.*) his, hers, its.
Ama-e-raw-chu, (*conj.*) nevertheless, still.
Ama-in, he himself, she herself, it itself, of itself.
Ama-ta, (*pro.*) his, hers, its.
An, (*pro.*) they, their.
An, (*s.*) the generic name for all edible leaves, green stuff of any sort.
A-na-rân-in, } in everything, upon every occasion, in vain.
A-na-zong-in, }
An-bong, (*s.*) a species of sorrel.
An' chhe lawh, } (*v. t.*) to curse.
An' chhia lawh, }
An' chhia dong, (*v.*) to be cursed.
Âng, (*s.*) the bosom, the lap, the space between the chin and knees.
Âng, (*v.*) to open the mouth, to abuse, to use abusive language, to nag.
Ang, (*s.*) sort, (*a.*) like, (*v.*) to be like.
Ang-chuan, (*conj.*) as if, as though, like as.
Ang dek, (*a.*) exactly resembling.
Ang êm chuan, } just as though, just as if.
Ang êm in, }
Ang-in, (*conj.*) as if, as though, like as.
Ang lo-vin, (*prep.*) contrary to.
Ang lo, (*adj.*) unlike.

Ang meo-vin,
Ang reng-in, } just as if, just as though, just as.
Ang tak na-ngial-in, just as, exactly as.
Ang zêl-in, (*prep.*) in, accordance with, according to, like as.
Ang zet-chuan,
Ang-zet-in, } just as if, just as though, just as.
Ân'hla, (*s.*) abusive language, abuse.
An-hlîng, (*s.*) the name of a plant with edible leaves.
Ani, yes (literally 'it is').
Ani, (*pro.*) he, she, it.
Ani-ang-e, (*adv.*) perhaps.
Ani-lo-leh, (*adv.*) else, then.
Ani-lo-vêk leh, (*adv.*) else.
Ani-na-a, (*conj.*) nevertheless, although this is so.
Ani-ta,
Ani-tawh, } ago, since.
Ani-ta, (*pro.*) his, her, its.
Ani-tak-e, so it is, it is really.
An-ku, (*s.*) the name of a tree with edible leaves.
An-ma-ni, (*pro.*) they, there, them.
An-ma-ni-ta, (*pro.*) theirs.
An-ni, (*pro.*) they, their, them.
An-ni-ta, (*pro.*) thiers.
An pâng-ṭhuam, (*s.*) the name of plant with edible leaves (when boiled with goat's flesh said to form a poison).
An' pui, (*s.*) a person or thing resembling another.
An-sa-pui,
An-sa-tê, } (*s.*) the name of an edible plant with yellow flowers.
An-ta, (*pro.*) theirs.
An-ṭam, (*s.*) a species of mustard plant.
An-ṭam bul bâl, (*s.*) a radish.
An-thûr, (*s.*) the name of a large edible plant.
An-vai-in, (*a.*) all.
An-za-in, (*a.*) all.
Ao, (*v.*) to scream, to cry out, to shout.
Ao, (*v.*) to call.
Ap, (*a.*) mouldy, mildewed, (*v.*) to get mouldy, etc.
A-piang, (*pro.*) whatever, whoever, whomever, as.
A-piang-a,
A-piang-in, } (*adv.*) whenever.
A pui a pang, (*s.*) old and young.
Âr, (*s.*) a fowl.
Ar, (*v.*) to spread out (as the hand, etc.,) to open (as a flower, etc.), to diverge (as lines, etc.)

Âr a fang-hma, (*s.*) the name of a creeper with a cucumber-like fruit.
Âr a khuan, } (*s.*) the name of a plant with a sweet smelling
Âr a tuk-khuan, } flower.
Âr awn rang-ka-chak, (*s.*) the peacock.
Âr chang, (*s.*) the long feathers in the tail of a cock.
Âr chang kei, (*a.*) curved, (*v.*) to be curved.
Âr chaw, (*s.*) fowl's food, the name of the insects which make the *tarpilu*.
Âr chhiar, (*s.*) a small fowl house under the eaves of a Lushai house.
Âr chhuang, (*s.*) the comb of a cock or hen.
Âr dah, (*s.*) the name of a tree the shoots of which are used as a medicine for toothache, etc.
Âr dan' bang, (*s.*) the name of a partition in a Lushai house.
Âr fêp, (*s.*) the long feathers near a cock's tail.
Âr hrik, (*s.*) a louse.
Âr hrik reh, (*s.*) the name of a tree the leaves of which are used to keep away lice.
Âr kai zân, (*s.*) the night of the full moon.
Âr kal, (*v.*) to walk on the hands.
Âr ke bawk, } (*s.*) the name of a creeper the root of which
Âr ke zung bawk, } is used as a medicine for burns.
Âr-la, (*s.*) a pullet.
Âr-mong-holh, (*s.*) the stick insect.
Âr-ngeng, (*s.*) the name of a plant, a pimple, a small boil.
Âr no, (*s.*) a chicken.
Âr pa, (*s.*) a cock.
Âr pa thei-rawl, (*s.*) a cockerel.
Âr phaw, (*s.*) the long feathers round a cock's neck which stand out like a shield when angry.
Âr pui, (*s.*) a full grown hen.
Âr-shi, (*s.*) a star.
Âr-shi thlawk, (*s.*) a shooting star, (*v.*) to shoot (as a star).
Âr tê, (*s.*) a chicken.
Âr tuk-khuan, (*s.*) the name of a plant with sweet smelling flowers.
A-rûk-in, (*adv.*) secretly, on the sly.
Ât, (*a.*) cut, reaped, (*v.*) to cut, to reap.
A-ta, (*prep.*) from.
A-ta, (*pro.*) his, hers, its.
A-tang-in, (*prep.*) from.
A-tawp a-tawp-a, in course of time, in the end.
A-thoi-in, (*adv.*) ambiguously, obscurely.

A-tûk-a, the next day.
A-vai-in, (*a.*) all.
A-za-in, (*a.*) all.
A-zeng-nge, (*pro.*) which ?

Aw

Aw, (*s.*) voice, yes.
Aw ! an interjection.
Aw a chhâng, (*v.*) to be hoarse.
Awh, (*v.*) to take up room, to occupy space, to seize or possess (as a spirit).
Awh zao, (*v.*) to take up much room.
Awh zîm, (*v.*) to take up little room.
Aw*k*, (*v.*) to hang by the neck or leg.
Awk, (*s.*) the name of a fabulous creature which is supposed to swallow the sun or moon during an eclipse.
Aw ka, (*s.*) the voice.
Awk-hlum, (*v.t.*) to hang.
Awk-hrawl, (*a.*) unreliable, dishonest, hypocritical, (*v.*) to be unreliable, etc.
Awk-in a lem, (*v.*) to be eclipsed (as sun or moon).
Awk lem, (*s.*) an eclipse.
Awk-pa-ka, (*s.*) the long opening in the *bahzâr* of a Lushai house, the entrance to a *zawlbuk*.
Awl, (*v.*) to rest, to have little to do.
Aw-lê, (*s.*) an alligator, a crocodile.
Aw-le, all right.
Awl-len-lai (or hun), the slack time after the *jhúm* is cut or when the weeding is over or after harvest.
Awm, (*s.*) the chest, the breast.
Awm-khaoh, (*a.*) burly, well made, (*v.*) to be burly, etc.
Awm ruh, (*s.*) the breast bone.
Awm-vêl, (*s.*) the name of a skin disease.
Awn, (*a.*) slanting, lopsided, (*adv.*) slantingly.
Awn-chep, (*s.*) the name of a tree.
Awng, (*s.*) a hole, an aperture.
Awng-phah, (*s.*) a mattress or anything spread for sleeping on.
Awt, (*s.*) a crab trap.
Aw-ze mi, }
Aw-zia, } (*s.*) a foreigner, one who speaks in a foreign tongue.
Aw-zia-mi, }

B

Ba, (*s.*) a tendril.
Ba, (*s.*) credit, (*v.*) to owe.

Ba'bun kho, (*s.*) the name of a basket.
Ba'den'suk, (*s.*) a wooden pestle for pounding arum bulbs for pigs' food.
Ba-hra, (*s.*) a yam.
Ba-hra thlum, (*s.*) the sweet potato.
Bah-zâr, (*s.*) an enclosed verandah at the back of a Lushai house, the platform at the upper end of a *zawlbuk.*
Bai, (*a.*) lame, (*v.*) to be lame, to walk lamely.
Bai, (*v.*) to cook with salt, (*s.*) anything cooked with salt.
Bai-ba-hlâng, (*v.*) to hop on one leg.
Bai-bing, (*s.*) the name of a species of arum.
Bâk, (*s.*) the bat.
Bâk, (*a.*) left unfinished, remaining, left to be done, (*v.*) to have on hand (to do, etc.), to have left (to do, etc.)
Bak, (*s.*) an elfin lock, hair immediately in front of the ear, mane.
Bâk-a le'uai, (*v.*) to hang upside down on a horizontal bar, etc.
Ba'kâng, (*s.*) a species of edible arum.
Bâ'khik, (*s.*) a species of wild arum.
Bak-kha-tê, (*s.*) the name of a plant with edible leaves.
Bak me'chem, } (*s.*) a razor.
Bak me'na, }
Bâl, (*a.*) dirty, (*v.*) to be or get dirty.
Bâl, (*s.*) an edible arum bulb and plant.
Bal, (*adv.*) off, (*a.*) having a piece off, chipped, (*v.*) to be chipped.
Bal-hla, (*s.*) a plantain.
Ban, (*s.*) a post (of house).
Ban, (*v.*) to reach out the hand, to reach, to arrive.
Ban, (*a.*) sticky, plastic, thick (as liquid), (*v.*) to be sticky, etc.
Bân, (*s.*) the arm.
Bân-bun, (*s.*) a bracelet.
Bân-chen, (*s.*) a measurement equal to the length of the arm.
Ba'nê, (*s.*) the young tubers of the arum.
Bâng, (*v.*) to cease, to stop, to hang up (as on a peg, etc.)
Bâng, (*a.*) left remaining.
Bang, (*s.*) a wall, a partition.
Bang-lai, (*s.*) the name of the partition in a Lushai house by the bed.
Bang-lai chhûng, (*s.*) the space behind the *banglai.*
Bang-rel, (*s.*) the framework of the walls of a house, wall battens.
Bang-tung, (*s.*) the perpendicular split bamboos in a mat wall.

Bang-zâl, (*s.*) the horizontal split bamboos in a mat wall.
Ban-pawl, (*s.*) a species of plantain.
Ban-phâk, (*v.*) to be able to reach.
Ban phar, (*s.*) the name of a tree.
Ban-puam, (*s.*) the muscle of the upper arm.
Ban-pui, (*s.*) a species of large plantain.
Bân-rêk, (*s.*) the wrist.
Ban-ria, (*s.*) a species of small plantain.
Bân zai, (*v.*) to vaccinate.
Baoh, (*v.*) to bark (as a dog), (*s.*) the bark (of a dog).
Ba'pui, (*s.*) the name of a large edible arum bulb.
Bâr, (*v.*) to stuff in the mouth.
Bar, (*v.*) to rest (a bamboo, etc.) against the fork of a tree.
Bâr-fa-ṭêk, (*s.*) the name of a bird.
Ba-rî, (*s.*) the parting of the hair.
Barî ṭhen, (*v.*) to part the hair.
Ba' sai kê, (*s.*) a species of edible arum.
Bat, (*v.*) to owe.
Bât, (*v.*) to hook, to catch (as briar), to cast or carry a cloth over the shoulder, to be hooked or caught.
Bât-ṭha, (*v.*) to adjust a cloth by throwing the ends over the shoulder.
Ba-thlâr, (*s.*) the place sheltered by the eaves.
Baw, (*s.*) semen.
Baw, (*v.*) a contracted form of *bua.*
Bawh, (*v.*) to lean upon, to pounce upon.
Bawh-bel, (*s.*) the beam on the top of the barrier at the entrance of a *zawlbuk.*
Bawh-chhiat, (*v.*) to break (as a custom or law), to lean upon and break.
Bawh-tah, (*s.*) the name of a certain kind of bamboo plaiting and cloth-weaving.
Bawh-thiang, (*s.*) the beam on the top of the barrier at the entrance of a *zawlbuk.*
Bawk, (*v.*) to swell, to come into a bump, (*s.*) a knot (in wood, string, etc.), an excrescence, a swelling.
Bawk, (*v.*) to tie up anything small in the corner of a cloth.
Bawk, } Bawk-tê, } (*s.*) a booth, a hut, a temporary house.
Bawl, (*s.*) to offer a sacrifice outside a village.
Bawl-hlo, (*s.*) the general name for the sacrificial furniture of the Lushais.
Bawl-tê-chhe-hnok, (*s.*) the name of a game played with the *koi* bean, (*v.*) to play at the above game.

Bawm, (*s.*) a box, case, basket, a vessel of any kind, a coop.
Baw*m*, (*v.*) to surround, to envelop, to cover (as sores).
Baw*m*-khat-lûk, (*v.*) to cover completely (as sores, dust).
Bawm-râng, (*s.*) the name of a basket.
Bawm-zo-sa-hnawh, (*s.*) the name of a game (similar to chess), (*v.*) to play at the above game.
Bawng, a contraction of *sebawng*.
Bawng, (*s.*) the name of a bird the male of which is scarlet and the female yellow.
Bawng-êk-lîr, the same as *pawng-êk-lîr*.
Bawng-khalh, } (*s.*) a bullock or cow-driver.
Bawng-pu, }
Bawng-tuh-thlawh, (*s.*) a large hoe, a *kodali*.
Bawr, (*s.*) a bunch, a cluster.
Bê, (*v.*) to bleat.
Bê, (*s.*) the generic name for different species of beans.
Be, a contracted form of *biak*.
Bê-ai-thang, (*s.*) the name of a wild fowl trap.
Beh, (*v.*) to wear in the ear.
Be-hliang, } (*s.*) the names of species of beans.
Be hloi, }
Bei, (*v.*) to do, to assault, to be engaged in doing anything, to begin, to appeal to (as in a lawsuit).
Bei, (*v.*) to stick, to adhere.
Bei-shei, (*v.*) to expect, think, consider, hope.
Bek, (*s.*) the side of the head.
Be-kang, (*s.*) the name of a bean.
Be-kar, (*s.*) a coolie, servant, workman.
Bek-bor, (*s.*) the side of the head.
Bel, (*v. t.*) to stick on (as paper, plaster, etc.), to plaster, to patch.
Bêl, (*s.*) a pot, a utensil.
Bêl, (*v.*) to depend upon.
Be-leoh, (*v.*) to yelp as a dog.
Belh, } (*v.*) to add to, to join, to swell the ranks by joining.
Belh-chhah, }
Bel-kâng, (*v.*) to become dry, as a scratch when healing.
Bêl-lei, (*s.*) clay.
Bel-mang, (*s.*) soot caused by the action of fire on pots, etc.
Bel-phuar, (*s.*) the name of a tree.
Bêl-thlêng, (*s.*) the name of a kind of saucer to cover pots.
Bel-vua-tu, } (*s.*) a potter.
Bel-vua*k* thiam, }
Beng, (*s.*) the ear, the handle (of cup, etc.), the eye (of a needle).

Beng, (*v.*) to press in (as salt in a measure), to blow (as wind the flames).
Bêng, (*v.*) to clap, to slap, to pat.
Beng-beh, (*s.*) a woman's earring.
Beng-bung, (*s.*) a Lushai dulcimer made of wood.
Beng-châh, (*s.*) the priming of a gun, (*v.*) to prime a gun.
Beng-chheng, (*s.*) a disturbance, a row, a noise, (*v.*) to make a noise, etc.
Beng-chhêt, (*a.*) deaf, (*v.*) to be deaf.
Beng-chhût-ngong, (*v.*) to pretend not to hear.
Beng kherh, (*s.*) otorrhœa, (*v.*) to have otorrhœa.
Beng-lût, Beng-lût-zawng, } (*a.*) interesting.
Beng-ngong, (*a.*) deaf, hard of hearing, (*v.*) to be deaf, etc.
Beng-thek, (*s.*) cymbals, a signal made of a split bamboo to give warning of the approach of an enemy, a bamboo cut so as to make a clapping noise to keep time when treading out grain.
Beng-tla-lo, (*a.*) cruel, stupid, vicious, bad, (*v.*) to be cruel, etc.
Beng-vâr, (*a.*) clever, enlightened, wise, sharp, quick of hearing, (*v.*) to keep a good look-out, to be clever, etc.
Ben'hon'silai, (*s.*) a snider rifle.
Ben-von, (*s.*) the name of a basket.
Be-pui, Be-pui-lei, Be-pui-sa-ríl, Be-pui-shen, } (*s.*) the names of various kinds of beans.
Ber, a superlative adjective particle, (*adv.*) very, most.
Berâm, (*s.*) a sheep.
Berâm-hmul, (*s.*) wool.
Berâm-huang, (*s.*) a sheep-fold.
Berâm-no, (*s.*) a lamb.
Berâm-pa, (*s.*) a ram.
Berâm-pu, (*s.*) a shepherd.
Berâm-pui, (*s.*) a ewe.
Berâm-vêngtu, (*s.*) a shepherd.
Be-raw, (*s.*) the name of a tree, a kind of resin.
Ber-bek, (*s.*) a burr.
Berh-bu, (*s.*) a bowl.
Be-ru, (*v.*) to whisper to, to speak secretly to.
Be-rûl, (*s.*) the snake-gourd (*trichosanthes anguina*).
Be-sal, (*s.*) a small undeveloped bean in the pod.
Bet, an affix signifying to hold or keep down, (*v.*) to stick, to adhere.

Be-tê, (*s.*) the name of a bean.
Bi, (*s.*) the keys of any musical instrument.
Bia*k*, (*v.*) to speak to, to speak, to propose (for marriage), to offer a sacrifice to.
Bial, (*a.*) round, spherical, square, (*adv.*) spherically.
Biâng, (*s.*) the cheek, the side post of a door.
Biang, (*s.*) a flying squirrel.
Biang-bôh, (*s.*) the mumps, (*v.*) to have mumps.
Biang-chhu, } (*s.*) a dimple.
Biang-khuar, }
Bih, (*v.*) to look into, to spy into, to look at, to examine.
Bih-thla, (*v.*) to look into on the sly.
Bîk, (*adv.*) more than others, specially, (*a.*) special.
Bil, (*a.*) blunt, (*v.*) to be blunt.
Bîl, (*s.*) the name of a tree.
Bil-baw-lawk, (*s.*) a knot, (*v.*) to tie a knot (in a single piece of string, etc.)
Bilh, (*a.*) sprained, (*v.*) to be sprained.
Bin, (*v.*) to throw over the head (as an antagonist in wrestling).
Bing, (*a.*) isolated.
Bîng, (*s.*) one of the stomachs of a ruminating animal.
Bing-bi-let, (*v.*) to turn over lengthways, to turn a somersault, (*adv.*) head over heels.
Bir, (*adv.*) vertically, perpendicularly, (*a.*) vertical, etc.
Bi-ru, (*v.*) to conceal or hide one's self.
Bo, (*a.*) lost, (*v.*) to be lost, (*adv.*) away.
Boih, (*s.*) a slave, a retainer.
Bok, (*adv.*) indeed, also, in a way.
Bok, (*v.*) to lie down (as animals), to recline with the head raised.
Bok-bawn, (*s.*) the egg fruit, brinjal.
Bok-khup-in, (*adv.*) forward, on the face.
Bok-phêk, (*v.*) to crouch.
Bok-vâk, (*v.*) to crawl.
Bol, (*s.*) a pimple, (*v.*) to have pimples.
Bol-hlawh, (*s.*) dirt, mire, filth, (*a.*) dirty, unclean (for sacrifice or food), (*v.*) to be dirty, etc.
Bol-hlawh-dûr, (*s.*) a rubbish heap.
Bon, (*a.*) dense (with undergrowth), (*v.*) to be dense.
Bop, (*s.*) a leg, the hind leg of an animal.
Bop-khaw-kherh-in ṭhu, (*v.*) to sit crosslegged.
Bop-pui, (*s.*) the claw (of a crab), the hind leg (of locusts, etc.)
Bor, (*a.*) a contracted form of *buar*.
Bo-ral, (*v.*) to be ruined, to be completely lost, to cease to exist, to come to nought, to perish.

Bo-ral-thei, (*a.*) perishable.
Bor-shom, (*a.*) unhealthy, (*v.*) to be in bad health.
Bo-ruak, (*s.*) the air, the atmosphere.
Bu, (*v.*) to bellow, to low.
Bu, (*s.*) a nest, a bunch, a cluster.
Buai, (*v.*) to be confused, to be muddled, to be in an uproar, to clamour.
Buai-thlâk, (*a.*) confusing, muddling.
Bua*k*, (*v.*) to be spilled, to pour out, to fall upon (as little pieces from the roof, &c.)
Bual, (*v.*) to bathe, to wallow.
Buan-chak-hlo, (*s.*) the name of a weed.
Buang, (*a.*) buff coloured.
Buar, (*s.*) the generic name for the thistle family.
Buar, (*a.*) swollen, bloated in the face (through sickness), (*v.*) to be swollen, etc.
Buar-pui, (*s.*) the fan palm, also a large species of screw pine.
Buat-saih, (*v.*) to prepare, to get ready.
Buh, (*s.*) rice.
Buh-bial, (*s.*) the name of a species of rice.
Buh-bih, (*s.*) a small hole made in the ground for planting rice.
Buh-chang-kuang, (*s.*) a small flute made of straw played by Lushai girls.
Buh-chi-ûm, (*s.*) a chrysalis.
Buh-fai, (*s.*) cleaned rice.
Buh-hawp, (*s.*) rice water, rice cooked very soft.
Buh-hmui, (*s.*) the name of a species of rice.
Buh hûm, (*s.*) unhusked rice.
Buh kem, (*s.*) small species of broken rice produced by the process of pounding.
Buh lâ*k*, (*v.*) to gather in the harvest.
Buh sa-nghâr, (*s.*) the name of a species of rice.
Buh sheng, (*v.*) to gather in the harvest.
Buh tlei, (*s.*) a piece of bamboo used for stirring cooking rice.
Buh-tun, (*s.*) millet.
Buh vorh, (*v.*) to toss, to gamble, (*s.*) the name of a game similar to knucklebones.
Buh zâm, (*s.*) the name of a species of rice.
Bui, (*a.*) bloated or flabby in the face (through sickness), swollen (through crying), (*v.*) to be bloated, etc.
Bui, (*s.*) the bamboo rat.
Bui-biang, (*s.*) the name of a plant with convolvulus-like flowers.
Bui-ke-lek, (*s.*) the mole.
Bui-luang-pâr, (*s.*) the hoary bamboo rat (*rhizomys pruinosus*).

Bui-lu-kham, (*s.*) the Indian rhododendron (*melastroma malabathricum*).
Bui-pui, (*s.*) the red cheeked bamboo rat (*rhizomys erythrogenys*).
Bui-shen, (*s.*) the chestnut bamboo rat (*rhizomys badius*).
Buk, (*v.*) to nod (the head).
Bûk, (*v.*) to weigh, (*s.*) a seer, two pounds.
Bûk, (*v.*) to tip up.
Bûk, (*s.*) a temporary house, a booth.
Buk, (*a.*) dishevelled, rough, bushy, (*v.*) to be dishevelled, etc.
Bûk khai-na, } (*s.*) scales, balance.
Bûk-na, }
Bul, (*s.*) cause, beginning, the root, stump or foot (of tree), the lower end (as of stick, post, etc.)
Bûl, (*a.*) having the top or head off, (*adv.*) off.
Bûl, (*s.*) the name of a durable tree.
Bul a ṭha, (*v.*) to have someone upon whom to rely, to have a powerful ally.
Bul-bâl, (*s.*) a bulb, a tuber.
Bul-bâl nei, (*a.*) bulbous, (*v.*) same as *bul nei*.
Bul-bawk, (*s.*) a bulb, a tuber.
Bul-bawk nei, (*a.*) bulbous.
Bul-lut, (*s.*) the imperial pigeon.
Bul-nei, (*v.*) to have someone upon whom to rely or fall back upon.
Bul tum, (*v.*) to bear the consequences or blame of anything, to offer or to be ready to bear the consequences or blame of anything.
Bum, (*v.*) to cheat, to deceive.
Bum-bôh, (*a.*) rough, rugged, uneven, (*v.*) to be rough, etc.
Bum-ro, (*v.*) to hinder.
Bum thlai, (*v.*) to deceive.
Bun, (*v.*) to lie in ambush, to ambush.
Bun, (*v.*) to pour out, to empty out.
Bun, (*v.*) to put on or wear (as ring, boots, etc.), to encircle.
Bung, (*s.*) a portion, a part, a chapter, (*adv.*) in pieces, (*v.*) to cut or chop in pieces.
Bûng, (*s.*) the name of a species of Indian fig tree.
Bung-rua, (*s.*) baggage, things, goods, luggage.
Bûr, (*v.*) to pierce, to stick in (as an arrow, etc.)
Bûr, (*s.*) a gourd, a vessel.
Bûr-chhe-lân, (*v.*) to swim or float, catching hold of the knees.
Buruk, (*s.*) a contrivance worked by the wind to scare away bears, etc. from a *jhûm*.
Bu-thuai-ram, (*s.*) the name of a tree the fruit of which intoxicates,
Bu-tu-puan, (*s.*) flannel, woollen cloth.

Ch.

Cha-bet, (*s.*) a burr.
Chah, (*v.*) to commission to tell, to ask to communicate, to ask to inform, to send for.
Chah, (*v.*) to bait, (*s.*) a bait.
Chai, (*s.*) the name of a dance, (*v.*) to engage in the above dance.
Chai, (*v.*) to romp, to play.
Chai-che', (*s.*) tongs, pincers, tweezers.
Chai-chîm, (*s.*) a mouse.
Chaih, (*v.*) to chase as the Lushais do a *gayal* before killing, etc. (A number of men have hold of one end of the rope by which it is secured and drive it about from place to place with much shouting.)
Châk, (*v.*) to want, to like, to be fond of (especially of eatables), to long for.
Chak, (*a.*) strong (physically), fast, swift, (*adv.*), fast, swiftly, (*v.*) to be strong.
Chak-ai, (*s.*) a crab.
Chak-ai fu, (*s.*) the name of a small edible plant.
Châk-khai, (*s.*) use, purpose, reason, a necessity, a requisite.
Châk-khai-zawng, (*s.*) anything necessary or requisite.
Chak lo, (*a.*) weak, (*adv.*) in a weakly manner, slowly, (*v.*) to be weak.
Cha-kok, (*s.*) a brake fern.
Chal, (*s.*) the forehead.
Chal, affix denoting the masculine gender.
Chal-ki-khât, (*s.*) a rhinoceros, the name of an insect.
Chal-lang, (*v.*) to be popular, (*a.*) popular.
Châl-tê, (*s.*) the name of a species of bamboo.
Chal-tlai, (*a.*) conceited, boastful, (*v.*) to be conceited, etc., (*adv.*) conceitedly, etc.
Cham, (*a.*) flat, level.
Châm, (*v.*) to remain in a place over a day and night, to sojourn.
Cham-phai-thei, (*s.*) a species of bilberry.
Cham-pha-phâk, (*s.*) anniversary.
Chân, (*v.*) to lose (as by death, fire, raid, etc.), to be deprived of.
Chan, (*s.*) lot, portion, luck, share.
Chan, (*v.*) to cut up, to slice up.
Chan, (*v.*) to make, convert or fashion into.
Chan-ai, (*s.*) a portion, a share.
Chan-chin, (*s.*) news.
Chang, (*v.*) to change into, to become.
Chang, (*s.*) the long feathers of a bird's tail.

Chang, (*a.*) hard, (not soft), ripe, mature, (*v.*) to be hard, ripe, etc.
Chang, (*v.*) to receive as a share or portion.
Chang, (*adv.*) freely, without fear.
Châng, (*v.*) to watch for, to waylay, to lie in wait, to lie in ambush.
Châng, (*s.*) a joint (as of fingers, bamboo, etc.), a verse of a song.
Châng, (*v.*) to warp.
Chang chang, (*adv.*) a little, slightly.
Châng châng-in, (*adv.*) occasionally, sometimes.
Châng-dam, (*s.*) the name of a cane.
Chang-êl, (*s.*) the wild plantain, sometimes used of cultivated plantains also.
Chang-hnih chen, (*s.*) a measurement, the distance from the tip of first finger to the second joint.
Chang-kêl, (*s.*) the fruit of the wild plantain.
Chang-kha, (*s.*) a vegetable (*momordica carantia*).
Chang-khat chen, (*s.*) a measurement, the distance from the tip of first finger to the first joint.
Chang-kor, (*s.*) stag moss.
Chang-lak-chen, (*s.*) a measurement, the distance from the tip of first finger to the middle of the second joint.
Chang-long, (*s.*) the heart of the plantain tree used as food.
Châng-man, (*s.*) a species of rice, used for making beer and spirits.
Chang-pât, (*s.*) a worm.
Chang-tîr, (*v. t.*) to alter, to transform.
Châng tum, (*v.*) to whistle with the knuckle in the mouth.
Chan-hrang, (*s.*) a portion, a share.
Chan-ve, (*s.*) a half, half-way.
Chan-vo, (*s.*) a portion, a share.
Chao, (*v.*) to be exhausted, to be tired out.
Chaoh, (*a.*) only, alone.
Chap, (*s.*) a cut *jhûm* before burning.
Chap-char, (*v.*) to complete, to finish cutting a *jhûm*, (*s.*) a cut *jhûm* before burning.
Chap-char kût, (*s.*) the name of a Lushai feast after the cutting of *jhûms*.
Cha-po, (*a.*) proud, (*v.*) to be proud.
Châr, (*a.*) dry, parched, (*v.*) to dry, to be dry, etc.
Châr, (*v.*) to stick.
Châr, (*v.*) to keep, to detain, to keep hold of.
Châr, (*s.*) the name of a tree.
Char, (*v.*) to hold out at arm's length, to straighten the arm.

Char-na, (*s.*) glue, gum, paste.
Châr chilh, (*v.*) to keep, to detain, to keep hold of.
Chat, (*v.*) to break (as a rope).
Chât, (*a.*) chapped, (*v.*) to be chapped, to have a corn.
Cha-tuan, (*a.*) ancient, eternal.
Cha-tuan-a, } (*adv.*) for ever, from the beginning, from time
Cha-tuan-in, } immemorial, eternally.
Chaw, (*s.*) cooked rice, food.
Chaw-bêl hmin lai, (*s.*) a measure of time equal to about one hour (literally, the time it takes for a pot of rice to cook).
Chaw-fâk, (*s.*) the midday meal, noon, (*v.*) to eat the midday meal.
Chaw-fak lai (or hun), (*s.*) midday, the time of the midday meal.
Chawh, (*v.*) to serve one right.
Chaw-hma, (*s.*) morning, forenoon.
Chaw-hma ban, }
Chaw-hma kal-na chen, } (*s.*) half a day's journey.
Chaw-hmeh, (*s.*) meat, vegetables, or anything eaten with rice.
Chaw-hnu, (*s.*) after noon.
Chawh-tolh, (*s.*) the name of a wooden basin for drawing beer in.
Chawk, (*adv.*) generally, as a rule.
Chaw*k*, (*v.*) to buy.
Chaw-kê, (*s.*) the name of a lizard, a gecko.
Chawl, (*v.*) to rest.
Chawm, (*v.*) to feed, to tend, to support.
Chawm hlum, (*v.*) to support a person for life.
Chawm-zil, (*s.*) the name of a flowering tree.
Chawn, (*s.*) cotton rolled ready for spinning.
Chawn, (*s.*) the calf of the leg.
Chawn zial, (*s.*) a kind of blind known in India as a 'chick,' a mat made of thin strips of wood, used for wrapping rolled cotton in.
Chaw-puan, (*s.*) the name of a Poi cloth.
Chê, (*v.*) to move.
Che, (*pro.*) to thee, from thee, for thee, thee.
Cheh-rep, (*s.*) the name of a trap which crushes its victims.
Chei, (*v.*) to tidy, to make or put tidy, to repair.
Chei-moi, (*v.*) to beautify, to adorn.
Chêk, (*v.*) to chop (with an axe), to hoe.
Chêk-sholh, (*v.*) to treat with contempt.

Chelh, (*v.*) to grasp, to hold, to detain, to restrain, to seize or possess (as a spirit).
Che-lo-vin, (*adv.*) without moving, motionlessly.
Chem, (*s.*) the Lushai chopper, a bill-hook, dao, etc.
Chem a kal, (*v.*) to be uneven (as the edge of dao).
Chem hrât-in, (*adv.*) by violence, by force of arms.
Chêm-i, (*s.*) a pet name for a little girl.
Chem-kal, (*a.*) fortunate in war, (*v.*) to be fortunate in war.
Chem-shei, (*s.*) a sword.
Chem-tê, (*s.*) a knife.
Chêm-tê, (*s.*) a pet name for a little girl.
Cheng, (*s.*) the lock (of a gun).
Chêng, (*s.*) a rupee.
Chên*g*, (*v.*) to stop, to continue, to remain.
Cheng-kek, (*s.*) the name of a tree with an edible fruit.
Chêng-kol, (*s.*) the name of a watersnail.
Chên' pui, (*v.*) to adopt, to keep (as a dog, boy, etc.), to entertain, to receive as a guest, (*s.*) a guest.
Che*p*, (*v.*) to nip, to clip.
Chep, (*a.*) small, cramped for room, (*v.*) to be small, etc.
Che-pa, (*s.*) the name of a squirrel.
Che*p* chhum, (*v.*) to cut (with scissors).
Chêr, (*a.*) thin, lean, (*v.*) to be thin, etc.
Chê*t*, (*v.*) to do, to act, to work, to perform.
Chêt zia, (*s.*) works, actions, deeds.
Che-u, (*pro.*) you, to you, from you, for you.
Chhah, (*a.*) thick (as wood, etc.), (*v.*) to be thick.
Chhaih, (*v.*) to tease.
Chhâk, (*v.*) to spit.
Chhak-a, (*adv.* and *prep.*) above, higher up.
Chhak-lam, (*s.*) the east.
Chhak-lam-a, (*adv.* and *prep.*) above, higher up.
Chhâl, (*v.*) to ask for an explanation of conduct, to question, to cross-examine.
Chhâl dang, (*v.*) to confute, to refute.
Chham, (*v.*) to run short of anything, to lack.
Chhâm-êk, (*s.*) the reddish deposit found at the bottom of some pools, or where water has run.
Chham phual, (*v.*) to supplicate, to pray, to repeat a prayer.
Chhan, (*v.*) to help, to rescue.
Chhan, object for, object of, reason for, reason of, meaning of.
Chhan-chhua*k*, (*v.*) to rescue.
Chhan-dam, (*v.*) to rescue, to save.
Chhân*g*, (*v.*) to answer, to reply, to accept.

Chhang, (*s.*) bread.
Chhang-bung, (*s.*) a brotheror sister next in age to one's self, either older or younger.
Chhang-chhe-pa (or nu), (*s.*) a man (or woman) encumbered with children.
Chhang-chhia*t*, (*v.*) to be encumbered with a family.
Chhang fûn, (*s.*) a loaf, a kind of ground rice dumpling.
Chhang hem-ro, (*s.*) toasted bread, toast, (*v.*) to toast bread.
Chhang-*in*, (*prep.*) instead of.
Chhang-khei, (*s.*) the name of a large squirrel.
Chhâng koi, (*v.*) to give an exasperating answer.
Chhang pêr, (*s.*) a pancake, a chapati, a loaf.
Chhang phut, (*s.*) flour.
Chhan him, (*v.*) to rescue, save.
Chhar, (*v.*) to find, to pick up.
Chhawh-chhi, (*s.*) a species of sesamum.
Chhawk, (*adv.*) in turns, (*v.*) to relieve of.
Chhawl, (*s.*) a broken off branch or twig.
Chhawn, (*s.*) a tuft of goat's hair dyed red, worn suspended round the neck as a charm.
Chhawn, (*v.*) to reply, to answer.
Chhawn, Chhawn-dawl, } (*s.*) a head-dress made of tufts of goat's hair dyed red, worn by men who have taken heads in war.
Chhawn-tual, (*s.*) the name of a tree.
Chhawng, (*s.*) a storey, a tier, (*adv.*) in storeys, in tiers, one above another, from one to another (in succession).
Chhawng hnot, (*s.*) the name of a feast, (*v.*) to keep the above feast.
Chhe-chham, (*v.*) to take an oath.
·Chhe har, (*a.*) durable.
Chhêk, (*v.*) to bring by instalments or by degrees.
Chhek-khawm, (*v.*) to collect or put together in one place.
Chhêk in, (*s.*) a house for storing rice.
Chhel, (*a.*) brave or patient under suffering, (*v.*) to be inured to, to endure patiently.
Chhêm, (*v.*) to kindle, to blow (with the mouth).
Chhem-thei, (*s.*) a hollow tube or bamboo used for blowing a fire.
Chhep, (*v.*) to pile up, to stack up, to build (as a bird its nest).
Chher, (*v.*) to forge, to sculpture.
Chher-chhuan, (*v.*) to put one on top of another, to put on top.
Chhe*t*, a contracted form of *chhia.*

Chhe tak-in ti, (*v.*) to treat badly, to do badly.
Chhi, (*v.*) to carry (a lamp, torch, etc.)
Chhia, (*a.*) bad, nasty, ugly, spoiled, old, degraded (in rank or power), (*v.*) to be bad, etc.
Chhia chham, (*v.*) to take an oath.
Chhiah, (*s.*) a butt (for ridicule, etc.)
Chhiah, (*s.*) a tax, (*v.*) to make an offering to the spirit of one departed.
Chhiah, (*v.*) to leave as a heritage.
Chhiah-hlawh, (*s.*) a servant.
Chhiah-hlawh pui, (*s.*) a fellow servant.
Chhiah khon tu, (*s.*) a tax collector.
Chhiah khua, (*s.*) a tributary state or village.
Chhiar, (*s.*) a small fowl house under the eaves of a Lushai house.
Chhiar, (*v.*) to count, to reckon, to read, to price, to ask a price.
Chhiar, } (*s.*) a granary.
Chhiar in, }
Chhiat, the same as *chhia.*
Chhia-ṭha, (*a.*) delicate, (*v.*) to be delicate.
Chhiat-shan, (*v.*) to make grimaces at.
Chhiat tawk, (*v.*) to meet with misfortune.
Chhi bung, (*s.*) a species of sesamum.
Chhih hri, (*s.*) a sieve, a strainer.
Chhim, (*v.*) to partake (of another's food).
Chhim, (*s.*) the south.
Chhim-bâl, (*s.*) a rainbow.
Chhim-buk, (*s.*) an owl.
Chhim-buk shial ki, (*s.*) the horned owl.
Chhim-chhak, (*s.*) the south-east.
Chhim-hruk, (*s.*) the name of a tree the juice of which is used for japanning.
Chhim-kêl lek, (*s.*) the tamarind.
Chhim-tai-vang, (*s.*) the name of an ant.
Chhim-thlang, (*s.*) the south-west.
Chhim-tîr, (*s.*) a musk rat.
Chhîn, (*s.*) a lid, a stopper, a cover, a cork, (*v.*) to close, to shut, to stopper, to cork.
Chhin, (*v.*) to try.
Chhin-chhiah, (*v.*) to mark, to count, to fix in the mind, to take special notice of so as to remember, (*s.*) a mark, a sign.
Chhin-chhiah-na, (*s.*) a mark, a sign.

Chhing, (*v.*) to shut (as the eye).
Chhîng, (*a.*) short (as a coat, rope, etc.), looped up, taut, (*v.*) to be short, etc.
Chhîn-khai, (*s.*) the lid of a woman's pipe.
Chhîn-na, (*s.*) a lid, a stopper, a cover, a cork.
Chhîn-ûp, (*v.*) to put a lid on (a pot when boiling to keep the steam in), to stopper or close (to prevent the contents from spurting out).
Chhîp, (*s.*) the top (of head, peak, etc.), summit, apex.
Chhîp chhua*k*, (*v.*) to abuse by bringing up a person's evil deeds or those of his ancestors.
Chhîp chhuan*g*, (*v.*) to carry or put on the head.
Chhi-pui, (*s.*) a species of sesamum.
Chhîp zawn, (*s.*) a measure, a conical heap of rice, etc., the apex of which will be level with the crown of an ordinary sized man's head.
Chhir, (*v.*) to kick, to kick against.
Chhi-ria,
Chhi-rial, } (*s.*) different species of sesamum.
Chhi-riat,
Chhi-tê,
Chhi-tê nai nai, } the Lushai call for a cat.
Chho, (*v.*) to ascend, to be steep (upwards), (*a.*) steep (upwards), (*adv.*) up.
Chho ha vei, (*s.*) debility, loss of strength, (*v.*) to be debilitated, etc.
Chho-he, (*s.*) the name of a tree.
Chho-hrei-vûng, (*s.*) part of the constellation of Orion.
Chhoih fa,
Chhoih fa thlawk, } (*s.*) a meteor.
Chhok, (*v.*) to toss from a sieve.
Chhok-hlei, (*s.*) the rhododendron.
Chhok-olh, (*a.*) bent, crinkled, (*v.*) to be bent, etc.
Chhom-dawl, (*v.*) to aid, to assist (as in work, food, etc.)
Chhon*g*, (*v.*) to face, to turn towards, to have the front towards.
Chhop, (*v.*) to bring by degrees or by instalments.
Chhor, (*v.*) to make use of, to use, to make (anything) pay.
Chho-tung-tu-rût, (*a.*) very steep (upwards).
Chhu, (*v.*) to notch.
Chhu, (*s.*) the vulva.
Chhuah, (*v.*) to make or convert into.
Chhuah-chhâl, (*v.*) to question, to cross-examine, to ask for an explanation of conduct.

Chhua*k*, (*v.*) to free, to let go, to release, to come or go out, to disembark, to originate, to come to light, to start (on a journey), to make into, to become, to finish, to feel (as in *ka mut a chhuak*—I feel sleepy), (*adv.*) out.
Chhua*k*-tîr, (*v.*) to put out, to eject, to let go.
Chhuan, (*s.*) a generation, an offspring, a meal.
Chhuang, (*v.*) to put on top of.
Chhuang, (*v.*) to be proud of, to be pleased with.
Chhuan lam, (*s.*) an excuse, (*v.*) to make an excuse.
Chhuan lam nei, (*v.*) to make an excuse.
Chhuar, (*s.*) the name of a shelf in a Lushai house.
Chhuar-pui, (*s.*) the name of a shelf on the rafters.
Chhuat, (*s.*) the floor.
Chhuh, (*v.*) to snatch away, to take away from.
Chhu hur, (*s.*) a fornicatress.
Chhuh sak, (*v.*) to snatch away, to take away from.
Chhui, (*v.*) to track, to trace.
Chhuih, (*v.*) to kick, to kick against.
Chhuk, (*v.*) to descend, to go down hill, (*a.*) steep (downwards), (*adv.*) down, downwards, down hill.
Chhûl, (*s.*) the afterbirth, the womb.
Chhûl khat kual pui, (*s.*) children of the same mother.
Chhûm, (*s.*) cloud, fog, mist.
Chhûm, (*v.*) to cook, to boil, to distil.
Chhum, (*v.*) to be severed, (*adv.*) off, apart.
Chhûm a zîng, (*v.*) to become foggy or misty.
Chhûn, (*s.*) day time.
Chhûn, (*v.*) to take after, to resemble (parents, etc.)
Chhun, (*v.*) to stab, to spear, to prick, to pierce, to shine into or upon.
Chhun, (*v.*) to reach as far as, to go to (as a road, telegraph wire, etc.)
Chhun, even then, even when, even what, even those, etc., as much as, such as.
Chhun-duk, (*s.*) a box (same as *sumduk*).
Chhûng, (*s.*) the same as *chhûng-te*.
Chhûn*g*, (*v.*) to cast (as metal), to pour in or out, (*a.*) cast (as iron, etc.)
Chhûng, (*s.*) the inside (of anything).
Chhûng-a, (*prep.*) within, inside, in.
Chhûng-chhun, (*v.*) to enter a house and kill its occupants.
Chhung-in, (*conj.*) as long as, all the time.
Chhûn*g*-kha*t*, (*v.*) to make an embankment, to fill in, to fill up, (*s.*) an embankment, a raised road.

Chhûng-mu, (*s.*) a kernel.
Chhûng-nung, (*a.*) inner.
Chhûng-nung ber, (*a.*) innermost.
Chhûng-phûm, (*s.*) a lining.
Chhûng pui, (*s.*) the inner room of a chief's house.
Chhûng te, (*s.*) family, household, near relations.
Chhûng-zong, (*conj.*) as long as, all the time.
Chhun-kal, (*v.*) to prop up.
Chhûn pelh, (*v.*) to pass through a village without putting up for the night.
Chhun-zom, (*v.*) to continue doing anything.
Chi, (*s.*) salt.
Chi, (*s.*) clan, caste, sort, seed.
Chiah, (*v.*) to put in water, etc., to soak, to dip.
Chiah pil, (*v.*) to immerse.
Chi-ai, (*v.*) to be at a loss what to do, to get excited or confused, to lose one's presence of mind.
Chiam, (*adv.*) hard, with one's might, vehemently.
Chiang, (*a.*) correct, proper, (*adv.*) correctly, properly.
Chiao, (*a.*) wet and dirty, thin, watery, (*v.*) to be wet and dirty, etc.
Chiar, (*s.*) the name of a creeper.
Chiat, (*adv.*) then, as in *nangma kal chiat roh*=then go yourself (*i.e.*, since you forgot to send the man), the same as *tal.*
Chi-bai bûk, (*s.*) a salute, a *salaam*, (*v.*) to salute, to *salaam.*
Chi-bai bûk na, (*s.*) a present.
Chi-cha, (*s.*) the indigo plant (*indigofera tinctoria*).
Chi chal, (*s.*) the name of a kind of Lushai salt.
Chih, (*v.*) to put on thatch, or roofing of any kind.
Chik, (*v.*) to spurt out.
Chik, (*v.*) to cut open (bamboos) and split them for matting, to pit, to dent, to chip, (*a.*) pitted, spotted, covered with small holes.
Chîk, (*v.*) to squeak.
Chi khawn, (*s.*) a cake of salt.
Chi khawn phel, half (of moon).
Chi khûr, (*s.*) a salt spring.
Chil, (*s.*) spittle, saliva.
Chîl, (*v.*) to trample under foot, to tread out (as grain), to tread or stamp upon, to throng.
Chil a phuan, (*v.*) to foam at the mouth.
Chîl bual, (*v.*) to trouble, to interrupt.
Chil chhâk, (*v.*) to spit.

Chil chik, (*v.*) to spit through the teeth.
Chilh, (*v.*) to pinch, to squeeze, to jam, to button, to tie, to fasten.
Chilh-na, (*s.*) a button, a fastening.
Chil phuan, (*s.*) foam (of mouth).
Chil phuan, a tla, }
Chil phuan a chhuak, } (*v.*) to foam at the mouth.
Chil pik, (*v.*) to spit through the fingers.
Chim, (*v.*) to collapse, to fall down.
Chîm, (*v.*) to submerge, to crowd round.
Chim-chok, (*s.*) the name of a tree.
Chim-hruk, (*s.*) see ***chhim-hruk.***
Chi-mit, (*v.*) to die out (as a race, etc.), to become extinct.
Chim-om, (*v.*) to be a nuisance.
Chin, (*conj.*) since, as far as.

Na-chin, where as in 'I do not know where it is,' '*a om-na-chin ka hre lo.*')
Ni-chin, how many days, }
Tam chin, how many, } same construction as above.
Hla-chin, how far, }

Chin-a, (*conj.* and *adv.*) since, after, as far as, up to.
Chi-nai, (*s.*) lime.
Chi-nai lung, (*s.*) limestone.
Ching, (*a.*) barren, impotent, childless, (*v.*) to be barren, etc.
Chîng, (*v.*) to plant, to sow, to be in the habit of using, etc.
Ching-al, (*s.*) potash, lye.
Ching-chip, (*s.*) the name of a large black spider.
Ching-hne, }
Ching-hnia, } (*s.*) the wild dog (*canis dhola*).
Ching-pir-i-nu, (*s.*) the name of a large owl.
Chip, (*adv.*) finely, in small pieces, to powder.
Chîp, (*v.*) to shut, to close (as a cut, mouth, etc.)
Chîp, (*s.*) the name of a small bird.
Chip-chiar, (*v.*) to grumble, to find fault with, (*a.*) grumpy, grumbling.
Chi pui, (*s.*) the name of a kind of Lushai salt.
Chir chir, (*v.*) the Lushai call for fowls.
Chirh-dawt, (*s.*) a snipe.
Chirh-diak, (*s.*) mud, mire, (*a.*) muddy, (*a.*) to be muddy.
Chirh-dûp, (*s.*) a bog, (*a.*) boggy.
Chi-ri chi-ri, the Lushai call for fowls.
Chi-thlah, (*s.*) posterity, a descendant.
Chi-thlum, (*s.*) sugar.
Chiu, (*v.*) to prick, to stab.

Chiu,
Chiu-hiah, } the Lushai call for a dog.

Cho, (*v.*) to dig a hole.

Cho-âk, (*s.*) a crow.

Cho-âk thi, (*s.*) the name of a plant.

Choi, (*v.*) to carry or nurse (as a baby), to lift, to draw (water), to pay a fine or tax, to take or give as a name.

Choi, (*s.*) a post (of a fence).

Choi-moi, (*v.*) to exalt, to promote, to glorify.

Choi-te hring, (*s.*) the name of a small bead.

Choi-tîr, (*v.*) to fine, to tax, to levy a tax.

Chok, (*v. tr.*) to stir.

Chok buai, (*v.*) to stir up, to cause a disturbance.

Chok-chaw-eng,
Chok-chaw-ong, } (*s.*) the crop (of a bird).

Chok-hnok, (*v.*) to stir up, to agitate, to cause a disturbance.

Chok-rual, (*v.*) to level, to make peace among.

Chol, (*s.*) yeast.

Chom, (*s.*) the name of an evil spirit.

Chom, (*a.*) fat, chubby, (*v.*) to be fat, chubby.

Chon'do, (*v.*) to help with provisions at the *chong* feast.

Chon-fâng-thla, (*s.*) the time of year ccrresponding nearly to June.

Chong, (*s.*) a species of euphorbia.

Chong, (*s.*) the name of a three days' feast, (*v.*) to make the above feast.

Chong-dum-a sai-ngho, (*s.*) the name of a flowering tree.

Chong-kor, (*s.*) the cobra de capello.

Chong-moi-i, (*s.*) the evening star,

Chong-nak,
Chong-nok, } (*s.*) the name of a blue striped cloth.

Chong-pe-reng, (*s.*) any stringed instrument played with the fingers.

Chong-te-thing, (*s.*) the name of a tree.

Chong-tlai, (*s.*) the name of a tree which grows out of the hollow of another tree.

Chong-zong, (*s.*) a sparrow.

Chop, used with the reflexive particle *in* for emphasis.

Chop-in, (*prep.*) along with, together with.

Chop-le-chil-in, (*adv.*) immediately.

Cho-pui bu, (*s.*) the name of a plant.

Chor, (*v.*) to sprout, (*s.*) a sprout.

Chot, (*adv.*) actually, without preparation, asking, permission, warning, cause, etc.

Chu, an emphatic particle, (*pro.*) who, which, that.
Chu-ai, (*v.*) to suspend a weight from the tip of the first finger palm downwards, (*s.*) a weight, as much as can be thus suspended.
Chuai, (*a.*) faded, old looking, (*v.*) to fade (as a flower, etc.), to get old-looking, enfeebled.
Chuai lo, (*s.*) a species of immortelle.
Chuan, (*conj.*) if, when (in reference to future time).
Chu-ân, (*v.*) to look at from a distance.
Chuang, (*adv.*) more (denoting comparative degree), more than others.
Chuang, (*v.*) to get on top of, to be on top of, to sit upon, to mount, to ride, to embark.
Chuan*g*, (*v.*) to be without an owner, to be left over, to be superfluous, to be useless, (*a.*) without an owner, left over, etc., (*adv.*) to no purpose, uselessly.
Chuan-in, (*conj.*) if, when (in reference to future time).
Chuap, (*s.*) the lungs.
Chuap hnûn, (*s.*) the windpipe where it enters the lungs.
Chuar, (*a.*) puckered, wrinkled, creased, (*v.*) to be puckered, etc.
Chu chu, (*a.*) that, this.
Chuh, (*v.*) to claim, to snatch up (as goods when house is on fire, etc.)
Chu*k*, (*v.*) to bite (as a snake), to peck, to peck up.
Chu*k*, (*v.*) to knock against (as with elbow, body, etc.)
Chuk-chu, (*s.*) a large species of cockroach.
Chuk-tuah, (*v.*) to join together.
Chuk-tuah-na, (*s.*) a joint.
Chûl, (*v.*) to stroke.
Chul, (*s.*) a *jhûm* more than one year old, (*v.*) to become old.
Chûl cham, } (*v.*) to level, to make peace among.
Chûl rual, }
Chul-thei hmu, (*s.*) a species of raspberry.
Chum, (*a.*) fat, chubby, (*v.*) to be fat, chubby.
Chûm, (*v.*) to punch, to strike with the fist.
Chûm, (*s.*) the bamboos in a roof going lengthways on the top of the rafters.
Chum-chi, (*s.*) the name of a brass girdle.
Chûm lok, (*v.*) to punch with the knuckles.
Chung, (*s.*) roof, top.

Chung-a, (*prep.*) above, upon, against (as in *i chunga thu-poi ka nei*,=I have a complaint against you), for (as in *keim a chunga a ṭap*,=he is crying for me), with (as in *i chunga a thinur e*,=he is angry with you), on account of, for, about, (as in *eng chunga nge i lokal*=what have you come about, or for?

Chunga pawh (or pôh), (*conj.*) even when, although.

Chung che'na, (*s.*) the long bamboos going lengthways on top of the thatch to keep it down.

Chûng chu, (*a.*) this, that, these, those.

Chung-dâl, (*s.*) flattened bamboos put on top of thatch to keep it down.

Chung-dûp-silai, (*s.*) a Martini-Henri rifle.

Chûng ho chu, (*a.*) these, those.

Chung-in, (*prep.*) during, (*conj.*) while.

Chung lêng, (*s.*) flying creatures, birds, insects, etc.

Chung-nung, (*a.*) upper.

Chung-nung ber, (*a.*) uppermost.

Chûng te chu, (*a.*) these, those.

Chung-u, (*s.*) a frog.

Chut, (*a.*) dull, quiet, undemonstrative, phlegmatic.

Chu-ta-chuan, (*adv.*) there, in that place, from there, from that place.

Chu-ti-chuan, (*conj.*) therefore, then, so that, so and so, this or that being so, (*adv.*) thus, in this or that manner.

Chu-ti êm chuan,
Chu-ti fa-hran chuan, } (*adv.*) so.

Chu-ti kha-ti, so and so, etcetera, this and that.

Chu ti-lo-chuan, (*conj.*) lest, that not being so.

Chu-ti-vâng-in, (*conj.*) for this or that reason, therefore.

Chuti-zât, so many.

Chu-vâng-in, (*conj.*) for this or that reason, therefore.

D

Da, (*v.*) to lose savour, to fade, to lose taste, (*a.*) without savour, faded.

Dah, (*a.*) addled, (*v.*) to be addled.

Dah, (*v.*) to put, to place, to take off (as cloth), to put off, to defer, to put by.

Dah ang-e, = lest, perhaps, may.

Dah kham, (*v.*) to give as security, to put by for.

Dah-law-maw, =lest, perhaps, may.

Dah-ne-maw, =lest not, perhaps not, may not.

Dah-shon, (*v. t.*) to move.

Dah-ṭha, (*v.*) to put in order, to put away, to preserve.
Dai, (*v.*) to wade.
Dai, (*v.*) to become cool, to cool down, to quiet, (*s.*) dew, rain water which has settled on leaves.
Dai, (*s.*) a fence, outskirts.
Dai, (*s.*) a dragon-fly.
Dai-a shu-lêp, (*v.*) to give a ride a-cock-horse.
Dai-dêp, (*s.*) the name of a lizard.
Dai-dul, (*s.*) the side of a river where there is but little current.
Daih, (*v.*) to last, to hold out, to be sufficient.
Daih-kat, (*s.*) the tailor bird.
Dai-hlim, (*s.*) shade, (*a.*) shady.
Dai-lêng, (*v.*) to defæcate.
Dai-pui, (*s.*) a stockade.
Dai-sâm, (*v.*) to clear jungle or weeds round a house or village.
Dai-vel, (*s.*) environs.
Dak, (*v.*) to congeal, (as fat, etc.)
Dâ*k*, (*v.*) to look out (as of a door), to look about one, to look upwards, to raise or lift the head.
Dâk-chhua*k*, (*v.*) to raise the eyes or head (after looking down), to look out (as of door, etc.)
Dak-da-lêk, (*v.*) to cackle.
Dal, (*s.*) membrane, skin (as inside of egg, etc.)
Dâl, (*v.*) to keep from, to prevent, to stop, to obstruct.
Dâl-na, (*s.*) an obstacle.
Dam, (*v.*) to be alive, to be well, to be saved, (*a.*) live, etc.
Dâm, (*s.*) land sheltered from the sun's rays and so kept continually damp.
Dâm, (*v.*) to be slightly depressed, to be concave.
Dam-chhan, (*s.*) an object in living, that which makes life worth living.
Dam-chhûng, (*s.*) lifetime.
Dam-doi, (*s.*) medicine.
Dam-lai, (*s.*) lifetime.
Dam-lo, (*a.*) ill, dead, (*v.*) to be ill, to be dead.
Dân, (*s.*) custom, way, manner, habit.
Dan-a, every, ***nikhatdan-a***, every other day, ***kum thum dan-a***, every three years.
Dang, (*s.*) the palate.
Dang, (*v.*) to move out of the way (*trans.*) = to stop, to intercept.
Dang, (*v.*) to be speechless.
Dang, (*a.*) another, other, different, more.
Dâng, (*a.*) pale, (*v.*) to be pale.
Dang-awk, (*v.*) to stutter, to stammer, (*a.*) stuttering, etc.

Dang-chat, (*v.*) to cut short, to silence a person when speaking.
Dang-da, (*a.*) transparent, very thin (as cloth).
Dang-dang-a, (or in), (*adv.*) separately.
Dang lam, (*a.*) another, other, different, (*v.*) to be changed, to be altered.
Dang-mawn, (*s.*) the uvula.
Dang nâl, (*v.*) to be talkative, to be glib, to chatter, (*a.*) talkative, etc.
Dang om, (*v.*) to get out of the way.
Dang râl, (*a.*) perishable, that which may be eaten or consumed.
Dang thla, (*v.*) to silence a person when speaking.
Dân-hrai, (*s.*) the name of a basket.
Dap, (*v.*) to feel after.
Dap, (*v.*) to break into perspiration just before dying, (*s.*) death dew.
Dap, (*s.*) a bevelled edge (of chopper, etc.)
Dâp, (*s.*) coarse bamboo matting.
Dâp-chi, (*s.*) the name of a kind of Lushai salt.
Dâr, (*s.*) brass, a bell, a gong.
Dâr, (*s.*) shoulder, the shoulder blade with flesh, etc., the foreleg of an animal.
Dâr-bak, (*s.*) braces, the straps worn across the chest by Lushais to help to support a load.
Dâr-bu, (*s.*) a nest of three gongs used for leading singing, dancing, etc.
Dâr-chhem-thei, (*s.*) a telescope, field glasses.
Dâr-chong-tual-a, (*s.*) the name of an ant.
Darh, (*v.*) to be dispersed, to be scattered, to be scattered abroad, (*a.*) scattered, etc.
Dâr-hlo, (*s.*) a percussion cap.
Dâr-khuang, (*s.*) a Burmese gong.
Dâr-loi, (*s.*) a bugle.
Dâr-long, (*s.*) the name of a tribe to the north-west of Lushai.
Dâr-mang, (*s.*) the name of a small brass gong used in war, tiger hunts, etc.
Dâr-ngiao, (*s.*) the name of a small gong.
Dâr-ruh, (*s.*) the scapula.
Dâr-shen, (*s.*) copper.
Dâr-she-thi, (*s.*) a bell.
Dâr-thla-lang, (*s.*) glass, looking glass.
Dâr vai, (*v.*) to row.
Dâr-zai, (*s.*) thin brass wire.
Dawh, (*v.*) to hold out (as the hand, cloth, etc., for receiving anything), to make anything which is raised above the ground, such as a table, bed, bridge, shelf, etc.

Dawh, (*s.*) the bamboos in a noose trap which when pressed upon release the trigger and allow the sapling to fly up.

Dawh, (*a.*) patient, forbearing, (*v.*) to be patient, etc.

Daw'ha, (*v.*) to get or sell under false pretences or misrepresentations.

Daw'ha-in, (*adv.*) under false pretences.

Dawh-kân, (*s.*) a table.

Dawh-kilh, (*s.*) a hairpin.

Dawh-thei, (*a.*) patient, forbearing, (*v.*) to be patient, etc.

Dawh-thlêng, (*s.*) a seat in front of the hearth in a Lushai house.

Dawk, (*v.*) to come off, to slip off (as the edge or binding of anything).

Dawl, (*v.*) to bear, to bear the strain.

Dawm, (*v.*) to support (from below).

Dawn, (*s.*) a tube, a pipe-stem.

Dawn, (*v.*) to consider, to think of, to think or consider beforehand.

Dawng, (*s.*) the name of a succulent plant.

Dawng, (*s.*) something thrown in free when buying or selling.

Dawng, (*s.*) a new shoot or branch, (*v.*) to shoot out a new branch.

Dawng, (*v.*) to be unfortunate, to be taken in, to be swindled, to be defrauded, to be deprived of anything.

Dawng-dah, (*a.*) lazy, idle, (*v.*) to be lazy, etc.

Dawn thlawn, (*v.*) to be unfortunate, etc., same as *dawng*, only with a more intensive meaning.

Dawn-thlek, (*s.*) the name of a species of small frog.

Dawn-ta, almost, nearly, about to.

Dawn-tep-in, on the point of, just about to.

Dawn-zem, (*s.*) the name of a kind of creeping fern.

Dawp, (*v.*) to notch a tree when felling so as to ensure it falling in the right direction.

Dawr, (*v.*) to bargain with.

Dawr, (*s.*) a bazar, a market, a shop.

Dawr-hmun, (*s.*) a market place, a bazar.

Dawr in, (*s.*) a shop.

Dawr kai, (*s.*) a shop, a bazar.

Dawr-pui, (*s.*) a fair, a mela.

Daw-ron, (*s.*) the name of a basket.

Dawt, (*a.*) false, untrue.

Dawt, (*s.*) a tube, a pipe.

Dawt, (*v.*) to suck up (as cattle do water, etc.)

Dawt shoi, (*v.*) to lie.

Dawt' hei, (*s.*) a liar, (*v.*) to lie, to be a liar.

Dawt thu, (*s.*) a lie.
Dawt thu shoi, (*v.*) to lie.
Deh, (*v.*) to crack (a flea) on the finger nail.
Dêk, (*v. t.*) to tickle.
Dek, (*v. t.*) to feel, to touch.
Dek, exactly resembling.
De*k* chhua*k*, (*v.*) to produce, to get by the labour of one's own hands.
De*k* ral, (*v.*) to spend (as money), to sell, to dispose of.
Delh, (*v.*) to fall upon or against, to lean upon or against.
Dem, (*v.*) to accuse, to blame, to find fault with.
Dem, (*v.*) to banter, to poke fun at.
Dem-chhia*t*, (*v.*) to jest at, (*s.*) a jesting stock.
Dem-fiam, (*v.*) to banter, to poke fun at.
Dêng, (*v.*) to throw, to stone, to hammer, to pound, to cast or let down (as a net).
Deo, (*adv.*) slightly, rather, somewhat, more.
Deo deo, (*adv.*) gradually, little by little, by degrees.
Deo-lo, (*adv.*) not quite.
Dep, (*v.*) to be close, to touch.
Dep-a, (*prep.*) near, close to, against, over against.
Dep-dê, (*a.*) unreliable, dishonest, untrustworthy, (*v.*) to be unreliable, etc.
Der, (*v.*) to pretend to, (*adv.*) falsely, (*a.*) false, sham.
Dêr, (*adv.*) quite, soundly (as in quite dead, soundly asleep, etc.)
De-re, (*s.*) a two-anna piece.
Der-ken, (*s.*) a marigold.
Dêr lo, (*adv.*) not at all.
Di, (*s.*) thatching grass.
Diak, (*a.*) muddy, (*s.*) mud, (*v.*) to be muddy.
Dial, (*adv.*) signifying plurality.
Diâr, (*s.*) a turban.
Di chih, (*v.*) to thatch.
Di chim, (*v.*) to rejoice at another's misfortune, to say a thing serves another right.
Di chim om, } (*a.*) rejoiceful, serving one right.
Di chim tlâk, }
Dik, (*a.*) right, accurate, true, proper, righteous, (*v.*) to be right, etc.
Dik lo, (*a.*) wrong, inaccurate, untrue, improper, unrighteous, (*v.*) to be wrong, etc.
Dîl, (*v.*) to ask for, to beg.
Dîl, (*s.*) a lake.
Dîl, (*s.*) the inside part of a bamboo or cane.

Dîl chhût, (*a.*) inquisitive, (*v.*) to be inquisitive.
Dîl chiam *vak*, (*v.*) to beseech, to pray.
Dîl lui, (*v.*) to beseech, to pray.
Dîl shût, (*a.*) inquisitive, (*v.*) to be inquisitive.
Dîl tê, (*s.*) a pond, a tank.
Dîl tlat tlat, (*v.*) to beseech, to pray.
Dîm, (*v.*) to be careful, to take care.
Dim-a chim-lo, an idiom used as follows:

Ka huat dim-a a chim lo—There is no word to express my hatred.

Ka en dim-a chim lo—I cannot see too much of him.

Dîm dêm, (*adv.*) fussily, particularly.
Ding, (*a.*) right (opposite to left).
Ding, (*v.*) to stand, to be upright, to stop.
Ding chung nat, (*s.*) a slight illness not sufficient to confine one to bed, (*v.*) to be slightly ill, to be out of sorts.
Ding-di, (*s.*) the name of a flowering plant.
Ding-di hlîp, (*v.*) to stand on tip-toe.
Ding-di puan-tah, (*s.*) a configuration formed by Capella and three other stars in Auriga.
Ding lam, (*s.*) the right-hand side.
Dîp, (*v.*) to get or be in the way.
Dip, (*adv.*) into powder, (*a.*) finely powdered.
Dîp, (*a.*) almost broken through, slightly or imperceptibly cracked, (*v.*) to be almost broken through, etc.
Dîp, (*v.*) to hint, to sound (as to one's opinions, etc.)
Dîp, (*v.*) to notch a tree so as to ensure it falling in the right direction.
Di-riam, (*a.*) rejoiceful, serving one right, (*v.*) to rejoice at another's misfortune, to say a thing serves another right.
Di-riam om, } Di-riam tlâk, } (*a.*) rejoiceful, serving one right.
Di-sho, (*s.*) the long leaves protruding from the roof of a Lushai house.
Di-thla-far-fêm, } Di-thli-far-fêm, } (*s.*) the edge of the eaves.
Di-ton, (*s.*) the name of a creeper, a sprig of which when stuck in the hair at night is said to ensure the sight of a loved one in one's dreams.
Do, (*v.*) to be at enmity with, to prop up.
Do, (*v.*) to go or be out (in the rain).
Do-dâl, (*v.*) to withstand, to oppose, to be against.
Doi, (*s.*) witchcraft, magic, (*v.*) to bewitch, to practise magic or witchcraft.

Doi-dim, (*s.*) yeast.
Doih, (*a.*) cowardly, (*v.*) to be cowardly, to be afraid.
Doih-lok, (*a.*) an intensive form of *doih.*
Doi thiam, (*s.*) a witch, a wizard, a sorcerer, a magician.
Dok, (*v.*) see *dawk.*
Dok-lak, (*v.*) to be addicted, accustomed or used to.
Do-la-tu, (*s.*) an aggressor in war.
Dolh, (*v.*) to bolt (as a bird its food) to swallow (used generally of long things).
Dolh, (*a.*) tall and well built (as a man).
Dol-hnah, (*s.*) the leaves of the edible arum.
Do-lung, (*s.*) an anvil.
Dom, (*v.*) to hold, to catch hold of.
Don-fawh, (*s.*) a species of water melon.
Dong, (*v.*) to catch (as ball, etc.) to take up (as spinning top).
Dong-rawl, (*s.*) anything obtained by false pretences or as a reward or perquisite.
Dong-rawl duh, (*v.*) to be mercenary.
Dong-rawl duh a vâng-in, (*adv.*) with a mercenary motive.
Don-kawn, (*s.*) a syphon.
Don'thlêng, (*s.*) a piece of bamboo, bone, etc., for taking up a spinning top.
Dop, (*s.*) the feathers under the tail of a bird, the place covered by such feathers.
Dor, (*a.*) cracked, starred, (*v.*) to be cracked, etc.
Dot, (*a.*) next, (*adv.*) next.
Dot-tu, (*a.*) next, (*s.*) the next one.
Do-vân kai, (*v.*) to pay homage to, to humble one's self before.
Duai, (*a.*) dull, cloudy, stormy-looking, (*v.*) to be dull, etc.
Duai, (*a.*) out of the common.
Duai-dim-lo, } (*v.*) to be not below the ordinary standard. (*a.*) uncommon, extraordinary.
Duai lo, } (*adv.*) not a little, not a few.
Duang, (*s.*) a hank of coloured yarn.
Duat, (*v.*) to tend with care, to humour, to spoil (as a child), to treat with indulgence.
Duh, (*v.*) to want, to wish, to like.
Du-âm, (*a.*) greedy, (*v.*) to be greedy.
Duh-dah, (*adv.*) carelessly.
Duh-om, (*a.*) desirable.
Duh-sak bîk, (*v.*) to favour one more than another.
Duh-tak, (*a.*) beloved.
Duh-thu sàm, (*v.*) to say what one would like, to build castles in the air, to express one's desires, (*s.*) desire.

Duh-ting, (*v.*) to attempt, to want (although the thing desired does not come up to one's expectation).
Duh ting lo, (*v.*) to not want a thing, because it does not come up to one's expectation.
Duh tui, (*a.*) fastidious, (*v.*) to be fastidious.
Duh zawng, (*s.*) anything wished for, wanted or acceptable, (*a.*) acceptable, beloved.
Dûk, (*v.*) to slip off, to slip through.
Duk, (*a.*) dark or dull in colour, (*v.*) to get or be dark or dull.
Dul, (*v.*) to be loose, to be slack, to sag, to go in (as the sun), (*a.*) loose, etc.
Dul, (*s.*) the belly.
Du-li, (*s.*) an eight-anna piece.
Dûm, (*s.*) a pool in a stream.
Dum, (*a.*) black, dark (in colour).
Dum-bawm, Dum-bûr, } (*s.*) tobacco box.
Dum-dê, (*s.*) a firefly.
Dum-ei, (*s.*) tobacco.
Dum-ei zial, (*s.*) a cigar, cigarette.
Dûn, both, two, both together.
Dung, (*s.*) length.
Dung, (*s.*) the top of a range of hills, the course of a river.
Dung lam, Dung zawng, } (*adv.*) lengthway, along.
Dûp, (*a.*) soft, yielding to the touch, (*v.*) to be soft, etc.
Dûr, (*a.*) soft, (as the earth in a *jhúm* after being burnt), glowing with heat (as embers and ashes).
Durh, (*v.*) to blister, (*s.*) a blister.
Dur suih, (*v.*) to chuck on the back part of the leg, to have a feeling of weakness in the knees.
Dût, (*v.*) to suck up, (as cattle, etc., do water).

E

E, a word used in introducing a sentence.
E, an interjection.
E-hei, an interjection.
Ei, (*v.*) to eat.
Ei bâng, (*s.*) food left over after eating.
Ei in bâr, (*v.*) to eat and drink.
Ei-tîr, (*v.*) to feed.

Ei-tûr, (*s.*) food.
Êk, (*s.*) excrement, dung.
Êk, (*v.*) to defæcate.
Ek, (*v.*) to split wood with an axe.
Êk-dûr, (*s.*) a dung-heap.
Êk-in vûr, (*v.*) to manure.
Èk shûk bêl, (*s.*) the name of a Bengali pot, a lota.
El, (*v.*) to emulate, to vie with.
E-leh, a word used to introduce a sentence.
Elh, (*v. t.*) to bend.
Elh-tliak, (*v. t.*) to break, to snap in two.
E-lo, an interrogative particle.
Em, (*v.*) to scorch, to shine upon, (*a.*) scorched up.
Em, an interrogative particle.
Êm, (*s.*) a basket (without a lid).
Êm, (*adv.*) exceedingly, very, certainly, (*a.*) great, much, many.
Emaw, (*conj.*) whether, or, (*adv.*) about (as in *shom emaw ka duh*, =I want about ten).
Emaw-chu, (*conj.*) whether, whether or not, or not.
Emaw-lai, (*adv.*) about.
Emaw ti, (*v.*) to think, to suppose.
Êm êm, (*adv.*) exceedingly, very, certainly, (*a.*) great, much, many.
Em-ni, an interrogative particle.
Êm-pai, (*s.*) the name of a basket.
En, (*v.*) to look.
En-bel, (*v.*) to judge or form an opinion according to appearances.
Eng, (*s.*) the breast.
Eng, (*pro.*) what ?
Eng, (*a.*) yellow.
Êng, (*v.*) to shine, to give light, (*a.*) bright, shining.
Êng, (*s.*) light.
Eng-a, (*pro.*) what ?
Eng-a a to, (*v.*) to be perpetually in the mind, to rankle in the mind.
Eng-a emaw, in some or certain respects.
Eng-a-nge, (*adv.*) why ? what for ? wherefore ?
Eng ang hla nge, how far ?
Eng-a tân nge, (*adv.*) why ? what for ? wherefore ?
Eng-a-ti-nge, (*adv.*) why ? what for ? wherefore ?
Eng-a ti ta nge, what has happened ?
Eng-chen-nge, how much ? how long ?

Eng-chen-hla nge, how far?
Eng-e-maw, something, some, certain.
Eng-e-maw-chang, sometimes, at other times.
Eng-e-maw-zong, something.
Eng-hun-a-emaw, at some time (in future).
Eng-hun-pawh-in,
Eng-hun-pôh-in, } at any time (in future).
Eng-kim, all sorts of things, everything, etcetera.
Eng-lai-in-emaw, at some time (in past).
Eng-lai-ma-in, not at anytime (in past).
Eng-lo, (*s.*) something, anything.
Eng-ma,
Eng-ma...lo, } (*s.*) nothing.
Eng-maw, (*pro.*) what?
Eng-nga, (*pro.*) what?
Eng-nge, (*pro.*) what?
Eng-nge-maw-zât-lai, how many, how much.
Eng-pawh, anything, any, anyone.
Eng-pawh apiang, (*pro.*) whatever.
Eng-pawh-ni-roh-se,
Eng-pawh-ni-she-la,
Eng-pawh-ti-la, } howbeit, nevertheless, be it as it may, come what will.
Eng-pôh, the same as *eng-pawh.*
Eng thawl, (*a.*) blessed, prosperous.
Eng-tia-hla-nge, how far?
Eng-tik-a,
Eng-tik-a-nge, } (*adv.*) when?
Eng-tik-a-ma,
Eng-tik-a-ma ... lo, } not for a long time, not at any time.
Eng-tik-a pawh,
Eng-tik-a poh, } at any time, any time.
Eng-tik-ma,
Eng-tik-ma ... lo, } not for a long time.
Eng-ti-nge, how much? how many? how long (time)?
Eng-tin-ma
Eng-tin-ma ... lo, } no how, not any how, not at all.
Eng-tin-nge, how? what?
Eng-to-a nei, (*v.*) to keep or have perpetually in the mind, to have rankle in the mind.
Eng-zât, how many? how much?
Eng-zâ*t*-emaw-lai, some number, a certain number.
Eng-zâ*t*-nge, how many? how much?
Ên-khal, (*v.*) to dazzle.
En-kil, (*v.*) to superintend, to look after.

En-kil-tu, (*s.*) an overseer, a superintendent.
En-kol, (*v.*) to nurse, to tend, to look after.
Ên-na, (*s.*) a light, a luminary.
En-nom, (*s.*) a show, a spectacle, anything pleasing to look at.
En-shan, (*v.*) to forsake, to give up, to leave to one's own ways or devices.
En-thei, (*a.*) patient, forbearing, (*v.*) to be patient, etc., to put up with.
En-thla, (*s.*) a scout, a spy, (*v.*) to watch, to scout, to spy.
En-thla-tu, (*s.*) a scout, a spy.
En-tîr, (*v.*) to show.
En-tlang, (*s.*) a telescope, field-glasses, (*v.*) to look through.
En-tlang thei, (*a.*) transparent.
En-ton, (*v.*) to copy, to compare.
Ên-tu, (*s.*) a light, a luminary.
Eo, (*v.*) to lean back, to bend back,
Êo, an interjection, (*v.*) to point at in contempt.
Ep, (*v.*) to face, to have the front or face towards, to be arrayed against.
Ep-a, (*prep.*) facing.
Er, (*v.*) to be warped, to be turned up, to be bent back, to bend back.
Er, (*v. t.*) to melt.
E-raw-chu, on the other hand.
Êr êr, a suffix denoting a small quantity.
Er fu, (*v.*) to melt the fat off meat, (*s.*) meat with the fat melted from it.
Er-ur, a suffix denoting much.

F

Fa, (*s.*) offspring, son or daughter, a man's brother's child, a husband's brother's child.
Fa a chhia*t*, } (*v.*) to have a miscarriage.
Fa a tla-sual, }
Fah, (*s.*) the name of a tree.
Fah, (*v.*) to feed with the mouth, as Lushai women do their babies, and as birds their young.
Fa-hlawk kum, (*s.*) a prosperous year with good harvests.
Fa-hrah, (*s.*) an orphan.
Fa-hrah-ben'in bên*g*, (*v.*) to slap with the open hand.
Fa-hron, (*s.*) an adopted son or daughter.
Fah-thing, (*s.*) the name of a durable tree.

Fai, (*a.*) clean, (*v.*) to be clean.
Fai-fûk, (*v.*) to whistle.
Fai-khiat, (*s.*) a vessel for measuring rice.
Fai-rêl, (*s.*) a vessel for holding cleaned rice.
Fai-rêt, (*adv.*) completely, also expressing entirety or absoluteness.
Fai-thlâk, (*s.*) a vessel for measuring rice.
Fak, (*v.*) to praise, to report, or speak well of.
Fa-kâng, (*s.*) the name of a species of rice.
Fal, (*s.*) the name of a trap.
Fâl, (*a.*) apart, isolated, detached, (*adv.*) apart, only, (*v.*) to be apart, etc.
Fa-lak, (*s.*) a bastard whose father is unknown.
Fal-pui, (*s.*) a tiger trap.
Fa-lung, (*s.*) the name of a lucky stone supposed to ensure an abundant crop of rice.
Fa-mal, (*s.*) an only child.
Fam-kim, affix signifying in every respect, in everything, completeness.
Fân, (*a.*) elastic, (*v.*) to stretch, to be elastic.
Fan, (*adv.*) always, frequently, continually, often, constantly.
Fan, (*v.*) to work in part payment for a wife.
Fa-nao, (*s.*) children, sons and daughters collectively.
Fan-fan, (*adv.*) somehow or other.
Fang, (*adv.*) only.
Fang, (*s.*) a grain, a drop, a single one.
Fang, (*v.*) to inspect, to itinerate, to go from place to place.
Fang-hma, (*s.*) a species of large cucumber.
Fang-hmîr, (*s.*) an ant.
Fang-ra, (*s.*) a species of large bean.
Fa-nu, (*s.*) a daughter, a man's brother's daughter, husband's brother's daughter.
Fa-pa, (*s.*) a son, a man's brother's son, husband's brother's son.
Fa-phîr, (*s.*) twins.
Far, (*s.*) a drop, (*v.*) to drip, to leak.
Fâr, (*s.*) the fir tree, the pine.
Fa-rêl, (*s.*) a species of rice.
Far-nu, (*s.*) a man's sister.
Far-ṭuah, (*s.*) the name of a tree (*Erythrina indica*).
Fa-suar, (*s.*) a platform on which rice is trodden out; a threshing floor.
Fa-toi, (*s.*) a species of rice.
Fa-tu, (*s.*) one who presides at a feast.
Fa-tum-bu, (*s.*) a large bundle (of rice, etc.) done up in a cloth in the shape of a bolster.

Fa-vah, (*s.*) the Bengali bill hook, a reaping hook.
Fa-vai, (*s.*) husk of grain, chaff.
Fa-vâng, (*s.*) the autumn.
Fa-zu, (*s.*) a species of rice used for making beer.
Fawm, (*adv.*) as well, (*prep.*) along with.
Fawn, (*v.*) to roll (as a ship), to surge, to move up and down (as water).
Fawn buak, (*v.*) to slop over (as water, etc.).
Fawp, (*v.*) to kiss, to suck.
Fe, (*adv.*) fairly, rather.
Feh, (*v.*) to go to the *jhûm.*
Feh-reh hun (or lai), (*s.*) the time when all have gone to the *jhûms* and the village is quiet, about 8 or 9 o'clock.
Fei, (*s.*) a spear.
Fei, (*a.*) strong (as rope).
Fei-chhor, (*s.*) the spike on the tail end of a spear.
Fêk, (*a.*) slender (as the waist), squeezed in, (*v.*) to be slender, to be squeezed in.
Fel, (*a.*) just, accurate, correct, proper, convenient, (*adv.*) justly, accurately, etc.
Fem, (*a.*) sickly.
Fêm, (*s.*) a fringe.
Fên-hlîm, (*s.*) a trap made by Lushai boys to surprise girls as they walk along the path.
Feng, (*adv.*) much.
Fên-thuah, (*s.*) an apron, a cloth or skirt worn by women over the *puanfên* to protect it from dirt while working.
Fêp, (*v.*) to suck (as sugarcane).
Fiah, (*a.*) plain, distinct, (*adv.*) plainly, distinctly, (*v.*) to prove, to test, to make plain.
Fiak, (*a.*) high-pitched (as the voice), shrill, (*adv.*) in a high tone, (*v.*) to be high-pitched, etc.
Fiam, (*a.*) funny, joking, (*adv.*) in fun, jokingly, (*v.*) to play about with.
Fiam-thu, (*s.*) a joke.
Fiam-thu shoi, (*v.*) to joke.
Fian, (*s.*) a spoon.
Fian-thlîr, (*s.*) a ladle made from a gourd.
Fik, (*v.*) to cut through at one blow, (*adv.*) at one blow.
Fîm, (*a.*) clear, transparent, (*v.*) to be clear, etc.
Fîm-khur, (*v.*) to be careful, to be wary, to keep a good lookout, to take heed to one's self, (*a.*) careful, etc.
Fin, (*adv.*) together.
Fing, (*a.*) wise, clever, artful, (*v.*) to be wise, etc.

Fîng, (*s.*) a measurement, about a furlong.
Fing lo, (*a.*) ignorant, (*v.*) to be ignorant.
Fîp, (*a.*) hard, solid.
Fîr, (*a.*) mean, stingy, miserly, (*v.*) to be mean, etc.
Fo, (*adv.*) always, often, constantly, frequently, continually.
Fong, (*s.*) the name of a basket, a handle.
Fom, (*v.*) to gather (as sticks, firewood, etc., or as a bird its food).
Fu, (*s.*) sugarcane.
Fu, (*v.*) to alight, to settle, to roost, to perch.
Fual, (*v.*) to sag, to hang low, to be loose or long (as a coat, etc.), (*a.*) sagging, long.
Fuan, (*v.*) to gather together, (*s.*) a company, a swarm of fish gathered together for spawning.
Fuan khawm, (*v.*) to gather together.
Fuh, (*adv.*) just at the right time or in the right place, in the nick of time, straight so as to hit the object aimed at.
Fuih, (*v.*) to advise, to encourage, to urge, to set on (as a dog).
Fuk, (*a.*) erect, (*v.*) to be erect.
Fu-ke, (*s.*) a leg (of a quadruped).
Fu-lia-fa, (*s.*) a quadruped.
Fûn, (*v.*) to wrap up (in a parcel or bundle), to enclose (as fish in a net), to bring (cooked food) with one, wrapped up in a leaf, etc.
Fung, (*s.*) sharpened spikes used in war time for concealing in the path, to injure the feet and legs of an enemy, a stick.
Fung-ki, (*s.*) a powder horn.
Fûn-na, (*s.*) a wrapper.
Fûn-pui er, (*v.*) to cook a quantity of food for a journey.
Fûr, (*s.*) the rainy season.
Fûr-chon-thla, (*s.*) the time of year corresponding nearly to June.

H

Ha, (*s.*) a tooth, the teeth, the edge (of a dao, etc.) the handle of a hoe, etc.)
Ha a tîm, (*v.*) to have the teeth on edge through eating acid fruit.
Ha a ziao, (*v.*) to have the teeth on edge.
Ha-bul, (*s.*) the fang of a tooth.

Ha-chhek, (*s.*) a small axe.
Ha-chhiao, (*v.*) to sneeze.
Hah, (*v.*) to be tired, to be fatigued.
Ha hlam, (*s.*) the milk teeth.
Ha hmai, (*s.*) the incisor teeth.
Ha hni, (*s.*) the gums.
Ha hni puam, (*s.*) a gumboil.
Hah-thlâk, (*a.*) tiring, troublesome.
Hah-tîr, (*v. t.*) to tire.
Hai, (*v.*) to be giddy, to be dizzy.
Hai, (*v.*) to mistake, to forget.
Hai, (*v.*) to scratch up, to unearth by scratching.
Hai-dai, (*s.*) a species of large mangoe.
Hai-der, (*v.*) to connive at, to pretend not to know, to overlook intentionally.
Hai favâng, (*s.*) a species of mangoe.
Hai-haih, (*v.*) to be confused, to be excited, to be at a loss what to do, to lose one's presence of mind.
Hai hot, (*a.*) forgetful, absentminded, (*v.*) to be forgetful, etc.
Hai-tê, (*s.*) a small ladle made from a gourd.
Hak, (*v.*) to make much of, to wheedle, to make up to.
Hâ*k*, (*v.*) to put wood, rice, etc., on the fireshelf.
Hâk, (*v.*) to swallow the wrong way, or so as to choke, to catch one's breath.
Hâ*k*, (*v.*) to put on, to wear (as a coat).
Hâ*k*-ṭang, (*v.*) to dry wood, etc., on the fireshelf.
Hâl, (*v.*) to burn, to set on fire, to ignite, to char.
Hal, (*v.*) to hate.
Hâl pua*k*, (*v.*) to blast, to blow up.
Ham, (*v.*) to claw, to scratch, to gape.
Hâm, (*s.*) the diaphragm.
Ham-chhia, (*a.*) unfortunate, unlucky, (*v.*) to be unfortunate, etc.
Ham-da, (*s.*) a caul, membrane, skin.
Ham-haih, (*v.*) to be confused, to be excited, to be at a loss what to do, to lose one's presence of mind, to be absentminded, to be beside one's self (with rage, etc.)
Ham-hrul, (*s.*) the name of a toy, a blow-gun.
Ham-puar, } (*v. t.*) to inflate.
Hâm-puar, }
Ham-ṭha, (*a.*) fortunate, lucky, (*v.*) to be fortunate, etc.
Ham-thal, (*s.*) the dart of a blowgun.
Hân, (*v.*) to cease (as rain, etc.)
Han, a verbal prefix signifying motion upwards, and also motion towards the speaker.

Hâng, (*a.*) brown, dark complexioned, (*v.*) to be brown, etc.
Hâng, (*a.*) having a taste like meat, maize, bread, vegetables, etc.
Hao, (*v.*) to abuse, to reproach, upbraid.
Haoh, (*v.*) to bespeak.
Haoh-lo, (*adv.*) not at all.
Hao-hûk, (*s.*) a black ape, a species of gibbon.
Hao-sak, (*a.*) rich, (*v.*) to be rich.
Hap, (*v.*) to bite, to snap, as a dog, etc.
Ha-pui, (*s.*) the molar teeth.
Har, (*adv.*) late, a long time.
Har, (*a.*) difficult.
Hâr, (*s.*) pewter, solder.
Harh, (*v.*) to cheer up, to revive, to be refreshed, to wake, to be fully awake.
Harh vâng, (*v.*) to sleep lightly, (*s.*) a light sleeper.
Hər-sha, (*a.*) difficult, (*v.*) to be difficult.
Ha-rual, (*s.*) the name of a tree with edible fruit.
Ha ṭha, }
Ha thar, } (*s.*) the permanent teeth.
Ha ti-ziao, (*v.*) to set the teeth on edge.
Ha ui-ngho, (*s.*) the canine teeth.
Haw, (*v.*) to come, to go or return to one's village or home.
Haw, (*v.*) a contracted form of *huat.*
Hawh, (*v.*) to borrow when the identical article is to be returned.
Hawh, }
Hawh-oi, } interjections, like 'Here I take this.'
Hawh-te, }
Hawh-tîr, (*v.*) to lend when the identical article is to be returned.
Hawk, (*v.*) to unroof.
Hawk-dâk, (*v.*) to look about one, to be inattentive, to be inquisitive, to be fond of pleasure, (*a.*) inattentive, etc.
Hawng, (*s.*) bark, shell.
Hawng, (*v.*) to come, to go back to one's village or home, to take to one's home or with one.
Hawng-shen, (*s.*) the name of a tree.
Hawng-ṭial, (*s.*) the name of a tree.
Hawp, (*v.*) to eat with a spoon.
Hawp-khop, (*s.*) sufficient food to last for a year.
Heh, (*s.*) the lower lip.
Heh, (*v.*) to get through a lot (of work, food, etc.)
He-hi, (*a.*) this.
Heh-pe'in, (*adv.*) with all the might, resolutely.
Heh pet, (*v.*) to bite the lips, to make up the mind to bear anything (such as pain).

Hei, (*a.*) this.
Hei-hah, (*v.*) to make a grunting noise when carrying a load.
Hei-hi, (*a.*) this.
Hêk, (*v.*) to be consumed, to be used up.
Hêk, (*v.*) to speak against, to slander, to accuse to another.
Hêk-hok, (*v.*) to cut off an excrescence, to take a large quantity.
Hek lo, (*conj.*) neither, nor, (*adv.*) not at all.
Hêk thei lo, (*a.*) exhaustless.
Hel, (*a.*) unripe, raw, (*v.*) to be unripe, etc.
Hêl, (*v.*) to go round, to pass by, to walk round about, to walk up and down in front of.
Helh, (*v.*) to bolt food so that it hurts when passing down the gullet, to hurt when passing down the gullet, to upset (as bad news), to be upset, tc provoke, to be provoked.
Hel-leh, (*v.*) to revolt, to get the upper hand after being subjugated.
Hem, (*v.*) to dry, to roast, to scorch.
Hêm, (*v.*) to hit (as with a bough, etc., when suddenly released).
Hêm, (*v.*) to split with a wedge, (*s.*) a wedge.
Hêm, (*v.*) to wag, to wave about.
Hem dum,
Hem hâng, } (*v.*) to tan (as sun).
Hem hmin, (*v.*) to roast, to bake, to toast.
Hem ro, (*v.*) to toast, to dry.
Hem-ung, (*v.*) to scorch.
Hem-ût, (*v.*) to roast or toast so as to burn, to scorch much, to burn.
Hêng-hi, (*a.*) these.
Hêng ho hi,
Hêng te hi, } (*a.*) these.
Hêo, (*a.*) spoiled, wasted, (*v.*) to lose in weight, value, etc.
Her, (*v.*) to turn round, to revolve, to screw, to gin (as cotton).
Her-awt, (*s.*) a cotton gin.
Herh, (*v.*) to twist round.
Herh-chhua*k*, (*v.*) to turn up (as a lamp).
Herh-lût, (*v.*) to turn down (as a lamp).
Herh-she, (*s.*) the nageshwar tree (***mesua ferrea***).
He-ta,
He-ta-hian, } (*adv.*) here.
He-tia,
He-ti-ang, } (*adv.*) so, thus, like this.
He-ti-chen, so much, this much.
He-ti-zât, so many.
Hiao, (*adv.*) expressing entirety.
Hiar, (*a.*) stinging (to the tongue).

Hiat, (*v.*) to scratch.
Hik, (*v.*) to tingle, to ache (with cold, etc.)
Hîk, (*v.*) to skin, to strip off bark, etc.
Hil, (*a.*) nearly dry, dry on the top (as mud).
Him, (*a.*) without a flaw, unharmed, saved, safe, perfect, (*adv.*) safely, etc., (*v.*) to be without a flaw, etc.
Hîng, (*a.*) sour.
Hîp, (*v.*) to attract, to suck up, to draw (a breath).
Hîp lû*t*, (*v.*) to absorb.
Hit, (*v.*) to tingle, to ache as with cold.
Hla, (*adv.*) far, (*v.*) to be far.
Hla, (*s.*) a song, a poem, poetry.
Hlai, (*v.*) to flay, to skin, to split (as cane).
Hlai, (*s.*) a species of oak.
Hlai, (*a.*) large (used only of flat things,—paper, leaves, etc.)
Hlai-rah, (*s.*) an acorn.
Hla-kai-zia, (*s.*) a tune.
Hlam, (*s.*) a measurement, the distance between the tip of the fingers on the right hand to the same on the left with the arms extended, (*v.*) to measure by *hlams*.
Hlam, (*s.*) the afterbirth.
Hlam sam, (*s.*) the first hair at birth.
Hlam zuih, (*v.*) to die and not have a pig sacrificed at the burial, (*s.*) a person so dying.
Hlân, (*s.*) a ladder, a support from one tree to another.
Hlân, (*v.*) to give, to offer.
Hlâng, (*s.*) a bier, a stretcher, a support made to keep a corpse in a sitting posture.
Hlâng, (*v.*) to lift (across, over, up or down).
Hlâng chho, } (*v.*) to lift up and put upon a higher level.
Hlâng chhuak, }
Hlâng chhuk, (*v.*) to lift down.
Hlâng kai, (*v.*) to lift up and put upon a higher level.
Hlâng thlâ*k*, (*v.*) to lift down.
Hlân-in, (*prep.*) while, during.
Hlao, (*v.*) to fear.
Hlaoh, (*adv.*) haply, by chance.
Hlao-om, (*a.*) fearful, awful, dangerous, (*v.*) to be in danger of.
Hlao-pui, (*v.*) to fear for.
Hlao-thawng, (*v.*) to distrust, to fear.
Hlao-thawn'om, (*a.*) perilous.
Hlao-thawn'om tak-in om, (*v.*) to be in jeopardy or peril.
Hla phuah, (*v.*) to compose poetry or songs.
Hla phuah thiam, (*s.*) a poet.

Hla sha, (*v.*) to sing a song.
Hlawh, (*s.*) wages.
Hlawh, (*v.*) to serve for, to receive as wages, to work for wages, etc.
Hlawh chham, (*v.*) to be unsuccessful, to fail to accomplish, (*adv.*) unsuccessfully.
Hlawh-fa, (*v.*) to work for wages, (*s.*) one who works for wages, a hireling.
Hlawh tling, (*v.*) to be successful, to succeed, to reach an age when one can begin to work, (*a.*) of full size, (*adv.*) successfully.
Hlawh tlin'tîr, to answer (as prayer), to accede to a request.
Hlawk, (*adv.*) at a profit, cheaply, (*v.*) to increase (as grain).
Hlawm, (*v.*) to knead, (*a.*) matted together, (*adv.*) in a mass.
Hle, (*adv.*) very much, very, quite, exceedingly.
Hle hle, (*adv.*) still, (as 'keep *still*').
Hleih nei, (*v.*) to slight.
Hlei kap shen, (*s.*) the name of a squirrel.
Hlei lo, not particularly.
Hlei lu bial, (*s.*) the name of a squirrel.
Hlei mual rang, (*s.*) the name of a squirrel.
Hlei nga, (*v.*) to be full (as the moon).
Hlei nga zan, (*s.*) the night of the full moon.
Hlei tu lûm, } (*s.*) the names of different species of squirrels.
Hlei zawng, }
Hlel deo, (*adv.*) not quite, enough, not exactly, not particularly.
Hlel lo, (*adv.*) without fail, all in good time.
Hlem hle, (*a.*) untrustworthy, unreliable, (*v.*) to be untrustworthy, etc.
Hlên, (*adv.*) over, (*v.*) to go or pass over.
Hlen, (*adv.*) right on, on, for good, (*v.*) to carry out or fulfil a promise.
Hlep, (*v.*) to cut off a piece, to pare.
Hlêp, (*v.*) to make profit, to keep for one's self.
Hlêp-ru, (*v.*) to extort, to keep back part of a price for one's self.
Hli, (*a.*) self sown.
Hlia, (*v.*) to hide from sight, to screen, to overshadow, to obscure, (*a.*) hidden from sight, etc.
Hliam, (*v.*) to wound, (*a.*) wounded.
Hliao, (*v.*) to lick (as flames do a pot).
Hlim, (*s.*) a picture, shadow, shade.
Hlim, (*a.*) happy, joyful, (*v.*) to be happy, etc.

Hlim, (*adv.*) newly, freshly, just now, (*a.*) fresh, new.
Hlîm, (*v.*) to turn up or lift up (as a coat sleeve, cloth, or any covering).
Hlim-in, directly, immediately upon.
Hlim lâk, (*v.*) to photograph, (*s.*) a photograph.
Hlim lâk na, (*s.*) a photographic camera.
Hlim om, (*a.*) pleasing, joyful.
Hlim ve-leh, directly, immediately upon.
Hlîng, (*s.*) a thorn, a prickle.
Hlîng, (*v.*) to noose, to lasso, to tie a rope round the leg or the neck of an animal to lead it.
Hling-khang, (*s.*) a species of mimosa, the bark of which is used for poisoning fish.
Hling-shi, (*s.*) the soap-nut tree (the fruit is used for washing and as a preventative against leech bites, and as a remedy in *nao pang hri*).
Hlîp, (*v.*) to take off (as a coat), to remove (as a cloth).
Hlîr, (*adv.*) only, (*v.*) to divide or separate one kind from another.
Hlo, (*s.*) a drug, a weed, medicine.
Hlo-bet, (*s.*) grass, short weeds.
Hlo-châng-vom, (*s.*) the name of a small plant.
Hlo-fang-hma-tê, (*s.*) the name of a creeper.
Hloh, (*v.*) to lose.
Hloi, (*v.*) to cut off, to strip off (as leaves, &c.)
Hlo-kei-lei, (*s.*) the name of a small plant.
Hlol, (*adv.*) just.
Hlom, (*adv.*) in numbers, also has the idea of many, all or several.
Hlo-ni-en, (*s.*) the name of a plant, the shoots of which incline towards the sun.
Hlo-thun, (*a.*) loaded (as a gun).
Hlo-tung, (*s.*) the name of a reed.
Hlo-zak-thei, (*s.*) the sensitive plant.
Hlu, (*a.*) valuable, (*v.*) to be valuable.
Hlui, (*a.*) old, (not new), (*v.*) to be old.
Hlui, (*v.*) to serve (with food), to set before (as food).
Hlum, (*s.*) a ball, clay ready kneaded for making pots, etc.
Hlum, adverbial affix signifying 'dead.'
Hlum-kha, (*s.*) the name of a clay used as a remedy for cuts, etc.
Hlut, }
Hlut-sak, } (*v.*) to take pleasure in.
Hma, (*adv.*) early, soon.

Hma, (*s.*) the edge (of a knife blade, etc.)
Hma-a, (*prep.*) in front, before, prior to.
Hma-bâk, (*v.*) to have on hand (to do, etc.), to have left (to do, etc.)
Hma-chhon, (*v.*) to face.
Hma-chhuan, (*v.*) the same as *hmabâk.*
Hma-hliah, (*s.*) the name of a plant, the leaves of which are used to clean beads.
Hma-hruai, (*v.*) to pioneer, to go before, to lead the way, to take the lead (in work, etc.)
Hma-hruai-tu, (*s.*) a pioneer, a forerunner, a leader.
Hmai, (*s.*) the face.
Hmaih, } (*v.*) to overlook, to forget.
Hmaih-ṭhelh, }
Hma-in, (*prep.*) in front, before, prior to.
Hmai-phûm-tui-hleoh, (*v.*) to swim with the face under water.
Hmai-thing-hawng, (*a.*) brazen-faced, (*v.*) to be brazen-faced, to brave a thing out, to put a bold face upon anything.
Hmai-tluak, (*a.*) long-faced.
Hmai-zah, (*s.*) a fan.
Hma-khaw-ngai, } (*v.*) to set the heart or mind upon, to think about.
Hma-khua-ngai, }
Hma-lo-chuan, } (*conj.*) until.
Hma-lo-zong, }
Hman, (*v.*) to have leisure.
Hmân-a, (*adv.*) formerly, a long time ago, in olden times, some time ago.
Hman-châk-a, for something, for anything, for a purpose.
Hmang, (*v.*) to use, to be used or in the habit of.
Hma-ngai, (*v.*) to like, to be fond of, to love.
Hmang-tlâk, (*a.*) useful.
Hmang-tlâk-lo, (*a.*) useless.
Hman-hmaw, (*v.*) to hurry, to hasten, to be quick, (*adv.*) hurriedly, etc.
Hmân-lai, (*adv.*) formerly, in olden times, a long time ago, some time ago.
Hman-rua, (*s.*) materials for building, etc.
Hman-rua, } (*a.*) useful.
Hman-zia, }
Hmar, (*s.*) the name of all the tribes who wear their hair in a knot at the back of the head.
Hmâr, (*s.*) the name of a tribe of Kukis in the north of Lushai and in Manipur.
Hmâr, (*s.*) the north.

Hmâr-cha, (*s.*) a capsicum, a chilli.
Hmâr-chhak, (*s.*) the north-east.
Hmâr-lam-a, northwards.
Hmâr-thlang, (*s.*) the north-west.
Hma-sha, (*adv.*) in front, before, (*a.*) front, first.
Hma-sha-ber, (*adv.*) first, (*a.*) first.
Hma-tawng, (*a.*) to take the lead, (*s.*) a leader.
Hma-theh, (*s.*) the priming of a gun, (*v.*) to prime a gun.
Hma-thlâk, (*v.*) to carry a child in front of one.
Hma-ton, (*v.*) to face.
Hma-zawh-a, } Hma-zawn-a, } (*prep.*) opposite, opposite to, in front of.
Hma-zil, (*s.*) the name of a melon.
Hmawng, (*s.*) a species of Indian fig tree.
Hmawng-hnai, (*s.*) the sap of the *hmawng* tree used as bird lime.
Hmawr, (*s.*) border, edge, point, end, tip.
Hmeh-bûr khon, (*v.*) to beg from house to house.
Hmeh-bur khon mi, (*s.*) a beggar.
Hmei, (*s.*) a concubine.
Hmei-chhia, (*s.*) a woman.
Hmei-chhia nao-pang, (*s.*) a girl.
Hmei-thai, (*s.*) a widow, divorced woman or spinster living by herself.
Hmei-thai-thei, (*s.*) the name of a tree with small edible fruit.
Hmel, (*s.*) face, appearance, shape, form.
Hmel a chhia, (*v.*) to be ugly.
Hmel a ṭha, (*v.*) to be good looking, handsome.
Hmel-chhia, (*a.*) ugly.
Hmel duh, (*v.*) to be in love with, to be friendly with.
Hmel hriat, (*v.*) to recognise, to be acquainted with, to know by sight.
Hmel-hriat-mi, (*s.*) an acquaintance, a slight acquaintance.
Hmel-hriat-lo-mi, (*s.*) a stranger.
Hmel-ma, (*s.*) an adversary, an enemy.
Hmel mâk, (*v.*) to hate.
Hmel-ṭha, (*a.*) good-looking, handsome.
Hmer'per-na, (*s.*) the trigger of a gun.
Hmer, (*v.*) to grasp tightly, to squeeze, to encircle with the fingers, (*s.*) a measurement equal to the circumference of the thumb and the middle finger joined.
Hmet, (*v.*) to feel, to pinch, to squeeze, to knead.
Hmet-ri, (*v.*) to snap the fingers.
Hme'zial, (*s.*) the balsam plant.

Hmîm-thei, (*s.*) the name of a reed.
Hmin, (*a.*) ripe, cooked, mature, (*v.*) to be ripe, etc., to subjugate, to be subjugated.
Hmin-ṭuah, (*a.*) fully ripe.
Hming, (*s.*) a name.
Hming-a, in the name of.
Hming-chhâl, (*v.*) to take the name of another, to call one's self by another's name.
Hming-chhâl-in, falsely in the name of.
Hming-chhia, (*s.*) a nickname.
Hming-chhiat, (*v.*) to be disgraced, to lose one's good name.
Hming-chhia vua, (*v.*) to nickname.
Hming-der, (*s.*) a nickname.
Hming-der vua, (*v.*) to nickname.
Hming hliao, (*v.*) to be disgraced, to lose one's good name.
Hming-in, in the name of.
Hming-lem, (*s.*) a nickname.
Hming-lem vua, (*v.*) to nickname.
Hming-ṭha, (*a.*) reported or spoken well of.
Hming-thang, (*a.*) famous, renowned, (*v.*) to be famous, renowned.
Hming ti-chhiat, (*v.*) to give one a bad name, to disgrace.
Hmol, (*s.*) a morsel, a piece, a small piece or stick of wood, bamboo, etc.
Hmom, (*v.*) to put in the mouth whole, to put into the mouth.
Hmom-som, (*s.*) refreshment.
Hmu, (*v.*) to see, to get, to receive, to find.
Hmuak, (*v.*) to meet, to go to meet anyone.
Hmuam, (*v.*) to chew (as tobacco), to suck in the mouth, to retain in the mouth.
Hmuar, (*s.*) mildew, mould, (*a.*) mildewed, mouldy, (*v.*) to get mildewed or mouldy.
Hmui, (*a.*) savoury smelling, strong smelling (as burning feathers, fat, etc.).
Hmûi, (*s.*) the upper lip, bill, beak.
Hmui-fa-ril, (*s.*) the name of a tree.
Hmûi-hmul, (*s.*) the moustache.
Hmui-thal, (*s.*) a cotton spindle worked with a wheel.
Hmui-thla, (*s.*) an apparition, a wraith, a ghost.
Hmui-thlur, (*s.*) a cotton spindle worked by hand.
Hmul, (*s.*) hair, fur, wool, feathers.
Hmul-chhia, (*s.*) the hair with which a child or animal is born.
Hmul kawng, (*a.*) bald, unfledged.
Hmul thi, (*s.*) small hairs on the body.

Hmun, (*s.*) place, kind, sort, part, site.
Hmun-a, on the premises.
Hmun khat, (*a.*) alike, the same.
Hmun phiah, (*s.*) a broom, the name of a grass from which brooms are made.
Hmun phiat, (*v.*) to sweep.
Hmu-pa, (*s.*) a species of blackberry.
Hmûr, (*s.*) point, end, tip, prow.
Hmu-shit, (*v.*) to despise.
Hmu-ṭao, (*s.*) a species of yellow raspberry.
Hmu-tîr, (*v.*) to show.
Hmu-tu, (*s.*) one who sees, an eye-witness.
Hna, (*s.*) the source (of a stream), a spring.
Hna, (*s.*) work.
Hna, (*s.*) an anna.
Hnah, (*s.*) a leaf.
Hnah-bial-hrui, (*s.*) the name of a creeper.
Hnah-chang, (*s.*) the name of a wild plantain.
Hnah-fun, (*s.*) a species of small tailor bird.
Hnah-hlun, (*s.*) a species of Indian fig tree.
Hnah-hrat, (*s.*) the name of a species of grass.
Hnah-khâr, (*s.*) the name of a tree.
Hnah-khat, (*a.*) single, unmarried, (*s.*) the name of a bulbous plant with but one leaf, used as a remedy for burns and *phurthak.*
Hnah-khawr, (*s.*) a species of small tailor bird.
Hnah-kiah, (*s.*) the name of a tree, the bark of which is used to dye bamboo, etc., red.
Hnah-tha, (*s.*) the name of a plant.
Hnah-thial, (*s.*) the name of a class of plants some of which have large tough leaves, used for wrapping up food, etc.
Hnah-thlâk, (*s.*) descendants, the various clans of a single tribe.
Hnai, (*s.*) juice, sap, pus.
Hnai, (*a.*) near.
Hnai lo, no, not so.
Hnai-shai-lo, (*a.*) useless, worthless.
Hnam, (*s.*) a clan, a nation, a strap passing across the forehead to carry loads.
Hnam-chom, (*s.*) the common people, all save those belonging to the ruling clan.
Hnâm-tûr, (*s.*) the name of a creeper the roots of which are poisonous.
Hnâng, (*s.*) cane, etc., split for tying.
Hnâng, (*a.*) thick (as liquid).

Hnang, (*a.*) speechless with pain, overwhelmed with pain, (*v.*) to be speechless with pain, etc.
Hnap, (*s.*) mucus from the nose.
Hnap-hnît, (*v.*) to blow the nose.
Hnap-hnît-na puan, (*s.*) a handkerchief.
Hnap-khawn, (*s.*) the slug.
Hnap-khawn-râl, (*s.*) the name of an insect supposed to be the special enemy of slugs.
Hnap-shut, (*v.*) to sniff.
Hnâr, (*s.*) the nose, the source of a stream.
Hnâr, (*v.*) to snore.
Hnar, (*v.*) to deny admission, to forbid to come, pass, etc., to thrust from one, to not welcome or receive.
Hnâr a fing, (*v.*) to be keen-scented.
Hnâr a kem, (*v.*) to have a turned-up nose.
Hnâr a kul, (*v.*) to have an aquiline nose.
Hnâr a pêr, (*v.*) to have a flat nose.
Hnâr kawn, (*s.*) the indentation just above the nose.
Hnar-kîr, (*v.*) to thrust from one, to disbelieve, to refuse to believe.
Hnâr te-ngeng, (*s.*) the flaps of the nose.
Hnar-thla, (*v.*) the same as *hnar-kîr*.
Hna-thawk, (*v.*) to work, (*s.*) work.
Hnawh, (*v.*) to fill in (as a hole, etc.), to insert, to tamp.
Hnawh, (*v.*) another form of *hnot*.
Hnaw-kâl, (*s.*) a raincoat used by the Pois.
Hnawl, (*v.*) to push, to push along, to graze, to strike at an angle and slip along.
Hnawm, (*a.*) filthy, covered with mire and filth.
Hnawng, (*a.*) damp, moist.
Hneh, (*v.*) to win, to overcome.
Hneh-chhiat, } (*v.*) to treat badly, to oppress.
Hneh-sawh, }
Hnêk, (*v.*) to suck (the breasts).
Hnêk-chuan, } (*conj.*) than, in comparison with.
Hnêk-in, }
Hnem, (*a.*) many, much, (*s.*) a large quantity, a lot.
Hnêm, (*v.*) to comfort.
Hnêna, (*prep.*) with, to, along with, from.
Hnêna-ta, (*prep.*) from.
Hnep-hnol, (*s.*) refuse, rubbish.
Hni, (*s.*) a pouch underneath a crab for holding its young.
Hniak, (*s.*) a foot-print, (*v.*) to make a foot-print.
Hnial, (*v.*) to contradict, to gainsay, to make excuse, to refuse.
Hniam, (*a.*) low, short.

Hnial-kalh, (*v.*) to contradict.
Hniar, (*a.*) combed out, not entangled.
Hnih, (*a.*) two.
Hnim, (*v.*) to dip.
Hnim, (*s.*) a plant, a weed, undergrowth, (*a.*) overgrown.
Hnîm, (*v.*) to smell.
Hnim-lût, (*v.*) to dip, to join in with.
Hnim pet, (*v.*) to browse.
Hnip, (*a.*) soft.
Hnoih, (*v.*) to smear, to rub on.
Hnok, (*v.*) to be obstructed, to be encumbered, to be in the way.
Hnok-sak, (*a.*) obstructive, in the way, (*v.*) to be obstructive, etc.
Hnom, (*a.*) damp.
Hnon*g*, (*v.*) to be refused admission, to be excommunicated.
Hnon*g*-tîr, (*v.*) to send away, to forbid to enter or to come near, to excommunicate.
Hno*t*, (*v.*) to drive away (the shortened form is pronounced *hnawh*).
Hno*t*-chhua*k*, (*v.*) to drive out, to expel, to banish.
Hno*t*-daih, (*v.*) to drive away.
Hno*t*-thut, (*v.*) to drive away suddenly.
Hnu, (*s.*) a print, a foot-print, an impression.
Hnu-a, (*prep.* and *adv.*) after, behind.
Hnuai, (*s.*) the underneath.
Hnuai-a, (*prep.*) beneath, under.
Hnuai-lam-a, (*prep.*) beneath, under.
Hnuai-vâk, (*s.*) creeping things, creatures which walk upon the earth in contradistinction to those which fly.
Hnual, (*a.*) untempered.
Hnual-shuat, (*v.*) to disapprove.
Hnu chhui, (*v.*) to track.
Hnuh, (*s.*) the first crop of weeds on a *jhúm*, the sprouts of a bamboo which has been cut down.
Hnuh-hrâm, (*s.*) the second crop of weeds on a *jhúm*.
Hnuh la, (*v.*) to pull up the first crop of weeds on a *jhúm*.
Hnu-hnûng, } (*a.*) last.
Hnu-hnûng-ber, }
Hnuk, (*s.*) an imaginary cord which is supposed to snap at death.
Hnûk, (*v.*) to pull, to drag.
Hnuk a chat, (*v.*) to die.
Hnuk a fei, (*v.*) to be tenacious of life.
Hnûm, (*s.*) a species of walnut tree.
Hnûm-rah, (*s.*) a kind of walnut.
Hnûn, (*s.*) a stalk of flower, fruit, etc.

Hnung, (*s.*) the back.
Hnung-a, (*prep.* and *adv.*) after, behind, presently, afterwards.
Hnung-khirh, (*v.*) to tie the hands behind the back.
Hnung-lama, (*adv.*) behind, presently, afterwards.
Hnung-tolh, (*v.*) to walk or move backwards.
Hnung-zâng, (*s.*) the back.
Hnung-zui, (*s.*) a fellow traveller, a follower.
Hnûn-thlum, (*s.*) the name of a flowering tree.
Hnut-chhiat, (*v.*) to leave behind, to leave, to give away when going away.
Hnu-tê, (*s.*) the bosom, the breasts, udder, milk.
Hnu-tê hmûr, (*s.*) a nipple, a teat.
Hnu-tê sawr, (*v.*) to milk.
Hnu-tê tui, (*s.*) milk.
Hnu zui, (*v.*) to track.
Ho, a plural affix, (*s.*) a flock, a herd, a company.
Ho, (*a.*) abrupt, impulsive, not plastic, (*v.*) to be abrupt, etc.
Hoi, (*v.*) to turn (as head or body).
Holh, (*v.*) to push or poke in, to probe.
Holh-fung, (*s.*) a ramrod.
Holh-khâk, (*v.*) to ram down, to ram in.
Hol-ri-vâp, (*s.*) lime.
Hol-ri-vâp lung, (*s.*) limestone.
Hong, (*v.*) to open, to take off a covering.
Hon'sha, (*a.*) open, ready open.
Horh, (*v.*) to have a hole in (as a bund), to leak, to unstop (a hole, pipe, etc.), to make a hole in, (*s.*) a hole.
Horh-zao, (*v.*) to enlarge (as a hole).
Hot, (*v.*) to stir (as with a spoon, etc.).
Ho-te, (*s.*) those under the supervision of a superior, a household, a company.
Ho tu, (*s.*) a master, commander, overseer, officer, anyone acting as the head of a company, the head of a family.
Ho-va te, (*s.*) the same as *ho-te.*
Hrai, (*v.*) to feed.
Hrai, (*s.*) the name of a basket.
Hrai-hlum, (*v.*) to kill by poisoning the food.
Hral, (*v.*) to sell, to spend, to expend.
Hram, (*a.*) without gloss, dry (as unoiled hair).
Hram, (*v.*) to try to, to do one's best to do anything, (*adv.*) scarcely, with difficulty, somehow or other.
Hrâm, (*v.*) to cry as an animal, to chirp, to mew, etc., to nag, to talk a great deal.
Hrâm, (*v.*) to thin out, as plants, etc.

Hrâm-hrâm, (*adv.*) somehow or other, by hook or by crook.
Hrang, (*a.*) different, separate, another, (*adv.*) separately, etc.
Hrang, (*s.*) a piece, a slice.
Hrâng, (*a.*) brave.
Hrâng-chhuan-a, (*s.*) a planet.
Hrât, (*a.*) brave, persevering, able to suffer privations.
Hrât-khaw-khêng, (*a.*) famous, renowned for bravery.
Hre, (*v.*) another form of *hriat.*
Hre-chhuak, (*v.*) to know well.
Hre-chhuak leh, (*v.*) to recollect.
Hreh, (*v.*) to dislike, to object, to think a trouble, to not want.
Hreh-om, (*a.*) troublesome, horrible, miserable, uncomfortable, wretched.
Hrei, (*s.*) an axe.
Hrei-ha-tluk, (*s.*) a measurement equal to the length of an axe.
Hrei-ha zawn, (*s.*) a measure, a conical heap of rice, etc., the apex of which will be level with the head of an axe held high above the head of an ordinary-sized man.
Hrei-pui, (*s.*) an axe.
Hrei-rawt, (*s.*) the name of a tree with edible fruit.
Hrei-tê, (*s.*) a small axe.
Hre-lawk, (*v.*) to foresee, to foreknow.
Hre-leh, to recollect.
Hrem, (*v.*) to punish.
Hrên, (*s.*) a loincloth, a dhooty.
Hrên'a la, (*v.*) to take as security.
Hrêng, (*v.*) to detain forcibly, to keep as a security or hostage, to keep in a pound.
Hrêng, (*a.*) dense as jungle, (*v.*) to be dense.
Hrêng-a pêk, } (*v.*) to give as security.
Hrêng-tîr, }
Hrên'na in, (*s.*) a pound for stray animals.
Hrên' tûr-in lâk, (*v.*) to take as security.
Hreo, (*a.*) dishevelled (as hair, etc.)
Hreoh, (*v.*) to burrow.
Hrep, (*adv.*) hard, with force.
Hre-reng, (*v.*) to remember, to keep in mind.
Hre-tîr, (*v.*) another form of *hriat ter.*
Hre-tu, (*s.*) a hearer, a witness.
Hri, (*s.*) the spirit supposed to cause sickness.
Hri, (*v.*) to sift (through a sieve).
Hria, (*v.*) see *hriat.*
Hri a lêng, (*v.*) to be prevalent (as sickness).

Hriam, (*a.*) sharp (not blunt), (*s.*) a weapon, tool, implement, arms.
Hriam keng, } (*v.*) to be armed, to have implements with one.
Hriam shin, }
Hriang, (*s.*) the birch tree.
Hriang-fâng, (*s.*) a species of birch tree.
Hriang pui, (*s.*) the alder tree.
Hriang-zao, (*s.*) a species of birch.
Hriao, (*s.*) a needle.
Hriao-hmawr-bawk, (*s.*) a pin.
Hria*t*, (*v.*) to hear, to feel, to understand, to know, to surmise, to remember.
Hriat fiah-na, (*s.*) a proof.
Hriat-leh, (*v.*) to recollect.
Hriat-na, (*s.*) a proof.
Hriat-pui, (*v.*) to remind, to bear witness.
Hria*t*-reng, (*v.*) to remember, to bear in mind.
Hriat-tîr, (*v.*) to explain, to cause to know, to show how to do.
Hrih, (*adv.*) for a little while, for a time or season, for the present, at present.
Hrik, (*s.*) a louse, parasitical insects.
Hril, (*v.*) to tell, to inform.
Hril-fiah, (*v.*) to explain.
Hrilh, (*v.*) to tell, to inform, to teach.
Hrilh, (*v.*) to keep or observe a holiday or rest day.
Hril-lawk, (*v.*) to prophesy, to foretell, to forewarn.
Hril-leh-chhawng, (*v.*) to repeat to another what has been heard.
Hrim lo, (*adv.*) not at all.
Hring, (*a.*) fresh, green (not withered).
Hrin*g*, (*v.*) to bear, to beget, to bring forth.
Hring chhuak, the formula used in warding off the evil eye.
Hring-ei, (*s.*) a cannibal.
Hring-hlum, (*a.*) still-born, (*v.*) to give birth to a dead offspring.
Hring kîr, (*s.*) a young widow or divorced woman.
Hri-pui, (*s.*) an epidemic, a pestilence.
Hri-shêl, (*a.*) healthy, well.
Hri-shen, (*s.*) the name of a disease.
Hri-tlân*g*, (*v.*) to have a cold, to be unwell, (*s.*) a cold, sickness.
Hri vei, (*v.*) to get or contract any disease.
Hrok, (*s.*) the throat, the gullet.
Hrok a dawng, (*v.*) to live poorly.
Hrok a tlai, (*v.*) to live well or sumptuously.
Hrok bawk, (*s.*) Adam's apple.
Hrok hrawl, (*s.*) the windpipe, the larynx.

Hrok puar, (*s.*) a goitre.
Hrok ti dawng, (*v.*) to deprive one's self of food.
Hrok ti tlai, (*v.*) to pamper one's self with all kinds of food.
Hrol, (*a.*) big, large.
Hron, (*v.*) to lodge, to lodge with, to live with.
Hrot, (*adv.*) hard.
Hruai, (*v.*) to conduct, to lead, to escort, to take with.
Hruai-hrang, (*v.*) to lead away, to take on one side.
Hrual, (*v.*) to roll up in the hand, to twist.
Hrual-a, (*prep.*) against, close by, near.
Hrui, (*s.*) a threshing floor.
Hrui, (*s.*) a creeper, cane, rope, string.
Hrui-chûn, (*s.*) the name of a creeper.
Hrui-duk, (*s.*) the name of a creeper with a bean-like fruit.
Hrui-hrual, (*s.*) string, rope.
Hrui-khao, (*s.*) rope made from the bark of the *vaisa* tree.
Hrui-pawl, (*s.*) the name of a creeper used as a remedy when the teeth are set on edge through eating acid fruit.
Hrui-pui-thei, (*s.*) the name of a creeper with edible fruit.
Hrui-thui, (*s.*) the name of a creeper, also the juice of the same which is used for japanning.
Hrui-tung, (*s.*) the name of a cane used for tying, the young shoots and pith of which are edible.
Hrui valh, (*s.*) a loop.
Hrui-zên, (*s.*) string, rope, cable.
Hrû*k*, (*v.*) to rub, to wipe.
Hrû*k*-fai, (*v.*) to scour, to dust, to rub clean.
Hrûl, (*v.*) to go along close by (as by a wall, the bank of a river, etc.), to go along by the edge or side of.
Hrûm, (*s.*) the name of the knot of hair of the Poi tribe.
Hrûm-hriao, (*s.*) the name of a tree.
Hrûm-kun, (*s.*) the name of a clan of Pois.
Hrût, (*v.*) the same as *hrûl*.
Hu, (*v.*) to be worth (so much money, etc.)
Hu, (*s.*) breath, (*v.*) to breathe upon.
Huai, (*s.*) an evil spirit, (*a.*) haunted, (*v.*) to be haunted.
Huai, (*a.*) bold, brave, victorious, (*v.*) to be bold, etc.
Huai-shen, (*a.*) brave, (*v.*) to be brave, (*s.*) a brave man.
Hual, (*v.*) to surround, to besiege.
Hual, (*v.*) to lay claim to, to bespeak.
Hual-rêo, (*v.*) to cry (as the gibbon ape).
Huam, (*v.*) to dare, to be prepared (to do anything).
Huam haoh, (*a.*) greedy.
Huam hap, (*v.*) to be greedy.

Huan, (*s.*) a garden.
Huang, (*s.*) a fence.
Huang, (*s.*) a yard, enclosure, pen, fold.
Huang chhûng, (*s.*) a yard, enclosure, pen, fold.
Huang-tao, (*v.*) to be ill-behaved, over-familiar, unruly, to take liberties, (*a.*) ill-behaved, etc.
Hua*t*, (*v.*) to hate, to dislike, to have an idiosyncrasy under the influence of certain drugs, venomous bites, etc.
Huat-thla-la, (*a.*) objectionable, bad, rude.
Huat-zawng, (*s.*) a despised one, one who is hated, *bête noir.*
Huh, (*a.*) wet, (*v.*) to be wet, to get wet.
Hûi, (*v.*) to whistle as the Lushais do when carrying heavy loads, etc.
Hui-chhuk thli, (*s.*) a cold wind which blows down into the valleys from the hill tops.
Huih, (*v.*) to rake, to scrape.
Hui-hui, the Lushai call for *gayals.*
Huih-na, (*s.*) a rake.
Huih-thlâk, (*a.*) level full (as a measure), (*v.*) to make level full, to level off the top of a measure full of grain, etc.
Hul, (*a.*) dry, watertight (as a roof), (*v.*) to be dry, to be watertight, to be not implicated, to be clear (of a crime).
Hul-hâr, (*a.*) unencumbered with children, (*v.*) to be unencumbered with children.
Hul-hliap, (*s.*) a verandah, the gable of a house, the part sheltered by the gable of a house.
Hul-hual, (*adv.*) under no circumstances, on no condition, not at all.
Hûm, (*v.*) to clench (the hand), to clasp, to grasp.
Hum, (*v.*) to defend, to protect, to give shelter to.
Hum, (*s.*) the well of a trap (*thang*) dug in the ground, a pitfall.
Hum-him, (*v.*) to save, to rescue.
Hun, (*s.*) time, season, (*adv.*) when (in the future).
Hun-a, Hun-chuan, Hun-chuan-in, } (*adv.*) when (in reference to future time).
Hûng, (*v.*) to stand a thing on its end, to stand a thing upright.
Hung, (*s.*) a clump (of bamboos, trees, etc.)
Hung, (*v.*) to fence in, (*s.*) a fence.
Hun-in, (*adv.*) when (with reference to future time).
Hu*p*, (*v.*) to cover (with the hand, etc.)
Hûp, (*v.*) to sip, to suck up, to draw in (as breath).

Hu*p*-hlum, (*v.*) to suffocate by stopping the nose and mouth.
Hu-phurh, (*v.*) to be jealous of.
Hur, (*v.*) to be on heat, to have sexual desire.
Hût, (*a.*) blighted.
Hût, (*s.*) worms (disease).
Hût pai, (*v.*) to have worms (disease).

I

I, (*pro.*) thou, thy.
Ie, an exclamation like 'I say!'
I-he, (*v.*) to gainsay, to grumble, to make a fuss.
In, (*v.*) to drink.
In, (*s.*) a house.
In, (*prep.*) by, of, on, with, by means of.
In, (*pro.*) you, your.
In, an affix indicating the nominative case when the subject is followed by a transitive verb.
In, a prefix denoting reciprocity, with one another, one another, each other, etc.
In, a reflexive pronominal prefix, himself, herself, themselves, etc.
In-bah, (*s.*) a game played by girls with the *koi* bean, (*v.*) to play at the above game.
In-bâ*t*, (*v.*) to be linked together.
In-bel-bom, (*v.*) to be stuck, bound, joined, or tied together.
In-bual, (*v.*) to bathe, to wallow.
In-buan, (*v.*) to wrestle.
In-chaih, (*v.*) to romp or play together.
In-chei, (*v.*) to make one's self tidy, to adorn one's self, to be tidy, (*a.*) tidy.
In-chei-lo, (*a.*) untidy.
In-chen, (*a.*) equal.
In-chhâl, (*v.*) to personate.
In-chhawh, (*v.*) to take turns.
In chhawk, (*adv.*) by turns, one after another.
In chhawng, (*s.*) the story of a house.
In-chhir, (*v.*) to kick against.
In-chhîr, (*v.*) to regret, to repent.
In-chîl, (*v.*) to go in a body to meet a contending party as the Lushais do before a wrestling tournament.
In-chu, (*v.*) to collide.

In-chuh, (*v.*) to scramble for, to quarrel over the possession of anything, to both lay claim to anything.
In-chuk-tuah-na, (*s.*) a join, a joint.
In chun, (*s.*) roof rafters.
In chung, (*s.*) a roof.
In-dawr, (*v.*) to buy and sell, to barter, to bargain.
In-den'chen, (*v.*) to put or throw a weight, as in gymnastics.
In-dîp, (*v.*) to be in one another's way.
In-do, (*v.*) to be at enmity or war with one another.
In-don, (*v.*) to buy and sell, to barter, to bargain.
In-dot, next to each other.
In-dot-tak-in,
In-dot-zêl-in, } (*adv.*) in order, consecutively.
In-dot-zia-in,
In-el, (*v.*) to squabble, to strive together to excel or rival one another, to emulate one another, to vie with one another.
In-ep, (*v.*) to be opposite each other, to be in array one against the other.
In-fak, (*v.*) to boast, to praise one's self.
In-fan, (*v.*) to get married without parents' consent, to cohabit.
In-fin, (*v.*) to merge into one, to join together, to run into one another (as rivers), to gather together.
In-fin-na, (*s.*) the confluence of rivers, the place where things or persons are gathered together.
In-hal, (*v.*) to disagree with one another, to be incompatible (as different drugs, etc.)
In-hao, (*v.*) to quarrel, to abuse one another.
In-hen, (*v.*) to be quits, to be equal.
In-hîp, (*v.*) to sigh, to sob, to snivel.
In-hlân, (*v.*) to pass on from one to another.
In-hlawh-fa, (*v.*) to work for wages, (*s.*) one who works for wages, a hireling.
In-hliam, (*v.*) to be wounded, to wound one's self.
In-hlu, (*v.*) to exalt one's self, to be conceited, to think highly of one's self, to be proud.
In-hma-ton, (*v.*) to be face to face.
In-hnial, (*v.*) to argue, to contradict one another, to discuss, to dispute.
In-hnîp, (*v.*) to sob, to snivel.
In-hnok, (*s.*) the name of a game played by boys with the ***koi*** bean, (*v.*) to play at the above.
In-hnot-tong, (*v.*) to be huddled together so as to hinder one another, to follow close one upon another, to come in (as money).

In-hoi-ton, (*v.*) to be face to face.
In-hrûk-na puan, (*s.*) a towel, a cloth for wiping off perspiration.
In-hu, (*v.*) to be of equal value or price.
In-kai-kêp, (*v.*) to counterbalance, (*s.*) something given in when buying a quantity.
In-kam-bet, (*v.*) to mutually support or hold up, to be mutually dependent.
In-kam-ki, (*v.*) to stand up for or by one another, to help.
In-kâ*p*, (*v.*) to fight, to shoot at one another.
In-kawm-ngeih, (*v.*) to associate with, to make up after a quarrel.
In-khawm, (*v.*) to assemble, to come together.
In-kherh, (*a.*) twisted together, (*v.*) to be twisted together.
In-khing, (*v.*) to share (between two), to go halves, to be in pairs.
In-khual-te-lem, (*v.*) to go for a picnic, to play at being grown-up persons, (*s.*) a picnic.
In-koi, (*s.*) the name of a game somewhat resembling chess, (*v.*) to play at the above game.
In-kop, (*v.*) to be friends with; to be or cause to be of the same mind; to come into conjunction; to be in pairs.
In-kulh, (*v.*) to lodge at a place and provide one's own food.
In-lâr, (*v.*) to appear; to show one's self (as a spirit).
In-lu-khung, (*v.*) to live together as husband and wife without being legally married; to cohabit.
In-ngai, (*v.*) to be in love with one another, to love one another, to copulate.
In-ngai-hlu, }
In-ngai-na, } (*v.*) to exalt one's self, to think much of one's self.
In-ngai-tlawm, (*v.*) to humble one's self, to be humbled, to feel small or insignificant.
In-ngeih, (*v.*) to become friends after being at enmity, to agree together.
In-nghir-ngho, (*v.*) to be at enmity, to be at loggerheads.
In-om-lem, (*v.*) to play, to play at being grown-up people.
In-phu, (*v.*) to be in right proportion, to be properly matched, to match.
In-phu-tawk, (*v.*) to be in right proportion.
In-phung-châng, (*v.*) to be on friendly terms.
In-pu-tawk, (*v.*) the same as ***inphutawk***.
In-rawn, (*v.*) to consult together, to reason together, to ask advice of one another.
In-rem, (*v.*) to be at peace.
In-ring, (*v.*) to keep a good look out, to look out for, to get or be ready, to make preparation for, to prepare beforehand.

In-ron, (*v.*) to do anything one after the other or together.
In-shang-mar, } (*v.*) to make one's muscles stiff.
In-shang-mar-rual, }
In-shem, (*v.*) to divide, to portion out.
In-shi, (*v.*) to be contiguous.
In-shiak, (*s.*) the name of a game, played by spinning a spindle, (*v.*) to play at the above game.
In-shiam, (*v.*) to be or get ready.
In-shon, (*v.*) to move.
In-shu, (*v.*) to knock together.
In-shûm, (*v.*) to be temperate, to restrain one's self, to desist.
In-shûm kâr nei lo, (*a.*) intemperate.
In-shûm-thei, (*a.*) temperate, abstemious.
In-soi-zoi, (*v.*) to take exercise, to practise austerity.
In-sual, (*v.*) to fight, to quarrel, to come to blows.
In-suih-fin, (*v.*) to merge into one.
In-sûl-pêl, (*v.*) to overlap one another, to go by different roads and so miss one another.
In-ta, (*pro.*) yours.
In-taoh, (*v.*) to knock together (as heads).
In-tawk, (*v.*) to meet one another.
In-tawm, (*v.*) to share, to use or have in common.
In-tawng, (*v.*) to pelt one another.
In-then, (*v.*) to separate.
In-ṭhian, (*v.*) to make friends.
In-thian, (*v.*) to purify, to cleanse, to make one's self ceremonially clean.
In-thi-chilh, (*v.*) to die, as when two men are fighting and each kills the other.
In-thlah-dah, (*v.*) to be untidy, slovenly.
In-thleng, (*v.*) to exchange.
In-thoi, (*v.*) to offer a sacrifice when one is sick or to ensure good health.
In-thuah, (*v.*) to be double, to be twofold, (*a.*) doubled, twofold.
In-thup, (*v.*) to hide one's self, to be hidden.
In-tiang, (*v.*) to be one on top of another, to be piled up.
In-tiam, (*v.*) to make a contract.
In-ti-bîk, (*v.*) to be taken up with one another to the exclusion of others.
In-ti-dawng, (*v.*) to practise austerity, to deprive one's self of anything.
In-ti-hmai-bâl, } (*v.*) to do one's self harm, to make one's self
In-ti-hmai-mawk, } disliked.
In-tin-a, from house to house, in every house.

In-ṭing, (*s.*) soot, (*a.*) sooty.
In-tlâk, (*a.*) drinkable.
In-tlân-shiak, (*v.*) to run a race, to race.
In-tlon, (*v.*) to be on good terms with one another.
In-tluk, (*v.*) to be equal.
In-tok, (*s.*) the name of a game played with a top, (*v.*) to play at the above game, to collide.
In-tok, (*a.*) touching, (*v.*) to be touching.
In-tong, (*v.*) to meet one another, to come across one another.
In-tûr, (*s.*) drink.
In-vet, (*v.*) to be complicated.
In-zawl, (*v.*) to be on good terms.
In-zawn, (*v.*) to be in a straight line.
In-zen, (*v.*) to commit fornication.
In-zom, (*v.*) to be joined together, to be contiguous.
In-zom-na, (*s.*) a joint, a join.
In-zui, (*v.*) to walk or go one after another, to walk in Indian file.
Îp, (*v.*) to draw in (as stomach), to keep in or back, to retain (as urine).
Ip, (*s.*) a sack.
Ip tê, (*s.*) a satchel, bag, pocket, pouch.
Ir, (*s.*) the part of the breast above the sternum, sometimes applied also to the part where the sternum is situated.
Irh, (*v.*) to belch, to eructate.
Irh a a nam, (*v.*) to have the taste of anything eaten rise into the mouth.
Irh-fiak, (*v.*) to hiccough.
Ir leh ir chuk-tuah, (*v.*) to fall on each other's neck, to embrace.
Ir-ruh, (*s.*) the sternum.
Ît, (*v.*) to covet, to want very much.
I-ta, (*pro.*) thine.
Ît-om, (*a.*) desirable.
Ît-shîk, (*v.*) to envy, to be jealous of.
Ît-shîk-om, (*a.*) enviable.

K

Ka, (*pro.*) I, my.
Ka, (*s.*) the mouth.
Ka, (*v.*) to open (as the legs).
Ka'chik, (*s.*) a syringe.
Kah-pa-thîr, (*s.*) steel.

Kah-sa-mar, (*s.*) blue vitriol.
Kah-teh, (*s.*) a measure for measuring charges of gunpowder.
Kai, (*v.*) to take as a substitute, to pull, to spin (cotton, top, etc.), to assist in walking, to hold up, to lead (as by hand or rope).
Kai, (*s.*) a bamboo, rope, creeper, tree, or anything which facilitates climbing a large tree, etc., or crossing a river, etc., the ford of a river, the crossing of a river either by a bridge or ford, (*adv.* and *prep.*) across.
Kai, (*v.*) to stick to.
Kaih, (*v.*) to wear or put on (as a loincloth).
Ḳaih-dêp-silai, (*s.*) a Martini-Henri rifle.
Kai-harh, (*v. t.*) to wake.
Kaih-bu, (*s.*) a spinning top.
Kaih-hnoih, (*v. t.*) to implicate.
Kaih-kuah, (*v.*) to put the hand on the shoulder of another, to put the arm round the neck or waist.
Kaih-kulh, (*v.*) to secure a roof by wind ties, (*s.*) a wind tie.
Kai-hruai, (*s.*) a regent, (*v.*) to act as a regent for.
Kai-ki, (*v.*) to hang the head.
Kai-kuang, (*s.*) a prawn.
Kai-kuang-râl, (*s.*) the name of a bird.
Kai-kûn, (*v.*) to bury the face in the hands, to put the hand to the face or head (as when in perplexity or sorrow), to hang the head.
Kai-lawn, (*s.*) the ladder leading up to a Lushai house.
Ka-in chelh, (*v.*) to detain by persuasion, to restrain.
Kai-phi-hrît, (*s.*) the name of a weed.
Kai-ṭen, (*s.*) the steps leading up to a Lushai house.
Kai-thawh, } (*v. t.*) to wake, to help one rise, to cause to rise.
Kai-tho, }
Kai-za, (*s.*) the bend of the leg behind the knee.
Kai-za vêng, (*s.*) an attendant, a companion on a journey, a supporter, one who looks after another's interests.
Kâk, (*v.*) to cackle.
Kâk, (*s.*) the fork (of a tree, etc.), (*v.*) to be forked, (*a.*) forked.
Kâk-chhun, (*s.*) a measurement equal to the length of the first finger to the fork of the thumb.
Kâk-zawn, (*s.*) a measure, a conical heap (of rice, etc.) the apex of which will be level with the tips of a man's fingers when standing with the arm raised high above the head.
Kal, (*s.*) the kidneys, a kidney.
Kal, (*v.*) to go.

Kal-bo, (*v.*) to go away.
Kal-bo-pui, (*v.*) to take away, to carry off.
Kal-bo-shan, (*v.*) to desert, to leave.
Kal-bo-tîr, (*v.*) to send away.
Kal-chhet, (*s.*) stilts.
Kal-dung, (*s.*) rafters under the roof of a house running lengthways and lying immediately above the *kal-khang*.
Kalh, (*v.*) to oppose, to contradict, to act contrary to.
Kal-kong, (*s*) roadway, path.
Kal pah, (*v.*) to buy, get, visit, etc. while on the way to anywhere.
Kal-pah-in, (*adv.*) on the way.
Kal-pêl, (*v.*) to pass by.
Kal-pui, (*v.*) to take away, to remove, to accompany.
Kal-shan, (*v.*) to leave, to abandon.
Kal-tîr, (*v.*) to send away, to let go.
Kam, (*s.*) a bank, a shore, the mouth.
Kam, (*v.*) to set (a trap), to support from underneath, to prop up, to prevent rolling by wedging.
Kâm, (*v.*) to decrease.
Kam ka, (*v.*) to open the legs.
Kam-khat, (*v.*) to rebuke, (*s.*) a word or two.
Kam-ki, (*v.*) to help, to stand by or up for.
Kam-rah, (*s.*) a generic name for edible roots, leaves, fruit, etc., sometimes used also of vegetables.
Kam-tam, (*v.*) to gossip, to be talkative, to divulge a secret.
Kan, (*pro.*) we, our.
Kan, (*v.*) to visit.
Kân, (*v.*) to step over, to cross.
Kâng, (*v.*) to burn.
Kâng, (*adv.*) up.
Kang, (*v.*) to fry.
Kang, (*v.*) to decrease, to evaporate, to dry up.
Kâng-hlai, (*s.*) the crane (the saras).
Kâng-mang, (*s.*) the name of a creeper.
Kâng-ṭêk, (*s.*) the name of a tree the bark of which is used to poison fish.
Kâng-ṭhai, (*s.*) the name of a stinging nettle.
Kâng-thîng, (*s.*) the name of a Chin plaid.
Kâng-ût, (*v.*) to char, to burn, (*a.*) charred, burned.
Kâng-vâr, (*s.*) a *jhúm* between the burning and the springing up of the first seeds.
Kao, (*v.*) to cock a gun, to force or pull open, to open or be open (as the legs, earth, cut, etc.)

Kao-hnih, (*v.*) to fully cock (as gun).
Kao-khat, (*v.*) to half cock (a gun).
Kâ*p*, (*v.*) to fire (a gun), to shoot at.
Kap, (*v.*) to gag, to wedge open.
Kap, (*s.*) the fork of the legs.
Kâ*p*-fuh, (*v.*) to shoot (so as to hit).
Kâ*p*-hlum, (*v.*) to shoot dead.
Kap-kâr, (*s.*) the space between the legs.
Kap-na, (*s.*) a gag, a wedge.
Kap-parh, }
Kap-pharh, } (*v.*) to open (as an umbrella).
Ka'pup, (*s.*) a popgun.
Kâ*p*-thelh, (*v.*) to shoot and miss the mark.
Kar, (*v.*) to lever, to paddle with a stern oar, to wriggle about, to row.
Kar, (*s.*) the name of a trap which releases a spear or pointed bamboo or fires a gun.
Kar, (*v.*) to secure or demand on certain conditions or by distraint.
Kâr, (*v.*) to step, to pace, to stride.
Kâr-a, (*prep.*) between.
Kar-her-na, (*s.*) a rudder.
Kar-nân hrê*ng*, (*v.*) to distrain.
Kat, (*v.*) to stumble, to hop (as locusts, etc.), to go by bounds.
Kât, (*s.*) sulphur.
Kât-chât, (*s.*) a species of brake fern, the walking leaf-insect (*phyllium siccifolia*)
Kaû, (*adv.*) much, many.
Kaw-chhia, (*s.*) indigestion, diarrhœa.
Kaw-chhûng, (*s.*) the inside (of animal, man, etc.)
Kawh-mawh, (*v.*) to be self-willed, disobedient, (*a.*) self-willed, disobedient.
Kawh-mawh-bawl, (*v.*) to pick a quarrel, to aggress.
Kawh-mawh-bawl-tu, (*s.*) the aggressor in a quarrel, etc.
Kaw' hmu, (*v.*) to introduce, to point out.
Kawh-tê-bêl, (*s.*) the name of a tree, known also as *vombâl*, the fruit of the above tree and its fruit used for japanning.
Kaw*k*, (*v.*) to point, to point at.
Kaw khawh, (*s.*) a watery diarrhœa, (*v.*) to have diarrhœa.
Kawl, (*s.*) the horizon.
Kawl-a bêl, (*s.*) the name of a pot, the Bengali *kalshi*.
Kawl a phe, (*v.*) to lighten.
Kawl-ba-hra, (*s.*) the sweet potato.
Kawl-eng, (*s.*) the name of a yellow silk.

Kawl-êng, (*s.*) zodiacal light, also the light in the sky before sunrise and after sunset.
Kawl-fung, (*s.*) the name of a wild *gayal.*
Kawl-hnâm, (*s.*) a large knife, the 'Burmese dao.'
Kawl-hren, (*s.*) the name of a cloth used in Lushai as a turban.
Kawl-kar, (*v.*) the name of a tree used in sacrificing.
Kawl-khuang, (*s.*) a small drum.
Kawl-kil, (*s.*) the horizon, the utmost bounds of the earth.
Kawl-la, (*s.*) wool, the fibre from which sackcloth is made.
Kawl-la-ip, (*s.*) a gunnybag, a sack.
Kawl-la puan, (*s.*) sackcloth.
Kawl-mi, (*s.*) the Burmese.
Kawl-phe, (*s.*) lightning.
Kawl-vai, (*s.*) Hindustanis and Gurkhas in Burmah.
Kawm, (*s.*) a gutter cut in the ground under the eaves.
Kawm, (*s.*) an ear of maize on the cob, shell, pod, the stock (of a gun), the cover (of a book).
Kawm-kâr, (*s.*) the space or alley between two houses.
Kawm-sherh, (*v.*) to send to Coventry.
Kawm-tui, (*s.*) rain water from the roof of a house.
Kawn, (*s.*) a shallow valley, the saddle of a hill.
Kawng, (*s.*) the loins.
Kawng-beng, (*v.*) to put the arms akimbo.
Kawng-chilh, (*s.*) a small girdle worn by women to keep up the kilt.
Kawng-dom, (*v.*) to put the arms akimbo.
Kawng-fên, (*s.*) a girdle, a belt.
Kawng-hrên-na, (*s.*) a girdle, a belt.
Kawng-kaw-roi, (*s.*) the name of a large snail.
Kawng na, (*s.*) lumbago.
Kawr, (*s.*) the layers or rings in the stems of plantains and similar trees, the sheath of maize cobs.
Kawr-ong, (*v.*) to be hollow, (*s.*) a hollow, (*a.*) hollow.
Ke, (*s.*) a foot, a leg.
Ke âr-tui, (*s.*) the heel.
Ke bai, (*v.*) to be lame, (*s.*) a lame person.
Ke-chheh-ri, (*s.*) a footfall.
Keh, (*v.*) to be smashed, to be broken to pieces, to be broken, (*a.*) smashed, etc.
Keh-me, (*s.*) the flower of sungrass.
Kei, (*pro.*) I.
Kei-a, (*pro.*) my.
Kei-ata, (*pro.*) mine.
Kei-fâng, (*s.*) the kaphal tree and fruit (*myrica nagi*).
Keih, (*v.*) to bite.

Kei-ma, (*pro.*) I, my.
Kei-ma min, (*pro.*) me, to me, for me.
Kei-ma-ni, (*pro.*) we, our.
Kei-ma-ni min, (*pro.*) us, for us, to us.
Kei-ma-ni-ta, (*pro.*) ours.
Kei-ma-ta, (*pro.*) mine.
Kei-ni, (*pro.*) we, our.
Ke-in kal, (*v.*) to walk, to go on foot.
Kei-pui, (*s.*) a tree and fruit similar to the *keifâng*.
Kei-rim-nam, (*s.*) the name of a tree.
Kei-tê, (*s.*) a leopard.
Kê*k*, (*v.*) to separate (as cotton, long hair, etc.), to pluck (such things as maize, grass for brooms, rushes, reeds, etc.)
Ke khai, (*v.*) to lift up the foot.
Ke-kok, (*s.*) a boot, a shoe.
Ke-kor, (*s.*) trousers, knickerbockers.
Ke-kor a'na, } (*s.*) braces.
Ke-kor dâr-bak, }
Ke-kual, (*a.*) bowlegged, (*v.*) to be bowlegged.
Kêl, (*s.*) a goat.
Kel-a-sai-raw-phit, }
Kel-a-sai-raw pip, } (*s.*) the cape gooseberry.
Kel-a-sa-ri-phit, }
Kêl-be, (*s.*) the name of an offensive smelling plant.
Kêl-bu, (*s.*) the name of a creeper.
Kêl-doi, (*s.*) a kid.
Kêl-hmawng, (*s.*) a species of Indian fig tree.
Kêl-no, (*s.*) a kid.
Kem, (*s.*) a small piece of anything.
Kêm, (*v.*) to get, take, etc., at the same time, (*adv.*) at the same time.
Ke-mit, (*s.*) the ankle.
Keng, (*v.*) to take, to bring, to hold, to have with one or upon one's person.
Ke-ngha' chhan, (*s.*) a footstool.
Keo, (*v.*) to force or pull open, to force an opening through.
Keoh, (*v.*) throw down from the back (as a load of wood, etc.)
Kep, (*s.*) a bivalved mollusc, the gill (of a fish).
Kêp, (*adv.*) also, at the same time, too, as well, (*v.*) to do anything for another at the same time as doing it for one's self.
Ke-per-ri, (*s.*) footfall.
Ke-phah, (*s.*) the foot.
Ke-phah-hnuai, (*s.*) the sole of the foot.
Kep-pum, (*s.*) the conch shell.

Kep-tuam, (*s.*) the name of a large butterfly.
Kep-tum, (*s.*) the name of a bulbous plant.
Ker-kua, (*v.*) to hollow out.
Ke-tam-i-nu, (*s.*) a species of millipede.
Ke-tât-fai-na, (*s.*) a door mat, a scraper.
Ke-zung, (*s.*) a toe.
Ke-zung chal, (*s.*) the second toe.
Ke-zung-lai, (*s.*) the middle toe.
Ke-zung-pui, (*s.*) the big toe.
Ke-zung-ṭang, (*s.*) the toes.
Ke-zung-tê-u, } (*s.*) the fourth toe.
Ke-zung-u, }
Ke-zung-tê, (*s.*) the little toe.
Kha, (*s.*) the lower jaw.
Kha, (*pro.*) that, which, who, (*a.*) that, that by you.
Kha, (*a.*) bitter, (*v.*) to be bitter.
Kha, (*interjection*) 'Here!' as in 'Here! take this.'
Kha-be, (*s.*) the chin, the lower jaw.
Kha-be hmul, (*s.*) the beard.
Kha-bor, (*s.*) a double chin, the fat under the chin (as of a pig).
Kha chîp, (*s.*) lockjaw, (*v.*) to have lockjaw.
Kha-do, (*s.*) the name of a tree the timber of which is used for boat building.
Khai, an interjection.
Khai, (*v.*) to hang up, to suspend, to carry, to lift up, to draw (as water from a well), to draw up.
Khai-chhîn, (*s.*) the cover of a woman's pipe.
Khai-diat, (*s.*) a chain.
Khai-khin, (*v.*) to compare.
Khai-le, }
Khai-tawh, } it is sufficient, it is enough, stop.
Khai-tawh-le, }
Khâk, (*s.*) phlegm.
Khak, (*v.*) to contradict,
Kha kha, (*pro.* and *a.*) that, that by you.
Kha khawng, (*v.*) to gnash the teeth.
Khak-rak, (*s.*) see *Phakrak.*
Khâl, (*v.*) the name of various Lushai sacrifices.
Khâl, (*v.*) to play about with, to handle.
Khal, (*a.*) congealed, heavy (as bread), thick (as paste), plastic, waxy (as potatoes), (*v.*) to congeal, etc.
Khâl-chuam, } the name of a Lushai sacrifice.
Khâl-chuang, }
Khalh, (*v.*) to drive (as cattle), to outstrip, to get in front.

Khâl pui, (*s.*) the name of a Lushai sacrifice.
Khâm, (*s.*) a precipice.
Kham, (*v.*) to be tired or stiff (with standing in one position, etc.), to have had sufficient of.
Kham, (*v.*) to proclaim or appoint a holiday, rest day, etc., to place in a horizontal position, to define (as a boundary), (*adv.*) horizontally.
Kham, (*v.*) to give as an earnest, to bespeak by part payment, to mark as one's own.
Kham-phei, (*v.*) to place in a horizontal position, (*adv.*) horizontally.
Kham-tluan, (*s.*) a shelf for pots.
Khân, (*adv.*) when (in reference to past time).
Khan-chhuk, (*s.*) the cross beams in the roof of a house.
Khan-dai, (*s.*) a sword.
Khân-in, (*adv.*) when (in reference to past time).
Khan-kawn, (*s.*) a saddle joining two ridges.
Khang, (*a.*) congeal, (*v.*) to congeal.
Khâng, (*s.*) the sheaths round the knots of bamboos, a piece of string or wire round the leg of a bird, etc., to identify it.
Khang-ding, (*s.*) a creeper, the bark of which is used to kill fish.
Khâng-ho-kha, (*a.*) those, those near you.
Khâng-kha, (*a.*) those, those near you.
Khâng-te-kha, (*a.*) those, those near you.
Khao, (*s.*) a grasshopper, a locust, a cricket.
Khao-bop-pui-ṭial, } (*s.*) the names of different kinds of grass-
Khao-chem-pai, } hoppers.
Khao-chher, (*s.*) a small green cricket.
Khaoh, (*a.*) stiff, inflexible, strong (as the current of a river).
Khao-hnah-chang, (*s.*) a species of poisonous cricket.
Khao-hriang, (*s.*) a species of small cockroach.
Khao-khim, (*s.*) the name of a flowering tree with red blossoms.
Khao-khuap, (*s.*) a species of edible locust.
Khao-lu-zum, }
Khao-mâm, } (*s.*) the names of different kinds of grasshoppers.
Khao-phâr, }
Khao-pui, (*s.*) the name of a tree.
Khao-pûm-dêng, } (*s.*) the names of different kinds of grass-
Khao-sa-nghar, } hoppers.
Khao-sher, (*s.*) the name of a small green cricket.
Khap, (*v.*) to blink.
Khap, (*v.*) to prohibit, to restrain.
Khâp, (*v.*) to span with thumb and middle finger, (*s.*) a span as above.

Khâr, (*v.*) to shut.
Khâr, (*v.*) to congeal on the surface, to crust over, to have a thin coating of ice on the surface, to be frozen over.
Kha-ruam, (*s.*) the name of a tree.
Khat, (*a.*) full, one, (*v.*) to be full.
Khât, (*a.*) far apart, (*v.*) to be far apart, (*adv.*) occasionally, at long intervals.
Kha-ta, } Kha-ta-khân } (*adv.*) there, there in that place, there near you.
Kha-teh, (*interjection*) Here! as in 'Here! take this.'
Kha-tual, (*s.*) the name of a plant, a decoction of which is taken internally as a remedy for enlarged spleen and externally for sores.
Khaw, (*s.*) a contracted form of *khua.*
Khaw-cheng, (*s.*) very wet weather.
Khaw-chung, (*s.*) Kukis or Lushais living in the Cachar Hills and thereabouts.
Khaw-duai, } Khaw-dur, } (*a.*) stormy-looking, rainy-looking.
Khaw-êng, (*s.*) daylight.
Khaw-fîng cha*t*, (*s.*) the first break of dawn.
Khaw-fîng a cha*t*, (*v.*) to become daylight, to break (as day).
Khawh, (*v.*) to spear, to fall end downwards upon, to throw as a spear, &c., to make (a booth, or temporary house).
Khaw-har, (*v.*) to have time hang heavily, to be lonely, (*a.*) lonely.
Khaw-hâr-lên-pui ni, (*s.*) the day after a burial.
Khaw-hâr thlâk, (*a.*) lonely.
Khawh-ral, (*v.*) to spend (as money), to sell.
Khaw-hring, } Khaw-hring-in ei, } (*v.*) to be affected by the evil eye.
Khaw-hring nei, (*v.*) to have the evil eye, (*s.*) one having the evil eye.
Khaw-hring-nei tu, (*s.*) one having the evil eye.
Khaw-hring thiar, (*v.*) to ward off the evil eye, to perform the ceremony which averts the evil eye.
Khawk, (*v.*) to echo.
Khaw-kherh, (*v.*) to cross (as the legs, &c.), to fold (as the arms), to take another's arm.
Khaw-kherh, (*s.*) the walnut tree, the leaves of which are used for poisoning fish.
Khaw-kherh rah, (*s.*) a walnut.
Khawl, } Khawl-khawm, } (*v.*) to lay up, to accumulate, to store up.

Khaw-lam, (*s.*) a contracted form of *khualam*.
Khaw-lo, (*v.*) to be spoiled, to be perverted.
Khawm, (*v.*) to put or gather together, (*adv.*) together.
Khawm-tu-tûr, (*s.*) an heir to anything.
Khaw-mual, (*s.*) land (in contradistinction to water).
Khaw-mual-a chhuak, (*v.*) to land.
Khaw-mual-kai-kuang, (*s.*) a scorpion.
Khaw-mual-kai-kuang shuak, (*s.*) a small pseudo-scorpion.
Khawn, (*v.*) to drink through a tube.
Khawn-bawl, (*s.*) an elder, a mantri.
Khawng, (*v.*) to strike (with stick or flat of a *dao*).
Khaw-ngai, (*v.*) to love, to pity, to regard or treat with favour.
Khaw-ngai-tak-in, (*adv.*) kindly.
Khaw-ngai thei, (*a.*) pitiful, kind.
Khaw-ngai thlâk, (*a.*) pitiable.
Khaw-nge, (*adv.*) where? also used as an *interjection*.
Khawng-pui, (*s.*) a large trap which crushes its victim by letting a heavy beam or beams fall upon it.
Khawn-vâr, (*s.*) a candle, a lamp, a lantern.
Khawn-vâr bûr, (*s.*), a lamp glass or chimney.
Khawn-vâr-tui, (*s.*) lamp oil.
Khaw-om, (*s.*) dry or unusually dry weather.
Khaw-pal, (*s.*) one who has fits, an epileptic.
Khaw-per, (*s.*) a tributary village, a small outlying village.
Khaw-pui-ri, (*s.*) thunder, (*v.*) to thunder.
Khawr, (*v.t.*) to double up (as a leaf to form a drinking cup), to curl up, (*a.*) doubled up or turned over at the edge, dog-eared, curled up.
Khaw-rêng, Khaw-rêng-fâr, } (*s*) the names of very durable trees.
Khaw-sha, (*v.*) to manage.
Khaw-shak, Khaw-shak-zia, } (*s.*) circumstances, worldly estate.
Khaw-shâng, (*s.*) dry or unusually dry weather.
Khaw-shik, (*s.*) fever, cold.
Khaw-thiang, (*s.*) clear weather.
Khaw-thim, (*s.*) evening, nightfall, night, darkness.
Khaw-thlang, (*s.*) the west.
Khaw-thli, (*s.*) a species of oak.
Khaw-tin-a, everywhere, to or in every village,
Khaw-tlâng-lung-lên, (*v.*) to be melancholic, (*s.*) a hypochondriac.
Khaw-vàr, (*s.*) early dawn, daybreak, day, daylight.
Khaw-vár ṭian, (*s.*) early dawn.

Khaw-vâr tîr a-ta, from the first dawn of light, from the beginning of the world.
Khaw-vêl, (*s.*) a shortened form of *khuavêl.*
Khei, (*v.*) to prick as a blister, to pick out or dig out (as a thorn).
Khei, (*s.*) the name of a red paint.
Khei-mit, (*s.*) the ankle.
Khêk, (*v.*) to hoard, to put by, to save for the future, to put off, to defer.
Khêk, (*v.*) to cry (as an elephant or monkey).
Khel, (*s.*) the hips, the side of the upper part of the thigh.
Khêl, (*s.*) a false alarm, (*v.*) to be falsely alarmed.
Khêl, (*a.*) blind (as a road), (*adv.*) without completing.
Khel-ruh, (*s.*) the hip bone.
Khêl shiam, (*v.*) to make a false alarm.
Khêng, (*v.*) to kick out behind, to hammer in (as a nail), to nail.
Khêng, (*a.*) dry (as weather).
Khêng-bet, (*v.*) to nail to, to nail up, to nail down.
Kheoh, (*v.*) to pick (as a sore, &c.)
Kher,
Kher-hlaoh, } (*adv.*) by chance, haply.
Kher-mei, (*v.*) to be strict, particular, (*adv.*) strictly, particularly.
Kher-phei-in, (*adv.*) haply.
Khi, (*v.*) to crack, (*s.*) a crack.
Khi, (*a.*) that up there.
Khiang, (*s.*) the chilauni tree (*Schima wallichii*).
Khiang-moi, (*v.*) to begin to form in the bud (as rice, etc.)
Khiang-te-zawng-zîm, (*s.*) the name of a group of stars in Taurus near Aldebaron.
Khi khi, (*a.*) that up there,
Khim, (*v.*) to bind on (as a turban).
Khîn, (*v.*) to weigh, (*s.*) a seer.
Khing, (*s.*) one side (having another corresponding side).
Khing-hnih-in, with both hands.
Khîng-ho-khi, (*a.*) those up there.
Khing-khang ruh, (*s.*) the collar bone.
Khing-khat-in, with one hand.
Khîng-khi, (*a.*) those up there.
Khing-khih, (*s.*) the name of a weed.
Khing-pui, (*s.*) one on the opposite side, a defendant or plaintiff in a law case, a fellow, a mate, one of a pair.
Khîng-te-khi, (*a.*) those up there.

Khir, (*s.*) a scab, (*v.*) to scab.
Khirh, (*a.*) hard to bear (as pain), difficult (to accomplish, to say, etc.).
Khi-ta,
Khi-ta-khian, } (*adv.*) up there.
Kho, (*s.*) the name of a basket.
Khoi, (*s.*) a contracted form of *khuai*, 'a bee.'
Khoi, (*v.*) to tame, to domesticate, to cultivate, (*a.*) tame, etc.
Khoi-a, (*adv.*) where?
Khoi-a-emaw, (*adv.*) somewhere, in a certain place, somewhere or other.
Khoi-a-lam-a-nge,
Khoi-a-lam-a-ta-nge, } (*adv.*) whence?
Khoi-a-ma,
Khoi-a-ma ... lo, } (*adv.*) nowhere.
Khoi-a-mi-nge, (*adv.*) whence?
Khoi-a-nge, (*adv.*) where?
Khoi-a ... nge, (*adv.*) whence?
Khoi-a-pawh (or pôh), (*adv.*) anywhere.
Khoi-a-pawh ... na a-piang-a, (*adv.*) wherever.
Khoi-a-tal, (*adv.*) somewhere, anywhere.
Khoi-a-ta-nge, (*adv.*) whence?
Khoi-a-ṭang-in-nge, from where? as in 'from where did you see it?
Khoi-chuai, (*s.*) a contracted form of *khuai chuai.*
Khoi-dâng, (*s.*) a wasp.
Khoih, (*v.*) to touch.
Khoi-hli, (*s.*) a boil, an abscess.
Khoi-hli zang, (*s.*) the hard piece in the centre of a boil.
Khoi-hnun, (*s.*) bees' wax.
Khoi-hnûr, (*s.*) the round bead in the centre of an amber necklace, sometimes used for the whole necklace.
Khoi-i-nge, (*pro.*) which?
Khoi-lama-pawh ... na-a-piang-a, (*adv.*) wherever.
Khoi-nge, (*adv.*) where? also used as an *interjection*, somewhat similar to the English 'Now then!' 'Here!'
Khoi-roh,
Khoi-te, } *interjections*, similar to *khoi nge.*
Khoi-thlâr, (*s.*) honeycomb.
Khoi-tûr, (*s.*) the same as *khuai-tûr.*
Khoi-zu, (*s.*) honey.
Khok, (*v.*) to peel off, to pull off (as skin, bark, etc.) to be grazed, to have the skin or bark scraped off.

Khom-hma, (*s.*) the name of a tree the wood of which is used to make charcoal for gunpowder.
Khon, (*v.*) to collect.
Khong. (*v.*) to be stiff (as leg, neck, cloth, etc.)
Khop, (*v.*) to be sufficient, to be enough, (*adv.*) sufficiently, enough, (*s.*) a sufficiency.
Khor, (*a.*) deafened, (*v.*) to be deafened.
Khorh, (*v.*) to dish up, to serve out (as food).
Khu, (*a.*) that down there.
Khua, (*s.*) a village, weather, country.
Khua-a-cheng, (*v.*) to be very rainy, to be wet weather.
Khua-a-duai, } (*v.*) to be stormy or rainy-looking, to be cloudy.
Khua-a-dur, }
Khua-a-êng, (*v.*) to be or become daylight.
Khua-a-shik,(*v.*) to be cold, to have fever.
Khua-a-thiang, (*v.*) to be clear weather.
Khua-a-thim, (*v.*) to be or become dark.
Khua-a-vâr, (*v.*) to dawn (as day), to become light.
Khua fang, (*v.*) to itinerate, to go from village to village, to go all over a village.
Khua-hâr, (*v.*) to be lonely, to have the time hang heavily on one's hands, to wait for, to be impatient for.
Khuah-hrolh, (*s.*) a rail, a railing.
Khuah-khirh, (*v.*) to keep, to detain, to hinder.
Khuai, (*s.*) a bee, a wasp, a hornet.
Khuai-chuai, (*s.*) a cake of bee's wax weighing as much as can be supported when suspended from the tip of the forefinger, with the palm of the hand downwards.
Khua-in pal, (*v.*) to have an epileptic fit.
Khuai-thlâr, (*s.*) honeycomb.
Khuai-tûr, (*s.*) the name of a tree the fruit of which is used to kill fish, and the smoke of the burning bark for stupefying bees. The seeds are edible and yield oil.
Khual, (*s.*) see ***mi khual.***
Khua-lam, (*s.*) a country.
Khual-bûk, (*s.*) a rest-house for strangers, a dâk-bungalow.
Khua-leh-tui, (*s.*) a kingdom, a domain, a subject or subjects of a chief.
Khua leh Vâng, (*s.*) used by some as the name of an evil spirit, by others as the name of a good spirit.
Khual-lâm, (*s.*) the name of a dance, those who take part in the above dance.
Khual-thu-thang, (*s.*) false rumour, hearsay.
Khuang, (*v.*) to crow (as a cock), (*s.*) a drum.

Khuang chi-rît, (*s.*) the name of a kind of house cricket.
Khuang-choi, (*s.*) the name of a public feast given by chiefs and by well-to-do Lushais, (*v.*) to give the above feast.
Khuang-choi-thla, (*s.*) the time of year corresponding nearly with October.
Khuang-ruang, (*s.*) the name of a black ant.
Khuang-thli, (*s.*) the name of a tree.
Khuang-tîr, (*s.*) the name of a kind of house cricket.
Khuang-tum-fung, (*s.*) a drumstick.
Khua-om, (*s.*) dry or unusually dry weather.
Khuap, (*v.*) to dam up.
Khua-per, (*s.*) a small outlying village, a dependent village.
Khuar, (*s.*) a hole, a cavity.
Khuar-khu-rum, (*s.*) a hole, a hollow, a cavity (in the earth).
Khua shak, (*v.*) to manage.
Khua shâng, (*s.*) dry or unusually dry weather.
Khua-tlai, (*v.*) to make an offering of food or drink to the spirits before eating or drinking when in the jungle, (*s.*) an offering so made.
Khua-vâng, (*s.*) see *Khua leh Vâng.*
Khua-vâng-buh, (*s.*) the name of a species of grass.
Khua-vâng-chhin-chhiah, (*s.*) a mole, a spot.
Khua-vâng zawl, (*v.*) to be possessed by *Khuavâng*, (*s.*) one so possessed.
Khuh, (*s.*) a cover, (*v.*) to cover, to hide, to conceal.
Khuh, (*v.*) to cough.
Khuh-hîp, (*s.*) whooping cough.
Khuh-hriang, (*s.*) the name of a kind of saucer used as a cover for a cooking pot.
Khui, (*v.*) to stop crying.
Khuih, (*s.*) a comb, (*v.*) to comb.
Khuih-hniar, (*v.*) to comb out.
Khu-khu, (*a.*) that down there.
Khum, (*prep.*) upon.
Khum, (*s.*) a bedstead, a *machân*.
Khum, (*v.*) to carry on the head, to wear (as a hat), to put on (as a hat), to cover.
Khûm, (*prep.* and *adv.*) over.
Khum-ai, (*s.*) the bed near the front door in a Lushai house.
Khum-beo, (*s.*) the name of a Lushai hat.
Khum-fa, (*s.*) a bug.
Khum-ngiao, (*s.*) the name of a cloth.
Khum-pui, (*s.*) the bed in a Lushai house on the further side of the fireplace.

Khung, (*v.*) to put in, to imprison.
Khung, (*v.*) to uncock (a gun).
Khûng-ho-khu, }
Khûng-khu, } (*a.*) those down there.
Khûng-te-khu, }
Khun-tak-in hril, (*v.*) to explain thoroughly.
Khûp, (*s.*) the knee.
Khûp-al, (*s.*) the name of a flowering tree.
Khup-khang, (*s.*) the name of a cloth.
Khûp-koi, (*s.*) the patella.
Khûp-tuah, (*a.*) knock-kneed, (*v.*) to be knock-kneed.
Khûr, (*v.*) to tremble, to shiver, to shudder.
Khur, (*s.*) a hole, a cavity.
Khur-chhia, (*s.*) an unlucky cavity or subterranean passage.
Khu-ta, }
Khu-ta-khuan, } (*adv.*) down there.
Ki, (*s.*) a horn.
Kiam, (*v.*) to lessen, to be lessened, to be reduced, to be degraded.
Kiang, (*v.*) to disperse, to clear.
Kiang-a, (*adv.* and *prep.*) near.
Ki-bâr, (*s.*) the barb of an arrow, spear, etc.
Kik, (*v.*) to rap.
Ki-kiao, (*a.*) zigzag.
Kîl, (*s.*) an angle, a corner.
Kîl, (*v.*) to sit down to eat food, to surround.
Kilh, (*v.*) to button, to nail, to fasten.
Kilh, (*s.*) a measurement equal to the circumference of the two thumbs and two middle fingers joined.
Kilh-na, (*s.*) a button, a nail, a fastening.
Kilh-na ṭial, (*s.*) a screw.
Kil-koi, (*v.*) to look after, to superintend.
Kil-li, (*a.*) four-cornered, square.
Kil-tum, (*a.*) triangular.
Kim, (*v.*) to be sufficient, entire, enough, complete, (*adv.*) sufficiently, completely, etc.
Kim-ki, (*v.*) to bury the face in the hands, to put the hand to the face or head, to be downcast, to hang the head.
Kin, (*v.*) to be completed, or finished, to come to an end.
King-ha, (*a.*) chipped (as the edge of a knife, chopper, etc.)
Kip-a-koi-in, (*adv.*) thoroughly.
Kîr, (*v.*) to return, (*adv.*) back, again.
Kir, (*a.*) curly, (*v.*) to curl.
Ki-reo, }
Ki-riu, } (*s.*) the snippet.

Kit, (*v.*) to fell, to cut down.
Kiu, (*s.*) the elbow.
Ki-u, (*v.*) to bellow.
Kiu-hik, Kiu-hit, } (*s.*) the funnybone.
Ko, (*v.*) to call.
Ko, (*v.*) to have a good appetite, to be ravenous.
Ko, (*s.*) a mound, raised ground, the brow of a hill or incline.
Ko-bawk, (*s.*) a measurement from tip of middle finger to opposite shoulder with arm extended, the tip of the shoulder.
Ko-chhuak, (*v.*) to call out from, (*s.*) the same measurement as *kobawk.*
Ko-hrang, (*v.*) to call on one side.
Koi, (*a.*) crooked, bent, (*v.*) to be crooked, etc., (*s.*) a bend.
Koi, (*s.*) the seed of a creeper which is used as a plaything.
Koih-sa-pir, (*s.*) a crook, a hooked stick.
Koih-ṭhuang, (*s.*) the name of a tree.
Ko-khawm, (*v.*) to call together.
Ko-ki, (*s.*) the shoulder.
Ko-kim, (*v.*) to be complete (as guest at a feast, warriors at a fight, etc.), to call a sufficient number.
Kok-pui, (*s.*) a tree fern.
Kol, (*v.*) to keep, to have in possession, to receive or keep as a trust, to take care of.
Kol, (*s.*) fetters, manacles, stocks.
Kol-a, (*s.*) a pet name for a little boy.
Kol bun, (*v.*) to fetter, to put in stocks.
Kolh, (*a.*) ferocious, savage, (*v.*) to be ferocious, etc.
Kolh, (*a.*) bald, bare.
Kol-i, (*s.*) a pet name for a little girl.
Kol-te, (*s.*) a pet name for a child.
Kol-tir, (*v.*) to entrust with, to give into one's keeping.
Kol-tûk, (*v.*) to secure a roof by passing a bamboo over it and imbedding each end in the ground, (*s.*) the name of the above wind-tie.
Kom, (*v.*) to bend (the leg at the knee), to be bent.
Kom, (*a.*) miserly, stingy, mean, (*v.*) to be miserly, etc.
Kom-châr-a, (*prep.*) behind a house.
Kom-chhak-a, (*prep.*) above (spoken of a house on a hillside).
Kom-deo, (*a.*) provident, thrifty, (*v.*) to be provident, thrifty.
Kom-kaw-raw, (*s.*) a shell.
Kom-thlang-a, (*prep.*) below (spoken of a house on a hillside).
Kong, (*s.*) a path, a doorway, a way.

Kong awh, (*v.*) to block up the way, to be in the way, to cumber, to be profitable, to be of use.
Kong-ka, (*s.*) a doorway.
Kong-ka-biang, (*s.*) a door post, the side of a doorway.
Kong-khar, (*s.*) a door, (*v.*) to shut a door.
Kong-khâr-biang, (*s.*) a door post, the side of a doorway.
Kong-khêl, (*s.*) a blind path or road.
Kong-long, (*s.*) a species of rice.
Kong-nâk-pêk, (*s.*) a path running along the side of a steep mountain.
Kong-pêng, (*s.*) a branch road or path, the place where one path runs into another.
Kong shial, (*v.*) to make a road.
Kong-thuam, (*s.*) the place where several roads join.
Kop, (*adv.*) at one time, at one go, at the same time, at once.
Kop-kim, (*v.*) to be even in number.
Kop-kim lo, (*v.*) to be odd.
Kop-pui, (*s.*) a fellow, a mate.
Kop-thek, (*s.*) the name of a plant.
Kor, (*s.*) a coat.
Kor, (*s.*) a Bengali.
Kor, (*s.*) a small valley, a ravine.
Kor bân-bul, (*s.*) a waistcoat, a sleeveless vest.
Kor-dung, (*s.*) a small valley, a ravine.
Ko-ri-tu, (*v.*) to be of use or importance, to be careful of observing customs, to have respect for customs.
Kor-pum, (*s.*) a shirt.
Kor-thin-dêng, (*s.*) the name of a tree with large fruit.
Kor-tong hâ*k*, (*v.*) to wear a cloth in such a manner as to make it do duty for a coat.
Kor-vom-va, (*s.*) the name of a tree with edible fruit.
Kot, (.*s*) the space in front of a house.
Kot, (*v.*) to carry a load on each end of a stick the centre of which rests on the shoulder.
Kot-chhuah, (*s.*) the entrance to a village.
Ko-tîr, (*v.*) to send for.
Kot-lai,
Kot-lai thlêr, } (*s.*) a street, the space in front of a house.
Kot-thlêr,
Kua, (*s.*) a hole, the bowels.
Kua, (*a.*) nine.
Kua a khawh, (*v.*) to have diarrhœa.
Kua a puar, (*v.*) to have a feeling of fulness in the stomach.
Kua a ṭha lo, (*v.*) to have diarrhœa.

Kuah-khirh, (*v.*) to keep, to detain, to hinder.
Kua hreoh, (*v.*) to burrow.
Kuai, (*a.*) drooping, (*v.*) to pull down towards one (as a bough), to bend.
Kuai-ḳûr, (*v.*) to bend, to pull down towards one (as a bough).
Kua-in zût, (*v.*) to have diarrhœa.
Kual, (*s.*) a coil (as of rope), (*v.*) to make into a cylinder, to coil, to be winding, to be bent, (*adv.*) round about, (*a.*) winding, round about.
Kuam, } (*s.*) the channel (of a river, etc.), a groove.
Kuang, }
Kuang, (*s.*) a coffin, a trough.
Kuang-ngo, (*s.*) a species of rice.
Kuang-tuah, (*s.*) a coffin.
Kuang ur, (*v.*) to enclose a dead body in a hollow tree in the house until the flesh is all decayed.
Kuh-mûm, (*s.*) a bud, (*v.*) to bud.
Kuh-va, (*s.*) the areca palm and nut, the betel nut.
Kûk, (*v.*) to shriek.
Kûl, (*a.*) slanting from the roots upwards and drooping at the top (as bamboos).
Kulh, (*s.*) a stockade, a fort, a wall round a village, (*v.*) to fortify, to stockade.
Kulh a ṭang, (*v.*) to take the lead, to take the most prominent part, to set an example.
Kulh bîng, (*s.*) a blockhouse.
Kum, (*s.*) a year.
Kum, } (*a.*) concave.
Kûm, }
Kum, (*a.*) small and narrow (as the mouth of a bottle or other vessel).
Kum-in-a, this year.
Kum-khua, (*adv.*) always, at all times.
Kum-lêng, (*s.*) the name of a plant.
Kumpi-nu, (*s.*) the Lushai name for Queen Victoria (literally 'the Company's mother').
Kum-tin thla nei lo, (*s.*) the name of a species of wingless grass-hopper.
Kûn, (*v.*) to stoop, to lean or bend forward.
Kûng, (*s.*) a plant, a tree, the trunk of a tree, the stem of a plant.
Kûng-hmui, (*s.*) stubble, short stumps of bamboos, etc.
Kûng-pui mu-ṭhi, (*s.*) the name of a flowering plant.
Kûr, (*v.*) to bend down, to droop.
Kûr-tai, (*v.*) molasses.

Kut, (*s.*) the hand.
Kut bilh, (*v.*) to sprain the wrist.
Kut châng, (*s.*) a knuckle.
Kut-choi, (*s.*) a backsheesh, something thrown in as a present.
Kut dawh, (*v.*) to hold out the hand, to ask an alms.
Kut-dawh mi, (*s.*) a wayside beggar.
Kut-durh, (*s.*) the name of a beetle.
Kut-hmet-ri, (*v.*) to snap the fingers.
Kut-in hûi, (*v.*) to beckon.
Kut in-man, (*v.*) to shake hands.
Kut kem nei, (*v.*) to be a thief, to be given to stealing, (*s.*) a thief.
Kut-kor, (*s.*) a glove.
Kut phah, (*s.*) the palm of the hand.
Kut phah bêng, (*s.*) a measurement equal to the width of the hand.
Kut-phah kor, (*s.*) a glove.
Kut phah lêng-thla, (*s.*) a measurement from the tip of the middle finger to the opposite wrist with the arms extended.
Kut suih, (*v.*) to clasp the hands.
Kut thing ri, (*v.*) to snap the fingers by shaking the hand.
Kut thlâ*k*, (â.) to lay hands upon (with the intention of arresting, stealing, etc.), to strike, to touch.
Kut-tum, (*s.*) the fist, (*v.*) to clench the hand.
Kut ulh, (*v.*) to crack the knuckles, to sprain the wrist.
Kut ulh ri, (*v.*) to crack the knuckles.
Kut-ze en thiam, } (*v.*) to be skilled in palmistry.
Kut-zia en thiam, } (*s.*) one skilled in palmistry.
Kut-zung, (*s.*) a finger.
Kut-zung chal, (*s.*) the first finger.
Kut-zung lai, (*s.*) the middle finger.
Kut-zung pui, (*s.*) the thumb.
Kut-zung ţang, (*s.*) the fingers and thumb collectively.
Kut-zung tê, (*s.*) the little finger.
Kut-zung tê u, } (*s.*) the third finger.
Kut-zung u, }

L

La, (*s.*) cotton, yarn.
La, (*s.*) the spleen, (*v.*) see *lâk.*
La, (*adv.*) yet, still, by and bye, presently.
La a tla, (*v.*) to have enlarged spleen.
La-chawn, (*s.*) rolled cotton ready for spinning.
Lah, as for, but.

La-hlûm, (*s.*) a reel or ball of cotton.
La-hlûm-na, (*s.*) a cotton reel.
Lah-ui, (*s.*) the pineapple.
Lai, (*s.*) the centre, the middle, the navel.
Lai, (*v.*) to dig, to hoe, (*s.*) time, season, place (*prep.*) about (as in *ni shom lai*, about ten days).
Lai-a, (*adv.*) when (in reference to past time).
Lai-chîn, (*s.*) a relation, a fellow clansman.
Lai-fei, (*s.*) a bayonet.
Lai-herh, (*s.*) the name of a plant.
Lai-in, (*adv.*) when (in reference to past time).
Lai-khân, Lai-khân-in, } (*adv.*) when (in reference to past time).
Lai-kîng, (*s.*) the chameleon, the bloodsucker.
Lai-lên, (*s.*) the wagtail.
Lai lên tui pal, (*v.*) to make ducks and drakes on the water with flat stones, etc.
Lai-lung-dawt, (*s.*) a bayonet.
Lai-na, (*s.*) one who compassionates, a friend.
Lai-na*t*, (*v.*) to feel sorry for, to compassionate, (*a.*) compassionate.
Lai phîr, (*s.*) a double-barrelled gun.
Lal pui, (*s.*) a cannon.
Lai shuih, (*s.*) paper, reading and writing.
Lai-tel, (*s.*) the name of a lizard.
Lai-zawn, Lai-zawn-nu, } (*s.*) a female's sister.
Lâ*k*, (*v.*) to take, to fetch, to bring.
Lak-a, (*prep.*) from, because of, with.
La kai, (*v.*) to wind cotton.
La-kaih-na, (*s.*) a cotton winder.
La-kher, (*s.*) the name of a tribe in the south of Lushai.
La-khuih, (*s.*) a species of screw pine.
La-khuih-thei, (*s.*) the pineapple.
Lak-lawh, (*v.*) to be above or under the required weight, number, etc., to be engaged in doing something, to partly do a thing. (*adv.*) partly.
Lâk-sak, (*v.*) to confiscate, to take away.
Lal, (*s.*) a chief, (*a.*) great.
La-la, (*adv.*) at this or that very time.
Lalmanga nu hlaw roi thla, (*s.*) the time of the year corresponding nearly to April.
Lalruanga be-thi, (*s.*) the name of a plant.
Lalruanga peng-tawng, (*s.*) the name of a plant.
Lạm, (*s.*) way, direction, place.

Lam, (*v.*) to pronounce, to summon, to call for, to search or look for, to mention, to speak of.
Lam, (*conj.*) that.
Lâm, (*v.*) to dance, to drill.
Lam-bun, (*v.*) to come to meet and relieve of a load.
Lam-lian, (*s.*) a road.
Lâm-pâk, (*v.*) to welcome by a dance, to give a dance in one's honour.
Lam thuam, (*s.*) the place where paths meet, cross roads.
Lem thu zong, } (*prep.*) with regard or respect to, concerning.
Lam zong, }
Lân, (*v.*) to usurp or take the place of, to supersede, to excel, to eclipse.
Lâng, (*v.*) to become unpopular, to lose the esteem of others, to come into disrepute, to give place to, to float.
Lâng, (*v.*) to appear, to be visible.
La*ng*, if thou.
Lao, (*v. t.*) to slant, (*adv.*) at an angle, slantingly.
La-pui, (*s.*) the name of a stinging nettle.
Lâr, (*a.*) bright in (colour), clear (as amber, etc.), (*v.*) to be bright, clear.
La-shi, (*s.*) the fabled creator of animals, the spirit which presides over hunting.
La-tla, (*s.*) enlarged spleen.
La-tui, (*s.*) spun cotton on the spindle.
La-zai, (*s.*) cotton thread.
Law, (*v. a.*) contracted form of *lua*k.
Lawh, (*v.*) to pluck (as flowers or fruit).
Law*k*, (*adv.*) beforehand.
Lawk, (*v.*) to scoop or to shovel up, to take down from the fire shelf, to lift down a sitting hen, to lift anything on a tray.
Lawm, (*v.*) to assist a person to do anything in exchange for similar help received or to be received.
Lawm, (*v.*) to be pleased, to be pleased with, to have pleasure in, to be contented, to be happy, to be grateful, to be thankful.
Lawm-na, (*s.*) something to give pleasure.
Lawm-na chang hre, (*v.*) to be thankful, to be grateful, (*a.*) grateful, thankful.
Lawm-na chang hre lo, (*v.*) to be ungrateful, to be unthankful, (*a.*) ungrateful, unthankful.
Lawm-na chang hria, (*v.*) to be grateful, to be thankful, (*a.*) grateful, thankful.
Lawm-om, (*a.*) pleasurable, enjoyable, pleasing.
Lawm-zawng, (*a.*) anything which gives pleasure.

Lawn, (*v.*) to climb, to ascend, to embark.
Lawr, (*v.*) to collect, to gather here and there, (*adv.*) in different places, from different places, here and there.
Law-tuk, (*adv.*) too.
Leh, (*adv.*) again, then, (*conj.*) and, or, if.
Leh-khalh, (*v.*) to get in front of, to outstrip.
Leh lam, the other side, the opposite side or direction.
Leh lam leh lam, on either or both sides.
Leh-lân*g*, (*v.*) to go anywhere and return the same day, to go through and come out the other side or end.
Leh-pek, (*adv.*) again, (*a.*) next.
Leh-zual, (*adv.*) more.
Lei, (*v.*) to buy, to barter.
Lei, (*s.*) a bridge.
Lei, (*s.*) the tongue, a fine, a debt, a tax.
Lei, (*s.*) earth, ground.
Lei âr-chang, (*s.*) the name of a curved bridge.
Lei-ba, (*s.*) a tax, a tribute, a fine, a debtor.
Lei ba*t*, (*v.*) to owe a tax, etc.
Lei-chhia, (*s.*) a fine.
Lei-diak, (*s.*) mud.
Lei-dum, (*s.*) the name of a tree.
Leih, (*v.*) to pour out (as a fluid,) to water plants.
Lei-haoh, (*v.*) to bespeak.
Lei-hrui-shen, (*s.*) the name of a creeper.
Lei hrût-na, (*s.*) a plough.
Lei-ka, (*s.*) the platform in front of a Lushai house.
Lei-ka pui, (*s.*) a platform built at the side of the *lei-ka*.
Lei-kha, (*s.*) a species of white ant.
Lei-ko, (*v.*) to misrepresent.
Lei-kulh, (*s.*) earthworks for fortification, an entrenchment.
Lei-lawn, (*s.*) a bridge.
Lei-lung-lan' hun (or lai), (*s.*) early dawn when things are just beginning to become visible.
Lei lung pian tîr a-tâ, from the foundation of the world.
Lei min, (*s.*) a landslip.
Lei pui, (*s.*) a large suspended bridge.
Lei pui, (*s.*) a kitchen garden at a distance from the house.
Lei pui chen, (*s.*) a measurement of about a mile.
Lei phum, (*s.*) the foundation of a house, the part of a post buried in the ground, (*v.*) to bury in the ground.
Lei-ruang-tuam, (*s.*) an unlucky mound like a grave.
Lei shi, (*v.*) to bow down to the ground, to touch the head on the ground, (*s.*) the name of a creeper.

Lei ṭha, (*s.*) a debt, a tax.
Lei ṭha, (*s.*) a species of white ant, good soil.
Lei ṭha uih, (*s.*) the name of a small insect with an offensive smell.
Lei tlang, (*s.*) a debt, a tax.
Lei tlang, (*s.*) a clod, a lump of earth.
Lek, (*v.*) to be twisted.
Lek, (*v.*) to take or hold in the hand, to hold up, to wave.
Lekha, (*s.*) playing cards, a letter, paper, reading and writing.
Lekha-bu, (*s.*) a book.
Lekha-in-den' na, (*s.*) playing cards.
Lekha-tlân-pui, (*s.*) a dâk runner.
Lekha-tui, (*s.*) ink.
Lekha-tui bawm, } (*s.*) an inkpot.
Lekha-tui bûr, }
Lekha-ziak-na, (*s.*) a pen, a pencil.
Lekha-ziak-na tui, (*s.*) ink.
Lekha-ziak-tu, (*s.*) a writer, a clerk, a scribe.
Lek-lek, (*adv.*) on the point of, almost.
Le-len, (*s.*) a species of iris.
Lêm, (*s.*) the name of a species of palm.
Lêm, (*s.*) difference, (*v.*) to be different, (*adv.*) more than others.
Lem, (*s.*) a model, an image, a picture, imitation.
Lem, (*v.*) to swallow.
Lem-chuang, (*s.*) difference, (*v.*) to be different, (*adv.*) more than others.
Lên, (*v.*) to wave about.
Lên, (*s.*) a net.
Lên, (*v.*) to waft, to bear along.
Len, (*a.*) a contraction of *lian.*
Lên-chhawn, (*s.*) a plume worn by those who have slain men in a raid.
Lên-hlîng, (*s.*) a species of thistle.
Len-hmui, } (*s.*) the name of a tree and fruit, the Bengali 'kâlâ
Lên-hmui, } jâm.'
Lên fung choi, (*v.*) to swim upright, carrying a net and catching fish.
Lêng, (*v.*) to be prevalent (as a disease), to stroll, to walk, to take a walk, to float (in the air), to fly about.
Leng, (*v.*) to kick out, to kick about.
Leng, (*v.*) to penetrate, to enter, to go in (as one thing in another).
Lêng kir, (*s.*) a ledge of rock in a river bed over which the water falls.
Lêng-lai, (*s.*) the time of life before marriage.

Lêng-leh, (*s.*) a young widow or young woman who has been divorced, a young widower or young man who has been divorced.
Lêng-ma-shêr, (*s.*) the name of an aromatic herb.
Lêng-ṭûl, (*s.*) a spinster, a bachelor.
Lên' lai zai, (*s.*) the name of a song.
Lên' lâng, (*v.*) to float along.
Lên-lâng, (*s.*) the name of a tree.
Lên pât, (*s.*) the name of a species of tree moss.
Lep, (*v.*) to turn up, to roll up, to turn inside out.
Lep-chiah, (*a.*) full of animal spirits, frivolous, fond of joking, unreliable in character, unstable, desultory, capricious, (*v.*) to be full of animal spirits, etc.
Lep-she, (*v.*) to turn up, to roll up, to turn inside out.
Lêr, (*s.*) the top (of tree, post, etc.), the end (of a sentence).
Lêt, (*v.*) to alter, to transform.
Lêt, (*v.*) to return, to come back.
Let, (*v.*) to turn upside down, to capsize, to turn over.
Le*t*-ling, (*a.*) upside down, inside out, wrong way about, *vice versâ*, (*v.*) to be upside down.
Let-ling kal, (*v.*) to walk on the hands.
Le*t*-thlâ*k*, (*v.*) to get the better of, to turn aside, to refute.
Li, (*a.*) four.
Li, (*s.*) a deep pool (in a river).
Li, (*s.*) a spring (as of watch, gun, etc.).
Lia*k*, (*v.*) to lick, to lap.
Liam, (*v.*) to overflow, to go or be out of sight behind anything.
Liam, } beyond, more than.
Liam-a, }
Lian, (*a.*) large, eminent, great, (*v.*) to be large, etc., to increase in size.
Liang, (*s.*) a handle (of pot, spoon, etc.), a wall plate.
Lian-kual vai-hlo, (*s.*) the name of a plant with burrs.
Lian-pui, (*a.*) immense, gigantic.
Lian-rân, (*s.*) a species of rice.
Li luh, (*v.*) to dive, to plunge.
Lim, (*s.*) a picture, model, image, imitation.
Ling, (*a.*) red hot, (*v.*) to be red hot, to plant (as bulbous plants).
Lip, (*v.*) to flay.
Lîr, (*v.*) to roll.
Lîr a nghîng, (*v.*) to quake (as the earth).
Lîr nghîng, (*s.*) an earthquake.
Li teng shawl, (*s.*) a bay, a cove, a creek.
Lo, (*adv.*) not.
Lo, a verbal prefix signifying motion towards the speaker.

Lo, (*s.*) a Lushai cultivation, a *jhúm.*
Lo, (*v.*) to pluck (as flower, fruit, etc.)
Lo ang-in, (*prep.*) contrary to.
Lo beng vâr, (*v.*) to be on the alert, to be in readiness.
Lo chen, (*s.*) a measurement equal to about three or four miles.
Lo-chu, } (*prep.*) with the exception of, except, but.
Lo-chuan, }
Lo-ding, (*v.*) to stand.
Lo en, (*v.*) to search for a fit place for *jhúming.*
Lo haw, } (*v.*) to come.
Lo hawng, }
Lo hi, } (*prep.*) with the exception of, except, but.
Lo hian, }
Loi, (*s.*) a buffalo.
Loi, (*v.*) to conduct a bride to a bridegroom's house, to entice fowls into a coop, the act of a bride going to the bridegroom's house, to go into a coop (as fowls).
Loi-chal, (*s.*) a man who accompanies the bride to the bridegroom's house.
Loi-rawl, (*s.*) a bugle.
Lo-in-ring, (*v.*) to be on the alert, to be in readiness.
Loi-thlêm, (*v.*) to commit adultery with a woman by force or stratagem.
Lok, (*v.*) to punch or rap with the knuckles.
Lok, (*adv.*) soon, for a short time.
Lok, (*a.*) knobby, rugged.
Lo-kal, (*v.*) to come.
Lo-kalh, (*v.*) to contradict, to oppose.
Lo-kîr, (*v.*) to come back, to return.
Long, (*s.*) a boat.
Long ba'din'na, (*s.*) an anchor.
Long-barh, (*s.*) mica.
Long chelh ding tu, (*s.*) an anchor.
Lo-nghâk, (*v.*) to wait for.
Long-lêng, (*s.*) an open boat.
Long-pâr, (*s.*) a clove.
Lo-pawh, } (*prep.*) besides.
Lo-pôh, }
Lo pom, (*v.*) to select a site for a new *jhúm.*
Lor, (*v.*) to protrude.
Lo ring, (*v.*) to make preparation for eating, etc., to get or make ready.
Lo-sûl-haw*ng*, (*v.*) to return home from the field or from work.
Lo-sûl-thlen*g*, (*v.*) to arrive home from the field or from work.

Lo-thleng, (*v.*) to arrive, to befal.
Lo vât, (*v.*) to cut a *jhûm*.
Lu, (*s.*) the head.
Lu, (*v.*) to copulate with.
Lua, (*adv.*) too.
Luah, (*v.*) to occupy, to take possession of, to enter into possession of.
Lu a ha, (*v.*) to be giddy.
Luak, (*s.*) to vomit.
Luak-thei, (*s.*) the name of a tree with edible fruit.
Luak a chhuak, (*v.*) to feel sick.
Lu a na, (*v.*) to have a headache.
Luang, (*v.*) to flow.
Luang, (*s.*) the name of a reed, ekra.
Lua-tuk, (*adv.*) too.
Lu-dîp, (*s.*) the fontanel.
Luh, (*v.*) to importune.
Luh-lul, (*a.*) disobedient, obstinate, stubborn, self-willed, (*v.*) to be disobedient, etc.
Luh-thluk, (*v.*) to persuade by importunity.
Lui, (*adv.*) purposely, intentionally, in an insistent manner, (*v.*) to insist.
Lui, (*s.*) a stream, a river.
Lui-dung, (*s.*) a valley.
Lui hnâr lam-a, (*adv.*) upstream.
Lui-hrâm, (*adv.*) persistently, perseveringly.
Lui in-khan, (*s.*) a watershed.
Lui kai, (*s.*) a ford, bridge, or any crossing of a river.
Lui-liam, (*s.*) the name of a creeper.
Lui mong lam-a, (*adv.*) downstream.
Lui-pui, (*s.*) a river.
Lui-tîr, (*v.*) compel, force.
Lu-ka, (*s.*) the platform in front of a Lushai house.
Luka-pui, (*s.*) a platform to the side of the *lu-ka*.
Lu-kham, (*s.*) a pillow, a bolster.
Lu-khum, (*s.*) a hat, a cap.
Lu'khung, (*v.*) to cohabit with, to serve for a wife, to enter a house with the intention of killing, assaulting, or quarrelling with its inmates.
Lum, (*v.*) to roll.
Lum, (*a.*) warm, hot, (*v.*) to be warm, to be hot.
Lum, (*s.*) the name of a tree the roots of which are used for making a yellow or red dye.
Lum, (*v.*) to be, to do.

Lum-lêr, (*s.*) the name of a species of plum.
Lu mêt, (*v.*) to cut the hair.
Lu-mêt mi, } (*s.*) a barber.
Lu-mêt-tu, }
Lu na, (*s.*) headache.
Lung, (*s.*) a stone, a rock.
Lung, (*s.*) the heart.
Lung, (*s.*) a maggot, (*a.*) maggotty, (*v.*) to be maggotty.
Lung a lêng, (*v.*) to feel sad, to feel homesick, to let the mind wander, to ponder over the past.
Lung chhe, (*v.*) to be heartbroken, to be sad, to be hurt in the feelings.
Lung chhia, (*s.*) a rock.
Lung chhia*t*, (*v.*) to be heartbroken, to be sad, to be hurt in the feelings.
Lung chhiat pui, (*v.*) to feel sorry for anyone.
Lung chhiat thlâk, (*a.*) heartbreaking, sad, grievous.
Lung-dawh, (*s.*) a platform erected in memory of the dead.
Lung in, (*s.*) a prison, a stone house.
Lung kham, (*a.*) anxious, worried, troubled, (*v.*) to keep or have in the mind, to wish, to be anxious, worried, or troubled.
Lung lai-shuih, (*s.*) a slate for writing.
Lung lai-shuih ziak-na, (*s.*) a slate pencil.
Lung lekha, (*s.*) the same as *lung lai-shuih.*
Lung-li, (*s.*) the name of a very durable tree, the juice of which is used as a remedy for sores.
Lung muang, (*v.*) to have peace of mind.
Lung-ngai, (*v.*) to be sad, to grieve, to be sorrowful, discouraged or disheartened.
Lung ni, (*v.*) to be pleased, to be contented.
Lung ni lo, (*v.*) to be vexed, annoyed, displeased, or discontented.
Lung-oi, (*v.*) to be pleased, to be contented.
Lung-oi-lo, (*v.*) to be vexed, annoyed, displeased, or discontented.
Lung-pât, (*s.*) stone moss.
Lung-phur-buh-tun, (*s.*) the name of a grass.
Lung-râl, (*s.*) a pickaxe.
Lung-sam, (*s.*) a maidenhair fern.
Lung-tât, (*s.*) a hone, a grindstone.
Lung-ten, (*v.*) to dislike, detest, disown.
Lung-ṭhîl, (*s.*) gravel.
Lung-thu, (*s.*) a trivet, stones used to support a pot over the fire.

Lung ti chhia*t*, (*v. t.*) to hurt the feelings, to break the heart. to make sad.
Lung tu'hrât, } (*s.*) a pickaxe.
Lung tuk-na, }
Lung-vai chi, (*s.*) the name of a kind of Lushai salt.
Lun lai, (*s.*) the time when a thing is in full swing.
Lu-phut, (*s.*) scurf.
Lu'pui, (*v.*) to bring in.
Lu-ruh, (*s.*) a skull.
Lu-shûn, (*v.*) to put down the hair as a sign of mourning for the dead, to go into mourning, to neglect the personal appearance, clothing, etc., as a sign of mourning.
Lû*t*, (*v.*) to enter, to sink, to appeal to (as in a law case).
Lu tan, (*v.*) to decapitate.
Lu-tuk, (*adv.*) too.
Lu-virh, (*s.*) a headache which comes on every morning soon after sunrise.

M

Mah, (*adv.*) even (used only in the negative).
Mah-na, it may be, perhaps.
Mai, (*adv.*) merely, to no purpose.
Mai, (*s.*) a pumpkin.
Mai-châm, (*s.*) an altar.
Mai-hûn, (*s.*) a basin.
Mai-mai, (*adv.*) merely, uselessly, gratuitously, undeservedly, simply, causelessly.
Mai-maw, (*s.*) silk.
Mai-mit chhin*g*, (*v.*) to shut the eyes.
Mai-mom, (*s.*) a spider.
Mai-mom in, (*s.*) a spider's web, a cobweb.
Mai-mom rîl, (*s.*) a spider's thread, a cobweb.
Mai-pawl, (*s.*) the name of a pumpkin.
Mai-tâm-tok, (*s.*) the name of a vegetable (*mordica mixta*).
Mak, (*a.*) wonderful, (*adv.*) wonderfully, (*v.*) to be wonderful.
Mâ*k*, (*v.*) to divorce, to give up.
Mâ*k*-mawh, (*adv.*) certainly, without fail, also a particle joined to a verb with the meaning of 'compelling,' 'provoking,' as *oi-mâkmawh* = belief compelling.
Mâk-pa, (*s.*) a sister's or daughter's husband.
Mak ti, (*v.*) to be amazed, to be filled with wonder.
Mal, (*s.*) a drop, a grain, a single one.
Mal chung, (*s.*) the lap.

Ma-lêk, (*v.*) to not trouble, as in *kal malêkroh* = don't trouble to go.
Mal-mâk, (*v.*) to renounce upon oath, to abjure, to cast off for ever.
Mal-mal-in, (*adv.*) one at a time, one after another, one by one.
Mal-phêng, (*s.*) the side of the thigh.
Mal-pui, (*s.*) the thigh.
Mal-shawm, (*a.*) fortunate.
Mal-shawm sak, (*v.*) to bless, to call down blessings upon.
Mal ṭheoh-vin, } (*adv.*) one at a time, one after another, one by one.
Mal zêl-in, }
Mâm, (*a.*) smooth, (*v.*) to be smooth.
Mamawh, (*v.*) to have urgent business, to have imperative need of, to be imperatively necessary.
Mâm-rem, (*a.*) smooth, even (as a road, etc.)
Man, (*v.*) to seize, to hold, to grasp.
Man, (*s.*) price, reward, recompense, wages, (*v.*) to be good value for money, to be expensive.
Mang, (*v.*) to die, to die out, to become extinct.
Mang, (*adv.*) very, much.
Mang, (*s.*) a dream.
Mang-ang, (*v.*) to be bewildered, perplexed, amazed, troubled in mind, to be in a predicament.
Mang-an'thlâk, (*a.*) bewildering, perplexing.
Mang-khawh, (*v.*) to gather together the pieces of burnt wood, etc. after the burning of a *jhûm*.
Mang-khawng, (*s.*) a species of rice.
Mang-khawng, (*s.*) the name of a trap for rats in which the animal is killed by a falling beam.
Mang-khawng-dai, (*s.*) the name of a small palm.
Mang-khai râl-vêng, (*s.*) the plover.
Mang nei, (*v.*) to dream.
Mang phan, (*v.*) to dream of what one has been talking about.
Ma-ni, (*pro.*) own, self.
Man-tîr, (*v.*) to deliver up, to cause to be seized, to cause to seize.
Man-zâng, (*s.*) a species of edible arum.
Mao, (*s.*) a bamboo.
Mao âr-fêp, (*s.*) new shoots springing from the roots of old bamboos after a jungle fire.
Mao-buh, (*s.*) a species of rice.
Mao-hâk, (*s.*) a patch of bamboos not to be *jhûmed*, but preserved for building purposes.
Mao-hnu, (*s.*) the shoots of bamboos in a *jhûm*.
Mar, (*s.*) the pulse.

Mar, (*a.*) straight, even, stretched tightly, (*v.*) to be straight, even, stretched tightly.

Mar darh,
Mar ṭai, } (*s.*) an erratic pulse.

Ma-thei lo,
Ma-thei lo vin, } (*adv.*) certainly, without fail.

Ma-tu, (*s.*) the Kumi tribe.

Maw, an interrogative particle.

Mawh, (*v.*) to be unable ; affix like the English affix 'less' or the prefix 'un'.

Mawh-chhiat, (*v.*) to blame falsely, to lay blame upon.

Mawh phur, (*v.*) to bear the consequences or blame.

Mawl, (*v.*) to be plain, to be without adornment, without common sense, foolish, (*a.*) plain, etc.

Mawn, (*s.*) the *glans clitoris.*

Mawt, (*s.*) the name of a creeping cane.

Me, (*s.*) the liber cells of certain trees, the minute thorns on certain fruits and plants, (*v.*) to be covered with the above minute thorns, to be irritating (as flannel to the skin), (*a.*) covered with *me*, irritating.

Me, the Lushai call for goats.

Mei, (*s.*) fire, a tail, the stern of a boat.

Mei-alh, (*s.*) a flame.

Mei-hu, (*s.*) tinder.

Mei chhem, (*v.*) to light a fire, to blow a fire.

Mei chher, (*s.*) a torch, a firebrand.

Mei êk thiar, (*v.*) to snuff (candle, torch, etc.)

Mei-hle, (*s.*) the name of a tree similar to the sago palm.

Mei-hol, (*s.*) charcoal.

Mei khu, (*s.*) smoke.

Mei khu chhua'na, (*s.*) a chimney.

Mei khu long, (*s.*) a steamboat.

Mei ling, (*s.*) live embers.

Mei long, (*s.*) a steamboat.

Mei lung, (*s.*) a flint.

Mei-pêk silai, (*s.*) the name of a gun used by the Lushais before the advent of flintlocks, fired with a firebrand.

Mei pui, (*s.*) a bonfire anywhere outside a village.

Mei-shi, (*s.*) a spark.

Mei talh, (*s.*) a lucifer match, flint, steel, and tinder, (*v.*) to strike a light.

Mei talh bawm, (*s.*) a tinder box, a match box.

Mei-tei, (*s.*) a Manipuri.

Mei-tei ruk-ru, (*s.*) the sensitive plant.

Mei-thal-lawn, (*s.*) fireworks, a rocket.
Mei-thui, (*s.*) the name of a tree, the juice of the above tree which is used for japanning.
Mei-vâm, (*s.*) live embers.
Mei-vâp, (*s.*) ashes, burnt leaves.
Melh, (*v.*) to stare at, to look at steadfastly, to stare.
Meng, (*v.*) to wake, to be awake, to open (as eyes).
Men'lai, (*s.*) the time between supper and bedtime.
Meoh = self.
Mê*t*, (*v.*) to scrape, to shave, to cut (the hair).
Mi, (*s.*) a person, a man, a thing, one.
Mi-â, (*s.*) a fool, an idiot, a silly person, a mad person.
Mi dah bêl, (*s.*) the name of a large earthen pot.
Mi daw'thei, (*s.*) a liar.
Mi en-khal thei, (*a.*) dazzling.
Mi-fîr, (*s.*) a miser, a niggard.
Mi-hring, (*s.*) a man, a person.
Mi-khua, (*s.*) another village.
Mi-khual, (*s.*) a stranger, one belonging to another village.
Mi-khua mîm kût thla, (*s.*) the time of the year corresponding nearly to August.
Mi-lem, } (*s.*) a model, a picture, an image, a scarecrow.
Mi-lim, }
Mîm, (*s.*) Job's tears, a nut, see also ***mit a mîm.***
Mîm kût, (*s.*) the name of a Lushai feast.
Min, (*pro.*) me, us, for me, for us, to me, to us.
Min, (*v.*) to slip away (as the side of a hill, a path, etc.)
Mi-ngei, (*a.*) full of buoyant spirits, fond of joking.
Mi-pa, (*s.*) a male, a man.
Mi-pa naopang, (*s.*) a boy.
Mi-pui, (*s.*) a crowd, a multitude.
Mi-rang, (*s.*) a Magh.
Mi-rong, (*s.*) a Naga.
Mi-ruk-ru, } (*s.*) a thief.
Mi-ruk-ru-hmang, }
Mi-sual, (*s.*) a quarrelsome, foolish, or bad person, a sinner.
Mit, (*s.*) the eye.
Mit, (*s.*) a skein (of yarn, etc.)
Mît, (*s.*) the gall bladder.
Mi-tâng, (*s.*) a prisoner.
Mit a mîm, (*v.*) to have something in the eye.
Mit a vai, (*v.*) to be dazzled, to see one thing as if it were another, to see indistinctly.
Mit-del, (*v.*) to be blind, (*a.*) blind.

Mit doi vai, (*v.*) to conjure, to deceive the eyes.
Mit doi vai thiam, (*s.*) a conjurer, a magician.
Mit-dum, (*s.*) the iris of the eye.
Mit fe-rê, (*s.*) the name of a fly, the discharge on the lashes during a cold in the eye.
Mit-fîm, (*a.*) keen-sighted, (*v.*) to be keen-sighted.
Mi-thi, (*s.*) a corpse, a dead person.
Mi-thi buh, the same as ***khuavâng buh.***
Mi-thi chhiah, (*v.*) to make an offering to a departed spirit.
Mi-thi-in a thlûk, (*v.*) to have a fit.
Mi-thi-khua, (*s.*) the abode of departed spirits.
Mi-thi ngai, (*v.*) to mourn for the dead.
Mi-thi râl, (*v.*) to hold a wake, (*s.*) the men who assemble to drink at a burial.
Mi-thi-thlûk, (*s.*) a kind of fit.
Mit-hmul, (*s.*) the eyelashes.
Mit-kalh, (*a.*) crosseyed, (*v.*) to be crosseyed.
Mit khap, (*v.*) to blink the eye, (*s.*) a moment.
Mit-khap-kâr lo vin, (*adv.*) in an instant, instantaneously, in the twinkling of an eye.
Mit-khing-shiai, (*v.*) to wink, to shut one eye.
Mit-ko, } (*s.*) the eyebrows.
Mit-ko-tlâng, }
Mit-la, (*v.*) to take the fancy.
Mit lên, (*v.*) to look round about.
Mit-mal, (*v.*) to be afflicted with night blindness.
Mit mei, (*v.*) to watch, (*s.*) behaviour, manner.
Mit mei hmu, (*s.*) to have the approbation of.
Mit mei vên 'thiam, (*v.*) to know how to read a person's thoughts by his manner, (*s.*) one so skilled.
Mit meng-zia, (*s.*) behaviour, manner.
Mit-men'sak, (*v.*) to be drowsy, to cause drowsiness.
Mit-mu, (*s.*) the eyeball.
Mit nao-tê, (*s.*) the pupil of the eye.
Mit-shiai, (*v.*) to wink, to shut one eye.
Mit shîr-in melh, (*v.*) to watch out of the corners of the eyes.
Mit-thla, (*s.*) imagination.
Mit-thla-in hmu, (*v.*) to imagine, to see in imagination.
Mit ti-vai, (*v. t.*) to dazzle.
Mit-tlâng kawm, (*s.*) the edge of the eyelid.
Mit-tui, (*s.*) tears.
Mit vâr, (*a.*) keen-sighted, (*v.*) to be keen-sighted.
Mit vâr leh, (*v.*) to regain sight.
Mit vâr nei, (*v.*) to receive sight.

Mit vun, (*s.*) the eyelid,
Mit vun chuar, (*v.*) to frown.
Mo, (*s.*) a bride, a son's or brother's wife.
Mo-chal, (*s.*) a daughter's or sister's husband who goes to live in his wife's house.
Moi, (*a.*) pretty, (*v.*) to be pretty, beautiful, exalted, honoured, to be fit or proper.
Moi, (*a.*) beginning to form in the bud (as rice).
Moih, (*a.*) rotten, (*v.*) to rot, to be rotten.
Molh, (*adv.*) assuredly, certainly, specially.
Mo loi, (*s.*) the friend of a bride who accompanies her to her husband's house.
Mom, (*a.*) shining, glistening, polished, greasy, (*v.*) to shine, glisten, etc.
Mong, (*s.*) the bottom of anything, the posterior, the mouth of a river.
Mong-chep, (*s.*) an earwig.
Mong-choi, (*v.*) to commence cutting a *jhúm* at the lower end and working upwards.
Mong-er, (*s.*) the name of an ant.
Mong hur, } (*s.*) one who practises sodomy.
Mong khaw hur, }
Mong kua, (*s.*) the anus.
Mong-phu-hru, (*s.*) a false bottom.
Mong-thun-silai, (*s.*) a breechloading gun.
Mu, (*s.*) the hawk.
Mu, (*s.*) a seed, a kernel.
Mual, (*s.*) a mound, a hill, a spur (of a hill).
Mual-dung, (*s.*) a spur (of a hill).
Mual-pho, (*v.*) to be put to shame.
Muan, (*v.*) to encourage.
Muan*g*, (*v.*) to be encouraged, to take courage, to be in comfortable circumstances, to have no anxiety.
Muan*g*, (*v.*) to be slow, leisurely, or self-collected, to take things quietly, (*adv.*) slowly, leisurely, self-collectedly, steadily, quietly.
Muan*g* chang, (*v.*) to be slow, leisurely or self-collected, to take things quietly.
Mu âr la, (*s.*) the name of a species of hawk.
Mu beng nei, (*s.*) a vulture.
Mu-chhia, (*s.*) the name of a hawk.
Muk, (*a.*) pressed tightly together, close together, prosperous, (*v.*) to be pressed tightly together, etc., (*adv.*) tightly together, closely together.
Muk, (*s.*) the name of a tree with a durable heart.

Mûk, (*a.*) dull (of colour).
Mu-khao, (*s.*) the name of a tree.
Mu-lu kolh, (*s.*) a vulture.
Mûm, (*a.*) round, cylindrical.
Mûm, (*v.*) to close (as a flower), to be closed (as a flower).
Mu-mang, (*s.*) a dream.
Mu-mang-a mang, (*v.*) to dream.
Mu-mang-in hmu, } (*v.*) to dream of, to see in a dream.
Mu-mang lama hmu, }
Mu-mang nei, (*v.*) to dream, to have a dream.
Mûm-pal, (*a.*) perfectly cylindrical.
Mûm-shawl, (*a.*) cylindrical.
Mun*g*, (*v.*) to stew, to boil for a long time.
Mu-nghîl, (*v.*) to sleep, to be asleep.
Mu-nghîl dêr, (*v.*) to be fast asleep.
Mun*g*-koi, (*v.*) to boil or stew until the whole substance is dissolved.
Mûr, (*v.*) to be frosted (as the centre of amber bead), (*v.*) to have the appearance of goose skin.
Mu-ra, (*s.*) the name of a fabulous gigantic bird.
Mur-pui, (*s.*) a species of swallow.
Mu-shao, (*s.*) a slug for a gun.
Mu-shep, (*s.*) small shot, small, abortive or undeveloped seeds.
Mu*t*, (*v.*) to lie down, to recline, to sleep, to close (as a leaf at night).
Mût, (*v.*) to smoulder.
Mut a chhuak, (*v.*) to feel sleepy.
Mut-hîl, (*v.*) to sleep, to be asleep.
Mut-hîl dêr, (*v.*) to be fast asleep.
Mut-hmun, (*s.*) a sleeping place.
Mu-ṭih, (*s.*) the castor oil plant.
Mut thlû*k*, (*v.*) to fall asleep while sitting or standing, to be heavy with sleep.
Mu-vân-lai, (*v.*) the name of a kind of hawk which eats snakes.

N

Na, (*s.*) the outside (of bamboos, etc.)
Na, (*a.*) boisterous, scorching, intense, (*v.*) to be boisterous, etc., (*adv.*) boisterously, etc.
Na, (*prep.*) for, also an instrumental and causative affix, also an affix denoting 'place of.'
Na, see *nat*.
Na-a, (*conj.*) although, even though.
Na a nei, (*v.*) to be stringy (as beans, etc.)

Na-apiang-a, (*adv.*) wherever.
Na-chin, (*adv.*) whence, where.
Nâk, (*s.*) the side.
Nâk-a-lai-in, just when, when.
Nak-in-a, (*adv.*) by and bye, presently.
Nak-in-deo-va, } (*adv.*) by and bye, presently.
Nak-in-hnu-a, }
Nak-kum-*a*, (*a.*) next year.
Nâk-lâm, (*s.*) the name of a creeper the leaves of which are used to relieve pain in the side.
Nâk ruh, (*s.*) a rib, the ribs.
Nak-tiam-*a*, three days hence.
Nak-thai-*a*, the day after tomorrow.
Nak-thai-zân-*a*, the night after tomorrow night.
Nak-tip-*a*, the day after tomorrow.
Nak-tip-zân-*a*, the night after tomorrow night.
Nak-tûk-*a*, tomorrow.
Nak-tûk-tûk-leh-*a*, the day after tomorrow.
Nak-tuk zân-*a*, tomorrow night.
Nak-zân-*a*, tonight.
Nâl, (*a.*) slippery, smooth, (*v.*) to be slippery, etc.
Nam, (*v.*) to push, to knock against.
Nam, (*v.*) to smell of, to give forth a smell, to be high, to be strong smelling.
Na-mai, (*a.*) ordinary, common, any sort of, every sort of, all sorts of, (*pro.*) whoever, whomever, whatever.
Na-mên, (*a.*) ordinary, common.
Na-mên-lo, (*a.*) extraordinary, uncommon.
Nam-liam, (*v.*) to push over the edge.
Nam-nul-mai, (*v.*) to do a thing anyhow.
Nan, (*v. t.*) to wet, to fall upon (as rain).
Nân, (*prep.*) for.
Na-na-na-in, just as, exactly as.
Nan*g*, (*v.*) to get a glimpse of an animal when tracking, to overtake, to be in time, to meet.
Nang, (*pro.*) thou, thine, thee.
Nang-a, (*pro.*) thy.
Nang-a-ta, (*pro.*) thine.
Nang-ma, (*pro.*) thou, thy, thee.
Nang-ma-a-ta, (*pro.*) thine.
Nang-ma-ni, (*pro.*) you, your.
Nang-ma-ni-ta (*pro.*) yours.
Nang-ma-ta, (*pro.*) thine.
Nang-ni, (*pro.*) you, your.

Nang-ni-ta, (*pro.*) yours.
Nao, (*s.*) a younger brother or sister, a child, a paternal uncle's younger child, a maternal aunt's younger child, a younger brother's wife, a husband's younger sister or brother.
Nao a chhia*t*, (*v.*) to have a miscarriage.
Nao-bân, (*s.*) an orchid.
Nao-chaw-ṭhing-bawm, (*s.*) the name of a small red ant.
Nao-huai-hlo, }
Nao-huai-hrui, } (*s.*) the name of a flowering creeper.
Nao pai, (*v.*) to be with child.
Nao-pang, (*s.*) a child, a boy, a girl.
Nao-pang chal-â, (*a.*) childish.
Nao-pang hri, (*s.*) the name of a disease.
Nao-pan*g* lai, (*s.*) childhood.
Nao-shên, (*s.*) a baby.
Nao-thak, (*s.*) the name of a tree.
Nao-va-oi-mu, (*s.*) the name of a plant.
Nao vei, (*v.*) to labour with child.
Nao vei na, (*v.*) to travail with child.
Na-rân, (*a.*) ordinary, common, any sort of, every sort of, all sorts of, (*pro.*) whoever, whomever, whatever.
Na-rân-in, (*adv.*) whenever, wherever.
Na-sha, (*adv.*) exceedingly, (*a.*) immense, intense.
Na*t*, (*v.*) to pain, to ache, to feel pain, to be ill, (*s.*) pain, sickness.
Nat-ni-nei-in, (*adv.*) intermittently (as in fever).
Nat-tlun, (*s.*) ague.
Na-zia, an affix similar to the English affix 'able.'
Na-zong, (*a.*) ordinary, common, any sort of, every sort of, all sorts of, (*pro.*) whoever, whomever, whatever.
Na-zong-in, (*adv.*) whenever, wherever.
Naw' alh, (*s.*) a lucifer match.
Naw-chi-zuar, (*v.*) a harlot.
Naw'-fung, (*s.*) the bow of a Lushai fiddle.
Nawh-phuai, (*s.*) the name of a creeper.
Nawh-thuh, (*v.*) to bribe, (*s.*) a bribe.
Nawl, (*s.*) debris, drift, a heap of dust or rubbish.
Nawl, (*v.*) to graze, to strike at an angle and slip along (see *hnawl*).
Naw*t*, (*v.*) to rub, to scour.
Nawt-chik, (*v.*) to creak.
Nawt-fai, (*v.*) to clean by scouring or rubbing.
Naw-ti-zuar, (*s.*) a harlot.
Nawt-kiu, }
Nawt-ri, } (*v.*) to creak.

Nawt-tle, (*v.*) to polish.
Nê, (*s.*) the young tubers of bulbous plants.
Nei, (*v.*) to get, to have, to obtain.
Nei-tu, (*s.*) an owner.
Nek, (*s.*) a fellow, a term of contempt.
Nek, (*adv.*) with force, vehemently, very much.
Nêk, (*adv.*) to throng, to press against, to treat with unfairness or without respect, to disrespect the rights of, to take advantage of, to cause to bear the blame, to beat down, to offer a price lower than the one quoted.
Nêl, (*a.*) soft (as skin).
Nêl, (*v.*) to be used to, to be familiar with, to be not afraid of.
Nel, (*a.*) flexible, supple, (*v.*) to be flexible, to be supple.
Nêl-tlang, (*s.*) a clod of earth.
Nem, (*v.*) to press, to squeeze.
Nêm, (*a.*) fine in texture, soft, weak (as beer).
Nêm, (*adv.*) not.
Nem-i nu chhu uih, (*s.*) the name of a plant used by the Lushais as a medicine for worms.
Nem-in ziak, (*v.*) to print, to impress.
Nem-sawr, (*v.*) to squeeze liquid out of anything.
Nên, (*prep.*) with, equivalent to 'and'.
Nêp, (*v.*) to ask a price higher than the right value, to offer a smaller price than the one quoted, to pretend not to want in buying anything in hopes that the price will be reduced, to do without.
Ner, (*v.*) to mushroom out (as top of post when beaten with a mallet, bottom of walking stick, etc.)
Nga, (*a.*) five.
Ngah, (*v.*) to have much, to possess much.
Ngai, (*adv.*) ever.
Ngai, (*a.*) the same.
Ngai, (*v.*) to bear, to endure.
Ngai, (*s.*) the name of a kind of screw-pine.
Ngai, (*v.*) to love, to long after an absent one, to copulate, to listen, to obey, to take notice of, to think, to consider, to wait for, to be necessary, to have need of, to be customary, (*a.*) beloved.
Ngai-bei-shei, (*v.*) to expect.
Ngai-dam, (*v.*) to pardon, to forgive.
Ngaih-hih, (*s.*) a creeper, the roots of which are used to poison fish.
Ngai hlu*t*, (*v.*) to think much of, to value highly.
Ngai-hna-thiam, (*v.*) to forgive, to pardon.
Ngai-hrui, (*s.*) a string of black, red and white yarn tied round the wrist by friends when parting.

Ngai-koi, (*v.*) to put a wrong construction upon.
Ngai-lo, (*adv.*) never, (*v.*) to be not customary.
Ngai-mawh, (*v.*) to be unable to put up with or bear.
Ngai-na, (*v.*) to be fond of, to like, to set great store by.
Ngai-na hre, } (*v.*) to know how.
Ngai-na hria*t*, }
Ngai-na-rêng hre lo, (*v.*) to not know what to do, to be in a fix, to be at a loss, to be in suspense.
Ngai-na-rêng hre-lo-vin shiam, (*v.*) to put in a fix, to hold in suspense.
Ngai-nom, (*s.*) anything pleasant to hear.
Ngai-ruat, (*v.*) to calculate, to guess, to reckon, to put on one side for a set purpose.
Ngai-ruat-in, (*adv.*) according to calculation, reckoning, or guess.
Ngai-ruat-pui, } (*v.*) to advise.
Ngai-ruat-sak, }
Ngai-sak, (*v.*) to regard, to have respect to or for, to heed, to care about, to care for, to show respect to or for.
Ngai-sam, (*a.*) heedless, careless, (*v.*) to be heedless, careless.
Ngai-shâng, (*v.*) to be interested in, to take interest in, to regard, to respect (as word, etc.)
Ngai-shân' tlâk, (*a.*) interesting.
Ngai-tak, (*a.*) beloved.
Ngai-thei, (*v.*) to put up with, to suffer, to endure.
Ngai-thlâ*k*, (*v.*) to listen, to give heed to, to eavesdrop.
Ngai-tlawm, (*v.*) to disregard, to think of no account, to think little of another, to look down upon one as an inferior.
Ngai-tua, (*v.*) to consider, to ponder, to be anxious.
Ngai-tua-pui, (*v.*) to advise.
Ngai-tua reng, (*v.*) to remember.
Ngai-vêk, the same again.
Ngai-vên', (*v.*) to watch, to keep guard over, to look after, to listen to.
Ngai-vom, (*s.*) the name of a plant.
Ngal, (*s.*) the shin.
Ngal-châr, (*s.*) the shin.
Ngal-hem, (*s.*) a contrivance made by boys to hit people on the leg as they walk along the path.
Ngam, (*a.*) brave, daring, tame, (*v.*) to be brave, etc., to dare, to gain a victory, to be prepared to do a thing.
Ngam-pah, } (*v.*) to be familiar with, to be not afraid of.
Ngam-pao, }
Ngam-thlêm, (*v.*) to deal craftily with, to use stratagem.
Ngam-thlêm hmang, (*v.*) to be crafty, (*a.*) crafty.

Ngân, (*s.*) rice ready damped for making beer.
Ngan-bawm, (*s.*) the name of a tree.
Ngao, (*s.*) a grey monkey.
Ngap, (*a.*) gritty.
Ngaw, (*s.*) virgin forest.
Ngawt, (*s.*) the name of a painless swelling on the head.
Nge, (*conj.*) or (generally used in interrogative sentences only).
Ngei, self.
Ngei, (*adv.*) really, certainly.
Ngei, (*v.*) to make to feel sick, to make one turn against, to cause one to turn against, to nauseate.
Ngei-a-lom, an emphatic verbal particle.
Ngeih, (*v.*) to be acclimatized, to agree with.
Ngei-kha-le, an emphatic verbal particle.
Ngêk, (*v.*) to squeal.
Ngên, (*s.*) bell metal.
Ngên, (*v.*) to ask for, to demand, to ask.
Ngên chiam, (*v.*) to beseech.
Ngêt, (*s.*) the name of a boring insect.
Ngêt, (*v.*) to be eaten by insects, to decay (as teeth), (*a.*) eaten, decayed.
Ngha, (*s.*) a fish.
Ngha chhan, (*v.*) to rest upon or against, (*s.*) a rest of any kind for arms, feet, etc.
Nghai-sha, (*v.*) to destroy wilfully, to torture, to ill-treat, to mutilate, to handle, to work at.
Nghâk, (*v.*) to wait.
Nghâk-hlel, (*v.*) to be impatient, to be eager, (*a.*) impatient, eager.
Ngha-koi, (*s.*) a fish-hook.
Ngha-koi-ngul, (*s.*) a fishing rod.
Ngha-kuai, (*a.*) a fish-hook.
Ngha-kuai ngul, (*s.*) a fishing rod.
Nghâl, (*adv.*) immediately, straightway, while about it.
Nghal, (*a.*) ill-behaved, unruly, over-familiar, rude, (*v.*) to be ill-behaved, etc., to take liberties.
Nghal-chang, (*s.*) a large male wild boar.
Nghal-fek, (*s.*) the name of a stinging bee.
Ngha-lim, (*s.*) the name of a small fish.
Nghal-mal, (*s.*) a large male wild boar.
Nghal-pol, (*s.*) the name of a plant.
Nghal-pui, (*s.*) the name of a stinging bee.
Nghal-rual, (*s.*) the name of a wild boar.
Ngha-mi, (*s.*) a species of large cat-fish.

Ngha-ngiai, (*s.*) the name of a fish.
Ngha-phu, (*s.*) the mahseer fish.
Nghar-dai, (*s.*) the name of a bramble.
Ngha-rûl, (*s.*) an eel.
Nghat, (*v.*) to put down (as a load upon the ground) to rest against or upon.
Ngha-thu, (*s.*) Bengali dried fish.
Ngha-tun-bek-bor-tleng-in hleoh, (*v.*) to swim on the side.
Ngha-vok, (*s.*) the name of a fish.
Nghawng, (*s.*) the neck.
Nghawng-kol, (*s.*) a yoke worn by the Lushais when carrying loads, a silver neck ornament.
Nghawng-puar, (*s.*) a goitre.
Nghei, (*v.*) to fast.
Nghen'-chhan, (*v.*) to lean against.
Nghêng, (*v.*) to be in contact with, to knock or lean against, to touch, to depend upon.
Nghêng-a, } (*prep.*) against.
Nghêng-lama, }
Nghet, (*a.*) firm, rigid, prosperous, stable, (*v.*) to be firm, etc., (*adv.*) firmly, etc.
Nghet-lo, (*a.*) loose, unstable, (*v.*) to be loose, etc.
Nghîng, (*v.*) to shake, to wave.
Ngho, (*s.*) a tusk, a tooth.
Nghong, (*s.*) a measurement from the tip of the middle finger to the opposite elbow with arms extended.
Nghor, (*v.*) to shake, to boil galloping.
Ngial, (*adv.*) rather, fairly.
Ngiat, (*v.*) to want, to wish for, to ask for.
Ngîl, (*a.*) straight, (*v.*) to be straight, (*adv.*) straight.
Ngil nei, (*a.*) kind, thoughtful, considerate, unselfish.
Ngo, (*a.*) white, fair, of a light colour, (*v.*) to be white, etc.
Ngoi, (*s.*) a fish trap.
Ngoi, (*s.*) quiet, silent, (*v.*) to be quiet, silent, to stop, to pause.
Ngoi-choi, (*a.*) morose, quiet (in disposition, or through sickness,) (*v.*) to be morose, to be quiet.
Ngoi-hêm, (*s.*) the name of a tree.
Ngoi-tao, (*v.*) to sulk, to be sulky.
Ngol-tawt, (*a.*) obstinate, self-willed, stubborn, disobedient, (*v.*) to be obstinate, etc.
Ngong, (*a.*) slow of understanding, dull, stupid, (*v.*) to be slow of understanding, etc.
Ngor, (*s.*) consumption, any chronic or wasting disease, one so afflicted.

Ngorh, (*v.*) to keep on at, (*adv.*) continuously.
Ngorh chhên, (*v. t.* and *int.*) to keep on at, to keep on the go, (*adv.*) continuously.
Ngorh-shek, (*v.* and *adv.*) the same as 'ngorh.'
Ngot, (*a.*) crisp, short.
Ngot, (*adv.*) merely, actually, very much, also with the meaning of 'without preparation, warning, permission, cause, or taking heed.'
Ngo-te-kherh, (*s.*) the name of a cloth.
Ngot shiah shiah, (*a.*) crisp, short.
Nguai, (*v.*) to cause to feel sick or bilious.
Nguai, } (*a.*) listless, quiet, silent, downhearted, sad, miserable,
Ngui, } (*v.*) to be listless, etc.
Ngûk, (*v.*) to grunt.
Ngul, (*s.*) the barrel (of a gun), the stick or sapling bent down for a spring in making a noose trap, a rod.
Ngûm, (*s.*) the tail of a bird without the feathers, the lower end of the spine.
Ngûm fi-ruh, (*s.*) the coccyx.
Ngûm-hnâm, (*s.*) a sword.
Ngûm-ruh, (*s.*) the sacrum.
Ngûn, (*s.*) the name of a bracelet.
Ngun, (*v.*) to be careful, (*adv.*) carefully.
Ngûn-kual, (*s.*) a spiral, a spiral spring, the name of a creeper.
Ngur, (*v.*) to growl.
Ngût, (*adv.*) only, really.
Ni, (*s.*) the sun, day, a paternal aunt.
Ni, (*v.*) to be, (*adv.*) yes.
Ni-chin-a, (*adv.*) a short time ago.
Ni-chhua*k*, (*s.*) sunrise, (*v.*) to rise (as the sun).
Ni-chuang, (*v.*) to stay over a day and a night.
Ni-e, (*adv.*) yes.
Ni-êng, (*s.*) sunlight.
Ni-hlawh, (*a.*) fortunate, lucky, (*v.*) to be fortunate, to be lucky.
Ni-hliap, (*s.*) a sunshade, an umbrella.
Ni khat ban, }
Ni khat kal, } one day's journey.
Ni khat kong, }
Ni-khua, (*v.*) to thrive, to prosper.
Ni-kum-*a*, last year.
Ni-kum-hma-sha-*a*, the year before last.
Ni-lên', (*v.*) to spend or pass time.
Ni-lêng, }
Ni-lêng-in, } all day.

Ni-lêng kal na chen, (*s.*) a measurement, a full day's journey, about 15 to 20 miles.
Ni-lo, (*adv.*) no.
Ni-lum, (*s.*) sunshine.
Ni-ma-shela, (*conj.*) nevertheless, yet, still, but.
Ni-min-*a*, yesterday.
Ni-min-piah-*a*, the day before yesterday.
Ni-min-piah zân-*a*, three nights ago.
Niminzân-*a*, the night before last.
Nin*g*, (*v.*) to be tired of.
Nin-hlei, (*v.*) to fidget, (*a.*) fidgetty.
Nin-no, (*s.*) a burning glass, a magnifying glass.
Nin-om, (*a.*) fatiguing, monotonous, tiresome.
Ni-pui hun (or lai), (*s.*) the summer, the hot weather.
Ni-pui-pâr, (*s.*) the name of a creeper with scarlet flowers.
Ni-sari, (*s.*) a week.
Ni-sha, (*s.*) sunshine.
Ni-shu-e, (*adv.*) no.
Ni tlâ*k*, (*s.*) sunset, (*v.*) to set (as sun).
Ni-tin, } (*adv.*) daily, day by day.
Ni-tin-in, }
Ni tum-toi, (*v.*) to pass time quickly.
Ni tum-toi-na, (*s.*) a pastime.
Ni-zân-*a*, last night.
Ni-zawn-in, (*adv.*) day after day.
No, (*s.*) a cup, a vase, a jug.
No, (*s.*) the young of animals, birds, etc, (*a.*) young, soft, tender.
No a chhiat, } to have a miscarriage.
No a tla-sual, }
Noi, (*s.*) small pieces, small change, dregs, (*a.*) small, (*adv.*) in pieces.
Noi-nawk, (*s.*) the name of a plant with edible leaves.
Nom, (*a.*) a contracted form of *nuam*.
Non, (*s.*) the trunk (of an elephant, etc.)
Non, (*v.*) to do or say anything over and over again, (*adv.*) again and again, over and over again.
Nor, (*v.*) to butt, to push (as a pig), to collide with.
No-thei, (*s.*) a bamboo cup.
Nu, (*s.*) a mother, a maternal aunt, a paternal uncle's wife, a husband's mother, a female, a feminine affix.
Nu, (*a*) muddy, turbid, (*v.*) to be muddy, to be turbid.
Nuai, (*a.*) one hundred thousand.
Nuai, (*v.*) to brush, to rub, to blow about violently.
Nuai-eng, (*s.*) the balsam plant.

Nuai-phuan, (*s.*) the name of a shrub with white flowers.
Nuai-thang, (*s.*) the balsam plant.
Nuam, (*v.*) to wish, to want.
Nuam, (*a.*) comfortable, nice, (*v.*) to be comfortable.
Nuar, (*v.*) to sulk, to get into a temper, to be disappointed.
Nu-beng-chah, (*s.*) the name of a reed.
Nu-fa, (*s.*) mother and child, used also to express 'one and a half' and 'one hundred and fifty.'
Nu-hnûn, (*s.*) the papaw (*carica papaya*).
Nu-hron, (*s.*) a stepmother.
Nuhron ben' in beng, (*v.*) to slap with the open hand.
Nui, (*v.*) to laugh.
Nui-chhiah, (*s.*) a laughing stock.
Nui-shan, (*v.*) to laugh at, to mock, to scoff at.
Nui za, (*v.*) to feel like laughing.
Nui za-thlâ*k*, (*a.*) ridiculous, funny, laughable.
Nûl, (*v.*) to brush past, to rub against.
Nu-la, (*s.*) a maiden, a young woman.
Nun a nem, (*v.*) to be good-tempered.
Nun chhia, (*a.*) cruel, vicious, bad, (*v.*) to be cruel, etc.
Nun*g*, (*a.*) alive, (*v.*) to live, to revive (after fainting, chloroform, etc.)
Nun*g*-chan*g*, (*s.*) nature, mode of life, disposition, habit.
Nun-nem, (*a.*) good-tempered.
Nun'ning, (*v.*) to be tired of life.
Nu-pa, (*s.*) husband and wife.
Nu-pui, (*s.*) a wife.
Nu-pui nei, (*v.*) to marry a wife.
Nu-ṭa, (*s.*) a female's brother.
Nu tak ben'in beng, (*v.*) to slap with the hand hollow.
Nu-tar, (*s.*) the name of the Poi's religious rites.
Nu-thloi, (*s.*) a young woman either divorced or widowed.
Nu tlin*g*, (*s.*) a full-grown female, (*a.*) full grown, (*v.*) to be of age, to arrive at the age of puberty.

O

O, (*a.*) extensive (spoken of several *jhúms*, etc., joined together).
Oi, (*v.*) to hush a child.
Oih, (*a.*) steep.
Oih, (*v.*) to believe, to allow, to obey, grant.
Oih-lo, (*v.*) to disbelieve, to disallow, to disobey.
Oih-mâk-mawh, (*a.*) convincing.
Oih-mâk-mawh-in, (*adv.*) convincingly.

Oih-om, (*a.*) credible.
Oih-pui, (*v.*) to assent to.
Oih-sak, (*v.*) to believe (one's word).
Oi-tlâk, (*a.*) credible.
Oih-tlia', (*v.*) a shortened form of *uai tliak.*
Oi-mu, (*v.*) to hush to sleep.
Ol, (*a.*) easy, (*v.*) to be easy.
Om, (*v.*) to be, to remain, to exist, to have, to stop, to rest, to do no work, to wait.
Om-eo, (*a.*) capricious, desultory, (*v.*) to be capricious or desultory.
Om-lai, (*s.*) the name of the personification of death who is supposed to be the author of death and sickness.
Om-na, (*s.*) abode, home, place.
Om-na-chin, whereabouts.
Om-na-tlâk, Om-na-tui, Om-na-zia, } (*a.*) habitable.
Om ni, (*s.*) a day of rest, a holiday.
Om-pui, (*v.*) to adopt, to keep, to receive or entertain as a guest.
Om-pui-tu, (*s.*) a keeper, a master, an owner.
Om-tual, (*s.*) a fire in the open air in or near a village.
Om-zia, (*s.*) meaning, shape.
Ong, (*s.*) the crop (of a bird).
Ong-puar, (*s.*) a goitre.
Ong-rop, (*a.*) unsubstantial, badly constructed, unreliable, (*v.*) to be unsubstantial, etc.
Op, (*v.*) to brood over, to sit (as a fowl), to govern, to rule.
Op, (*v.*) to collapse, to break down.
Op chhia, (*a.*) to be addled.
Op-tlei, (*v.*) to bring up (as a child), to rear.
Op-tu, (*s.*) a ruler, a governor.
Op-tui, (*v.*) to be addled.
Or, (*s.*) the throat (outside).
Or, (*v.*) to wear round the neck.
Or-fual, (*s.*) the dewlap.
Or-puar, (*s.*) a goitre.
Or-râng, (*s.*) the name of a large black squirrel.
Ot, (*v.*) to covet, to envy.

P

Pa, (*s.*) a father, a husband's father, a paternal uncle, a maternal aunt's husband, a male, a masculine affix.
Pa, (*s.*) a fungus, a mushroom.

Pa-âr-dang, (*s.*) the name of a species of edible fungus.
Pa-chang, (*s.*) the name of a species of edible fungus.
Pa-chhe, (*a.*) poor, badly off.
Pa-chhia, (*s.*) a toadstool, an unedible fungus.
Pa-chhia, (*a.*) poor, badly off, (*v.*) to be badly off.
Pa-chuao, (*s.*) the name of a Lushai clan.
Pa-dawp, (*s.*) an hermaphrodite, a neuter.
Pa-hnah-kâr, (*s.*) the name of an edible fungus.
Pa-hnih, (*a.*) two.
Pa-hron, (*s.*) a stepfather.
Pai, (*s.*) a sheath, a scabbard.
Pai, (*v.*) to stagger.
Pai, (*v.*) to conceive, to have in one's inside or below the skin, to digest, to keep to one's self, to keep in.
Paih, (*v.*) to throw away, to abandon.
Pai-hol, (*s.*) a cowrie.
Pai-kawng, (*s.*) the name of a basket.
Pai-per, (*s.*) the name of a basket.
Pai-sha, (*s.*) a pice.
Pai-sha de-re, } (*s.*) a pie (money).
Pai-sha khing-phel, }
Pai-tê, (*s.*) the name of a tribe to the east of Lushai.
Pai-tung, (*s.*) the name of a powder-horn.
Pâk, (*v.*) to wheedle, to make up to, to make much of.
Pa-kai, (*v.*) to go over to the side of another, to join another party after deserting one's own.
Pa-kai shan, (*v.*) to desert in order to join another.
Pa-khang-bun, (*s.*) the name of an edible fungus.
Pa-khat, (*a.*) one.
Pa-kua, (*a.*) nine.
Pal, (*s.*) a fence.
Pal, (*v.*) to knock against with the lower part of the leg or with foot, to trip against.
Pa-lai, (*s.*) an ambassador, an emissary, (*v.*) to go as an ambassador.
Pa-lai tir, (*v.*) to send as an emissary or ambassador.
Pa-lang, (*s.*) a bottle.
Palh, (*adv.*) unintentionally, accidentally.
Pal-hni-fêng, (*s.*) the lower part of a fence which is made double to keep pigs and other animals out of a garden, (*v.*) to make the above.
Pa-li, (*a.*) four.
Pa-luang, (*s.*) a species of edible fungus.
Pal-tung, (*s.*) a fence made of upright posts.
Pa-lu-rûl, (*s.*) the perpetuator of a man's name.

Pal-za, (*s.*) a rail, a railing.
Pâm-ṭûl, (*v.*) to leave unfinished or incomplete, to leave without finishing, to abandon a *jhûm* without completing the cultivation of it.
Pan, (*a.*) thin (as paper, etc.)
Pân, (*s.*) a sore, a wound, (*v.*) to break into a sore.
Pan, (*v.*) to make for, to steer for, to go towards.
Pân-bawm, (*s.*) a small cane-work shield made to protect a sore on the leg when going through the jungle.
Pâng, (*a.*) to balance (on the tip of finger, etc.).
Pâng, (*s.*) the cotton tree.
Pang, (*adv.*) without delay, soon.
Pang, (*s.*) the body, the side (of a mountain, etc.)
Pa-nga, (*a.*) five.
Pa-ngai, according to, the same.
Pa-ngai-in, according to, the same as.
Pa-ngang, (*s.*) a caterpillar.
Pa-ngang bawm, } (*s.*) a chrysalis.
Pa-ngang bu, }
Pa-ngang dum-de, (*s.*) a glowworm.
Pang-chang, (*a.*) peevish, pettish, (*v.*) to be peevish, etc.
Pang-kai, (*s.*) the lutqua or bhooby tree (*baccaurea sapida*).
Pâng-la, (*s.*) a kind of cotton yielded by the *pâng* tree.
Pang-pâr, (*s.*) a flower.
Pâng-parh, (*s.*) a fin.
Pang-ti, (*s.*) substance, form.
Pân-ruang, (*s.*) a species of betel.
Pa-pâr, (*s.*) a species of edible fungus.
Pa-puan-veng, (*s.*) a species of edible fungus.
Pa-pui, (*s.*) a receptacle for storing rice.
Pâr, (*s.*) a flower, a blossom, (*v.*) to bloom, to blossom.
Pâr-âr-shi, (*s.*) the name of a plant with white flowers and edible leaves.
Pâr-di, (*s.*) the name of an aromatic herb.
Pa-reng, (*s.*) a receptacle for storing rice.
Parh, (*v.*) to open (as a flower, etc.)
Pa-riat, (*a.*) eight.
Pâr-lâk, (*v.*) to harvest by cutting off the ears of grain and leaving the stalks standing.
Pa-rol, (*s.*) a man divorced from his wife, a widower, a middle aged or old bachelor, a man living away from his wife.
Pâr-ṭhi-hrui, (*s.*) a garland of flowers.
Pâr-tlân, (*s.*) the name of a tree.
Pa-ruk, (*a.*) six.

Pâr-va, (*s.*) a pigeon.
Pa-sai-beng, (*s.*) the name of an edible fungus.
Pa-sal, (*s.*) a husband.
Pa-sal nei, (*v.*) to marry a husband.
Pa-sal tak-a-za, (*s.*) the name of a tree the leaves of which when bruised are used to heal sores.
Pa-sal-ṭha, (*s.*) a man who is brave and manly, (*a.*) brave, manly.
Pa-sari, (*a.*) seven.
Pa-shi, (*s.*) the name of an edible fungus.
Pa-son-tlung, (*s.*) the name of an edible fungus.
Pât, (*s.*) moss.
Pa-tê, (*s.*) a receptacle for storing rice.
Pât-êk, (*s.*) a species of water plant.
Pa-thian, (*s.*) God, the Giver and Preserver of Life.
Pa-thian biak, (*v.*) to worship God.
Pa-thlang-lam, (*s.*) the side of a house opposite the fireplace.
Pa-thloi, (*s.*) a young married man or widower, a man of marriage-able age.
Pa-thum, (*a.*) three.
Pa-thûr, (*s.*) the name of an edible fungus.
Pa-til, (*s.*) a woman who dresses and behaves like a man.
Pa-tling, (*s.*) a full grown male, (*a.*) full grown, (*v.*) to arrive at the age of puberty, to be of age.
Pa-zawng-beng, (*s.*) a species of edible fungus.
Paw, (*v.*) to carry on the back (as child, etc.)
Pawh, (*adv.*) also, even.
Pawh, (*v.*) to come up to, to reach.
Pawh-chhiat, (*s.*) the last crop of weeds on a *jhûm*.
Pawh-in, (*conj.*) although, notwithstanding.
Pawl, (*s.*) straw.
Pawl, (*s.*) a group, a flock, a herd, a pair, a company, a species, a kind, (*v.*) to company with, (*a.*) blue, covered with bloom (as fruit).
Pawl-bul, (*s.*) stubble.
Pawl-delh-ruah, (*s.*) the rain which falls soon after the gathering in of harvest.
Pawl-kût, (*s.*) the name of a Lushai feast after harvest.
Pawl-mi, }
Pawl-pui, } (*s.*) a companion.
Pawl-te, }
Pawl-tlâk lai (or hun), (*s.*) the time between the harvest and the cold weather.
Pawl-tu, (*s.*) a companion.
Pawn, (*s.*) the outside, (*a.*) shallow.

Pawn-a, Pawn-lama, } (*adv.* and *prep.*) outside.
Pawng, (*adv.*) by force, without paying for. (Is placed before the verb.)
Pawng, (*a.*) higher in one place than another, swollen, uneven.
Pawng-êk-lîr, (*s.*) the name of a dung beetle.
Pawng-hrâm, (*v.*) to speak unadvisedly, to gabble, to chatter.
Pawn-ta, (*a.*) outer.
Pawn-ta ber, (*a.*) outermost.
Pawn-to, (*v.*) to be out of doors in the evening or at night.
Pe, (*v.*) see *pêk.*
Peh, (*v.*) to break or to be broken (as the hole in the lobe of ear, a hole in wood, etc.), to have a piece of the edge off or to be split at the edge (as paper, cloth, etc.), to be frayed, (*a.*) broken, frayed, etc.
Peh-buk, (*s.*) a tassel.
Pei, (*v.*) to pinch.
Pei, (*v.*) to offer for sale at a profit.
Peih, (*v.*) to be ready, to be able, to complete, to have inclination to, to have strength or ability to, to have time to.
Pei-pung, (*v.*) to sell at a profit.
Pek, (*adv.*) again.
Pê*k*, (*v.*) to give, to offer.
Pê*k*-kîr, (*v.*) to give back, to return.
Pêl, (*v.*) to pass, to pass by, through or out, to allow to pass.
Pelh, (*s.*) the name of a plant.
Pelh-soih, (*a.*) dislocated, crossed (as pen, etc.), (*v.*) to be dislocated, etc.
Pêm, (*v.*) to migrate, (*s.*) one who has migrated.
Pem, (*v.*) to be wounded so that blood flows or bones are broken, (*s.*) a fresh wound.
Pên, (*v.*) to step, to stride, to pace, (*s.*) a step, a stride, a pace.
Pen, (*v.*) to fillip.
Pê*ng*, (*v.*) to turn (to the right or left when walking, etc.), to branch, to branch off, (*a.*) branching off, branch.
Peng-leng, (*s.*) the name of a bird resembling a swallow.
Pên'na, (*s.*) the place where roads, etc., meet, a branch road, an offshoot.
Pêr, (*a.*) flat and thin, (*adv.*) flat.
Per, (*v.*) to stamp, to hop, to spring.
Perh, (*v.*) to shoot with the pellet bow, to spring up or fly back (as a springy stick, etc.)
Perh-khet, (*s.*) a spring gun.

Perh-pawng, (*s.*) the name of a cricket.
Perh-pawng-chaw, (*s.*) the name of a plant.
Pêr-shen, (*s.*) the name of a weed.
Pet, (*v.*) see *hnim pet*.
Pe-tek, (*v.*) to stumble.
Phah, (*v.*) to spread (as cloth, etc.)
Phah, object of or for, cause of, meaning of, reason of or for, means of.
Phai, (*a.*) low-lying, low, (*v.*) to be or get low.
Phai, (*s.*) the name of a reed.
Phai-khaw hlûm, } (*s.*) a low range of hills.
Phai-khaw tlâng, }
Phai-phâk, (*s.*) the name of a plant.
Phai-pheng, (*s.*) the name of a reed.
Phai-phu-lêng, (*s.*) a concertina, an accordion.
Phai-sa-pui, (*s.*) a large tiger.
Phai-tual, (*s.*) the plains.
Phâ*k*, (*v.*) to overtake, to reach, to be able to reach.
Phak, (*a.*) rough (to the taste).
Phak-rak, (*s.*) split bamboos spread out under the floor matting or under the roof to keep it level.
Phal, (*s.*) a sheaf (of rice, etc.)
Phal, (*v.*) to permit, to allow, to grant.
Phân, (*s.*) the name of a durable tree.
Phan, (*v.*) to knit, to crochet.
Phâr, (*s.*) leprosy, (*v.*) to have leprosy.
Phar, (*v.*) to spread out or hold out (the arms or hands on either side), to straighten (the arm), to lift or hold up (the arm).
Phar, (*s.*) the name of a species of bamboo.
Pharh, (*v.*) to open (the hand, flower, etc.), to spread out or open out (as cloth, etc.)
Pha*t*, (*v.*) to confess and ask pardon, to apologise, to deny.
Phaw, (*s.*) a shield.
Phaw-hlaw, (*v.*) to cut off the outside of a tree, etc.
Phawk, (*v.*) to startle a bird or animal.
Phei, an emphatic particle.
Phei, (*s.*) a foot, a leg.
Phei, (*a.*) level, flat, (*v.*) to go along level ground, to go straight on without going up or down, (*adv.*) horizontally, evenly, neither up nor down.
Phei-chuan, } supposing if.
Phei-in, }
Phei khai, (*v.*) to lift the foot.
Phei-khong, (*s.*) the part immediately above the heel.

Phei-kok, (*s.*) a boot, a shoe, a clog.
Phek, (*a.*) strong looking, robust, well made, entangled, (*v.*) to be strong looking, etc.
Phêk, (*a.*) flat and thin, (*s.*) a page, a slice, a slab, (*v.*) to be flat and thin.
Phek-phe, (*s.*) the name of a tree.
Phek-phe-lên, (*v.*) to hold a child by the thighs and jump it up and down.
Phel, (*v.*) to split, to cut in halves.
Phelh, (*v.*) to undo, to loosen, to take off (as a coat), to unfasten.
Phelh-dul, (*v.*) to shut (as an umbrella), to loosen.
Phel-shêp, (*v.*) to split (a bamboo, etc., into four or more pieces), (*s.*) bamboos, etc., so split.
Phên, (*v.*) to get behind, to take shelter behind.
Phên-a, (*prep.*) in shelter of, under the lee of, behind.
Pheng, (*a.*) tough, robust, entangled, (*v.*) to be tough, etc.
Phêng, (*a.*) flat.
Phêng-long, (*s.*) a flute.
Phêng-phe-hlep, (*s.*) a butterfly, a moth.
Phe-phe, (*v.*) to work, to strive, to move.
Pher, (*s.*) the name of a mat.
Pherh, (*v.*) to spread (as a sore, etc.)
Pher-phek, (*s.*) the name of a bamboo mat.
Phe*t*, (*v. t.*) to trip up, to pull away a support from underneath, (*v.*) to have the legs slip away from underneath.
Phiar, (*v.*) to plot, to conspire, to plan.
Phiar, (*v.*) to knit, to plait, to crochet, to be crossgrained (as wood), to be knotted or prominent (as sinews), to be entangled, (*a.*) knitted, etc.
Phiar-thlu, }
Phiar-tlu, } (*v.*) to complete a plan, plot or conspiracy.
Phih, (*v.*) to jerk.
Phih, (*v.*) to wash (the face).
Phih-bal, (*v.*) to pull off or out with a jerk (as twig or tooth).
Phil, (*v.*) to steal and kill an animal, fowls, etc., for eating or sacrifice, to murder secretly, to assassinate.
Phil-hmang, (*s.*) one who steals and kills an animal, fowl, etc., for eating or sacrifice, an assassin, a secret murderer.
Phing-phi-hlîp, (*s.*) a winged white ant.
Phîr, (*a.*) forked, double (as gun, egg, nut, etc.), (*v.*) to be forked, etc.
Pho, (*v.*) to dry or air in the sunshine.
Phoi, (*v.*) to pull out, to extract, to unsheath.

Phok, (*v.*) to lift up on end, to raise, to turn over (as page of book etc.), to come off or take off (as hat or cover).
Phok, (*a.*) fond of joking, full of fun, fond of playing pranks, lively, (*v.*) to be fond of joking, etc., to play pranks, etc.
Phok, (*a.*) coarse, thick, (*v.*) to be coarse, etc., (*adv.*) coarsely, etc.
Pho-lêng, (*s.*) a landmark.
Pho-lêng târ, (*v.*) to make or set up a landmark.
Pho-lôh, (*s.*) the name of a species of rice.
Phong, (*v.*) to take off (as a cover, hat, etc.), to come or fall off.
Phorh, (*v.*) to take out, to exhume.
Phot, (*adv.*) certainly (only used in affirmative sentences).
Phu, (*a.*) suitable, (*v.*) to suit.
Phu, (*v.*) to beat (as heart, etc.)
Phuah, (*v.*) to compose, to make up.
Phuah-khawm, (*v.*) to put together evenly (as sticks, paper, etc.), to pleat.
Phuai, (*s.*) shavings.
Phuai-zia'-na, (*s.*) a knife for scraping.
Phuan, (*s.*) froth, lather, scum, foam, (*v.*) to froth, etc.
Phuan-ber, } (*s.*) the name of a tree.
Phuan-ber-pui, }
Phuan-puar, (*s.*) a bubble.
Phuar, (*v.*) to bind.
Phu-ba lâ*k*, } (*v.*) to avenge.
Phu-ba lam, }
Phu-hlip, (*s.*) scales (of fish, sores, etc.)
Phu-hru*k*, (*v.*) to insert, to fill in, to tamp.
Phui, (*a.*) closely woven, free from holes, airtight, (*v.*) to be closely woven, etc., (*adv.*) firmly, thoroughly, closely, etc.
Phui-hnam, (*s.*) the name of a plant with edible leaves.
Phui-hnam-chhia. (*s.*) the name of a plant with an offensive smell.
Phuk-phu-hlûm, (*s.*) the name of a puffball.
Phul, (*v.*) to sprinkle.
Phûl, (*v.*) to froth, to bubble up, to effervesce.
Phûl, (*s.*) an open tract of country generally covered with grass and with few or no trees.
Phu lâ*k*, } (*v.*) to avenge.
Phu lam, }
Phu lo, (*a.*) unsuitable, (*v.*) to be unsuitable.
Phûm, (*v.*) to bury.
Phun, (*v.*) to plant, to set up by burying one end in the ground.
Phun, (*v.*) to mutter, to murmur, to talk to one's self, to grumble, to find fault with.
Phun-chiar, (*v.*) to grumble, to find fault with.

Phun chong, (*s.*) the name of a tree yielding a kind of cotton.
Phung, (*s.*) a ghost.
Phung-chăng, (*s.*) a fellow clansman, a friend, (*a.*) friendly.
Phŭng-lem, (*s.*) the name of a game, blindman's buff.
Phŭng-sa-hmîm, (*s.*) the name of a bad-smelling fungus.
Phŭng zawl, (*v.*) to have a fit, (*s.*) a person subject to fits.
Phun-noi, (*v.*) to murmur.
Phun-ru, (*v.*) to whisper, to mutter, to murmur, to talk to one's self.
Phur, (*v.*) to carry on the back (as load), (*s.*) a load.
Phurh, } (*s.*) small-pox.
Phurh-hri, }
Phur-thak, (*s.*) the name of an itching sore on the feet.
Phut, (*adv.*) suddenly.
Phut, (*a.*) scurfy, floury, powdery, (*s.*) powder, dust.
Phŭt, (*v.*) to move (as the ears and nostrils).
Phŭt, (*v.*) to demand, to ask for, to hint at.
Phu-tăp, (*v.*) to go unavenged.
Phu-tĭr-zok, (*v.*) to startle, to surprise, to make to jump with surprise.
Phu*t*-zok, (*v.*) to be surprised or startled, to jump with surprise.
Pi, (*s.*) a grandmother, a greatgrandmother, a wife's female relation, a maternal uncle's wife or daughter, a term of respect for women.
Piah, (*prep.*) beyond.
Piah-a, } (*prep.*) beyond.
Piah-lama, }
Pial-lung, (*s.*) the barrel (of a gun).
Pial-răl, (*a.*) the Lushai paradise.
Pian*g*, (*v.*) to be born.
Piang-hlawh chham, (*v.*) to be afflicted from birth.
Pian*g*-sual, (*v.*) to have any great infirmity, to be deformed, to be maimed.
Pian-lung, (*s.*) the barrel (of a gun).
Pian-pui, (*s.*) an own brother or sister.
Pi-buh-dêng, (*s.*) the name of a long-legged spider.
Pi-khoi-zu, (*s.*) the name of a kind of bee.
Pil, (*s.*) bark (of tree, etc.)
Pil, (*s.*) depth, (*v.*) to sink.
Pilh, (*v.*) to chop or pull off small pieces of bark, skin, etc.
Pin-dan, (*s.*) a partition, a room.
Pin-dan-chhŭng, (*s.*) a room.
Pin*g*, (*a.*) closed up, (*v.*) to close up, to be closed up.
Ping-pih, (*s.*) a species of wild Job's tears.
Pip, (*s.*) the name of a basket.
Pi-pu, (*s.*) a swing.

Pir, (*v.*) to butt, to push (as a bull), to hit and scrape past (as a bamboo, etc., suddenly released).
Pir, (*v.*) to take a small quantity of anything with the finger or knife.
Pi-ring, (*s.*) a land snail.
Pît, (*s.*) the name of a small bird.
Pi-tar, (*s.*) an old woman, (*v.*) to become an old woman.
Pi-zon, (*s.*) a wife's mother, a wife's sister.
Pôh, (*adv.*) also, even (the same as *pawh* throughout).
Pôh-in, (*conj.*) although, when, notwithstanding.
Poi, (*v.*) to be of consequence, to matter, to be a pity, to be a misfortune.
Poi, (*s.*) the Chins and other tribes who wear their hair in a knot upon the top of the head.
Poi khoih, (*v.*) to do harm, to do mischief, to harm.
Poi-mawh, (*a.*) important, necessary, (*v.*) to be important, etc.
Poi-sha, (*s.*) a pice, see *pai-sha*.
Poi-sha, (*v.*) to respect, to regard.
Poi shoi, (*v.*) to make mischief, to speak to another's hurt.
Poi ti, (*v.*) to care, to regard.
Pok, (*v.*) to pop.
Pok, (*a.*) improvident, (*v.*) to be improvident.
Polh, (*v.*) to mix.
Pom, (*v.*) to embrace, to take hold of, to accept, to obey, to give heed to, to take.
Pon-to, (*v.*) to be out of doors in the evening or at night.
Pop, (*s.*) a hole, an aperture, (*v.*) to have a hole in.
Por, (*a.*) untidy, frayed, fluffy, rough, (*v.*) to be untidy, etc.
Por-nei, (*a.*) fluffy.
Pot, (*v.*) to pull, to pull up.
Pot-chhe, }
Pot-chhia, } (*v.*) to pull up the last crop of weeds on a *jhûm*.
Pu, (*s.*) a grandfather, great grandfather, a wife's male relation, a maternal uncle's son, a maternal uncle, one in charge of any one or anything, a term of respect for a man.
Pu, (*v.*) to have upon one's person (as dirt, sores, whiskers, etc.)
Pu, (*v.*) to carry on the shoulder, or in the mouth (as dog).
Pua, (*v.*) to make (as a blanket).
Puak, (*v.*) to carry on the back (as child, etc.)
Puak, (*v.*) to explode, to burst, (*s.*) explosion.
Puak-per-phur, }
Puak-phur, } (*s.*) a load, a carrier, a coolie, a porter.
Puak-phur-mi, (*s.*) a carrier, a porter, a coolie.
Puak-tam silai, (*s.*) a revolver, a repeating rifle.

Pual-eng, (*s.*) the name of a tree.
Puam, (*a.*) swollen, (*v.*) to swell, to be swollen.
Puan, (*s.*) a cloth, cloth.
Puan-bu, (*s.*) a weaving machine with partly woven cloth.
Puan-fên, (*s.*) a short petticoat or kilt worn by Lushai women.
Puan*g*, (*v.*) to tell of, to make known, to expose, to reveal, to spread (as sore, news, etc.)
Puan*g*-tîr, (*v.*) to spread abroad.
Puan-hrui, (*s.*) the name of a cloth.
Puan-kâng ṭhui, (*v.*) to buttonhole, (*s.*) buttonholing (a kind of sewing).
Puan-kop, (*s.*) the name of a cloth.
Puan-lai-choih, Puan-lai-shen, Puan-lai-ṭial, } (*s.*) the names of white cloths with stripes.
Puan-mawl, (*s.*) the name of a plain white cloth.
Puan-phei, (*s.*) the woof.
Puan-pui zûng ṭhui, (*v.*) to feather stitch, (*s.*) feather-stitching.
Puan-rîn, (*s.*) the name of a young woman's cloth.
Puan-tung, (*s.*) the warp.
Puan-vual, (*s.*) the name of a cloth.
Puar, (*v.*) to have had sufficient food, to be full.
Puar-peng, Puar-per, } (*s.*) the name of a creeper with edible fruit.
Puh, (*v.*) to blame, to accuse.
Puh-khêl, (*v.*) to accuse or blame falsely.
Pui, (*v.*) to help, to assist, (affix.) means of, cause of.
Pui, (*a.*) large, big, full grown (generally used of female animals, birds, etc., after having had young), (*v.*) to be large, to be full grown.
Pui noi, (*s.*) great and small (people).
Pui-thiam, (*s.*) an exorcist, a priest.
Pui-thu, (*v.*) to be religious, conscientious, superstitious, conservative or zealous for one's own customs, to observe or keep religiously, (*a.*) religious, conscientious, etc.
Pui-tlin', (*v.*) to accomplish, to carry out, to be successful.
Pui-tlin*g*, (*v.*) to reach maturity.
Pûk, (*v.*) to borrow (when the equivalent but not the thing itself is to be returned).
Pûk, (*s.*) a cave.
Pûk-bâk, (*s.*) the cave bat.
Pûk-tîr, (*v.*) to lend.
Pu-kul-a thang, (*s.*) the constellation Grus.
Pûl, (*v.*) to die of plague or pestilence.
Pûm, (*s.*) a raft.

Pûm, (*s.*) a smithy.
Pum, (*s.*) the abdomen, the belly.
Pum, (*a.*) whole, all.
Pum-hlûm, (*a.*) whole.
Pûm-hnâr, (*s.*) the tubes which run under ground from the bellows to the forge in a smithy.
Pûm-hrûl, (*s.*) the cylinders of a blacksmith's bellows.
Pûm-hrût, (*s.*) the name of a ferry, consisting of a raft and a rope spanning the river.
Pum-in, (*a.*) whole.
Pum-pa, an emphatic particle.
Pum-pelh, (*s.*) a short cut, (*v.*) to avoid, to escape
Pûm-phîr, (*s.*) the name of a reed.
Pum-pui, (*s.*) the stomach.
Pûm-thei, (*s.*) the cylinders of a blacksmith's bellows.
Pûm-za'na, (*s.*) the pistons of a blacksmith's bellows.
Pun', (*v. t.*) to assemble, to call to assist.
Pung, (*v.*) to increase in numbers or quantity.
Pung, (*v.*) to assemble, (*s.*) an assembly.
Pung-ho-te, (*s.*) an assembly.
Pung-khawm, (*v.*) to assemble.
Pung-pu-lût, (*v.*) to carry cock-shoulder.
Pu-pawl-a, (*s.*) the one who is supposed to stand on the road to *Mithi-khua* and shoot at spirits as they pass by on their way thither.
Pûr, (*v.*) to ask continually for.
Pûr-chaw, (*v.*) to buy rice, to get food from another person or country.
Pu-rûn, (*s.*) an onion.
Pût, (*v.*) to leak, to run out, to slip through or off, to push a way through, to squeeze through.
Pu*t*, (*v.*) to carry on the shoulder or in the mouth.
Pu-tar, (*s.*) an old man, (*v.*) to become an old man.
Pût-thla, (*v.*) to fall through.
Pu-vân-a, (*s.*) the name of a god.
Pu-vân-a sai-hlum, (*s.*) a wood louse, a sowbug.
Pu-vân-a shial, (*s.*) the name of a beetle.
Puvâna thleng-pui hnu' rîk, (*s.*) thunder.
Pu-zon, (*s.*) a wife's father or brother.

R

Rah, (*s.*) fruit, (*v.*) to bear fruit.
Rah-bi, (*s.*) notches made in a tree or hill to assist in climbing.

Rah-ka, (*s.*) steps, stairs.
Rai, (*a.*) pregnant, (*v.*) to be or become pregnant.
Rai-cheh, (*v.*) to die in giving birth to an offspring.
Rai-chhok, (*s.*) the name of a species of cane.
Raih lo, (*adv.*) certainly not, surely not.
Rai-ruang, (*s.*) elephant grass.
Rai-sheh, (*s.*) the name of a species of ant.
Rai-ṭeoh, (*v.*) to be great with young.
Rai-thei, (*s.*) the name of a tree with edible fruit.
Rak-zu, (*v.*) spirits, distilled *zu.*
Râl, (*s.*) bank, side.
Râl, (*v.*) to be at war, to war against, (*s.*) fighting men.
Ral, (*v.*) to pass away, to cease to be or exist, to burn out (as fire), to disappear, (*adv.*) away.
Râl-a, (*adv.*) at a distance, from a distance, (*prep.*) on the opposite bank of, on the other side of (a river or valley).
Râl-buh, (*s.*) the name of a species of rice.
Râl cha-bêl, } (*s.*) the name of a large earthenware pot.
Râl chaw-bêl, }
Râl-hrât, (*s.*) a warrior, one who distinguishes himself in battle.
Râl-khêl, (*v.*) to be falsely alarmed of a raid or an attack, (*s.*) a false alarm of a raid or attack.
Râl-khêl shiam, (*v.*) to raise a false alarm (of a raid, etc.)
Râl lem-a chang, (*v.*) to have a sham fight.
Râl-lem-chang, (*s.*) a sham fight.
Râl-tê, (*s.*) the name of a tribe of Lushais.
Râl-thawn', (*s.*) to attack suddenly.
Râl-vên'-bing, (*s.*) a blockhouse.
Râl-vêng, (*s.*) a sentry, a scout, (*v.*) to be a sentry, to scout.
Râl-vêng-bûk, (*s.*) a blockhouse.
Ram, (*s.*) forest, country.
Ram, (*a.*) brittle, (*v.*) to be brittle.
Ram, (*a.*) empty, deserted, uninhabited, (*v.*) to be empty, deserted, etc., to plunder, to ravage.
Ram, (*v.*) to tie together by a series of loops.
Ram-âr, (*s.*) a jungle fowl.
Ram-chhuak, (*v.*) to hunt, to go hunting.
Ram-chom, (*s.*) the name of a species of edible arum.
Ram-hnuai, (*s.*) forest.
Ram-huai, (*s.*) an evil spirit.
Ram hual, (*s.*) the principal men of a village.
Ram-kêl-chal, (*s.*) the name of a white insect, a larva of one of the *cicadidæ.*
Ram-pâr-va, (*s.*) a wood pigeon.

Ram-shial, (*s.*) a wild *gayal.*
Ram-ṭang, (*s.*) those of a household able to work, *jhûm*, etc.
Ram-thîng, (*s.*) a species of wild ginger.
Ram-tin-a, (*adv.*) everywhere, in different places, in several places.
Ram-zuan, (*v.*) to prepare a *jhûm* near to where a new village will be built the following season.
Ran, (*s.*) domesticated animals, poultry, etc.
Rang, (*a.*) quick, (*v.*) to be quick, (*adv.*) quickly.
Râng, (*a.*) slightly spotted, having a few patches of white, piebald, mottled, (*v.*) to be slightly spotted, etc.
Rang-ka-chak, (*s.*) gold, (*a.*) golden.
Rang-kha, (*s.*) the name of a woman's brass girdle.
Rang-va, (*s.*) a tin, tin, (*a.*) tin.
Ran-in biak, } (*v.*) to sacrifice to.
Ran-in luh, }
Ran-nung, (*s.*) an animal, an insect, living creatures.
Rao, (*s.*) a swarm (of bees), (*v.*) to swarm (as bees).
Rap, (*s.*) the shelf over the fire in a Lushai house.
Ra*p*, (*v.*) to tread upon, to tread.
Râp, (*v.*) to frighten, to scare, to terrify.
Ra*p*-be*t*, (*v.*) to trample under foot, to oppress, to lord over.
Rap-hâk, (*s.*) a bamboo mat used to dry rice, etc., upon.
Ra*p*-ri, (*s.*) a footfall.
Râp-thlâk, (*a.*) terrifying, fearful, (*v.*) to be terrifying, etc.
Raw-chhem, (*s.*) the name of a Lushai musical instrument.
Rawh, (*v.*) to heat, to roast, to bake.
Rawh-puak, (*v.*) to blast, as rocks.
Raw-kuai, (*s.*) a long bamboo set up in a village with the skin of a wild cat or other animal suspended from it.
Raw-lak, } (*s.*) names of species of bamboo.
Raw-mi, }
Rawn, (*v.*) to massacre, to ask advice, to consult, to ascertain a person's wishes, to make enquiries, to ask.
Raw-nâl, (*s.*) a species of bamboo.
Rawng, (*a.*) vicious, cruel, destructive, (*v.*) to be vicious, etc.
Rawp, (*v.*) to feel a desire for animal food after illness.
Rawp, (*v.*) to waste away (as in illness), to wither, to dry up.
Raw-pui, (*s.*) a species of bamboo.
Rawt, (*v.*) to cut off (as edge of thatch, bamboo stump, etc.), to massacre.
Raw-tê, }
Raw-ṭhing, } (*s.*) the names of various kinds of bamboos.
Raw-thla, }

Raw-tuai, (*s.*) the edible shoots of bamboo.
Reh, (*v.*) to stop, to abate, to fade.
Reh, (*a.*) oppressively silent, (*v.*) to be oppressively silent.
Rei, (*s.*) delay, long time, (*v.*) to delay, to be a long time, (*adv.*) slowly, for a long time.
Rei-lo-tean, after a short time.
Rei-ngial, (*adv.*) some time, some little time.
Rei-om-lo-vin, } without delay.
Rei-rial-lo-vin, }
Rei-ta-ngial, some time ago.
Re*k*, (*a.*) notched, more slender at one place than at another, (*v.*) to be notched, etc., to notch.
Rêk, (*v.*) to seize by the throat, to squeeze in.
Rê*k*-hlum, (*v.*) to throttle.
Re*k*-po*p*, (*v.*) to break through, to make a hole through.
Rel, (*v.*) to begin to build a house, to put up the framework of a house, (*a.*) unfinished (as house), (*s.*) the lowest beam under the floor of a Lushai house, framework.
Rêl, (*v.*) to backbite.
Rêl, (*v.*) to pay a debt, to pay for anything, to return the equivalent of a thing lent, to repay.
Rêl, (*v.*) to purpose, to plan.
Relh, } (*v.*) to escape, to run or go away secretly.
Relh-ru, }
Rêm, to stop flaring.
Rem, (*v.*) to be at peace.
Rem, (*a.*) convenient, proper, (*v.*) to be convenient, etc.
Rem-chång, (*s.*) opportunity, (*a.*) opportune, convenient, (*v.*) to be opportune, etc.
Rem-chång tîr, (*v.*) to permit, to consent, to make convenient.
Rem-hre-tak-in, (*adv.*) prudently, wisely.
Rem hria*t*, (*v.*) to be prudent, wise.
Rem ruat, (*v*) to advise, to plan, to devise.
Rem-ruat-pui, (*v.*) to advise.
Rem ti, (*v.*) to agree with or to, to consent, to permit,
Rem-tîr, (*v.*) to permit, to consent, to make convenient.
Ren, (*v.*) to economise, to take out,
Ren a chham, (*v.*) to be out of anything.
Rêng, (*adv.*) already, also an affix denoting previous action.
Reng, an affix denoting continuity.
Rêng-an, (*s.*) the name of a plant with edible leaves.
Rêng-chal, (*s.*) the name of a large chirping insect.
Reng-fei, (*s.*) the name of a tree.
Rêng-pui, (*s.*) the Raja of Hill Tipperah.

Reng-pui, }
Reng-tê, } (*s.*) the names of baskets for storing rice.
Rêp, (*v.*) to dry over the fire, to be sore or cracked (as the lips), (*a.*) dried over the fire, etc.
Re-raw, (*s.*) the name of a blackish dye and the tree from the bark and fruit of which it is made.
Re-thei, (*a.*) poor, unfortunate, miserable, tired, (*v.*) to be poor, etc.
Ri, (*s.*) a boundary, see also ***rîk.***
Ria, (*a.*) slender, slight (as a man).
Ria' bûk, (*s.*) a temporary hut in the jungle to spend the night in.
Riai lo, (*adv.*) surely not, certainly not.
Ria*k*, (*v.*) to put up for the night.
Rial, (*s.*) hail, glass, china, earthenware.
Rial, (*v.*) to give up coming or going for a time, to not come or go for a time.
Rial-hlen, (*v.*) to give up coming or going altogether.
Rial-no, (*s.*) a glass, a tumbler, an earthenware or china cup or mug.
Riang vai, (*s.*) a poor person, (*a.*) poor.
Riat, (*a.*) eight.
Rih, (*adv.*) for a little while, for the present, at present.
Rih, (*s.*) the name of a lake to the east of Lushai said to be passed by spirits on their way to *Mithikhua.*
Rih-mîm, (*s.*) a species of Indian fig tree.
Rî*k*, (*s.*) sound, (*v.*) to sound.
Ril, (*s.*) the bowels, entrails.
Ril (*s.*) the heart (of a tree, etc.) (*a.*) deep, profound (as a saying), difficult, weighty, important, (*v.*) to be deep, etc.
Ril-a-ṭâm, (*v.*) to be hungry.
Ril-ru, (*s.*) the mind, the thoughts.
Ril-ru a shei, (*v.*) to have thought for the future.
Ril-ru a toi, (*v.*) to have no thought for the future.
Ril-ru hmun-khat-in, with one mind.
Ril-rû*k*, (*v.*) to think of, to conceive (an idea), to purpose, to intend, to think, to ponder, to remember.
Ril-ru lam-let, (*v.*) to change the mind.
Ril-ru nei, (*v.*) to make up the mind, to decide.
Ril-ru ngai pu, (*v.*) to be in one's right mind, to be in one's former state of mind, to be of the same mind.
Ril-ru shon, (*v.*) to change the mind.
Ril-ṭâm, (*s.*) hunger.
Rim, (*a.*) tired, toilworn, exposed or subjected to friction or wear and tear, (*v.*) to be tired, etc., (*adv.*) hard, toilsomely.
Rim, (*s.*) smell, odour.
Rîm, (*v.*) to visit (a young woman), to court, to go courting.

Ri-mên-hoih, (*s.*) the name of a creeper with crimson flowers.
Rim hria*t*, (*v.*) to smell.
Rim-tong, (*v.*) to be overworked, to be thoroughly worn out with work.
Rîn, (*s.*) a line, a scratch, (*v.*) to draw a line, to scratch.
Rin, (*s.*) faith, belief.
Rin' chhan, (*v.*) to lean against.
Ring, (*s.*) the neck.
Rin*g*, (*v.*) to believe, to trust, to think, to suppose, to depend on, rely upon, to make or get ready, to make shift with, to lean against.
Ring, (*a.*) loud, (*adv.*) loudly.
Rin*g*-hlel, (*v.*) to doubt.
Ring-thar, (*s.*) a *jhúm* of the present year.
Rin'om, (*a.*) reliable, trustworthy, honest.
Rin'shoi, (*v.*) to guess, to express an opinion.
Rin'tlâk, (*a.*) reliable, trustworthy.
Rip, (*s.*) a cage or enclosure in which mad people, etc., are kept, a cage, a prison cell.
Ri ri, the Lushai call for pigs.
Rî*t*, (*v.*) to scrape with a hoe.
Rî*t*, (*v.*) to cultivate a *jhúm* two or more years in succession.
Rit, (*a.*) heavy, difficult, hard, profound, (*v.*) to be heavy, etc.
Ro, (*a.*) dry, dead, (*v.*) to be dry, etc., to lack.
Ro, (*s.*) treasure, property, (*v.*) to prize, to set store by, to treasure.
Ro chung, (*v.*) to take possession of.
Roi, a contracted form of *hruai*.
Roih, (*s.*) an employé.
Rok, (*adv.*) without permission.
Rok, (*v.*) to take away one's goods, to plunder, to loot.
Ro khawm, (*v.*) to inherit property.
Ro-khawm-tu, (*s.*) an heir.
Rol, (*a.*) stiff after work, (*v.*) to be stiff.
Rolh, (*v.*) to push in, to probe.
Rol-thar, (*s.*) a young man, (*a.*) young, (*v.*) to be young.
Ro luah, (*v.*) to inherit property.
Ro-luah-tu, (*s.*) an heir.
Rolura thlah-te mîm kût thla, (*s.*) the time of year corresponding nearly to August.
Ro-mei, (*s.*) haze.
Ron, (*v.*) to fire a volley, (*adv.*) together, one after another.
Ron, a verbal prefix signifying motion towards the speaker.
Rong, (*s.*) the mouth of a bottle, jar, etc.
Rong bawl, (*v.*) to minister, to serve, to attend upon.

Rong bawl tu, (*s.*) a minister, a servant, an attendant.
Ron-hawn, (*v.*) to bring.
Ron-hnai, (*v.*) to draw near.
Ron-shin, (*v.*) to bring.
Ron-thlen', (*v.*) to bring.
Rop, (*a.*) rotten and brittle, rotten (as cloth), (*v.*) to rot.
Ro-pui, (*a.*) mighty, marvellous, commanding, grand, magnificent, stupendous, great.
Ro pui-na, (*s.*) glory, anything which tends to one's greatness.
Ro-rêl, (*v.*) to judge, to arbitrate, to take counsel, to talk over a matter, to make arrangements, to govern, to manage.
Ro-rêl tu, (*s.*) a judge, an arbitrator, a manager.
Ro-rum, (*a.*) reckless, daring, (*v.*) to be reckless, etc., (*adv.*) recklessly, daringly.
Rot, (*v.*) to suggest, to suppose.
Rot-pui, (*v.*) to advise, (*s.*) an adviser.
Ru, (*s.*) the name of a creeper, the roots and leaves of which are used to poison fish, various roots, leaves, etc., used for poisoning fish, (*a.*) pungent, strong (as spirits, tobacco, etc.)
Rua, (*s.*) a bamboo.
Rua, (*a.*) unmanufactured, (*s.*) material for making anything.
Ruah, (*s.*) rain.
Ruah a shûr, (*v.*) to rain.
Ruah bing, (*s.*) a local shower.
Ruah kung, (*s.*) rain beginning in the distance and gradually advancing.
Ruah mal, (*s.*) a rain-drop.
Rua hman, (*v.*) to mark out, to plan.
Ruah mual-liam, (*s.*) a short sharp shower.
Ruah phing-phi-shiao, (*s.*) a drizzling rain, (*v.*) to drizzle.
Ruah-tui, (*s.*) rain water.
Ruah vâr-pui, (*s.*) a shower with large drops far apart.
Ruai, (*v.*) to employ.
Ruai, (*adv.*) almost, on the point of.
Ruai dong, (*v.*) to partake of a feast, to be a guest at a feast.
Ruai ṭheh, (*v.*) to make a feast.
Ruai-tu, (*s.*) an employer.
Ruai ṭuan, (*v.*) to prepare a feast.
Ruak, (*a.*) empty, hollow, naked, (*v.*) to be empty, hollow, naked.
Ruak, (*adv.*) lengthily, in streaks.
Ruak-lo, (*a.*) pregnant, (*v.*) to be pregnant.
Rual, (*a.*) worthy, possible, fit.
Rual, (*s.*) a herd, a flock.
Rual, (*a.*) even, level, (*adv.*) evenly, etc., together.

Rual ani lo, (*v.*) to be impossible.
Rual-rem, (*a.*) even, level.
Ruang, (*s.*) a dead body, a corpse.
Ruang-chai-che'thlâk, (*v.*) to get an enemy between two companies of an army.
Ruat, (*v.*) to set apart, to choose, to appoint, to fix upon, to ordain, to select, to believe, to consider, to think, to be of opinion.
Ruh, (*a.*) caked together, firm (as muscle), hard, (*v.*) to be caked together, etc.
Ruh, (*s.*) a bone, the framework of a house.
Ruh-sheh, (*s.*) rheumatism.
Ruh-sheh vei, (*v.*) to have rheumatism.
Ruh-tak-in tum, (*v.*) to be determined.
Ruh-tuah, (*s.*) a joint (of bones.)
Rui, (*v.*) to be drunk, to be intoxicated, (*a.*) drunk, intoxicated.
Rui-tîr, (*v.*) to intoxicate.
Ruk, (*a.*) six.
Rûk, (*v.*) to steal, (*adv.*) secretly, slyly, on the sly, stealthily.
Ruk-rak, (*s.*) the name of a plaid cloth.
Rûk-ru, (*s.*) a thief.
Rûl, (*s.*) a snake.
Rûl, (*v.*) to compensate, to recompense, to give in place of or instead of, to pay a debt, (*s.*) a compensation, a recompense.
Rul, (*a.*) springless, (*v.*) to be without or to lose springiness.
Rûl-hût, (*s.*) a tapeworm, worms, disease.
Rûl-hût pai, (*v.*) to have worms.
Rûl muk, (*s.*) the name of a poisonous snake.
Rûl ngân, (*s.*) the name of a poisonous snake.
Rûl ngawng shen, (*s.*) the name of a snake.
Rûl pui, (*s.*) the name of a large snake.
Rûl-pui lu din', (*v.*) to stand on the head.
Rûl-puk, (*s.*) the name of a plant with edible fruit, a species of *solanum*.
Rûl-ruah, (*s.*) the name of a creeper without leaves.
Rûl-ṭhi, (*s.*) the name of a plant.
Rûl-thûr, (*s.*) the name of a tree with edible fruit.
Rûl-tu-ha, (*s.*) the name of an ovoviviparous snake.
Rûl-vân-kai, (*s.*) a species of green snake.
Rûm, (*v.*) to groan, to growl, to purr, to hum.
Rum, (*a.*) suddenly.
Rûn, (*v.*) to raid, to attack, to exact a fine in lieu of work.
Run, (*v.*) to provoke, to offend, to aggravate, to exasperate, to grieve, to be provoked, offended, etc.
Rûn-hmui, (*s.*) the name of an aromatic plant.

Run-râl, (*v.*) the same as ***run.***
Run-thlâk, (*a.*) aggravating, grievous, provoking, exasperating, (*adv.*) aggravatingly, etc.
Ru-sakei, (*s.*) the name of a creeper used for poisoning fish.
Rût, (*v.*) to scoop up, to gather up.
Ru-thei, (*s.*) the name of a tree, the fruit of which is used for poisoning fish.

S

NOTE.—The initials *s* and *sh* are often interchangeable.

Sa, (*s.*) an animal.
Sa, (*s.*) religious rites and customs, religion.
Sa-beng-tung, (*s.*) an ass, a mule.
Sa bual, (*s.*) a hole where animals wallow.
Sa-bual hlo, (*s.*) the name of a plant.
Sa-fia, (*s.*) the name of an animal, probably the crab-eating mungoose.
Sa-hai, (*v.*) to bevel, to cut off at a slant, (*a.*) bevelled, etc., (*adv.*) slantingly.
Sa-hmai-ṭha, (*s.*) the name of a small animal (a species of mungoose).
Sa-hmîm, (*s.*) a netted haversack used with a skin cover.
Sa-hmîm khuh, (*s.*) the skin cover of a ***sahmîm.***
Sa-hmul, (*s.*) fur, hair of animals.
Sa-hmul phah thla, (*s.*) the time of year corresponding nearly with November.
Sa-hram, (*s.*) an otter.
Sa-hriak, (*s.*) oil, grease.
Sa-huai, (*s.*) the slow-paced lemur (*Nycticebus tardigradus*).
Sai, (*s.*) an elephant.
Sai, (*s.*) wormwood.
Sai-âr, (*s.*) a turkey.
Sai-doi-ûm, (*s.*) a bottle.
Sai-hlît, (*s.*) a water leech.
Sai-hlum, (*s.*) a clay pellet for the pellet bow.
Sai-hri, (*s.*) syphilis.
Sai-hum, (*s.*) an elephant trap.
Sai-hmâr-thûr, (*s.*) the name of a species of ant.
Sai-ip, (*s.*) a sack, a gunny bag.
Sai-khûp, (*s.*) the name of a bowl.
Sai-lung-vâr, (*s.*) the name of a white stone.
Sai-lu-târ, (*s.*) the name of a flowering tree.

Sai-man-thing, (*s.*) the name of a tree.
Sai-pân, (*s.*) a syphilitic sore.
Sai-phah, (*s.*) the name of a plate.
Sai-pir-hmer, (*s.*) a measurement, as much as can be encircled with the first finger and thumb.
Sai-pir-khâp, (*s.*) a span (with thumb and first finger), (*v.*) to span.
Sai-pir-kil, (*s.*) a measurement, as much as can be encircled by the thumbs and the forefingers of both hands joined together.
Sai-raw-kherh, (*s.*) the pellet bow.
Sai-rîl, (*s.*) the name of a cane.
Sai-shiak, (*s.*) the name of a tree,
Sai-shîk, (*v.*) to whistle through the teeth.
Sai-shîr, (*v.*) to put or get on the side, (*adv.*) sideways, on the side.
Sai-thei, (*s.*) the name of a tree with a non-edible fruit.
Sai-ṭhi, (*s.*) the name of small round red bead.
Sak (affix), for, from.
Sa-kei, (*s.*) a tiger.
Sa-khi, (*s.*) a barking deer (*Cervulus vaginalis*).
Sa-khi-chal, (*s.*) a stag.
Sâ-khua, (*s.*) the spirit who presides over the house, religion, religious rites and customs.
Sa-kor, (*s.*) a horse.
Sa-kor bak-cheh, (*s.*) scissors.
Sa-kor beng tung, (*s.*) a mule, an ass.
Sa-kuh, (*s.*) a porcupine.
Sak-rong, } (*s.*) the body.
Sak-ruang, }
Sal, (*s.*) a captive taken in war.
Sal-tui-hleoh, (*v.*) to swim with the hands behind the back.
Sam, (*s.*) the hair of the head.
Sâm, (*v.*) to cut down (weeds, trees, etc.), to clear (jungle), to massacre.
Sa-mak, (*s.*) a rhinoceros.
Sa-mang, (*s.*) a small species of bear.
Sa-mat, (*s.*) the Kasalong river.
Sa-mat dawr, (*s.*) Kasalong bazar.
Sam-chhawl-leng, (*s.*) hair which is too short to be gathered into a knot.
Sam-hram pu, (*v.*) to be unclean or in mourning for the dead, to have one's hair unoiled, (*s.*) one so unclean.
Sam-khai, (*s.*) a head-dress of beetles' wings, seeds, beads, etc., worn by girls on festive occasions.
Sam-khuih, (*s.*) a comb, (*v.*) to comb the hair.
Sam-tho, (*s.*) bristling hair, (*v.*) to stand on end (as hair).

Sam-ṭok, (*s.*) a species of *solanum.*
Sam-zai, (*s.*) a hair.
Sam-zial, (*s.*) a knot of hair, (*v.*) to put the hair up into a knot.
Sa-na, (*s.*) a watch, a clock.
Sa-na lâm thei, (*s.*) a watch, a clock.
Sang, (*v.*) to strain (tenesmus), to puff out the stomach.
Sa-ngai, (*s.*) the name of a deer.
Sa-ngha, (*s.*) a fish.
Sa-ngha dan'na, (*s.*) a fishing weir.
Sa-nghal, (*s.*) a wild boar.
Sa-nghar, (*s.*) a wild cat (*Felis marmorata*).
Sa-nghar-kuai, } (*s.*) a wild-cat skin suspended from a long bamboo
Sa-nghar-ngul, } in a Lushai village.
Sa-nghawng, (*v.*) see *sahai.*
San-tên, (*s.*) dysentery, (*v.*) to have dysentery.
Saoh saoh, (*adv.*) quickly.
Sâp, (*s.*) a corruption of *Sahib.*
Sâp berh-bu, (*s.*) the name of a bowl with the rim turned outwards.
Sâp-bok-bawn, (*s.*) the tomato.
Sa-pêl, (*v.*) to hunt, to go hunting.
Sa-per, (*s.*) the name of a tree.
Sa-phai, (*s.*) the python.
Sa-phi, (*s.*) the name of an animal.
Sa-phi-hrik, (*s.*) a tick.
Sa-phît, (*s.*) the name of a small plant used for dyeing hair, etc., red.
Sa-phi-vok, (*s.*) the hog badger (*Arctonyx collaris*).
Sa-phu, (*s.*) the pangolin or scaly ant-eater.
Sa-phun, (*v.*) to adopt the religious customs of another, (*s.*) a convert, a proselyte.
Sa-phût, (*s.*) the name of a tree.
Sa-pui, (*s.*) a tiger.
Sari, (*a.*) seven.
Sâr-in-thi, (*v.*) to die an unnatural death.
Sa-ri-tom, (*s.*) a crocodile.
Sa-ri-vai-thun, (*s.*) the name of an animal.
Sâr-thi, (*v.*) to die an unnatural death.
Sa-ruak, (*a.*) naked.
Sa-rual, (*s.*) a species of wild boar, a herd of animals.
Sa-sherh, (*s.*) the parts of a sacrificed animal set apart for the spirits.
Sa-shua, (*s.*) the name of an oak (*Quercus serrata.*)
Sa-tel, (*s.*) a tortoise.
Sa-thah-hneh, (*s.*) the name of a game something like draughts, (*v.*) to play the above game.

Sa-thang-dai, (*s.*) the name of a small palm, a fence made with small apertures in it for catching animals.
Sa-thâr, (*s.*) a wild goat.
Sa-thla, (*v.*) to refuse to believe, to disbelieve, to thrust from one.
Sati-kâng, (*s.*) Chittagong.
Sa-tliah, (*a.*) common, ordinary, (*adv.*) under any circumstances.
Sa-tlum, (*s.*) a large civet cat (*Viverra megaspela*).
Sa-va, (*s.*) a bird.
Sa-va-hmul, (*s.*) a feather.
Sa-vok len lon, (*a.*) thick set, short and strongly built (as man).
Sa-vom, (*s.*) a bear.
Sa-vom bu hreo, (*s.*) a bear's nest.
Sa-vun, (*s.*) hide, leather.
Sa-vung-a mîm kût thla, (*s.*) the time of year corresponding nearly to September.
Sa-za, (*s.*) a wild goat (*Nemorhœdus bubalina*).
Sa-zaw, (*s.*) the name of a species of civet cat (probably the small-toothed palm civet).
Sa-zu, (*s.*) a rat.
Sa-zuk, (*s.*) the sambar deer (*Rusa aristotelis*).
Sa-zuk-hnawng hlap, (*s.*) the name of a plant.
Sa-zuk thei, (*s.*) the name of a tree and fruit (*Randia dumetorum*).
Sa-zu-pui, (*s.*) a hare, a rabbit, a full-grown female rat.
Sa-zu thei-pui, (*s.*) a species of fig.
Saw, (*pro.* and *adj.*) that.
Sawh, (*v.*) to beat up (as eggs, etc.), to dump up and down, to mix up, to churn, to ram down or in.
Sawh-bawl, (*v.*) to stir up, to beat up.
Sawh-khâk, (*v.*) to ram (as with a ramrod).
Sawh-khal, (*v.*) to churn.
Sawh-khawk, (*v.*) to rebound, to bounce.
Sawh-mûk, (*v.*) to ram (as with a ramrod, etc.)
Sawh-thîng, (*s.*) ginger.
Saw lam-a, (*adv.*) there, in that direction.
Sawm, (*v.*) to ask, to invite.
Sawm-hmul-phah-thla, (*s.*) the time of year nearly corresponding to November.
Sawn, (*s.*) a bastard.
Sawng saw, (*a.*) that, those.
Sawr, (*v.*) to wring, to squeeze.
Saw saw, (*pro.* and *adj.*) that.
Sawt, (*v.*) to profit or benefit by, to increase (as money), to be profitable, (*a.*) profitable, beneficial, (*adv.*) quickly, to some purpose, not in vain.

Saw-ta,
Saw-ta-sawn, } (*adv.*) there.
Se-bawng, (*s.*) a cow, a bull.
Se-bawng no, (*s.*) a calf.
Se-bawng pa, (*s.*) a bullock.
Se-bawng pân, (*s.*) the name of a sore.
Se-bawng pui, (*s.*) a cow.
Se-bawng sha, (*s.*) beef.
Se-bawng til rek,
Se-bawng til ret, } (*s.*) an ox.
Se-bawng vêngtu, (*s.*) a cow-keeper.
Sêr, (*s.*) a lemon, a lime.
Sêr thlum, (*s.*) an orange.
Sêr-ṭok, (*s.*) a species of lemon.
Sha, (*s.*) flesh, meat.
Sha, (*a.*) hot, (*v.*) to be hot.
Sha, an affix signifying 'ready' and 'already', as ***shiam-sha***, ready-made.
Sha-buak, (*s.*) see ***sha-lum***.
Shah, (*v.*) to burst or break (as a dyke), to give way.
Sha-hâr, (*s.*) a chip.
Shak, (*a.*) hard (not soft), (*v.*) to be hard.
Sha-lum, (*s.*) an avalanche of stones used in war time.
Sham, (*a.*) easy.
Shan, (*v.*) to leave, also an affix used with an intransitive verb to make it transitive, similar to the English word 'at', ***min nui-shan***, 'he laughed at me.'
Shang, (*s.*) a thousand.
Shâng, (*a.*) dry, rainless.
Shâng, (*a.*) high, tall, (*v.*) to be high, etc.
Shâr, (*s.*) the name of the prismatic colours sometimes seen in the sky in fine weather, considered a bad omen.
Shâr, (*a.*) healthy looking, (*v.*) to be healthy looking.
Shâ*t*, (*v.*) to chop (with ***dao***), to cut, to build (a house), to make (a net).
Shâ*t* fik, (*v.*) to cut right through at one blow.
Shât rek, (*v.*) to notch.
Sha um, (*s.*) potted fat, (*v.*) to pot fat.
Shawl, (*a.*) oblong.
Shawng, (*v.*) to shrivel, to contract, (*a.*) shrivelled, etc.
She, (*s.*) a contracted form of ***shial***.
She-fa, (*s.*) bears, boars, rats, birds, and all animals which eat the crops.
Sheh, (*v.*) to bite, to sting.

She-hnap, (*s*) the name of a flowering plant.
She-hneh, (*s.*) the name of a tree with edible leaves.
She-hor, (*s.*) the name of a tree.
She-hrui shâ*t* chha*t*, (*v.*) to steal the affections of a woman already engaged to another and to cause the marriage not to take place.
Sheh-shen, (*s.*) the name of a tree from the leaves of which a dye is extracted.
Shei, (*a.*) long, (*v.*) to be long.
Shei lian, (*v.*) to grow up.
She-khup-thûr, (*s.*) a species of begonia.
She-ki, (*s.*) a four-anna piece, a gayal's horn.
She-ki buh chhuak, (*s.*) a fabled horn from which the owner could obtain anything he desired.
She-kot-rolh, (*s.*) a slip rail.
She-lê, (*s.*) a wild gayal.
She-loi, (*s.*) a buffalo.
She-lu, (*s.*) the fan palm, a gayal's head.
She-lu phan, (*s.*) a post upon which gayals' skulls are placed.
She-lu-tun, (*s.*) the name of a kind of plaiting.
Shem, (*v.*) to divide, to distribute.
Shen, (*a.*) red.
Shên, (*v.*) young.
Shên*g*, (*adv.*) completely, an affix meaning being able to finish.
Shên*g*, (*v.*) to use up, to spend (as money, strength, etc.), to give as a price.
Shen*g*, (*v.*) to gather up, to gather or take in.
Sheng-ma-tawk, (*s.*) the name of a thorny tree.
Shen-shiar, (*s.*) the name of a creeper.
Shen-te-lêk, (*s.*) red yarn.
Shen-te-zêl, (*s.*) the name of a flowering tree.
Sheoh, (*adv.*) completely, unreservedly.
Shêp, (*v. t.*) to dance up and down (as a child).
She-phûng, (*s.*) the name of a beetle.
She-pui-ki-a-tia, (*v.*) to be in the first quarter (as moon).
Sher, (*s.*) a scar, (*v.*) to scar.
Sherh, (*s.*) to keep, to observe a holiday, to swear not to do or say a thing.
Sherh; (*s.*) the parts of a sacrificed animal set apart for the spirits.
She-sam' (*s.*) the name of a plant.
Shi, (*v.*) to butt (as a bull), to rest the forehead on anything.
Shi, (*s.*) a fragment, (*a.*) blind, bad, barren (as a seed).
Shi, (*conj.*) yet, still, but, for, although.

Shi, a contraction of *arshi*, a star.
Shiak, (*s.*) the spur (of a cock), small stones, pieces of baked clay, etc., mixed with potter's clay before making pots.
Shiak, (*v.*) to syphon, to draw with a syphon.
Shiak-thûr, (*s.*) wood-sorrel.
Shial, (*s.*) the domesticated gayal (*gavœus frontalis*).
Shial-hma, (*s.*) the name of a tree.
Shial-lu, (*s.*) the fan palm, a gayal's head.
Shial-ring chi, (*s.*) the name of a kind of Lushai salt.
Shial-shîr, (*s.*) the name of a small hawk.
Shial-ṭang, (*s.*) a small Manipuri coin.
Shial-tuai, (*s.*) the name of a tree.
Shiam, (*v.*) to get ready, to make, to construct, to make arrangements, to appoint.
Shiam-mihring, (*v.*) to make a man of, to bring up (as a child), to assist into better circumstances.
Shiar, (*s.*) a copy, a resemblance.
Shiam-sha, (*a.*) ready made, (*v.*) to be ready or already made.
Shi-chak-ai, (*s.*) the configuration formed by a certain cluster of nebulæ and two stars.
Shih, (*s.*) a small spring.
Shi-hal, (*s.*) a jackal.
Shi-hlo, (*s.*) a species of reed.
Shi-hnok-khur, (*s.*) a configuration made by four stars in the constellation Delphin.
Shik, (*v.*) to pinch, to nip.
Shik, (*a.*) cold, (*v.*) to be cold.
Shi-kei-shen, (*s.*) the planet Mars.
Shi-ki, (*s.*) a four-anna piece.
Shi-koi-kâp, (*s.*) a configuration made by three stars in Aquila and four stars in Delphin.
Shik-sherh, (*s.*) fever, feverishness, (*v.*) to have slight fever, to be feverish.
Shik-shîl, (*s.*) the Lushai umbrella.
Shil-hlu, (*s.*) the emblic myrobalan (*phyllanthus emblica*).
Shil-ong, (*v.*) to be weakly-looking, to be deformed, to have something the matter with one.
Shim, (*v.*) to reform, to repent, to give up, to keep one's self from doing a thing.
Shi-mei-khu, (*s.*) a comet.
Shi-mei-talh, (*s.*) the configuration made by three small stars in the constellation of Orion.
Shin, (*v.*) to carry, to have with one (as money, etc.), to wear (as cloth), to hold.

Shin, an emphatic verbal particle.
Shîn, (*a.*) fine (as cotton), high (as voice), (*v.*) to be fine, etc., (*adv.*) finely, high.
Shîng, (*a.*) ten thousand.
Shing-ship, (*s.*) the name of an imaginary insect which is supposed to be humming when one has a buzzing or singing in the ears (as—*ka beng-a shing-ship a hrâm*, I have a singing in my ears, lit., a *shing-ship* is singing in my ears).
Shin-hlu, (*s.*) see *shil-hlu*.
Shîr, (*s.*) the side (of anything).
Shîr-kâm, (*s.*) the name of a tree.
Shi-ruk, (*s.*) the Pleiades.
Shi-shên, (*s.*) the name of a small red ant.
Shi-shêp, (*s.*) a winnowing fan.
Shi-ship, (*s.*) see *shing-ship*.
Shi-vok bawm, (*s.*) the name of a configuration of stars.
Sho, (*v.*) to boil, to bubble up, to effervesce, (*a.*) boiling, etc.
Shoi, (*v.*) to say.
Shoi-chhia, (*v.*) to run down, to speak against, to blaspheme, to speak evil of.
Shoi-hnawm, (*v.*) to speak depreciatingly of.
Shoi-koi, (*v.*) to speak away from the point.
Shoi-lawk, (*v.*) to foretell, to prophesy, to say beforehand.
Shoi-lian, (*v.*) to magnify by praising.
Shoi ngîl, (*v.*) to correct, to explain, to say correctly, to speak to the point.
Shoi-shei, (*v.*) to be prolix, to beat about the bush.
Shoi-shel, (*v.*) to raise objections, to find fault with, to make excuse, to speak against.
Shoi-shêl hmang, (*v.*) one given to raising objections, finding fault, etc.
Shom, (*a.*) ten.
Shom-hnih, (*a.*) twenty.
Shom leh pahnih, (*a.*) twelve.
Shom leh pakhat, (*a.*) eleven.
Shom leh pakua, (*a.*) nineteen.
Shom leh pali, (*a.*) fourteen.
Shom leh panga, (*a.*) fifteen.
Shom leh pariat, (*a.*) eighteen.
Shom leh paruk, (*a.*) sixteen.
Shom leh pasari, (*a.*) seventeen.
Shom leh pathum, (*a.*) thirteen.
Shom-kua, (*a.*) ninety.
Shom-li, (*a.*) forty.

Shom-nga, (*a.*) fifty.
Shom-riat, (*a.*) eighty.
Shom-ruk, (*a.*) sixty.
Shom-sari, (*a.*) seventy.
Shom-thum, (*a.*) thirty.
Shon, (*v.*) to move from one place to another, to change the mind or opinion, (*adv.*) in another place.
Shu = do not thou (imperative negative termination).
Shu, (*v.*) to collide with, to knock against.
Shua*k*, (*v.*) to ladle out.
Shuak, (*a.*) spurious, pseudo.
Shuan, (*s.*) lead.
Shuan, (*v.*) to take off the fire (as a pot).
Shuan-kâng, (*s.*) the name of an iron pot.
Shuan-kual, (*s.*) a pair of tongs for taking pots off the fire.
Shuar, (*s.*) a shallow place in a river, a rapid, a ford.
Shui, (*v.*) to scrape.
Shu*k*, (*v.*) to wash (clothes).
Shuk-tlong, (*s.*) the name of a durable tree.
Shûm, (*s.*) a measurement equal to twice the length of the closed fist.
Shum-bul, (*s.*) the name of a plant.
Shûn, (*v.*) to outlive.
Shun-hlu, (*s.*) see *shilhlu.*
Shûr, (*s.*) an aërial root, a branch growing downwards from the trunk (as in the fig tree).
Shût, (*s.*) a post inside a house supporting the ridge pole.
Sil, (*v.*) to wash.
Sil, (*a.*) maimed, wounded, disabled, injured, deprived of members, (*v.*) to be maimed, etc.
Si-lai, (*s.*) a gun.
Silai ai-bop, (*s.*) the hammer of a gun.
Silai beng-kua, (*s.*) the touch-hole of a gun.
Silai beng-thlêng, (*s.*) the pan of a gun.
Silai hlo, (*s.*) gunpowder, saltpetre.
Silai hlo thun, (*v.*) to load a gun, (*s.*) a loaded gun.
Silai hme' per-na, (*s.*) the trigger of a gun.
Silai holh-fung, (*s.*) a ramrod.
Silai kawm, (*s.*) the stock of a gun.
Silai kep tê, (*s.*) the nippers of a gun which hold the flint.
Silai khiang rah, (*s.*) the screw of the nippers of a gun.
Silai li-pui, (*s.*) the spring of a gun.
Silai li-tê, (*s.*) the small spring of a gun.
Silai mong pheng, (*s.*) the butt of a gun.

Silai mu, (*s.*) a shot, a bullet.
Silai mu-hnawh, (*s.*) a wad.
Silai pial-lung, (*s.*) the barrel of a gun.
Silai tho-chuan, (*s.*) the sight-piece of a gun.
Silai ui lei, (*s.*) the steel of a gun upon which the flint strikes.
Silai zawn, (*s.*) a measure, conical heap of rice, etc., the apex of which will be level with the end of a gun held high above the head of an ordinary-sized man.
Sil-fai, (*v.*) to wash, to wash clean.
Silh, (*v.*) to wear (as a cloth).
Silh-fên, (*s.*) clothes.
Sil-fên chhia, (*s.*) left off clothing, old clothes.
Si-pai, (*s.*) a sepoy, a soldier.
Soi, (*s.*) bird lime made from the sap of the *hmawng* tree.
Soi, (*v.*) to punish.
Soi-sha, (*v.*) to handle, to work at.
Soi-zoi, (*v. t.*) to exercise, to break in (as horse, etc.)
Sok, (*adv.*) violently.
Som, (*adv.*) in small pieces.
Son-tlung, (*s.*) a species of clay, raised by white ants into mounds.
Son-tlung-lei, (*s.*) a species of clay.
Sop, (*s.*) a contrivance for frightening birds, etc., worked from the *jhûm* house by means of a rope.
Sop, (*v.*) to wash clothes, etc., by squeezing and dashing them up and down upon anything.
Sop, (*v.*) to collapse.
Sop-rop, (*v.*) to be fragile, to be in bad order or condition, to be easily upset or made ill, (*a.*) fragile, etc.
Sor, (*v.*) to shake.
Sot, (*v.*) to go by bounds (as a mouse, rat, etc.)
Sua*k* sual, the same as 'sual.'
Sual, (*s.*) a fault, sin, (*a.*) bad, wicked, sinful, ill-dispositioned, faulty, wrong, (*adv.*) by mistake, in error, wrongly.
Sual pum hmom, } (*v.*) to be entirely evil without having any
Sua' sual pum hmom, } redeeming feature, (*a.*) entirely evil.
Suat, (*v.*) to thin out (as plants), to kill off, to decimate.
Suih, (*v.*) to tie in a weaver's knot, to tie, (*s.*) a knot, (*a.*) knotted.
Suih-bawk, (*v.*) to tie a knot in a single piece of string, etc., (*s.*) a knot.
Suih fin, (*v.*) to tie together.
Suih-hlih, (*v.*) to tie in a bow, (*s.*) a bow.
Suih tung-tu-rut, (*v.*) to tie in an ordinary knot, (*s.*) an ordinary knot.
Suk, (*s.*) a large pestle for pounding rice, etc., a pestle.

Sûk bûk lêm, } (*s.*) a swing made of a bough of a tree.
Sûk lêm, }

Suk-sawn, (*s.*) the name of a brass girdle.

Suk-tê, (*s.*) the name of a tribe to the east of Lushai (the same as Paitê).

Sul-pêl, (*v.*) to overlap, to miss anyone when going to meet him by taking the wrong road.

Sul-rûl, (*s.*) the name of a small maggot which is destructive to clothes, the name of a species of white-ant.

Sum, (*s.*) a large mortar for pounding rice, a mortar.

Sum, (*s.*) goods, chattels, furniture, possessions.

Sum dawng, (*v.*) to trade, to be fortunate in trading, to do a good stroke of business, to buy cheaply, to sell at a good price.

Sum-duk, } (*s.*) a box.
Sum-duk-bawm, }

Sum hmun, (*s.*) a verandah, the front verandah of a Lushai house.

Sun-rûl, (*s.*) see *sulrûl.*

Su-rai, (*s.*) file.

T

Ṭa' awh, (*v.*) to persuade by entreaty or tears, to entreat.

Ṭa' chhan, (*v.*) to weep over or about, (*s.*) a cause of weeping.

Tah, (*v.*) to weave, (*a.*) woven.

Ta-hâm, (*s.*) the name of a plant.

Ta-hian, (*adv.*) here.

Tah-râng, (*s.*) the name of a matting.

Tai, (*s.*) the lower extremity of the bowels.

Tai, (*v.*) to be at enmity with, to hate.

Tai, (*a.*) yellow or ripe (as fruit), ruddy, rosy, (*v.*) to be ripe, etc.

Tai, (*v.*) to push or butt with the tusks (as hog, etc.)

Tai, (*s.*) the waist.

Ṭai, (*s.*) the name of a species of rice.

Tai a tla, (*v.*) to have protrusion of the bowels.

Tai-fê, (*s.*) rice from which beer has been brewed.

Tai-kuang, (*s.*) a butt for holding pigs' wash, etc., made of a hollowed-out tree, a water butt, a tub.

Tai-ma, (*a.*) diligent, energetic, (*v.*) to be diligent, etc., (*adv.*) diligently, etc.

Ṭai-pui, (*s.*) the name of a species of rice.

Tai-rua, (*s.*) the name of a species of cane.

Tai-taw, (*s.*) see *toi-taw.*

Tai-tê, (*s.*) a pet name for a little boy, or used if the real name is unknown.

Tai-ṭêm, } (*s.*) the name of a stinging nettle.
Tai-ṭêng, }

Tai-vâng, (*s.*) the name of a large ant.

Tai-von', (*v.*) to wear in the belt (as a dagger), to keep in the belt (as money).

Tak, (*v.*) to increase in size or numbers (used of things under ground only, such as potatoes, etc.)

Tak, (*adv.*) very, really, exactly, (*a.*) real, exact.

Takam, (*s.*) the Chakma tribe.

Tak meoh, (*adv.*) really exactly, (*a.*) real, exact.

Tak-na-ngial-in, (*adv.*) just as, in exact accordance with.

Tak-sa, (*s.*) the body.

Tak-tak, (*adv.*) really, exactly.

Tak zet, (*a.*) real, exact.

Tal, (*v.*) to kill (an animal).

Tal, (*adv.*) at least, at any rate, even then (see *chiat*).

Tâl, (*v.*) to struggle, to move, to wriggle.

Talân, (*s.*) the name of a species of bamboo.

Talh, (*v.*) to strike together (as flint and steel, etc.)

Talh-ṭêk, (*v.*) to strike fire.

Tal-tum, (*s.*) a club, a mallet.

Tam, (*a.*) much, many, common, plentiful.

Tâm, (*v.*) to suffer famine, to be hungry.

Tam-kor, (*s.*) the name of a species of mustard.

Tam-tak, (*a.*) very much, very many.

Tan, (*v.*) to chop or cut off, to cross (as a river, etc.), (*adv.*) off, across.

Ṭan, (*v.*) to commence, to start.

Ṭan, (*v.*) to take one's part, to side with, to choose.

Tân, (*prep.*) for.

Ṭang, (*v.*) to deny.

Ṭâng, (*v.*) to put forth strength, to exert one's self.

Ṭang, (*a.*) dry.

Ṭang, (*v.*) to engage one's self to do, etc.

Ṭang, (*s.*) a twig, a small branch.

Ṭâng, (*v.*) to stick in, to catch in, to lodge in, to be imprisoned.

Ṭang-in, (*prep.*) from.

Ṭang-ka, (*s.*) money, a rupee, (*a.*) silver.

Ṭang-kai, (*a.*) useful, (*v.*) to be of use.

Tang-ka pui, (*s.*) a medal.

Tang-ka rua, (*s.*) silver, white metal.

Tang-ka rua chher-tu, (*s.*) a silversmith.

Tang-ka sum, (*s.*) money, riches.

Tang-kawng, } (*s.*) the names of a species of large lizard.
Tang-keo, }

Ṭâng-kham, (*v.*) to support, to hold up (a sick person, etc.)

Ṭang-kun, (*s.*) the name of a tribe, probably the Tangkhul Nagas.

Ṭâng-phel, (*s.*) a measurement from the tip of the middle finger to the breast-bone with the arm extended.

Tang-rah, (*s.*) a vegetable or fruit arrested in growth.

Ṭang-rual, (*v.*) to band together.

Ṭang-thawm, (*a.*) cold (as weather after rain), (*v.*) to be cold.

Ṭâng-ṭial, (*s.*) the name of an edible spider.

Ṭang-tîr, (*v.*) to engage, to employ.

Ṭang-tlâng, (*v.*) to band together.

Ṭan-pui, (*v.*) to side with, to help, to be witness for, (*s.*) an ally, a helper, a witness for.

Ṭan-tîr, (*v.*) to commence, to start, to begin.

Ṭan-zawng-in, (*adv.*) across, crosswise.

Tao, (*v.*) to be cross, displeased, angry.

Taoh, (*v.*) to be cross with, to appear displeased with.

Taoh, (*v.*) to butt (as goat), to knock with the head, to knock the head against.

Tao-hmang, (*v.*) to be in the habit of getting cross, (*a.*) cross, disagreeable.

Tâp, (*v.*) to be lost, to be missing, to be detained or delayed, (*a.*) lost, etc.

Ṭa*p*, (*v.*) to cry, to weep.

Ṭap, (*s.*) a Lushai fireplace, a hearth.

Tap-chal, (*s.*) the mound of earth at the back of a Lushai fireplace to protect the wall from fire.

Tap-chhak, (*s.*) a Lushai fireplace, a hearth.

Tap-kawm, (*s.*) the wooden framework of a Lushai hearth.

Târ, (*v.*) to stick on a pole, to make or set up a landmark, to hang up.

Tar, (*a.*) old (in age), (*v.*) to become old.

Tar-â, (*v.*) to be childish with age, to be in one's dotage.

Tar-mit, (*s.*) spectacles, eyeglasses.

Tar-pi lu, (*s.*) the name of an ant's nest used for burning in order to keep away sand-flies.

Tar-tiang, (*s.*) the name of a small palm resembling the areca.

Ta-shing, (*s.*) the name of a species of grass.

Tât, (*v.*) to rub, to besmear.

Tât-fai, (*v.*) to rub clean, to rub (as the feet on a mat or scraper).

Tât-hriam, (*v.*) to sharpen.

Tât-kawng, (*s.*) a species of jack fruit.

Ta-tûr, (*prep.*) for.
Tawh-êk, (*s.*) the name of a large ant.
Tawh-lo, (*adv.*) never (used only in the future).
Tawk, (*v.*) to meet.
Tawk, (*adv.*) enough, sufficiently, (*v.*) to be enough, to be sufficient.
Tawk chao, (*v.*) to be exactly enough, to be ample, (*adv.*) exactly enough, amply.
Tawk fang, about the right quantity, size, etc., about sufficient.
Tawk-fang-in, (*adv.*) moderately.
Ṭawl, (*s.*) the heart of a tree from which the outside has rotted, (*v.*) to die unknown and uncared for and to go without burial.
Taw-lai, (*s.*) a kind of stretcher or seat of cloth on a pole used for carrying sick persons.
Taw-lai-lîr, (*s.*) a cart, a carriage, a barrow or any conveyance with wheels, a wheel.
Ṭawn, (*v.*) to tie, to bind.
Ṫawn, (*v.*) to push on one side, to run up against, to approach.
Tawng, (*v.*) to attack, to fight, to assault.
Tawp, (*s.*) conclusion, end, finish, (*a.*) last, (*v.*) to conclude, etc.
Tawt, (*a.*) tight fitting, tight, crowded, (*v.*) to be tight fitting, etc.
Taw-taw-rawt, (*s.*) a bugle.
Taw-taw-rawt hâm-tu, } (*s.*) a bugler.
Taw-taw-rawt pu, }
Tê, (*a.*) small, little, (*v.*) to be small, to get small.
Te, (*adv.*) exactly.
Te, a plural suffix.
Ṭeh, (*v.*) to disperse.
Ṫeh, (*v.*) to measure, to compare, to liken unto.
Teh-khawng, (*s.*) a measure, (*v.*) to compare.
Teh-khin, (*v.*) to compare, to liken to.
Teh-khin thu, (*s.*) a parable, a proverb.
Teh-lul, (*adv.*) even, also an emphatic particle.
Teh-lul êm-in, an expression of incredulity.
Tei, (*v.*) to twist (a single thread of yarn, etc.), (*a.*) twisted.
Têi, (*a.*) self.
Ṭêk, (*s.*) a meteorite, a thunderbolt, (*v.*) to make sparks, to break into sparks, to throw out sparks.
Ṭêk-em, (*s.*) the name of a tree.
Ṭêk-râl, (*s.*) the name of a species of mantis.
Ṫêl, (*s.*) a bundle, a bunch, (*v.*) to tie up into a bundle, etc.
Tel, (*v.*) to accompany, to join with, to be one of a company, to form part of, to take part in, to be present, to be added, to add.

Tel-hawng, (*s.*) a species of arum.
Telh-telh, (*adv.*) gradually, little by little.
Ṭelh-ṭelh, (*adv.*) just a little, slightly.
Ṫel khaw-mual, (*s.*) the name of a tortoise.
Tel-pui, (*s.*) the name of a large tortoise.
Tel-râng, (*s.*) the name of a small tortoise.
Tem, (*v.*) to taste.
Ten, (*v.*) to detest, to dislike, to abominate, to loathe, to have an aversion to.
Ten*g*, (*v.*) to obtain salt from a salt spring by evaporation.
Te-ngeng, (*s.*) a small round bell.
Ten*g*-khal, (*v.*) to evaporate salt water to obtain salt.
Ten-om, (*a.*) detestable, abominable, disgusting, loathsome.
Ṭeoh, (*v.*) to chip, to be uneven (as edge of a knife), to be slightly bad, also an affix signifying 'many' or 'much.'
Ṭeoh hriam, (*v.*) to sharpen (a flint, etc.) by chipping.
Ṭet, (*a.*) torn, (*v.*) to be torn.
Ṫha, (*s.*) a sinew, strength.
Ṭha, (*a.*) good, well-to-do, advantageous, beneficial, well, (*v.*) to be good, etc., (*adv.*) well, thoroughly.
Tha a chat, (*v.*) to get cramp.
Tha dah, (*v.*) to be idle, to do a thing listlessly because not working for one's self.
Tha-do, (*s.*) the name of a tree, the same as 'kha-do.'
Ṭha-hnem, (*adv.*) much, largely, in large quantities, (*s.*) much, a lot, a large quantity, (*a.*) useful, very good, (*v.*) to be useful, etc.
Ṭha hnem ngai, (*a.*) ambitious, earnest, greedy, zealous, thorough, (*v.*) to be ambitious, etc., (*adv.*) thoroughly, well, carefully.
Tha hrui nei, (*a.*) strong, mighty, (*v.*) to be strong, etc.
Thai, (*v.*) to scratch up, to scrape up or to scrape together (with the fingers or feet).
Thai-chhawni-nu, (*s.*) the cat-fish.
Thak, (*v.*) to itch, to be pungent, to be hot (as pepper), (*a.*) pungent, hot.
Thak-pui, (*s.*) the name of a stinging plant.
Thak-thing, (*s.*) the cinnamon tree, cinnamon.
Thal, (*s.*) an arrow, a dart.
Ṭhâl, (*s.*) the dry season.
Ṫhâl, (*v.*) to scoop or dip up (water, etc.)
Ṭhâl, (*s.*) the groin.
Ṭhâl-bê, (*s.*) the gland in the groin.
Ṭhâl-bê-a mi, (*s.*) posterity.
Ṫhal-hrit, (*s.*) lac, sealing wax.

Thal-ngul, (*s.*) a bow (weapon).
Ṭha-lo, (*a.*) bad, disadvantageous, not beneficial, (*v.*) to be bad, etc.
Thal-teh, (*s.*) the name of a tree.
Thal-thîng, (*s.*) lemon grass.
Ṭhâl-vuai-fu, (*s.*) the name of an inferior kind of sugarcane.
Ṫham, (suffix) of sufficient size, number or importance.
Tham, (*v.*) { to reward, to give in return for service rendered, to bribe, (*s.*) a reward, a bribe.
Ṭhâm, (*v.*) to claw, to take up in the fist or fingers.
Ṫhang, (*v.*) to sojourn (in a strange place), to remain (in another place or country).
Thâng, (*a.*) having a smell like raw flesh, dried pulse, etc., having a metallic taste or smell.
Thang, (*s.*) a trap, a snare.
Thang, (*a.*) greasy, (*v.*) to be greasy.
Than*g*, (*v.*) to spread (as fame), to be rumoured abroad, to become known, to be renowned, (*a.*) renowned, etc.
Ṭhan*g*, (*v.*) to grow.
Ṭhan*g*, (*v.*) to be accustomed to, to be used to.
Ṭhâng, (*s.*) the bamboo grass.
Ṫhang-chhuah, (*s.*) a title given to a man who has killed a certain number of animals in the chase, or to one who has given a public feast. Such a one is entitled to make a window in his house.
Thang-chhuah puan, (*s.*) the name of a cloth.
Thang-fên, (*s.*) the name of a blue bird.
Ṭhang-harh, (*v.*) to wake up.
Ṫhang-khawk, (*v.*) to echo, (*s.*) an echo.
Ṭhang-thar, (*s.*) the present generation, a new generation.
Ṫhang-ṭung, (*s.*) the name of a species of palm, the fibre of which is used for fiddle strings.
Thang-zang, (*s.*) the name of a weed.
Ṭhan'kin, (*a.*) full grown, (*v.*) to be full grown, to stop growing.
Ṫhao, (*s.*) fat, grease, mucus, (*a.*) fat, corpulent, (*v.*) to be fat.
Thap, (*a.*) rough (as wood), (*v.*) to be rough.
Ṭhâp, (*v.*) to sift in a *thlangra.*
Thar, (*a.*) new, (*v.*) to be new, (*adv.*) anew.
Tha-suih-hlo, (*s.*) the name of a small plant with a purple flower, a decoction of which is used by the Lushais as a lotion for cut sinews.
Tha*t*, (*v.*) to kill.
Ṭha*t*, see *ṭha.*
Ṫha-tak-in ti, (*v.*) to treat well, to do well by, to do well.
Ṭha-tawk-in, (*adv.*) according to ability.

That-chhia, (*a.*) lazy, (*v.*) to be lazy, (*adv.*) lazily.
Ṭhat-fam-kim, (*a.*) perfect, faultless, excelling in everything.
Ṫha thla, (*v.*) to be idle, to do a thing listlessly because not working for one's self.
Tha-zâm, (*s.*) veins, arteries, nerves.
Thaw, (*adv.*) almost, nearly.
Thaw'chham, } (*v.*) to be short of breath.
Thaw'dang,
Thawh, (*v.*) to rise (the same as *tho*).
Ṫhawh, (*v.*) to contribute, to subscribe.
Thaw hlop-hlop, (*v.*) to pant.
Thawh khawm, } (*v.*) to contribute, to get up a subscription.
Thawh lawm,
Thaw*k*, (*v.*) to breathe, to breathe out, to sigh.
Thaw*k*, (*v.*) to work, to do, to perform.
Thawk-khat-a, (*adv.*) suddenly.
Thawk-rim, (*v.*) to labour, to work hard, to toil.
Thawl, (*a.*) loose fitting, (*v.*) to be loose fitting.
Thawm, (*s.*) a sound, a voice.
Ṭhawn*g*, (*v.*) to attack or seize suddenly.
Ṭhawng-a lei vir, (*s.*) a whirlwind.
Ṫhawp, (*a.*) spongy, light (as bread), pithy (as radish, sugarcane, etc.), (*v.*) to be spongy, light, etc.
Thaw-pik, (*a.*) embarrassed, not prosperous, having a confined situation, (*v.*) to be embarrassed, etc.
Thaw-pik-thlâk, (*a.*) embarrassing, depressing.
Thaw-sha, (*a.*) hot, close, (*v.*) to be hot, etc.
Thaw-ven*g*, (*a.*) prosperous, having a high and open situation, (*v.*) to be prosperous, etc.
Ṭhe, a contracted form of *ṭhiat*.
Ṭhe, (*a.*) stale, dry, (*v.*) to be stale, etc.
Ṭhe, (*s.*) a bundle, (*v.*) to tie in bundles.
Ṫheh, (*v.*) to sprinkle, to splash.
Ṭheh, (*v.*) to offer, to give (as something to eat or drink).
Ṫheh-chhua*k*, (*v.*) to bring forth or out.
Ṭhe-hlân, (*s.*) a shelf in a Lushai house on the rafters, a loft.
Ṭhe-hlei, (*s.*) a squirrel.
Ṭhei, (*v.*) to chew, to masticate.
Ṫhei, (*v.*) to be able.
Thei, (*s.*) edible fruit.
Thei-âr-lung, (*s.*) the name of a tree with edible fruit.
Thei-bâl, } (*s.*) species of figs.
Thei-ba'tê,
Thei-chhûng-shen, (*s.*) the name of a tree with edible fruit.

Thei-fei-mûng, (*s.*) the name of a tree with edible fruit, only bears very occasionally.
Thei-hai, (*s.*) the mangoe.
Thei-hmu, (*s.*) a raspberry, a blackberry.
Theih-nghil, (*v.*) to forget.
Thei-kêl-êk, (*s.*) the name of a tree with edible fruit.
Thei-kêl-ki, (*s.*) the name of a creeper with edible fruit.
Thei-khuang-chawm,
Thei-khuang-thlûp,
Thei-kum, } (*s.*) the names of trees with edible fruit.
Thei-la-khuih, (*s.*) the pineapple.
Thei-pa-buan,
Thei-pa-ling-kawh,
Thei-pan*g*-kai, } (*s.*) the names of trees with edible fruit.
Thei-pui, (*s.*) a species of fig.
Thei-rah, (*s.*) edible fruit.
Thei-ria,
Thei-sa-khi,
Thei-sa-ruh, } (*s.*) the names of trees with edible fruit.
Thei-she-chal, (*s.*) the Indian medlar (*Pyrus pashii*).
Thei-sheh-rêt, (*s.*) the name of a tree with an edible fruit.
Thei-son-tlung, (*s.*) the name of a creeper with fragrant flowers and edible fruit.
Thei-tât, (*s.*) the name of a tree with edible fruit.
Thei-tawk-in, (*adv.*) according to ability.
Thei-tawp-in, (*adv.*) according to utmost ability.
Thei-tê, (*s.*) the peach.
Thei-thît, (*s.*) a species of fig.
Thei-vok-mit,
Thei-zawl, } (*s.*) the names of trees with edible fruits.
Thel, (*v.*) to blaze (with a hatchet, etc.), to strip off bark.
Ṭhelh, (*v.*) to extinguish or partially extinguish fire, to quell, to put a stop to (as quarrel, etc.)
Ṭhelh, (*adv.*) nearly, almost, (*v.*) to miss (not to hit, etc.)
Ṭhel-rêt, (*s.*) a contraction of *ṭhial-rêt*.
Ṭhel-rêt puan, (*s.*) waterproof cloth.
Ṭhem, (*s.*) a small or sample piece of anything, a piece.
Ṭhem-bu, (*s.*) a weaving machine.
Ṭhem-dawh, (*v.*) to put in splints.
Ṭhem-dawh-na, (*s.*) splints.
Ṭhem-thiam, (*a.*) expert, clever, skilful, (*v.*) to be expert, etc., to practise, to compete with one another, (*s.*) a skilled workman, a craftsman.
Thên, (*adv.*) exactly.

Thên, (*s.*) the name of a tree.
Thên, (*v.*) to swing to and fro.
Then, a contracted form of *thian.*
Ṭhen, (*v.*) to smile, to grin, to make grimaces.
Ṭhen, (*v.*) to divide, to separate, to leave, to take leave of, to separate from, (*adv.*) separately, apart.
Ṭhen, (*pro.*) some, others, (*s.*) part.
Then-fai, see *thiang-fai.*
Ṭhen khat, (*pro.*) some, others.
Then-ngo, (*s.*) the name of a tree.
Ṭhen-om, (*s.*) a neighbour.
Ṭhen-shan, (*v.*) to grin at, to smile at, to make grimaces at.
Then-shen, (*s.*) the name of a tree.
Thên-zawl hlo, (*s.*) the name of a species of grass.
Thêo, (*v.*) to make a fence or lattice, to fence in.
Thêo, (*a.*) dishevelled, (*v.*) to be dishevelled.
Ṭheoh, (*pro.*) each, everyone, everywhere.
Thep, (*v.*) to wait or sneak about, to walk about aimlessly.
Thêp, (*v.*) to sink in, to be sunken, to contract.
Ther, (*s.*) a splinter, a jagged edge, (*v.*) to be jagged.
The-reng, (*s.*) the generic name for all chirping insects.
Therh, (*s.*) a civet cat.
Thi, (*v.*) to die, (*a.*) dead.
Thi, (*s.*) blood, menses, (*v.*) to bleed.
Ṭhi, (*s.*) a bead, a bell worn by cattle.
Thial, (*v.*) to chew, to masticate, to grate the teeth.
Thial, (*s.*) the gizzard.
Ṭhial-pawn, (*s.*) the temples, the lock of the jaw.
Ṭhial-rêt, (*s.*) india-rubber, the india-rubber tree.
Ṭhial-rêt puan, (*s.*) waterproof cloth.
Thiam, (*v.*) to know how to, to know.
Thiam, (*v.*) to be not guilty, to be justified, to be in the right, to be innocent, to be indulgent, to pronounce not guilty, to justify, etc., (*a.*) innocent, indulgent, etc.
Thiam chang, (*v.*) to be cleared of guilt, to be justified.
Thiam-chang tîr, (*v.*) to pronounce guiltless or right, to clear of guilt.
Thiam hawn, (*v.*) the same as *thiam chang.*
Thiam-hon-tîr, (*v.*) the same as *thiam-chang tîr.*
Thiam-lo, (*v.*) to be guilty, to be in the wrong, to pronounce guilty, to condemn, (*a.*) guilty.
Thiam-na thu shoi, (*v.*) to make a defence.
Thiam-thai-nu mong-talh, (*s.*) the name of a small sand-burrowing insect.

Thian, (*s.*) a friend, a companion.
Ṫhian, (*s.*) the name of a creeper with white flowers resembling the convolvulus.
Ṫhian fai, (*v.*) to clear up, to clear away.
Thian*g*, (*a.*) clear (as atmosphere), clean, lawful, right, (*v.*) to be clear, to be clean, etc., to take out (as dust from the eye), to cleanse, to clean up.
Thiang, (*adv.*) side by side.
Ṫhiang-hlim, (*a.*) clean, ceremonially clean, without blemish, holy, (*v.*) to be clean, etc.
Thiang-lo, (*a.*) unlawful, wrong, (*v.*) to be unlawful or wrong.
Thian-hmul, (*s.*) the name of a creeper with yellow flowers resembling the convolvulus.
Ṭhian-kom-ngeih, (*s.*) bosom friends.
Ṫhian-lo, (*a.*) unclean, (*v.*) to be unclean.
Thian-nu, (*s.*) see *thian-hmul.*
Thiar, (*v.*) to pick out, to pick over, to take out, to remove from one place to another, to clean up.
Thiar-chhua*k*, (*v.*) to unload (as a boat, etc.), to take out.
Thiar-lut, (*v.*) to load (as a boat, etc.), to put inside.
Ṭhi-âr-ngal, (*s.*) the name of a small red bead.
Ṫhiat, (*v.*) to tuck in, to stick in.
Ṭhiat, (*v.*) to undo, to take to pieces, to dismantle.
Ṫhi-a-tlin*g*, (*v.*) to have a bruise.
Ṭhi-be, (*s.*) a man's ear-bead.
Ṫhi chhawng-in lum, (*v.*) to lie dying.
Thi chhawng-in om, (*v.*) to be dying.
Thi-dang, (*v.*) to faint.
Thi dawn lo, (*v.*) to risk or hazard one's life, to be regardless of death.
Thih, (*v.*) to anoint.
Ṫhi-hmu, (*s.*) the name of a black bead.
Ṭhi-hna, (*s.*) an amber bead or necklace, amber.
Ṭhi-hrui, (*s.*) a necklace.
Ṫhih-thiap, (*s.*) name of an animal.
Thîk, (*v.*) to be jealous of.
Thi kîr, (*v.*) to staunch blood by charming.
Thîl, (*v.*) to be swollen out (as ears of rice, etc.)
Ṭhîl, (*s.*) a species of oak.
Ṫhil, (*s.*) a thing.
Thil, (*v.*) to thread, to skewer.
Thi-lâ*k*, (*v.*) to bleed by cupping.
Thil dang-a, in other respects, in other things.
Thil phal, (*a.*) generous, (*v.*) to be generous.

Thil-tê, (*s.*) the name of a species of cane.
Thil-thek, (*s.*) the name of a plant the leaves of which are used by the Lushais for thatching.
Thîl thing, (*s.*) the name of a tree.
Thil ti, (*s.*) works, doings, deeds.
Thil ti thei-na, (*s.*) power, ability.
Thim, (*a.*) dark, (*v.*) to be dark, to be benighted, to be overtaken by night, (*s.*) darkness.
Thîm, (*v.*) to wither, to wilt, to be languid, to be slightly unwell, (*a.*) withered, etc.
Thîm, (*v.*) to cut off a small piece.
Thîm, (*s.*) an insect which destroys clothes and leather.
Ṭhi-mal, (*s.*) a cornelian bead.
Thim-hlim, } (*s.*) twilight.
Thim-hmul, }
Ṭhim-kual, (*s.*) the name of a brass hairpin.
Thim-tham, (*s.*) darkness, a dark place.
Thin, (*s.*) the liver.
Ṭhîn, (*adv.*) always, continually, also a verbal affix with the meaning of 'used to,' 'in the habit of.'
Thi-na, (*a.*) poisonous.
Thin a chhia, (*v.*) to be bad-natured, irritable, surly.
Thi-na hlo, (*s.*) poison.
Thin a ṭhawng, (*v.*) to be startled, to receive a shock by bad news, etc.
Thin chhe, (*a.*) bad-natured, irritable, surly, (*v.*) to be bad-natured, etc.
Thi-nei, (*v.*) to have menstrual discharge.
Thing, (*s.*) a tree, wood, (*a.*) wooden.
Thing, (*v. t.*) to shake.
Ṭhîng, (*v.*) to collect a debt from, to ask for anything owing.
Ṭhing, (*a.*) stale, cold, not eaten the same time as cooked, (*v.*) to get stale, cold, etc.
Thîng-dîm, (*s.*) the name of a dance and those who take part in it, (*v.*) to perform the above dance.
Thing-dol, (*s.*) the name of a tree.
Thing-fâk, (*s.*) firewood.
Thing-fang-hma, (*s.*) the papaw.
Thing-hâr, (*s.*) a chip of wood.
Thing-hnah-chang, (*s.*) the name of a tree.
Thing-hmar-cha, (*s.*) a pepper corn, pepper.
Thing-kha, (*s.*) the name of a tree.
Thing-khim, (*s.*) the name of a durable tree.
Thing-khuai-lu, (*s.*) the name of a durable tree.

Thing-khuang, (*s.*) the flat buttress-like roots at the foot of some trees.
Ṭhing-kual, (*s.*) see '*ṭhim-kual.*'
Ṫhing-lu-bul, (*s.*) a short undeveloped tree supposed to be haunted.
Thing-lung, (*s.*) the name of a durable tree.
Thing mâm-na, (*s.*) a plane, tool.
Thing-parh, } (*v.*) to shake out, to shake open.
Thing-pharh, }
Thing-phur-na chen, (*s.*) a measurement of about one mile.
Thing-puan-chhia, (*s.*) the name of a tree.
Thing-pui, (*s.*) the tea tree, tea.
Thing-pui rah, (*s.*) tea seed.
Thing-pui thing, (*s.*) the name of a tree.
Thing-rem, (*s.*) a box, wooden furniture of any kind.
Thing-rem shiam-tu, (*s.*) a carpenter.
Thing-ri, (*s.*) the name of a tree.
Thing-sai hrua, (*s.*) a tree of a certain peculiar growth supposed to be haunted.
Thing-sai phaw, } (*s.*) the names of trees.
Thing-sa-phu, }
Thing-sha-um-bûr, (*s.*) the name of a tree resembling the sago palm.
Thing-shia, (*s.*) a species of chestnut tree.
Thing-shia-mîm, (*s.*) a chestnut.
Thing-ṭawl, (*s.*) the heart of a tree from which the outside has rotted away.
Thing-thel-na ṭom, (*s.*) shavings.
Thing-ṭhi, (*v.*) to kneel.
Ṫhing-thiang, (*s.*) the name of a tree.
Thing-thu, (*s.*) wood with one end burnt, partly burned wood.
Thiing-thu-pui, (*s.*) the name of a tree.
Thing-tlâng, (*s.*) mountainous country.
Thing-tuai, (*s.*) a young tree, a shrub.
Thing-tum-bu, (*s.*) the name of a tree.
Thing-ui-ha-hni, (*s.*) the name of a tree.
Thing-vân-dawt, (*s.*) the name of a very tall tree.
Thing-zai-na, (*s.*) a saw.
Thing-zai-noi, (*s.*) sawdust.
Thing-zung-thlâr, (*s.*) the same as *thing khuang.*
Thin-lung, (*s.*) the heart, the mind.
Thin-lung a hlm, (*v.*) to feel elated, happy, joyful.
Thin-lung a khiei, (*v.*) to be cut to the heart so as to cause great anger.

Thin-lung a sha, (*v.*) to be angry, to be in a temper.
Thin-lung a ṭha, (*v.*) to be good-natured, to be good.
Thin-lung shon, (*v.*) to change the mind.
Thin-lung-ṭha, (*a.*) good natured, good.
Thin-nel, (*a.*) easy going, good tempered, (*v.*) to be easy going, etc.
Thin ram, (*a.*) touchy, easily made angry, quick-tempered, (*v.*) to be touchy, etc.
Thin-rim, (*a.*) angry, (*v.*) to be angry.
Thin tawt-in puak-keh lek lek, (*v.*) to be bursting with rage.
Thin-ur, (*a.*) angry, (*v.*) to be angry.
Thîp, (*s.*) the name of a species of grass.
Thîp, (*v.*) to smart, to be pungent.
Thîr, (*s.*) iron.
Thîr-bawm, (*s.*) a tool-basket, a basket in which old tools and pieces of iron are kept.
Thîr-chak-ai, (*s.*) an anchor.
Thîr-chher-thiam, } (*s.*) a blacksmith.
Thîr-dêng, }
Thîr-hrui, (*s.*) wire, iron wire.
Thîr-khen, (*s.*) a chisel.
Thîr-kilh-na, (*s.*) a nail, an iron nail.
Thîr-tlawn, (*s.*) a bar of iron, a jumper, a crowbar.
Thîr-tu'lung, } (*s.*) an iron jumper.
Thîr-tu'-ṭhulh, }
Thi-sawn, (*v.*) to die from exposure, to die a natural death (used of domestic animals), to die and not have the usual sacrifice offered.
Thi-shen, (*s.*) blood.
Thi-shen, (*v.*) to offer a sacrifice for the dead.
Thi-shen chhua*k*, (*v.*) to shed blood.
Ṭhi-ṭek, (*s.*) the name of a yellow bead.
Ṭhi-tling, (*s.*) a bruise.
Thi-thlo-chao, just enough to keep alive.
Thla, (*s.*) the moon, a month.
Thla, (*s.*) a spirit, one's double.
Thla, (*s.*) a wing.
Thla a chhuak, (*v.*) to rise (as moon).
Thla a de, (*v.*) to be a new moon.
Thla-bâr, (*v.*) to receive a great shock or fright.
Thla-bâr-in na, (*v.*) to be ill through a shock or fright.
Thla-bâr-in thi, (*v.*) to die of fright or as the result of a shock.
Thla-do, (*s.*) the name of a tree, the same as *khado.*

Thlah, (*s.*) a descendant, posterity.
Thlah, (*v.*) to let go, to release.
Thlah, (*v.*) to accompany part way, to see off.
Thla-hlui, } last month.
Thla hma-sha, }
Thla-hnak, (*v.*) to comfort, to cheer.
Thla-hual, (*s.*) the halo round the moon, *a in-in thla a hual*, there is a halo round the moon, literally, 'the moon is encircled by its house.'
Thla hual, (*v.*) to offer a sacrifice to quiet one's mind.
Thlah-thlam, (*v.*) to leave, to abandon, to forsake, to neglect, to leave to one's own devices, to leave in the lurch, to let alone.
Thlah-tu, (*s.*) an ancestor, a progenitor.
Thlai, (*s.*) vegetables.
Thlai-chhiah, (*v.*) to sacrifice an animal at the death of anyone, to accompany the departed spirit to the other world.
Thlai-zong, (*s.*) the wild cherry.
Thlâk, an affix denoting 'causing' or 'begetting,' as in *khaw-ngai-thlak*, pitiable (lit., pity causing).
Thlâ*k*, (*v.*) to relieve, to take another's place, to act as a substitute, to lower, to let down, to throw down, to drop.
Thlâ*k*-hlel, (*v.*) to hold dear, to be attached to, to be reluctant to part with or give up.
Thlâk-kha*t*, (*s.*) an embankment, a road on an embankment, (*v.*) to make an embankment.
Thlâk-thla, (*v.*) to let down, to drop down, to lower.
Thlâk-thlen*g*, (*v.*) to change, to exchange.
Thlâk-tu, (*s.*) a substitute, a successor.
Thla-leh, (*s.*) next month.
Thla-ler, (*s.*) uninhabited country, waste region, desert, wilderness, (*a.*) desolate, uninhabited, waste, (*v.*) to be or become desolate, etc.
Thlâm, (*s.*) a *jhúm* house.
Thla mang lai (or hun), the time when there is no moon.
Thla-muan, (*v.*) to comfort, to cheer.
Thla-muang, to be comforted, to cheer up, to have peace of mind.
Thlân, (*s.*) a grave.
Thlan, (*s.*) perspiration.
Thlan a sha, (*v.*) to perspire.
Thlan dai, (*v.*) to be cool, to get cool, to feel cool.
Thlang, (*adv.*) lower, down, (*s.*) the west.
Thlang, (*v.*) to choose, to select.

Thlang-a, (*prep.*) below, lower down.
Thlang-dâr-rim-chhia, (*s.*) the name of a beetle.
Thlang-lam, (*s.*) the west.
Thlang-lam-a, (*adv.* and *prep.*) below (lower down).
Thlang-ra, (*s.*) a Lushai sieve.
Thlang-tiang, (*s.*) the name of a reed.
Thlân-nghah ni, (*s.*) the day after a burial.
Thla noi, (*s.*) the last quarter of a moon.
Thlan-thla-chang, (*s.*) a crest of feathers worn as a sign that the owner has given a public feast.
Thlan-vong, (*s.*) the name of a flowering tree the wood of which is used for making troughs, plates, etc.
Thlao, (*v.*) to forsake.
Thlaoh, (*v. t.*) to drop unintentionally, to leave behind (as a slain comrade in battle).
Thlao-thla, (*v.*) to forsake, to give up.
Thla-phâng, (*v.*) to be exceedingly anxious, to be in anguish, to be in fear of death.
Thla-phur, (*s.*) the time of year corresponding nearly to the month of May.
Thlar, (*s.*) a bunch (as of plantains, keys, etc.)
Thla-rao, (*s.*) a spirit, the spirit, the soul.
Thla-rao hmu, (*v.*) to see a vision.
Thla-rao in-lar, (*s.*) a vision.
Thla-rao in-lâr hmu, (*v.*) to see a vision.
Thla-sherh, (*s.*) the time of year corresponding nearly to September.
Thla-shik, (*s.*) the cold weather.
Thla-shik kong, (*s.*) the milky-way.
Thla thar, (*s.*) the new moon.
Thla-vâr, (*a.*) phosphorescent, (*v.*) to be phosphorescent.
Thlawh-bua, (*s.*) a disused *jhûm*, land which has been *jhûmed*.
Thlawh-hlawh, (*v.*) to weed a *jhûm*, etc., for wages.
Thlawh-hma, (*s.*) a *jhûm*, crops.
Thlawh-hma chen, (*s.*) a measurement of about two to four miles.
Thlawk, (*v.*) to fly.
Thlawk-bir, (*v.*) to swoop down.
Thlawn, } Thlawn-in, } (*adv.*) to no purpose, in vain, gratuitously, uselessly.
Thlê, (*v.*) to move on one side (as the body or head), to turn head, to lean on one side (as body or head) to be lopsided, (*a.*) lopsided.

Thlei, (*v.*) to sift, to separate, to divide, to distinguish between, to have respect of persons, to make a distinction between.
Thlêm, (*v.*) to comfort, to persuade, to try to persuade, to pacify, to appease, to entice, to tempt.
Thlêm chiam, (*v.*) to beseech, to try hard to persuade.
Thlêm-thlu, (*v.*) to persuade, to succeed in persuading, comforting, appeasing, enticing or tempting.
Thleng, (*v.*) to change.
Thleng, (*v.*) to arrive, to put up, to lodge, to board, to cause to arrive, to escort, to appeal in a law case.
Thlêng, (*s.*) a plate, a trough.
Thleng-in, (*prep.*) as far as, up to, all the way to.
Thleng-reng, (*s.*) the name of a tree.
Thleng thleng-in, (*prep.*) all the way to, as far as, so far as, up to.
Thlen'in, (*s.*) a temporary lodging.
Thle*p*, (*v.*) to fold up.
Thlêr, (*v.*) to tear, to split, to rip up.
Thlêr, (*s.*) a street between two rows of houses.
Thler, (*v.*) to cross at an angle.
Thler-zawng-in, (*adv.*) crosswise, at an angle.
Thli, (*s.*) wind, a drought.
Thlia*k*, (*v. t.*) to snap, the same as *ti-tliak*.
Thliar, (*v.*) to divert the water of a river, to catch fish by diverting the water of a river.
Thliar, (*v.*) to slight.
Thliar-kâr, (*s.*) an island.
Thliar-thla, (*v.*) to slight.
Thli-fim, (*s.*) a breeze.
Thlik-thli-dîr, (*s.*) the crest (on a bird's head).
Thlik-thli êk bawm, (*s.*) the name of a parasitical plant.
Thlim, (*v.*) to glance at stealthily to see if being watched, to listen stealthily, to hear if any one is coming, to watch stealthily, to leave stealthily.
Thling, (*s.*) marrow.
Thli-pui, (*s.*) a wind storm.
Thlîr, (*v.*) to look at from a distance, to look, to look at, to view.
Thli*t*, (*v.*) to strain through a strainer, to pour out slowly, to pour off (as water).
Thli*t*-fai, (*v.*) to winnow by pouring from a height slowly and allowing the wind to blow away the chaff.
Thli ûp, (*v.*) to be free from or sheltered from the wind.
Thlo, (*v.*) to weed.

Thloh, (*s.*) a woodpecker.

Thloh-kor-ha,
Thloh-pui,
Thloh-pui-lu-eng,
Thloh-sai,
Thloh-tê,
Thloh-ṭial, } (*s.*) the names of different species of woodpeckers.

Thlon, (*v.*) to fall out, to come out (as teeth, horns, etc.), to come off (as the stalk of a fruit), to pull out (as tooth, etc.)

Thlop, (*v.*) to support, to stand up for or on behalf of, to stand by, in time of need, to befriend.

Thlor, (*v.*) to make saltpetre or lye.

Thlor-bêl,
Thlor-bûr, } (*s.*) a funnel for making saltpetre and lye.

Thluak, (*s.*) the brain.

Thluak-nem, (*a.*) good-natured, good-tempered, (*v.*) to be good-natured, etc.

Thluam, (*a.*) smooth, (*v.*) to be smooth, (*adv.*) smoothly.

Thluang, (*v.*) to straighten (the leg).

Thlu-hial, (*adv.*) contrary to expectation, on the contrary, an affix signifying that something contrary to expectation has taken place.

Thluk, (*s.*) the back of the head, the nape of the neck.

Thlûk-zia, (*s.*) tune, tone.

Thlum, (*a.*) sweet, strong (as beer), (*v.*) to be sweet, etc.

Thlum a pawn, (*v.*) to be weak (as beer).

Thlung, (*v.*) to tie up (as an animal), to stretch from one place to another (as a wire, rope, etc.), to suspend (a rope, etc.)

Thlûr, (*v.*) to spin (with a hand spindle), to pursue for a long distance.

Tho, (*s.*) a fly.

Tho, (*v.*) to get up, to rise (same as *thawh.*)

Tho, (*a.*) not fully fermented (as rice for beer), (*v.*) to be not fully fermented.

Tho-â, (*v.*) to be dazed or stupid upon waking from sleep.

Thoi, (*v.*) to exercise, to doctor.

Thoi, (*v.*) to slightly graze, to go or pass close to (as shot), to go round about or up and down in front of.

Thoi, (*a.*) ambiguous, (*adv.*) ambiguously, in parables.

Ṭhol-ṭhu, a contracted form of *ṭhualṭhu.*

Thom-hnaw, a contracted form of *thuvmhnaw.*

Ṭhom-mawl, (*s.*) a pile or post (under a house).

Thon, (*v.*) to send.

Thon-thu, (*s.*) a story, a fable, a tale.

Tho-shi, (*s.*) a mosquito.
Tho-shi lèn, (*s.*) a mosquito curtain.
Thu, (*s.*) a word, a saying, news, (*prep.*) about, concerning.
Thu, (*a.*) half burnt, partly charred, (*v.*) to be half burnt, etc.
Thu, (*s.*) fluid which comes from a corpse.
Thu, (*a.*) greasy.
Ṭhu, see *ṭhut.*
Ṫhuah, (*s.*) a layer, (*a.*) of more than one thickness, (*adv.*) in layers, one on top of another.
Thuah-riat, (*s.*) the name of a tree.
Thuai, (*adv.*) quickly.
Ṭhuai, (*adv.*) under no circumstances, on no condition.
Thuai-a, (*prep.* and *adv.*) underneath.
Thuai thuai, (*adv.*) quickly.
Ṭhual-ṭhu, (*s.*) the name of a tree the kernel of the fruit of which is eaten as an aperient and as an anthelmintic.
Thuam, (*s.*) goods, things, property, articles.
Thuam-chhia, (*s.*) a cloth for covering clothes during work.
Thuam-hnaw, (*s.*) things, articles, goods, property, implements.
Ṭhuam-pui, (*s.*) the name of a tree.
Ṭhuam-riat, (*s.*) the name of a tree the juice of which is used as a medicine for sores.
Ṭhuang-ruah, (*s.*) the rain which sometimes falls after *jhûm* cutting.
Thu-buai, (*s.*) a question, a complaint, a dissension.
Thu dawn lo-vin, (*adv.*) rashly, inconsiderately.
Ṭhuei-chhum, (*v.*) to twist, to wrench.
Ṫhu hmu, (*v.*) to receive authority.
Thu-hmun, (*a.*) alike, same, equal, (*v.*) to be alike, etc.
Thu-hnuai-rolh, (*a.*) humble, (*v.*) to speak humbly.
Thu-hre-tu, (*s.*) a witness for.
Ṭhui, (*v.*) to sew, (*s.*) a seam.
Ṫhui, (*adv.*) far, high.
Ṭhui-hruai, (*v.*) to act as a regent for, (*s.*) a dependant, one under authority, a follower, a regent.
Ṭhui-op, (*s.*) the name of a large ant.
Ṫhuk, (*s.*) a grate, a stove, a fireplace, the place enclosed by the three stones which support the pot on a Lushai fireplace.
Thûk, (*a.*) deep, (*v.*) to be deep.
Thuk duk, (*s.*) fire, live embers.
Thu-khat vua-in, (*adv.*) unanimously, with one mind, with one desire.
Thu-khat vua*k* (or vaw), (*v.*) to be unanimous or of one mind.

Thu-khawh-châng shoi, (*v.*) to converse, to gossip, (*s.*) gossip talk.

Thu*k*-ru*k*, (*v.*) to conceal, to hide.

Thuk-thai, (*s.*) fireirons (poker, shovel, etc.)

Thûl, (*s.*) the name of a large basket with a cover.

Ṭhulh, (*v.*) to not do a thing, to leave undone, to omit to, to be prevented.

Ṭhulh-tîr, (*v.*) to prevent, to cause or tell not to do, say, etc.

Ṭhûm, (*v.*) to scoop up with both hands, (*s.*) a double handful.

Ṫhûm, (*a.*) deep, gruff, (*v.*) to be deep, etc.

Thum, (*a.*) three.

Ṭhu-mi, (*s.*) a kind of pigeon.

Ṭhum vawr, (*v.*) to augur, to cast lots.

Ṭhum-vawr thiam, (*s.*) an augur, one skilled in augury.

Ṫhun, (*v.*) to put in (to anything long and narrow as bottle, etc.) to load (as gun).

Thu nei, (*v.*) to receive authority.

Thu-nei-a shiam, (*v.*) to give authority to.

Thu nei pê*k*, (*v.*) to give authority.

Thu-nei-tu, (*s.*) one in authority.

Thu-nei-tu ang-in, (*adv.*) authoritatively.

Thung, (*adv.*) now, after this, an affix with the idea of taking one's turn.

Thu-nun, (*v.*) to bring into subjection, to cause to obey, to break in, to train.

Thup, (*v.*) to conceal, to hide.

Thu-pê*k*, (*v.*) to command, to give permission.

Thu-pha choi, (*v.*) to apologise, to confess, to capitulate.

Thu-phiar, (*v.*) to plot, to conspire, to plan, (*s.*) a plot, a conspiracy, a plan.

Thu-poi, (*s.*) a complaint, a judicial case.

Thu*p*-ruk, (*v.*) to conceal, to hide.

Thu-pui, (*a.*) important.

Thûr, (*a.*) acid, sour, (*v.*) to be acid, etc.

Thur, (*a.*) rough (as hair), (*v.*) to be rough.

Thu ral-kah, (*s.*) an irrelevant speech.

Thu rem-tu, (*s.*) a judge, a magistrate, an arbitrator.

Thu rîl, (*s.*) a mystery, a deep saying.

Ṭhu-ro, (*s.*) a dove.

Ṫhûr-pui, (*s.*) the name of a creeper with an acid fruit.

Thûr-shiak, (*s.*) wood-sorrel.

Thu-rual, (*v.*) to be unanimous or of one mind.

Thu-rual-in, (*adv.*) unanimously, with one mind or desire.

Thu-ruk, (*s.*) a secret.

Thu-rum, (*a.*) foolhardy, reckless, fearless, daring, (*v.*) to be foolhardy, etc.
Thut, (*adv.*) suddenly.
Ṭhu*t*, (*v.*) to sit, to sit down, to succeed to a chieftainship.
Ṭhu*t* chhuak, (*v.*) to sit up, to sit upright.
Thu-thang, (*s.*) a report, a rumour, (*v.*) to get reported or rumoured.
Thu-thlun*g*, (*v.*) to make a covenant, agreement, or contract, (*s.*) an agreement, a covenant, a contract.
Thu-thu, (*s.*) command, pleasure, wish.
Thu-thu-in om, (*v.*) to be subject to, to obey.
Thu thiam, (*v.*) to command, to order, to threaten, to promise, (*s.*) a command, etc.
Thu ti-tlu, (*v.*) to give a verdict, to pass sentence, to wind up a case, to settle a case.
Ṭhut-na, (*s.*) a seat, a stool, a chair.
Ṭhu*t*-ngîl, (*v.*) to sit up, to sit upright.
Ṭhut-phah, (*s.*) a seat, a stool, a chair.
Ṭhu*t*-sop, (*v.*) to sit right down.
Ṭhut-thlêng, (*s.*) a seat, a stool, a chair.
Ṭhu*t*-tung, (*v.*) to sit on the haunches.
Thu vei vir, (*v.*) to misrepresent (so as to stir up strife).
Thu zêp, (*s.*) a secret.
Ti, (*v.*) to do, to say, to act towards.
Ti, (*prefix*) used to make intransitive verbs transitive, to cause to be.
Ṭi, (*v.*) to fear, to be nervous, to be timid, (*a.*) nervous, timid.
Ṭi, (*s.*) muscle, flesh, lean, substance, form, complexion.
Tia, as, like, as much as, same size as.
Tiak, (*v.*) to come to an end, to finish.
Ṭiak, (*s.*) a sprout, (*v.*) to sprout.
Ṭial, (*s.*) the thread of a screw, a screw.
Ṭial, (*a.*) spotted, striped, of various colours, tattooed, (*v.*) to be spotted, etc., (*s.*) spots, stripes, markings, tattoo.
Tiam, (*v.*) to promise, to threaten, to command, to appoint (a day etc.), to allow, to be ready, to be willing.
Tiang, (*s.*) a stick, a staff.
Tian*g*, (*v.*) to pile up, to put one on top of another, (*adv.*) one on top of another.
Tian' hrâng thlân, (*s.*) a Poi grave, a vault.
Ṭiao, (*s.*) sandy shingle.
Ṭiao, (*v.*) to disperse.
Ṭiao-chhum, (*s.*) morning mist.
Ṭiao-lung, (*s.*) shingle.

Ṭiao-mi, (*s.*) the name of a beetle which is said to produce madness if eaten.
Ṭiao-pho, (*s.*) a beach, a shingly beach, a sandbank.
Ṭiao-vai-vut, } (*s.*) sand.
Ṭiao-vut, }
Ṭiar, (*s.*) the name of a tree.
Tia-ve, (*a.*) half (lengthwise).
Ti a za, (*v.*) to feel creepy.
Ti-awn, (*v. t.*) to slant.
Ti-bal, (*v. t.*) to chip.
Ti-bâl, (*v.*) to make dirty.
Ti-bâng, (*v. t.*) to staunch, to stop.
Ti-bet, (*v.*) to hold down, to keep down.
Ti-bo-ral, (*v. t.*) to ruin, to lose.
Ti bua, (*v. t.*) to spill, to upset.
Ti-buai, (*v. t.*) to worry, to disturb, to set in an uproar.
Ti-bum, (*v. t.*) to swindle, to deceive.
Ti-chhe, } (*v. t.*) to destroy, to damage, to spoil, to degrade.
Ti-chhiat, }
Ti-chi-mit, (*v. t.*) to exterminate, to extinguish.
Ti-chhuak, (*v. t.*) to put out, to eject, to originate, to bring to light, to bring out, to institute.
Ti-chhuak-tu, (*s.*) one who brings out or puts out, a founder, an originator, a composer, an institutor.
Ti-dam, (*v.*) to make well, to save.
Ti-dang, (*v.*) to make speechless, to refute, to confute.
Ti-dang-lam, (*v. t.*) to alter.
Ti-dap, (*v. t.*) to bevel.
Ti-dawng, (*v.*) to take in, to swindle, to deceive, to deprive.
Ti-der, (*v.*) to pretend, to deceive, to do out of a thing.
Ti-dîm-dêm, (*a.*) fussy, particular, (*v.*) to be fussy, etc.
Ti-dip, (*v.*) to make into fine powder.
Ti-duh-dah, (*v.*) to oppress, to ill-use, to persecute, to do anything carelessly or lazily, to be idle.
Ti-dul, (*v. t.*) to shut (as umbrella), to slacken, to loosen.
Ti-el, (*v.*) to ridicule, to scoff, to speak sarcastically.
Ṭih, the same as '*ṭi*.'
Tih, (*conj.*) that, also a particle used with the interrogative pronoun to give it the force of a relative.
Ti-hah, (*v. t.*) to fatigue.
Ti-harh, (*v. t.*) to revive, to strengthen, to refresh, to cheer up, to wake up, to enlighten.
Ti-hêk, (*v. t.*) to chip.
Ti-hek, (*v. t.*) to use up, to consume, to waste, to eat a lot of.

Ti-hel-leh, (*v.*) to cause to revolt after being subjugated.
Ti-him, (*v.*) to preserve from harm.
Ti-hlum, (*v.*) to kill, to extinguish.
Ti-hmin, (*v. t.*) to cook, to ripen, to bring into subjection.
Ti-hmu, (*v.*) to set an example.
Ti-hniam, (*v.*) to lower.
Tih-oih, (*a.*) obedient, (*v.*) to be obedient.
Ti-hril-hai, (*v.*) to confound, to put to shame.
Tik-a, (*adv.*) when.
Ti-kâng, (*v. t.*) to raise.
Ti-keh, (*v. t.*) to break.
Ti-khat, (*v. t.*) to fill.
Ti-khaw-lo, (*v. t.*) to spoil, to pervert.
Ti-khaw-tlai, (*v.*) to waste time.
Ti-kher kher, (*a.*) particular, fussy, (*v.*) to be particular, etc.
Ti-khok, (*v. t.*) to graze, to scrape up skin or bark.
Ti-khol-kham, (*v. t.*) to hinder, to prevent.
Ti-khong-khaw-bai, (*v.*) to hop on one leg.
Ti-kiam, (*v. t.*) to lessen, to reduce.
Ti-ki-li, (*s.*) an ordinary muzzle-loading gun with percussion cap.
Ti-kin, (*v. t.*) to bring to a close, to finish.
Ti-koi, (*v. t.*) to bend.
Tik-tik, (*s.*) the name of a bird.
Tîl, (*v.*) to fall off (as leaves, hair, etc.).
Tîl, (*v. t.*) to roll about (as the tongue).
Til, (*s.*) testicle, the testicles and scrotum.
Ti-lam-dang, (*v. t.*) to alter.
Ti-let, (*v. t.*) to turn round, to turn over or upside down.
Ti-lian, (*v.*) to magnify.
Til lâk, (*v.*) to castrate.
Til-mu, (*s.*) a testicle.
Til rek, (*v.*) to castrate.
Til-rîl, (*s.*) a male born with but one or no testicles.
Ti-lui, (*v.*) to insist upon doing or saying.
Ti-lung-ni-lo, (*v. t.*) to displease, to offend.
Tîm, (*v.*) to be careful, to be wary, to beware, to be cautious, to shrink from, (*a.*) careful, wary, cautious, etc.
Ti-mang, (*v. t.*) to exterminate.
Ti-mang-ang, (*v. t.*) to amaze, to worry, to put in a fix.
Ti-mawh, (*a.*) self-willed, stubborn, obstinate, disobedient, (*v.*) to be self-willed, etc.
Ti-mit, (*v.*) to extinguish.
Ti-mual-pho, (*v. t.*) to put to shame.
Ti-mûk, (*v. t.*) to press closely together.

Tin, (*v.*) to try.
Tin, (*v.*) to threaten, by gesture.
Tin, (*a.*) every.
Tin, (*s.*) a nail, a claw, a talon, a hoof.
Tin, then, and so. (Used to introduce a sentence.)
Ṭîn, (*v.*) to disperse, to break up.
Ti-nâ, (*v. t.*) to hurt.
Ti-na, (*s.*) meaning.
Tin ai-choi, (*s.*) the claw on the under toe of a tiger or other animal.
Ti-na-zia, (*s.*) meaning.
Tîng, (*a.*) springy, (*v.*) to be springy.
Ṭing, (*s.*) the hill or Assam indigo (*Strobilanthes flaccidifolius*) yarn dyed blue.
Ting, (*v.*) to make as if, to pretend.
Ṭing dum, (*s.*) blue yarn, (*v.*) to dye blue.
Ti-nghor, (*v.*) to cause to shake.
Ti-ngîl, (*v. t.*) to straighten.
Ti-ngoi, (*v. t.*) to quiet.
Ṭing-shen, (*s.*) red yarn.
Ṭing-ṭang, (*s.*) the one-stringed Lushai fiddle, a fiddle.
Tin-hna, (*s.*) the quick of the nail.
Tin-hna ai-hni, (*v.*) to have a hangnail, (*s.*) a hangnail.
Tin-kim-dawn, (*v.*) to consider a subject in all its bearings beforehand.
Ti-noi, (*v.*) to pulverize, to make into small pieces.
Tin-reng, (*a.*) all sorts of, all kinds of.
Ṭîn-ṭîr, (*v.*) to dismiss, to cause to break up.
Ti-nuam, (*a.*) obedient, (*v.*) to be obedient.
Ti-nung, (*v.*) to save, to make well, to bring to life, to bring round after chloroform, to keep or make alive.
Ti-parh, (*v. t.*) to spread out (as cloth, hands, tail, etc.)
Ti-pawm, (*v. t.*) to mix.
Ti-peh, (*v. t.*) to break (as the lobe of the ear), to split the edge, to pull a piece off the edge of any soft material (as book, cloth, etc.), it corresponds to 'chip' in hard materials.
Ti-pelh-solh, (*v. t.*) to dislocate.
Ti-pem, (*v. t.*) to wound.
Ti-pheng, } (*v.*) to entangle.
Ti-phiar, }
Ti-phu-zok, (*v. t.*) to surprise, to startle.
Ti-poi, (*v. t.*) to mar, to spoil.
Ti-polh, (*v. t.*) to mix.
Ti-puang, (*v. t.*) to spread abroad.

Tîr, (*v.*) to cause, to send, to permit, to ask to do, to bid, to commission, to enable.
Tir-chhiah, (*v.*) to order about, (*s.*) a drudge.
Ti-reh, (*v. t.*) to staunch, to stop, to quiet.
Tirh-nuam, Tirh-oih, } (*a.*) obedient, (*v.*) to be obedient.
Tîr-in, (*adv.*) at first, first of all, at the beginning.
Tir-ko, (*s.*) a messenger.
Ti-ro-pui, (*v.*) to glorify.
Ti-rûi, (*v. t.*) to intoxicate.
Ti-sha, (*s.*) flesh.
Ti-shi-she, (*a.*) particular, fussy, (*v.*) to be particular, etc.
Ti-sil, (*v.*) to maim, to injure, to wound, to disable.
Ti-som, (*v. t.*) to make into pieces.
Tît, (*s.*) a centipede.
Ti-tak-a, Ti-tak-in, } (*adv.*) exactly, truly.
Ti-tao, (*v.*) to throw about in anger, to do anything in a tantrum.
Ṭît-êk, (*a.*) flyblown, (*v.*) to be flyblown.
Ti-ṭhaih, (*v. t.*) to frighten, to startle.
Ti-thi, (*v. t.*) to kill, to extinguish.
Ti-thiam, (*v.*) to count, reckon or pronounce just or right.
Ti-thi-tling, (*v. t.*) to bruise.
Ti-thlêr, (*v. t.*) to split, to rip up.
Ti-thlû*k*, (*v. t.*) to knock over, to push over, to knock down.
Ti-ti, (*s.*) history, news.
Ti-tlai, (*v.*) to treat, to stand treat.
Ti-tlat, (*v.*) to say emphatically, to charge strictly.
Ti-tlawm, (*v. t.*) to put out of power, to depose, to abase.
Ti-tliak, (*v. t.*) to snap, to break.
Ti-tlolh, (*v. t.*) to prevent.
Ti-tlu, (*v.*) to settle.
Ti-tui, (*v. t.*) to melt.
Ti-ul, (*v. t.*) to scorch slightly.
Ṭi-ûp, (*v. t.*) to shelter from the wind.
Ti-ût, (*v. t.*) to scorch much, to burn.
Tï-vui, (*v. t.*) to offend, to insult, to hurt one's feelings.
Ti-vûm, (*v. t.*) to pile up (as when measuring grain, etc.).
Ti-za, (*v. t.*) to tickle.
Ti-zak, (*v. t.*) to put to shame.
Ti-zâm, (*v. t.*) to frighten, to make afraid.
Ti-zia, (*a.*) opportune, good, just what is wanted.
Ti-ziao, (*v. t.*) to set on edge (teeth).
Ti-zuam, (*v. t.*) to assure, to give confidence.

Tla, (*v.*) to make answer the purpose, to make shift with, to make suffice.

Tla, (*v.*) to graze, to pasture, to search for food.

Tla, (*v.*) to be, to exist (similar to *om*).

Tla, (*v.*) see *tlâk.*

Tla-bung, (*s.*) Demagree.

Tla-chham, (*v.*) to run out of anything, to lack.

Tla-holh, (*v.*) to put the foot through, to fall through.

Tlai, (*s.*) a score, a standard of reckoning equal to twenty rupees.

Tlai, (*v.*) to be late, (*adv.*) late.

Tlai, (*v.*) to be fully satisfied (with food), to be full.

Tlai-berh, (*s.*) the bulbul.

Tlai-lam, (*s.*) the afternoon, the evening.

Tlai-vâr, (*v.*) to remain awake all night.

Tlak, (*s.*) chalk.

Tlak, (*v.*) to boil or cook without salt.

Tlak, (*v.*) to make a clicking noise.

Tlâ*k*, (*v.*) to fall from a height, to set (as sun, etc.), to be born prematurely, to complete (as one's time for working), to finish paying a debt.

Tlâk, (*v.*) to be worthy, fit, proper.

Tlâk-dêng, (*v.*) to face west and get the full rays of the setting sun.

Tlâk-lam, (*s.*) the side of anything facing the west.

Tlâk-tlai, (*a.*) useful, beneficial, serviceable, (*v.*) to be useful, etc.

Tlâk-tlum-tîr, (*v.*) to receive with approbation, to like.

Tla-lam, (*v.*) to make suffice, to make answer the purpose, to make shift with.

Tlâm-êm, (*s.*) the name of a basket.

Tlân, (*v.*) to run, to take shelter, to eat or drink anything, to be in the habit of eating or drinking anything.

Tlan, (*v.*) to ransom.

Tlân-bo, (*v.*) to run away, to escape.

Tlân-chhua*k*, (*v.*) to run out, to escape.

Tlang, (*adv.*) through.

Tlang, (*s.*) a lump of anything.

Tlâng, (*adv.*) unanimously, all together, with one consent, it has also the same meaning as *hlom.*

Tlâng, (*s.*) a mountain, a hill.

Tlâng, (*s.*) border, tip, edge, brim, mouth (of pot, etc.)

Tlâng, (*s.*) the public, the people.

Tlang, (*adv.*) without violence, peaceably, quietly, willingly, in a straightforward manner, without gainsaying.

Tlâng-ao, (*v.*) to herald, to proclaim, (*s.*) a village crier whose duty it is to make known the orders of the chief.
Tlâng-chîl, (*v.*) to administer punishment in which the whole village joins, to punish or attack in a body.
Tlâng-dung, (*s.*) a range of hills.
Tlâng-hriam, (*s.*) a mountain range without level ground at the top.
Tlâng in-khan-na, (*s.*) the place where two ranges join.
Tlâng-nêl, (*a.*) cheeky, brazen-faced, bold, forward, not shy or bashful, free and easy, (*v.*) to be cheeky, etc.
Tlâng-pui-dung, (*s.*) a large range of hills.
Tlâng thu, (*s.*) public opinion, the word of the people.
Tlâng-tlir, (*v.*) to fire a volley near a village when returning from hunting.
Tlang-vâl, (*s.*) a young man.
Tlâng-zawl, (*s.*) a plateau.
Tlar, (*adv.*) in a row, (*s.*) a row.
Tla-sual, (*v.*) to be born prematurely.
Tlat, (*adv.*) fast, firmly, emphatically.
Tla'-tlum, (*v.*) to be received with approbation, to be liked.
Tlaw, (*s.*) a skeleton, bones, a dead body lying unburied in the jungle or in the open.
Tlawh, (*v.*) to visit, to call upon.
Tlawh, (*v.*) to kick (with the bottom of the foot).
Tlawh-bet, (*v. t.*) to trample upon, to oppress, to hold in bondage, to look down upon, to despise.
Tlawh-chhan, (*s.*) a support for the feet used when weaving, a footstool, (*v.*) to rest the feet upon.
Tlawm, (*v.*) to lose prestige, to be deposed, to lose power, to be beaten, to fall from power, to be abased, to beat or excel one who is superior.
Tlawm-ngai, (*v.*) to persevere, to endure patiently.
Tlawm-ngai tak-in, (*adv.*) perseveringly, patiently.
Tlawn, (*a.*) straight and long, (*s.*) a bar.
Tlawn-tlai, (*s.*) shape, form, figure (of a living creature).
Tle, (*a.*) polished.
Tleh, (*v.*) to blow (as the wind).
Tlei, (*a.*) good (used of a baby that does not cry), (*v.*) to be good (as a baby).
Tlei-rawl, (*v.*) to attain to the time of life between childhood and puberty, (used also of animals and birds), (*s.*) one who has attained the above age.
Tlei-tla, (*v.*) to complete, to finish, to accomplish, to be completed, finished or accomplished.
Tlêm, (*a.*) little, few.

Tlêm-tê, (*adv.*) little (quantity), few.
Tlêm tlêm-in, (*adv.*) gradually, little by little.
Tleng, (*v.*) to slide.
Tleng, (*s.*) the large bamboo on a noose trap which slips down over the animal's leg and prevents it from gnawing itself free.
Tlêng, (*v.*) to clean by pouring water over.
Tleng-tle, (*s.*) the name of an iridescent beetle.
Tleo, (*v.*) to slip.
Tliak, (*v.*) to be snapped, to be broken, (*a.*) broken.
Tliang, (*a.*) polished, glossy, to be polished, etc.
Tling, (*v.*) to collect (as water in a pool), to accumulate.
Tling, (*v.*) to reach, to reach to, to amount to.
Tling-tlâk, (*v.*) to complete, finish or accomplish, to be completed, finished or accomplished.
Tlip,
Tlip-phar, } (*s.*) the names of species of stinging horse-flies.
Tlo, (*a.*) durable, strong, (*v.*) to be durable, to be strong, to be a long time (in doing, etc.)
Tlok-tlaw, (*a.*) dull of intellect, unable to acquire knowledge, inexpert, (*v.*) to be dull, etc.
Tlolh, (*v.*) to miss fire (as a gun), to be prevented, to omit to, to not do,—see *thulh.*
Tlon, (*v.*) to be on good terms with, to be friendly with.
Tlong, (*s.*) the Delaswari river.
Tlong-dawr, (*s.*) Changsil.
Tlor, (*a.*) greasy, glossy, sleek, (*v.*) to be greasy, etc.
Tlorh, the same as *tlor.*
Tlu, (*v.*) to fall down (not from a height), to be settled.
Tluan, (*s.*) a complete length, a whole length or row.
Tluang-hrui, (*s.*) an endless band.
Tluang-rel, (*s.*) bamboos going crosswise under the floor in a Lushai house, immediately above the *kaldung.*
Tluan-thîr, (*s.*) the name of a species of edible arum.
Tluk, (*v.*) to equal.
Tlum, (*v.*) to draw in (the head, etc.), to go in, to sink in.
Tlum-pui, (*s.*) the large civet cat (*Viverra migaspila*).
Tlum-therh, (*s.*) the lesser civet cat (*Viverra malaccensis*).
Tlun, (*v.*) to have ague.
Tlûng, (*s.*) a ridge pole.
Tlung-pi, (*s.*) a white-ant (wingless).
To, (*a.*) expensive, dear, (*v.*) to be expensive.
Ṭo, (*v.*) to grow, to shoot up.
Tôh-lawt, (*s.*) a rocky excrescence on the side of a mountain, (*a.*) projecting, (*v.*) to be projecting, to project.

Toi, (*a.*) short, (*v.*) to be short.
Ṭoi, (*a.*) symmetrical and having many branches, (as horns, trees, etc.)
Ṭoih, (*a.*) rotten, decomposed, putrid, (*v.*) to rot, etc.
Toi-taw, (*s.*) the hogplum (*spondia mangifera*).
Toi-taw zâm, (*s.*) the name of creeper, the bruised shoots, leaves, etc., of which are used as a poultice for tiger bites and sores.
Ṭok, (*a.*) blebby, red and spotted (as the nose), (*v.*) to be blebby, etc.
Ṭok, (*a.*) sour, (*v.*) to be sour.
Tok-tarh, (*s.*) a bait, (*v.*) to bait.
Tol, (*v.*) to move along.
Tol-lôh, (*s.*) the name of a young woman's cloth.
To-lo, (*a.*) cheap, (*v.*) to be cheap.
Tom, (*v.*) to crouch, to be rucked up, to be crumpled, to be drawn together, to be contracted, to be shrunken, to ruck up, to crumple, etc., to bend (as the finger, arm or leg).
Ṭom, (*a.*) untidy, dirty, littered, (*v.*) to be untidy, etc., (*s.*) litter, rubbish, the withered leaves of such plants as sugarcane, rice etc.
Tom-im, (*v.*) to crouch, to cringe, to keep out of one's way (for shame, etc.)
Ton, (*v.*) to wear (in the hair).
Tong, (*v.*) to meet, to come across, to arrive.
Tong, (*v.*) to knock against, to collide with, to knock the top of the head against.
Tong, (*s.*) a cubit, (*v.*) to measure by cubits.
Ṭong, (*v.*) to speak, to talk, (*s.*) language, speech.
Ṭong-â, (*v.*) to talk in sleep or in delirium.
Ṭong-chhilh, (*v.*) to interrupt by speaking, to drown another's voice by speaking.
Ṭong-ka, } (*s.*) disposition, mode of speech.
Ṭong-kam, }
Tong-khong, (*v.*) to be cramped for room.
Ṭong-ṭai, (*v.*) to make supplication for, to pray to God.
Ṭong-ṭha-in thlah, (*v.*) to bid farewell, to wish God-speed.
Ṭong-thei, (*s.*) a fluent person, a chatterbox, (*a.*) fluent, etc., (*v.*) to be fluent, etc.
Ṭong-tla-holh, (*v.*) to speak unadvisedly, to speak boastfully.
Tong-tong-in. (*adv.*) for no purpose, cause or reason.
Ṭong-vai, (*v.*) to talk in sleep or in delirium.
Ton-taw-thleng, (*v.*) to have a very abundant harvest.
Ton'-tîr, (*a.*) first, first reached or met with, nearest.

Top lo, (*adv.*) under no circumstance, not at all, in no wise, not in the least.
To-ruah, (*s.*) storms preceding the rainy season.
Tu, (*s.*) a grandchild, a sister's child, a husband's sister's child, a paternal aunt's child.
Tu, (*pro.*) who?
Tuah, (*v.*) to tend a fire, to put wood on a fire.
Tuai, (*v.*) to temper (as steel).
Tuai, (*a.*) of medium growth, not full grown.
Tuai, (*s.*) a man who dresses and acts like a woman.
Tuai-bûr, (*s.*) a species of hart's tongue fern.
Tuai-ha-bet, (*s.*) the name of a tree with edible fruit.
Tuai-om, (*v.*) to be tempered (as steel).
Tuai-ram, (*s.*) the name of a tree with edible fruit.
Tuai-thlêng, (*s.*) the name of a tree.
Tuak, (*v.*) to save up, to accumulate.
Tuak, (*s.*) a pair, a couple, (*a.*) both.
Ṭuak, (*a.*) gray, white (as hair), (*v.*) to be or become gray or white.
Tuak-khawm, (*v.*) to save up, to accumulate.
Tual, (*s.*) a fellow villager, a friend (not a foe), (*a.*) belonging to the village, native.
Tual-chai, (*v.*) to gambol, to skip.
Tual Poi, (*s.*) a Poi who lives among the Lushais.
Tual-shiam, (*a.*) country-made (not imported).
Tual-sum-su, (*s.*) a ghost which hops about on its head with its feet in the air.
Tual-tha*t*, (*v.*) to murder.
Tuam, (*v.*) to bandage, to wrap round, to brood over (as a fowl).
Tuam-na, (*s.*) a bandage.
Ṭuan-fûm, (*a.*) slow (at work, etc.), (*v.*) to be slow.
Ṭuan-rang, (*a.*) quick (at work, etc.), (*v.*) to be quick.
Ṭuar, (*v.*) to endure.
Tuar-zia a om, (*v.*) to be tolerable, to be bearable.
Tu-bâl, (*s.*) the name of a species of arum.
Tu-baoh, } (*s.*) a hammer.
Tu-bôh, }
Tu-e-maw, (*pro.*) someone, a certain man, (*a.*) certain.
Tu-e-maw tal, (*pro.*) anyone, someone.
Tu-e-maw zong, (*pro.*) someone.
Tu-fâr, (*s.*) the name of a tree.
Tuh, (*v.*) to plant (seed).
Tuh-dâl, (*s.*) a large hoe, a kodali.
Tuh-thlawh, (*s.*) a small hoe.

Tuh-thlawh-ha-zawn, (*s.*) a measure, a conical heap of rice, etc., the apex of which will be level with the end of a *ṭuhthlawh* held high above the head of an ordinary-sized man.
Tuh-ṭhulh, (*s.*) a spud.
Tui, (*s.*) water, juice, an egg, (*v.*) to melt, to lay an egg.
Tui, (*a.*) nice (to taste or smell), fit, worthy, (*v.*) to be nice, etc.
Tui-alh, (*s.*) kerosine or any other mineral oil.
Tui-a tla-hlum, (*v.*) to drown.
Tui-bûr, (*s.*) nicotine water.
Tui-bûr hmuam da, (*s.*) about half an hour, that is, the time a Lushai can keep a sip of nicotine water in his mouth.
Tui-bûr-lai, (*s.*) a woman's pipe.
Tui-chhe-in, an expression used when swearing by the water spirits.
Tui-chhuar, (*s.*) a kind of seat on the verandah of a Lushai house.
Tui-chhun-chhuah, (*s.*) a well.
Tui choi, (*v.*) to draw water.
Tui-choi-kawng, (*s.*) the name of a basket.
Tui-choi-tu, (*s.*) a water carrier.
Tui-don, (*s.*) an aqueduct.
Tui dung chhir, (*v.*) to walk water.
Tui-êk, (*a.*) rusty, (*v.*) to be rusty, (*s.*) rust.
Tui-fawn, (*s.*) a wave.
Tui-fin-rist, (*s.*) the sea.
Tui-hâl, (*a.*) thirsty, (*v.*) to thirst.
Tui-hawk, (*s.*) rainwater either running or standing in puddles, a puddle.
Tui-hawk-tling, (*s.*) a puddle.
Tui-hawr, (*s.*) a gutter, a ditch.
Tui-hleoh, (*v.*) to swim.
Tui-hlim, (*a.*) new laid (as egg), (*v.*) to be fresh laid.
Tui-hnah, (*s.*) water plants.
Tui-hnai, (*a.*) tempting (to eat).
Tui-hna-paih-na, (*s.*) the name of a kind of fishing weir.
Tui-hna-shiam-tu, (*s.*) a water spider.
Tui-hnoih-lo puan, (*s.*) the name of a cloth.
Tui-hri, (*s.*) cholera.
Tui-hu, (*s.*) steam.
Tui-khawh-thla, (*s.*) a waterfall.
Tui-khuang bêng, (*v.*) to make a booming sound in water with the hands.
Tui-khua*p*, (*s.*) a dam, (*v.*) to dam up water.
Tui-khur, (*s.*) a well, a waterhole.

Tui-kuk, (*s.*) the Tipperah tribe.
Tui-kun-luk, (*s.*) a cocoanut, a hookah.
Tui lai râp ang-in om, (*v.*) to be in suspense, to be in a fix.
Tui lai râp ang-in om tîr, } (*v.*) to hold or keep in suspense,
Tui lai râp ang-in shiam, } to put in a fix.
Tui leih, (*v.*) to water (as flowers, etc.), to pour out water.
Tui lêt, (*s.*) a flood, (*v.*) to be a flood.
Tui-lo, (*a.*) nasty (to the taste or smell), unfit, unworthy, (*v.*) to be nasty, etc.
Tui-pui, (*s.*) a large expanse of water, the sea.
Tui-pui sa-tang, (*s.*) a water newt.
Tui-pui shul-hlah, } (*s.*) a species of willow.
Tui-pui shut-hlah, }
Tui-pui tang-kawng, (*s.*) a water newt.
Tui-pum, (*v.*) to be swollen out (as an ear of rice).
Tui-rial, (*s.*) the Sonai river.
Tui-ruang, (*s.*) the Barak river.
Tui-sa-tel, (*s.*) the name of a water turtle.
Tui-sha-in leih, (*v.*) to scald.
Tui-shuk, (*s.*) cholera.
Tui-tai, (*s.*) a stream which dries up in the dry season, a rain torrent.
Tui-thawl, (*s.*) a water bottle or flask.
Tui-the, (*s.*) the name of a dragon fly.
Tui-thlâr, (*v.*) to outcast, to cast off (a relative, etc.), (*s.*) a water-fall.
Tui-tla, (*v.*) to be received with approbation, to be liked.
Tui-tlân, (*s.*) a water supply.
Tui-tla lo, (*v.*) to be disliked.
Tui-va-long, (*s.*) the name of several species of water birds.
Tui-va-rak, (*s.*) a wild duck.
Tui zang, (*s.*) the current of a river.
Tui-zawn, (*s.*) an aqueduct.
Tui-zu, (*s.*) a water rat, the flesh of which is eaten by the Lushais as a remedy in cholera.
Tu*k*, (*v.*) to make or cut anything out of wood, to cut (a bee's nest) out of a tree, to cut or chop (bough, etc.) off a tree.
Tuk, (*v.*) to command, to promise, to order, to ask a larger price.
Tuk, (*s.*) a knot of hair on the nape of the neck.
Ṭuk, (*v.*) to cluck.
Ṭuk-buk, (*s.*) a temporary hut or enclosure made of boughs of trees, etc., bamboos sprouting up from the roots.
Tuk-chîk, (*s.*) a small knot of hair.
Tuk-chorh, (*s.*) the sprouting stump of a felled tree.

Tu-ki-li, (*s.*) an ordinary muzzle-loading gun, used with a percussion cap.
Tûk-in-a, this morning.
Tuk-khum, (*s.*) the back of the head, the nape of the neck.
Tuk-khum-khur, (*s.*) the nape of the neck.
Tuk-lo, (*s.*) the name of a species of woodpecker.
Tuk-rop, (*s.*) large bamboos notched and bent over the ridgepole to support the thatch.
Tuk-ṭhuan, (*s.*) the morning meal, breakfast.
Tuk-tin, every morning.
Tu-ku-li, (*s.*) see *tukili.*
Tuk-verh, (*s.*) a window.
Ṭûl, (*v.*) to be high time, to be busy, to have on hand, to have a lot of work to do, to have need of, to need.
Ṭûl, (*a.*) rank, jungly, covered with weeds, (*v.*) to be rank, etc., to be old before getting married.
Tûl, (*s.*) a skewer, a kind of two-pronged fork.
Tu-lûm, (*s.*) the name of an evil spirit said sometimes to take possession of a dead body and cause it to speak.
Tu-lung, (*s.*) a rammer.
Tûl-zum, (*v.*) to be ready to burst (as a rice bud, etc.)
Tum, (*v.*) to wish, to want, to intend, to attempt, to try, to purpose, to be about to.
Tum, (*v.*) to play (a musical instrument).
Tum, (*v.*) to do, to do as one's special work, (*s.*) work, special or allotted work or task.
Ṭum, (*v.*) to jump with both feet together.
Ṫûm, (*v.*) to sulk, to be sulky, to pout, to look cross.
Tûm, (*s.*) the sago palm.
Tu-ma, } (*pro.*) no one.
Tu-ma...lo, }
Tum-bu, (*s.*) the plantain flower in bud (edible).
Tum-bung, (*s.*) half.
Tum-chhang, (*s.*) a sago cake.
Tum-fung, (*s.*) the bow of a fiddle, a drum stick, striker of a gong.
Tum-hrâm, } (*v.*) to strive, to try hard, to be determined, to be resolved.
Tum lui hrâm, }
Tum-pang, (*s.*) a wild *gayal.*
Tum-ruh, } (*v.*) to be determined, to be resolved.
Tum-sa-ruh, }
Tum-thang, (*s.*) the name of a plant with edible leaves and blossoms.
Ṭum-ṭhe, (*s.*) a sour drink made from the *fangra* bean.
Ṭum-tla, (*v.*) to complete, to accomplish, to finish, to conclude.

Tum-tlat, (*v.*) to be determined.
Tûn-a, (*adv.*) now, by now.
Tûn-a chin-a, (*adv.*) henceforth.
Tûn-a hian, (*adv.*) now.
Tûna-pang-in, (*adv.*) now already, now at once.
Tûna-pawh, } (*adv.*) still, even now, yet.
Tûna-pôh, }
Tûna-tei, (*adv.*) now at this moment.
Tûna-zong, (*adv.*) now by this time.
Tûn-chin-a, (*adv.*) henceforth.
Tung, (*v.*) to prick up (as ears), to stand on end or upright.
Tung-chaw, (*s.*) a Lushai bedpost.
Tung-chaw-kua, (*s.*) a hole made in a Lushai bedpost to serve as a receptacle for small articles.
Tu-nge, (*pro.*) who? whom? to whom? whose?
Tung-thawh, } (*v.*) to raise to a sitting posture.
Tung-tho, }
Tûn-hnu-a, (*adv.*) hereafter.
Tûn-lai, (*adv.*) nowadays, now.
Tûn lai ṭhang-thar, (*s.*) the present generation.
Tûn-la-la-a, } (*adv.*) now at this moment, now (emphatic).
Tûn-law-law-a, }
Tûn-pang-a, (*adv.*) now already, now at once.
Tûn-thla, this month.
Tûn-thleng-in, (*adv.*) yet, up to the present time, hitherto.
Tûn-thleng-pawh-in, } (*adv.*) still, even now, yet.
Tûn-thleng-pôh-in, }
Tu-nu, (*s.*) a granddaughter, a sister's daughter, a husband's sister's daughter, a paternal aunt's daughter.
Tu-pa, (*s.*) a grandson, a sister's son, a husband's sister's son, a paternal aunt's son.
Tu-pa-an ṭang, (*v.*) to take the lead, to take the most prominent part, to set an example.
Tu-pa-ber, (*s.*) a ringleader.
Tu-pa-rong, (*s.*) an iron spud made with a place to receive a wooden handle.
Tu-pawh, (*pro.*) anyone.
Tu-pawh a-piang, (*pro.*) whoever.
Tu-pôh, (*pro.*) the same as *tupawh.*
Tûr, (*s.*) poison.
Tûr, (*a.*) strong, pungent smelling (as spirits, etc.)
Tûr, a verbal affix.
Tûr a-ṭha, (*a.*) very poisonous (as snake, nettle, etc.), (*v.*) to be very poisonous.

Tûr nei, (*a.*) poisonous, (*v.*) to be poisonous.
Tûr-shing, (*s.*) the name of a species of bamboo used for making the bowls of men's pipes.
Tut, (*s.*) the Gutur river.
Tu-tal, (*pro.*) anyone.
Tu-tal-e-maw, (*pro.*) someone, anyone.
Tu-ta-nge, (*pro.*) whose?
Tu-te-e-maw, certain persons, certain.

U

U, (*s.*) an elder brother or sister, a husband's elder brother or sister, an elder brother's wife, a paternal uncle's elder child, a maternal aunt's elder child.
U, (*v.*) to whine (as a dog).
Uai, (*v.*) to swing.
Uai, (*a.*) withered, wilted, (*v.*) to wither, to wilt.
Uai-tlia*k*, (*v.*) to break off through having too great a weight upon it (as bough, peg, etc.)
Uak, (*v.*) to retch.
Uâng, (*v.*) to boast.
Uap, (*v.*) to make feel hot or depressed, to be sultry, to be depressing, to confine (such things as rice, etc., in an overfull basket), by forming a barricade of leaves, etc., round the edge, or by covering with a cloth and tucking in, (*a.*) sultry, depressing, hot.
Uar, (*v.*) to emphasise, to exaggerate.
Ui, (*s.*) a dog.
Ui, (*v.*) to forbid, to be reluctant to part with or give up, to try to dissuade, to beseech or ask not to, to grudge.
U-i, an interjection expressing wrath or contempt.
Ui-bâng, (*v.*) to dissuade, to put a stop to.
Ui-fawm, (*s.*) the praying mantis.
Ui-fawm-ring, (*s.*) the name of a weed.
Uih, (*a.*) stinking, high, strong smelling, (*v.*), to stink, etc.
Ui-hli, (*s.*) a flea.
Ui-om, (*v.*) to be a pity, to be a loss.
Ui-rê, (*s.*) an adulteress, (*v.*) to commit adultery (used only of a woman).
Ui-sa-le'lin, (*v.*) to turn a somersault on a bar.
Ui sa-thiam, (*s.*) a dog able to track game.
Ui-sûl, (*s.*) the name of a creeper.
Ui-tê-mê, (*s.*), the name of a creeper with a bean-like fruit.

Ui-thak, (*s.*) the itch.
Ui-thin-thâng, (*s.*) the name of a plant with a flower resembling the convolvulus.
Ui-tho-buh, (*s.*) a species of rice.
Ui-ṭhut, (*v.*) to sit on the haunches with the fore legs upright (as a dog, etc.)
Ui-tui-hleoh, (*v.*) to swim like a dog.
Uk, (*a.*) dirty, discoloured, karki coloured, (*v.*) to be dirty, etc.
Uk, (*v.*) to make a noise, as a rat when being suffocated by smoke in its hole.
Ul, (*a.*) slightly scorched, (*v.*) to be slightly scorched.
U-la, U-lang, U-lang-in, } if you, also a participial termination used when two or more imperatives come together.
U-leoh, (*s.*) the name of a flying lizard.
Ulh, (*v. t.*) to sprain, to bend.
Ulh tliak, (*v. t.*) to break, to snap.
Ulh-tliak silai, (*s.*) a breech-loading gun.
U-long, (*s.*) a tadpole.
U-luk, (*a.*) tidy, prim, particular in dress, etc., (*v.*) to be prim, to make tidy, to take pride in, to be particular.
U-luk-tîr, (*v. t.*) to make tidy.
Ûm, (*s.*) the name of a pumpkin, a gourd, a bamboo or other receptacle for holding liquids.
Ûm, (*v.*) to chase, to pursue, to hunt.
Um, (*v.*) to preserve by boiling and potting, to pot, to put fruit in a pot to hasten its ripening.
Um, (*v.*) to develop or enlarge (as the breasts).
Um-khal, (*s.*) the name of a tree.
Un, (*a.*) old (as village, books, etc.), (*v.*) to be old.
U-nao, (*s.*) a relation, a brother, sister or cousin.
Ung, (*a.*) mouldy smelling, (*v.*) to smell mouldy.
Ung, (*a.*) discoloured, kharki coloured, dirty, (*v.*) to be discoloured.
Ûp, (*v.*) to be sheltered or free from the wind.
Up, (*v.*) to put a lid on a pot when boiling on the fire to keep the steam in.
U-pa, (*s.*) an elder, a chief man, a mantri, (*v.*) to be old, to be elderly.
U-phâr, (*s.*) a toad.
Ur, (*v.*) to be angry.
Ur, (*v.*) to distil, to brew (as beer).
Urh, (*a.*) burnt (in cooking), smelling like burnt meat, (*v.*) to burn (as meat).
Ur-ur, (*adv.*) denoting many or much.

Ût, (*a.*) scorched badly by the fire, burnt, (*v.*) to scorch badly, to burn.
U-ṭok, (*s.*) a toad.
U-ṭok-hni, (*s.*) the name of a plant.

V

Va, (*adv.*) how. (Used only in exclamatory sentences.)
Va, verbal prefix signifying 'going,' generally on level ground, or from one place to another of equal elevation.
Va-bak, (*s.*) the night jar.
Va-cha, (*s.*) a heron.
Va-chirh-dawt, (*s.*) a snipe.
Vah, (*s.*) a woman's brother's child.
Va-hai, (*s.*) a species of hornbill.
Va-hla, (*s.*) the hill partridge.
Va-hlut, (*s.*) a species of flying squirrel.
Va-hmîm, (*s.*) a quail.
Va-hmîm bûng-pui, (*s.*) the name of a plant.
Vah-nu, (*s.*) a woman's brother's daughter.
Vah-pa, (*s.*) a woman's brother's son.
Va-hrit, (*s.*) the black pheasant.
Va-hûi, (*s.*) a wood pigeon.
Vai, (*v.*) to search for.
Vai, (*v.*) to row, to paddle.
Vai, (*s.*) a foreigner, a Hindustani, (*a.*) foreign.
Vai, (*s.*) parched rice.
Vai, (*v.*) to wave, to wave back with the hand, to wave the arm or anything horizontally, to cut or chop off horizontally.
Vai-bêl, (*s.*) a man's pipe.
Vai-bêl-til, (*s.*) the projection on the bowl of a Lushai man's pipe immediately below where the stem enters.
Vai buh, (*s.*) a species of rice.
Vai-cha, (*s.*) an oar, a paddle.
Vai-der-ken, (*s.*) the zinnia.
Vai-dip, (*s.*) bran.
Vaih, (*adv.*) haply.
Vai-hlen-hlo, (*s.*) the Kuki weed.
Vai-hlo, (*s.*) tobacco.
Vai-hmi-tê, (*s.*) a sandfly.
Vai-hren-hri, (*s.*) the itch.
Vai-in, (*a.*) all.

Vai-lian-hlo, (*s.*) the same as ***vai-hlen-hlo.***
Vai-lung-hlan, (*v.*) to pass on from one to another.
Vai-lung-thlâr, (*s.*) the name of a game played with stones and holes in the ground.
Vai-mîm, (*s.*) Indian corn, maize.
Va-in-ro-nghâk, (*s.*) the name of a bird which frequents houses.
Vai-phaw-hlo, (*s.*) the name of a tree and also the juice of the same, which is used by the Lushais for japanning.
Vai-va, (*s.*) the hill mainah.
Vai-vut, (*s.*) dust.
Vai-vut khu, (*s.*) dust (suspended in the air).
Vai-vut ti-khu, (*v.*) to make a dust.
Vai-za, (*s.*) the name of a flowering tree, the bark of which is used to make rope, and is then known as ***hrui khao.***
Vak, (*adv.*) with force, hard, vehemently.
Vâk, (*v.*) to go, to walk, to wander about.
Va-kel-chal, (*s.*) the name of a small bird.
Va-kep, (*s.*) the name of a plant.
Va-ki, (*s.*) a parrot.
Va-ki-ria, (*s.*) the name of a headdress made of parrots' feathers, beetles' wings, seeds, etc., worn on festive occasions.
Va-ko, (*s.*) the name of a mauve flowering creeper.
Va-kul, (*s.*) the bhimarâj.
Va-kul chang, (*s.*) a head-dress made of the long tail feathers of the bhimarâj, also the long tail feathers of the same bird.
Vâk-vai, (*s.*) a homeless person, a wanderer, a vagabond, (*v.*) to be homeless, to wander, etc.
Val, (*v.*) to go into rings or circles, (*a.*) circular.
Vâl, (*s.*) a ring of cane to put under a pot to keep it from rolling.
Va-la, (*v.*) to fetch.
Valh, (*s.*) a slip knot, a noose, a loop, (*v.*) to make a slip knot, noose or loop.
Va-lîm-chho, (*s.*) a small woodpecker.
Vâm, (*a.*) red-hot, live, (*v.*) to be red-hot.
Vâm, (*v.*) to crunch between the teeth.
Va-mûr, (*s.*) a swallow, a martin.
Vân, (*s.*) the sky.
Vân, (*v.*) to stretch one's self.
Vân-a-ṭhat, (*v.*) to be prosperous.
Vân-chhe-ko-vin, through you, etc., because of the curse of heaven upon you, etc.
Vân-duai, (*a.*) unfortunate, unlucky, (*v.*) to be unfortunate, etc.
Vang, (*s.*) the name of a species of acacia.

Vâng, (*a.*) scarce, scanty, uncommon, rare, (*v.*) to be scarce, etc.
Vâng, (*s.*) breadth.
Vâng-a, see *vâng-in.*
Vâng a zao, (*v.*) to be broad.
Vâng-in, (*prep.*) on account of, because of, for the sake of, because.
Vâng-lai, (*s.*) the time when a thing is at its best, the time of greatest prosperity.
Vâng-lam-a, (*prep.* and *adv.*) across.
Vâng-tlâng, (*a.*) average, medium, moderate.
Vâng-tlâng hmu-in, } (*adv.*) publicly, openly.
Vâng-tlâng hriat-in, }
Vâng-tlâng-mi, (*s.*) the general public, the people.
Vâng-tlâng zîng-a, (*adv.*) publicly, openly.
Vang-vat, (*s.*) a land-leech.
Vang-vat hlo, (*s.*) the name of a small plant.
Vâng-zawng-in, (*prep.* and *adv.*) across.
Van-i-an, (*s.*) the name of a plant with edible leaves.
Vân-kai-chaw, (*s.*) the last food a person eats before dying; the first offering of food made to a departed spirit.
Vân-kai-hrui, (*s.*) the name of a creeper.
Vân-khai-a, through (your) favour, because of heaven's favour upon (you, etc.)
Vân-lai-fong, (*s.*) the name of a basket.
Vân-lai in, (*s.*) a house with a roof sloping in four directions.
Vân-lai zawl, (*s.*) the zenith.
Vân-lung, (*s.*) the front room of a large Lushai house used as servants' quarters.
Vân-nei, (*a.*) fortunate, lucky, (*v.*) to be fortunate, etc.
Vân-ni-chang, (*v.*) to prosper.
Vân-ni-chhâl, (*v.*) to swear an oath by heaven.
Vân pui sai hrua, the name of a bow-like configuration, formed by Castor and Pollox in Gemini, Procyon in Canis Minor, Sirius, and a few other stars.
Vân-shâng-a ṭâk, (*v.*) to make a great trouble over nothing, to get angry without adequate cause.
Vân-vorh, (*v.*) to throw into the air.
Vao, (*v.*) to threaten, to adjure.
Vao-be, (*s.*) the name of a flowering tree (*Bauhinia variegata*).
Vao-dai, (*v.*) to threaten or frighten into compliance.
Va-ok, (*s.*) the name of a large bird.
Vao-kam, (*s.*) the bank (of a river), the edge (of a mug, etc.)
Va-pai hrui, (*s.*) the name of a creeper.
Va-pual, (*s.*) a hornbill.

Var, (*a.*) thin. (as bamboo), (*v.*) to be thin.
Vâr, (*a.*) keen (of sight, hearing, etc.), white, (*v.*) to be keen (of sight, etc.), to be white, to be light (not dark), (*s.*) light.
Var, (*adv.*) perfectly, quite, entirely.
Va-ṭak, (*s.*) a duck.
Va-ri-haw, (*s.*) the peacock pheasant.
Var-lo, (*a.*) thick (as bamboo), (*v.*) to be thick.
Vâr-lo, (*a.*) dim (as sight), (*v.*) to be dim (as sight).
Vâr-parh, (*s.*) the morning star.
Vâr-ṭian, (*s.*) early dawn.
Va-rung, (*s.*) the partridge.
Va-suih, (*s.*) the name of a small bird.
Vât, (*v.*) to cut (*jhúm*).
Va-tawk, (*s.*) a goose.
Va-te-khuai-zu, (*s.*) the name of a plant.
Va-vu, (*s.*) a pheasant.
Vaw, a contracted form of *vuak.*
Ve, (*adv.*) also, too, as well.
Veh, (*v.*) to watch stealthily, to seize stealthily.
Veh-bûr khon, (*v.*) to beg from house to house.
Veh-bûr khon-mi, (*s.*) a beggar.
Vei, (*v.*) to go or walk backwards and forwards, or to and fro.
Vei, (*adv.*) presumptuously. A suffix denoting that something presumptuous has been done.
Vei, (*v.*) to contract or catch (a disease), to have (a disease), to pass away (as a month, year, etc.)
Vei lam, (*s.*) the left-hand side.
Vei-nên, (*adv.*) withal.
Vek, (*adv.*) expressing entirety.
Vêk, (*adv.*) again, over again.
Vêl, (*v.*) to beat, to strike.
Vêl, (*v.*) to surround, to go round, (*adv.*) around, round.
Vêl, (*v.*) to put leaves round the top of a basket to prevent the contents from spilling.
Vêl-a, (*prep.*) round, on all sides of, throughout, in the neighbourhood of, round about.
Ve-leh, (*conj.*) directly, immediately, when.
Vêl-in, (*prep.*) see *vêla.*
Vêng, (*v.*) to watch, to look after.
Vêng, (*s.*) a village, vicinity, neighbourhood, a neighbour.
Veng, (*v.*) to gird round the waist (as cloth).
Vêng-te, (*s.*) a neighbour, neighbours.
Vêng-ṭu, (*s.*) a watcher, a keeper.

Verh, (*v.*) to drill a hole, to make a hole through.
Verh-awng, (*v.*) to drill or make a hole through.
Ver-ther, } (*v.*) to be a hypocrite, to be double-faced, to act so as
Ver-vêk, } to deceive, to be unprincipled or mean, (*a.*) hypocritical, etc.
Vet, a term of reproach or contempt.
Vêt, (*v.*) to put round.
Ve-ve, each (of two), both.
Viah, (*adv.*) entirely, perfectly, quite.
Vial, (*v.*) to curl up, to coil, to encircle (as a snake), (*s.*) a coil.
Vial-tîr, (*v.*) to coil.
Viao, (*adv.*) very, exceedingly.
Vil, (*v.*) to attend to cooking.
Vîn, (*a.*) ill-tempered, irritable, (*v.*) to be ill-temperred, etc.
Vir, (*v.*) to rotate, to revolve.
Vir, (*v.*) to have an intense longing for animal food.
Vir-kîk, (*v.*) the same as the above with a more intense longing.
Vir-vêt, (*v.*) to wind round and in and out.
Vir, (*v.*) to bore, to pierce through.
Vôh, (*v.*) to favour, to treat well.
Voi, (adverbial prefix for numerals) time, times.
Voih, (*v.*) to break wind.
Voi-hnih, (*adv.*) twice.
Voih-ui-hrui, (*s.*) the name of a creeper which is chewed by the Lushais as a remedy for toothache.
Voi-khat, (*adv.*) once.
Voi-khat-an, (*adv.*) suddenly, unexpectedly.
Voi-li, (*adv.*) four times.
Voi-in, to-day.
Voi-in-a, to-day.
Voi-thum, (*adv.*) thrice.
Vok, (*s.*) the domestic pig.
Vok-hmia'-zon' thla, (*s.*) the time of year corresponding nearly to June.
Vok-pui, (*s.*) a sow.
Vok pui ruang ruh, (*s.*) a species of mimosa.
Voksha, (*s.*) pork, bacon.
Vom, (*a.*) dark, tawny, black.
Vom, (*s.*) an old unit of value equal to about four annas.
Vom, (*v.*) to throw (stone, ball, etc.)
Vom, (*s.*) contraction of *savom*.
Vom-bâl, (*s.*) the name of a flowering tree and the juice of the same, which is used by the Lushais for japanning.

Vom-bâl-hnah-shîn, (*s.*) the name of a tree and the juice of the same, which is used for japanning.
Vom-buh, (*s.*) the name of a tree.
Vom-kûr, (*s.*) the name of a succulent plant.
Vom-lu, (*s.*) a bear's head, used of the moon when only three quarters is visible.
Vom-tlâk, (*s.*) a bear trap.
Vom-va, }
Vom-va-pui, } (*s.*) the names of trees with edible fruit.
Von a shor, (*v.*) to have diarrhœa.
Vong, }
Vong-reng, } (*v.*) to keep, to preserve, to take care of, to receive, to have upon one's person or with one.
Vorh, (*v.*) to scatter, to throw up, to toss.
Vot, (*a.*) cold, chilly, (*v.*) to be cold, etc.
Vua, (*adv.*) perfectly, entirely, quite.
Vua'fai, (*v.*) to bathe (as with lotion).
Vuah, (*v.*) to name.
Vuai, (*v.*) to wither, to wrinkle, (*a.*) withered, wrinkled.
Vua*k*, (*v.*) to beat, to strike, to thresh (grain), to poison (fish), to wear (as spectacles, etc.)
Vuak-fung, (*s.*) a stick for driving cattle.
Vual, (*s.*) a weal, (*v.*) to weal.
Vual, (*s.*) the name of a large grub.
Vuan, (*v.*) to catch hold of, to hold, to grasp, to seize or possess (as a spirit).
Vui, (*v.*) to bury or dispose of the dead in any manner.
Vui, (*v.*) to be offended, to be hurt in the feelings.
Vui, (*v.*) to ear (as grain), (*s.*) an ear (of grain).
Vul, (*s.*) the Indian medlar (*Pyrus pashii*).
Vulh, (*v.*) to keep or rear (domestic animals).
Vulh-hlawh, (*v.*) to keep or rear (domestic animals) for wages.
Vûm, (*v.*) to be piled up (as measure, etc.), (*a.*) piled up.
Vun, (*s.*) skin.
Vûn*g*, (*v.*) to swell, (*a.*) swollen, (*s.*) a mound, a swelling.-
Vûr, (*s.*) snow, ice, hoar frost.
Vûr, (*v.*) to earth up, to fill in (as hole), to pile up on top of.
Vur-vur, (*adv.*) entirely, perfectly, quite.
Vut, (*s.*) ashes, dust, (*v.*) to be reduced to ashes or dust.
Vut-lawh, }
Vut-luah, } (*s.*) a fire shovel.

Z

Za, (*v.*) to tickle, to have the pins and needles.
Za, (*a.*) a hundred.

Za, (*a.*) all.
Za-chham-in a la, "Zacham took him," an expression used to signify that a person has died suddenly in his sleep.
Zah, (*v.*) to reverence, to revere.
Zah-ngai, (*v.*) to have or show mercy.
Zah-ngai-thei-tak, (*a.*) merciful.
Zah-om, (*a.*) reverence begetting, commanding, compelling respect, respectable.
Zah-thlâk, (*a.*) disgraceful, shameful.
Zai, (*s.*) a single thread (as of cotton, hair).
Zai, (*s.*) a song, tone, (*v.*) to sing.
Zai, (*v.*) to cut.
Zai, (*a.*) of the same thickness all the way up (as bamboo, etc.)
Zai, (*v.*) to tell, to inform.
Zai dam, (*a.*) goodtempered, goodnatured, (*v.*) to be goodnatured etc.
Zai-hri, (*s.*) a species of Indian fig tree.
Za-in, (*a.*) all.
Zai-rum, (*s.*) the name of a tree.
Zai-zawh, (*s.*) the name of a tree.
Zai-zir, (*v.*) to make signs.
Zak, (*a.*) shy, modest, bashful, ashamed, (*v.*) to be shy, etc.
Zak, } (*s.*) the arm-pit.
Zak-hnuai, }
Zak kao, (*v.*) to lift up the arm so as to expose the arm-pit, the part of a coat, etc., under the armpit.
Zak-ze', (*v.*) to carry under the arm or on the hip, to have under one's wing.
Zak-zum, (*a.*) shy, bashful, diffident, (*v.*) to be shy, etc.
Zalh, (*v.*) to lay out a dead body, to lay in the grave, to dress up a dead body and place it in a sitting posture.
Zâm, (*v.*) to spread, to creep (as a creeper).
Zâm, (*v.*) to be terrified, to be panic-stricken, to be demoralized.
Zam, (*v.*) to suspend, to fasten.
Zama-diai, (*s.*) the name of a red bead.
Zâm-kai, (*v.*) to climb (as a creeper).
Zâm-pher, (*s.*) the name of a finely woven bamboo mat, the Bengali '*shital pati.*'
Zâm-phu, (*s.*) the name of an animal.
Zâm-zo, (*s.*) a species of amaranthus.
Zân, (*s.*) night.
Zâng, (*s.*) the back.
Zâng, (*a.*) light (not heavy), (*v.*) to be light.

Zang, (*s.*) the penis, the sting (of bee, etc.), the tang (of knife etc.), the tongue (of a reed in a musical instrument), the spout (of a kettle, etc.)
Zâng-bawk, (*a.*) hunchbacked, (*v.*) to be hunchbacked.
Zang-khua, (*s.*) the constellation of the Great Bear.
Zang-kol-tuk, (*s.*) the name of a tribe of Nagas.
Zâng kûl, (*a.*) hunchbacked, bent, (*v.*) to be hunchbacked, etc.
Zâng ruh, (*s.*) the backbone.
Zâng ruh thlîng, (*s.*) the spinal cord.
Zang-shi, (*s.*) the trigger or catch of a noose trap.
Zang tan, (*v.*) to circumcise.
Zang thal, (*v.*) to lie on the back, (*adv.*) on the back, backwards.
Zang thal tui hleoh, (*v.*) to float on the back.
Zân-in-*a*, to-night.
Zân-khua-in, all night.
Zân-lai, (*s.*) midnight.
Zân riah, (*s.*) the evening meal, supper.
Za nu-fa, one hundred and fifty.
Zân-zawn-in, night after night.
Zao, (*a.*) large, extensive, (*v.*) to be large, etc.
Zao, (*s.*) the name of a house sometimes attached to the dwelling of a wealthy Lushai.
Zao-o, (*a.*) very extensive, (*v.*) to be very extensive.
Zao tawp, (*s.*) the furthest *jhúm* from a village.
Zao tawp chen, (*s.*) a measurement. As far as the furthest *jhúm*, varying from 4 to 12 miles.
Zâ*p*, (*v.*) to fan,'to winnow, to flap, to flutter.
Za' pui, (*v.*) to be ashamed of.
Zâr, (*s.*) a bough, a branch.
Zâr, (*v.*) to hang up (as cloth on line, etc.), to spread (as sall).
Zar, (*v.*) to tickle (as a fly, straw, etc.)
Zâr-a, Zâr-in, } (*prep.*) because of, by favour of, (*conj.*) since, as, because.
Zar-pâk, (*v.*) to try to persuade,
Zar-pâk zo (or zawh), (*v.*) to succeed in persuading.
Zâr zo, (*v.*) to be a partaker of honours, etc., conferred upon one whom one follows, to receive perquisites, (*s.*) one who receives perquisites.
Zât leh zât, equal shares.
Zât-ve, (*s.*) a half.
Zât-ve khing-phel, (*s.*) a quarter.
Zawh, (*v.*) to finish, to complete.
Zawh, (*v.*) to go (on water in a boat, etc.), to walk along, to observe or keep as a command.

Zawh, (*v.*) to be able, etc., (another form of *zo*, 'see there').
Zawh-in, having finished, when, after.
Zawh-tê, (*s.*) the domestic cat.
Zawk, (*adv.*) more, rather, more likely.
Zawl, (*a.*) level, (*v.*) to be level.
Zawl, (*v.*) to be possessed (by a spirit, etc.)
Zawl, (*v.*) to be friendly with.
Zawl-ai di, (*s.*) the name of a philtre.
Zawl-bûk, (*s.*) a guest house, the large house where all the young unmarried men of the village sleep at night.
Zawl-zong, (*s.*) a species of green cricket.
Zawm, (*v.*) to obey, to become a follower of, to join, to join in, to accede to a request, to believe.
Zawn, (*v.*) to carry (between two persons).
Zawn, (*prep.*) opposite to.
Zawng, (*s.*) a monkey.
Zawng, (*pro.*) that which.
Zawng, (*s.*) direction, position.
Zawng-ai-thing, (*s.*) a species of wild ginger.
Zawng-an-thûr, (*s.*) name of a plant.
Zawng-awm-pawng, (*s.*) a species of gourd resembling the *loofah.*
Zawng-bal-hla, (*s.*) the name of a tree with edible fruit.
Zawng-be-tê, (*s.*) the name of a creeper.
Zawng-bilh-tah, (*s.*) the name of a kind of lattice work.
Zawng-dai kalh, (*s.*) the name of a lattice work, (*v.*) to make the same.
Zawng-dul-i-un, (*s.*) the Gangetic dolphin (*Platanista Gangetica.*)
Zawng-fian, (*s.*) the name of a mauve flowering creeper.
Zawng-hri, (*s.*) small-pox.
Zawng-kâng-ṭhai, (*s.*) the name of a stinging plant.
Zawng-khâr-khep, (*s.*) the name of a monkey trap in a *jhûm* house.
Zawng-tah, (*s.*) the name of a tree and its fruit, which resembles a large bean.
Zawng-tlâk, (*s.*) the name of a monkey trap.
Zawng-zawn, (*v.*) to carry lashed to a pole between two persons.
Zawt, (*v.*) to ask, to enquire.
Zawt-chhawng, (*v.*) to ask what another said, to ask for information in order to pass it on to another.
Zawt thu, (*s.*) a question.
Ze, a contracted form of *zia.*
Zeh-lung, (*s.*) flint.
Zêl, (*adv.*) continuously, right on, one after another.
Zêl, (*v.*) to put into a trance.

Zêl-din-a-thu bawl, } (*v.*) to say what one only imagines as if it were
Zêl-din-thu bawl, } really true.

Zêm, (*s.*) a large bamboo receptacle for storing rice.

Zem, (*v.*) to entwine (as creeper), to bind, to twist or wind round and round.

Zên, (*s.*) gunpowder.

Zen, (*v.*) to thrust the arm into (as a hole, coat-sleeve, etc.)

Zen, (*v.*) to commit fornication with.

Zên-chong, (*s.*) a small measure for measuring a charge of gunpowder.

Zeng, (*a.*) withered, paralysed, useless (as limb), (*v.*) to be withered, etc.

Zeng-e-maw, some kind of.

Zeng-nge, (*pro.*) which? what?

Zeng-zât-e-maw, some number, some quantity.

Ze*p*, (*v.*) to tuck in.

Zê*p*, (*v.*) to prevaricate, to lie, to keep anything back, to suppress, to conceal.

Zet, (*adv.*) very, exceedingly, really.

Zet, (*adv.*) first, previously.

Zi, (*v.*) to stretch one's self.

Zia, (*s.*) engraving, colouring, (*a.*) variegated, of various colours.

Zia, mode of, manner of. It is sometimes used as an affix to adjectives to form abstract nouns. It is also affixed to verbs with the meaning of 'ought' or 'fit'.

Zia, (*adv.*) exactly.

Ziak, (*v.*) to write, to engrave.

Zia'-kur, (*s.*) a piece of bamboo bent like a horse shoe and used for scraping beans.

Zial, (*a.*) rolled up, done up in a knot (as hair), (*v.*) to roll up, etc.

Ziao, (*v.*) to be on edge (as teeth).

Zia*t*, (*v.*) to scrape.

Zih-nghal, (*s.*) the name of a tree, the shoots of which are used as a remedy for stomach ache.

Zîk, (*s.*) a new shoot.

Zîk a chhuak, (*v.*) to feel like stretching one's self.

Zîk chhua*k* tak-in, (*adv.*) in order from beginning to end.

Zîk-no, (*s.*) a young leaf or shoot.

Zîk zuah, (*v.*) to strip a tree of all its leaves except a small bunch at the end of each bough or to cut off all the boughs except the topmost, and stripping that of its leaves except a bunch at the tip. A favourite pastime of the Lushais.

Zilh, (*v.*) to correct, to admonish, to reprove, to exhort, to instruct.

Zilh-hao, (*v.*) to scold.

Zîm, (*v.*) to surround (an animal in hunting, etc.)

Zîm, (*a.*) narrow, small, close together, (*v.*) to be narrow, etc., (*adv.*) closely together, frequently, at short intervals, little.
Zin, (*v.*) to go on a journey, to visit a distant village.
Zîng, (*v.*) to accumulate, to gather (specially used of clouds on hill tops and in valleys).
Zing, (*adv.*) closely together, frequently, (*v.*) to be close together.
Zîng-a, in the early morning.
Zîng-a, (*prep.*) among, with, along with.
Zir, (*v.*) to learn, to copy, to imitate.
Zir-sak, (*v.*) to imitate, to mock.
Zi-za, (*s.*) jute.
Zo, (*v.*) to be able, to be sufficient for.
Zo, (*s.*) the name of the Lushais and surrounding hill tribes.
Zo, (*a.*) high, of great elevation, (*v.*) to be high, etc.
Zo-âr-chhuang, (*s.*) a species of *Zâmzo*, the cockscomb plant.
Zo-chal, (*s.*) a cord resembling chenille made of dyed goat's hair, worn round the head in the form of a turban.
Zo-eng, (*s.*) a species of yellow amaranthus.
Zo-hniar, (*s.*) a species of amaranthus.
Zoi, (*a.*) limp, flexible, (*v.*) to be limp.
Zoi, (*a.*) slow.
Zoih zoih, (*adv.*) bitterly (cry), much.
Zoi-in, (*adv.*) slowly, gently, by degrees.
Zoi-tê-in, (*adv.*) slowly.
Zoi-zoi-in, (*adv.*) slowly, gradually, gently.
Zom, (*v.*) a contracted form of *zawm*.
Zom, (*v.*) to join, to be joined.
Zom-thaw, (*a.*) lazy, (*v.*) to be lazy.
Zom-zat, (*adv.*) without intermission.
Zong, an emphatic and distinguishing particle, for my part, for your part, etc., on the other hand.
Zong, (*v.*) to search.
Zong-chal, (*s.*) see *zochal*.
Zong-chhang, (*v.*) to be accustomed, addicted or used to.
Zong-in, (*conj.*) if.
Zong-zong, (*a.*) all.
Zop, (*a.*) damp, (*v.*) to be or get damp.
Zo-phei, (*s.*) the strong stick in a noose trap for keeping the sapling which is used as a spring from flying back.
Zo-thing hâng, (*s.*) the name of a tree.
Zo-zai, many, much, more than necessary.
Zu, (*s.*) beer.
Zuah, (*v.*) to spare, to leave.
Zual, (*adv.*) more.

Zual-ko, (*s.*) a messenger, (*v.*) to bear a message.
Zual-ko, (*v.*) to misrepresent.
Zuam, (*a.*) sure, confident, (*v.*) to be sure, to be confident, to have assurance.
Zuan, (*v.*) to pounce upon, to spring upon.
Zuan*g*, (*v.*) to leap, to jump, to gallop, to canter.
Zuang, (*v.*) the name of a tree the bark of which yields a blue-black dye.
Zuang-thla, (*v.*) to jump down.
Zuao, (*a.*) fussy or impatient in sickness or suffering, (*v.*) to be fussy or impatient.
Zuar, (*v.*) to offer for sale, to sell.
Zu-bêl, (*s.*) a beer pot, a water pot.
Zu-fâng, (*s.*) fermented rice.
Zu-fe, (*s.*) rice from which beer has been brewed.
Zu-hrei, (*s.*) the name of a large rat.
Zui, (*v.*) to follow, to go with, to accompany.
Zuih, (*a.*) tapering, (*v.*) to taper.
Zû*k*, (*v.*) to suck, to suck through, to smoke (as pipe), to bite (as a leech).
Zu*k*, a verbal prefix denoting motion downwards.
Zuk-buh, (*s.*) the name of a tree.
Zûk-bûr, (*s.*) a cup of bamboo or horn used for drawing blood.
Zuk-chal, (*s.*) a stag (see *sazuk*).
Zuk-pui, (*s.*) a hind (see *sazuk*).
Zum, (*a.*) pointed, (*v.*) to sharpen to a point.
Zun, (*s.*) urine.
Zun bawm, } (*s.*) the bladder.
Zun-bu, }
Zun*g*, (*v.*) to urinate.
Zung, (*s.*) a finger, a toe, a root.
Zung-bun, (*s.*) a finger ring.
Zung-chal, (*s.*) the first finger or toe.
Zung-khat-bêng, } (*s.*) a measurement equal to the width of one
Zung-khat-hmet, } finger.
Zung-lai, (*s.*) the middle finger or toe.
Zu-ngol-vei, (*s.*) a boisterous drunkard.
Zung-pui, (*s.*) the thumb, the big toe.
Zung-pui bêng, } (*s.*) a measurement equal to the width of the
Zung-pui-hmet, } thumb.
Zung-ṭang, (*s.*) the toes or fingers collectively.
Zung-tê, (*s.*) the little finger or toe.
Zung-tê-u, } (*s.*) the third finger or toe.
Zung-u, }

Zung-za-bêng, } (*s.*) a measurement equal to the width of four
Zung-za-hmet, } fingers.

Zung-zâm, (*s.*) a friend, one upon whom one can rely.

Zun im, } (*s.*) a stoppage of urine, (*v.*) to have a stoppage of
Zun in, } urine.

Zun im pui, (*s.*) stone in the bladder.

Zun-tui, (*s.*) urine.

Zu-peng, (*s.*) a bottle made of a gourd.

Zu-pui, (*s.*) steamed, fermented or unfermented rice for making beer.

Zûr, (*a.*) wizened, wrinkled, (*v.*) to wrinkle, to be wrinkled.

Zût, (*v.*) to stroke.

Zu-va, (*s.*) rats and birds, a term which includes all animals and birds which destroy the crops.

PART IV.—DICTIONARY.

ENGLISH - LUSHAI.

A

A, (*adj.*) pakhat.
Abandon, (*v.*) kal shan, paih, (habit, etc.) shim thlah-thlam.
Abandoner, (*s.*) kal shan tu.
Abase, (*v.*) li-tlawm.
Abased, (*v.*) (to be) tlawm.
Abate, (*v.*) reh.
Abbreviate, (*v.*) ti-toi.
Abdomen, (*s.*) pum.
Abhor, (*v.*) ten.
Abide, (*v.*) om, om reng.
Ability, (*s.*) thei-na, thil ti thei-na, (according to ability) thei-tawk-in.
Abjure, (*v.*) mal-mâk.
Able, (*v.*) (to be) thei, thiam, peih, zawh, zo.
Abode, (*s.*) omna.
Abominable, (*a.*) ten-om.
Abominate, (*v.*) ten.
About, (*prep.*) lai (as in 'ni-shom lai' = about ten days), emaw-lei, thu, chanchin, chung-a, (about to) dawn, dawn ta, tum.
Above, chung-a, chung-lam-a, chhak-a, (a house on hill side) kom-chhak-a.
Abrupt, (*a.*) ho.
Abruptly, (*adv.*) ho.
Abscess, (*s.*) khoi-hli.
Abscond, (*v.*) relh-ru, tlân-bo.
Absent, (*a.*) om lo.
Absent-minded, (*a.*) hai-hot, ham-haih.
Absolve, (*v.*) ngia-dam.
Absorb, (*v.*) hîp-lût.
Abstain, (*v.*) in-shûm.
Abstemious, (*a.*) in-shûm-thei, (*v.*) (to be) in-shûm.
Abundant, (*a.*) tam.
Abuse, (*s.*) ân-hla, (*v.*) hao, âng.

Acacia, (*s.*) vang.
Accede, (*v.*) hlawh tlin'tîr, zawm.
Accept, (*v.*) chhân*g*, nei, lâ*k*, pom.
Acceptable, (*a.*) dûh-zawng, (anything acceptable) duh-zawng.
Accidentally, (*adv.*) pal.
Acclimatized, (*v.*) (to be) ngeih.
Accompany, (*v.*) kal-pui, tel, zui, (part way) thlah.
Accomplish, (*v.*) tlei-tla, thin*g*-tlâ*k*, ṭum-tla, pui-tlin.
According to, (*prep.*) pa-ngai, pa-ngai-in.
Accordingly, chu mi a-vâng chuan.
Accordion, (*s.*) phai-phu-lêng.
Account, (*prep.*) (on account of) vâng-in, vâng-a.
Accumulate, (*v. t.*) khawl, khawl-khawm, tuak, tuak-khawm' (*int.*) tling, zîng.
Accurate, (*a.*) dik, fel.
Accurately, (*adv.*) dik tak-in, fel tak-in.
Accuse, (*v.*) dem, puh, (to another) hêk, (falsely) puh-khêl.
Accustomed to, (*v.*) ṭhan*g*, zong-chhang, nêl.
Ache, (*v.*) na, na*t*.
Achieve, (*v.*) ti hlawh tling.
Acid, (*a.*) thûr,
Acknowledge, (*v.*) oih.
Acorn, (*s.*) hlai rah, sa-shua rah, khaw-thli rah, ṭhîl rah.
Acquaint, (*v.*) hril.
Acquaintance, (*s.*) hmel-hriat-mi.
Acquainted with, (to be) hmel hria*t*.
Acquire, (*v.*) nei.
Acquit, (*v.*) thlah.
Acrid, (*a.*) thûr.
Across, (*adv.*) tan, tan-zawng-in, vâng-lama, vâng-zawng-in, kai.
Act, (*v.*) chê*t*, ti,
Action, (*s.*) chêt-zia, thil ti.
Actually, (*adv.*) chot, ngot.
Adam's apple, (*s.*) hrok bawk.
Add, (add to) belh, belh-chhah.
Adder, (*s.*) rûl,
Addicted, (*v.*) dok-lak, zong-chhang,
Addle, (*v. t.*) op-tui.
Addled, (*a.*) ḍah, op-tui.
Address, (*v.*) bia*k*, be.
Adequate, (*a.*) tawk.
Adhere, (*v.*) bei, bet.
Adherent, (*s.*) ṭan-pui.
Adhesive, (*a.*) bet thei, châr thei.

Adieu! dam tak in om roh! dam tak in kal roh!
Adjacent to, (*prep.*) kianga.
Adjoin, (*v.*) in-shi, in-zom.
Adjure, (*v.*) vao.
Adjust, (*v.*) ti ṭha, bât ṭha.
Administrator, (*s.*) ro-rêl tu, ho tu.
Admire, (*v.*) duh.
Admit, (*v.*) lût tîr.
Admonish, (*v.*) zilh.
Adopt, (*v.*) chên'-pui, om-pui.
Adorn, (*v.*) chei-moi, ti-moi, (one's self) in chei.
Adornment, (*s.*) chei moi, ti moi na.
Adult, (*s.*) pa-tling, nu-tling.
Adulteress, (*s.*) ui-rê.
Adultery, (*v.*) (to commit) (used only of woman) in-rê, (by stratagem, used of man) loi-thlêm.
Advantageous, (*a.*) ṭha.
Adversary, (*s.*) hmêl-ma.
Advice, (to ask) rawn.
Advise, (*v.*) fuih, ngai-ruat-sak, ngai-tua-pui, ngai-ruat-pui, rem-ruat, rem-ruat-pui, rot-pui.
Adviser, (*s.*) rot-pui.
Adze, (*s.*) rhei-pui.
Aërial root (*s.*) shûr.
Aërolite, (*s.*) ṭêk.
Afar, (*adv.*) hla.
Affable, (*a.*) zai-dam.
Affectionate, (*a.*) ngai thei.
Affirm, (*v.*) ti tlat.
Afflict, (*v.*) ti na.
Affright, (*v.*) râp, ti-ṭhaih, ti-zâm.
Afoot, (*adv.*) ke-in.
Aforetime, (*adv.*) hmân-a.
Afraid, (*v.*) hlao, (for another) hlao pui, (not afraid) nêl, ngam-pao, ngam-pah.
After, (*conj.*) chin-a, (*prep.*) hnu-a, hnung-a, zawh-in.
Afterbirth, (*s.*) chhûl, hlam.
Afternoon, (*s.*) chaw-hnu, tlai-lam.
Afterwards, (*adv.*) hnung-a, hnung-lama.
Again, (*adv.*) leh, leh-pek, pek, kîr, vêk.
Again and again, (*adv.*) non.
Against, (*prep.*) chung-a, dep-a, nghêng-a, nghêng-lama, hrual-a.
Aged, (*a.*) tar.

Aggravate, (*v.*) run, run-râl.
Aggravated, (*v.*) (to be) run, run-râl.
Aggressor, (*s.*) (in war) ɖo-la-tu, (in quarrel) kawh-mawh bawl-tu.
Agitate, (*v.*) chok-hnok.
Aglow, (*a.*) ling.
Ago, ani-ta, ani-tawh.
Agony, (*s.*) na.
Agree, (*v.*) (with) ngeih, rem ti.
Agreement, (*v.*) (to make) thu thlung ; also noun.
Ague, (*s.*) nat-tlun, (*v.*) (to have) tlun.
Ahead, (*adv.*) hma-sha.
Aid, (*v.*) (in work or food) chhom-dawl.
Ail, (*v.*) dam lo, bor-shom.
Ailment, (*s.*) na.
Air, (*s.*) bo-ruak, (*v.*) (in sunshine) pho.
Air-tight, (*a.*) phui.
Akimbo, (*v.*) (to put the arms) kawng-dom, kawng-beng.
Alarm, (false) (*s.*) khêl, also to be falsely alarmed, (falsely) (*v.*) khêl shiam.
Alder, (tree) hriang-pui.
Ale, (*s.*) zu.
Alert, (to be on) lo in-ring, lo beng-vâr.
Alien, (*s.*) aw zia mi.
Alight, (*v.*) fu.
Alike, (*a.*) thu-hmun, hmun-khat.
Alive, (*a.*) dam, nung.
All, an-za-in, a-za-in, a-vai-in, zong-zong, za, za-in, vai-in, an-vai-in, tlâng, (whole) pum, pum-in.
Allay, (*v.*) ti reh, ti bâng.
Alley, (*s.*) kawm-kâr.
Alligator, (*s.*) aw-le.
Allot, (*v.*) chang-tîr.
Allow, (*v.*) oih, phal, tiam.
All right, aw-le.
Ally, (*s.*) ṭan-pui.
Almost, (*adv.*) lek-lek, ruai, thaw, dawn-ta, thelh.
Alms, (*v.*) (to ask an) kut dawh.
Alone, (*adv.*) chaoh-vin.
Along, (*adv.*) dung-zawng, dung-lam.
Along with, (*prep.*) hnêna, chop-in, fawm, zîng-a.
Aloud, (*adv.*) ring-tak-in.
Already, (*adv.*) tûna pawh.
Also, (*adv.*) bok, pawh, pôh, ve.
Altar, (*s.*) mai-châm.

Alter, (*v. t.*) chang-tîr, ti-dang-lam, lêt, ti-lam-dang, (*int.*) dang-lam.
Alternately, (*adv.*) chhawk.
Although, (*conj.*) pawh-in, chung-a-pawh, na-a, shi. Although this is so, ani-na-a.
Altitude, (*a.*) (of great) zo.
Always, (*adv.*) fan, fo, thîn, kum-khua.
Amaranthus, (*s.*) zâm-zo.
Amaze, (*v.*) ti-mang-ang.
Amazed, (*v.*) (to be) mak ti.
Amazing, (*a.*) mak.
Ambassador, (*s.*) pa-lai.
Amber, (*s.*) ṭhi-hna. (Also amber bead or necklace.)
Ambiguous, (*a.*) thoi.
Ambiguously, (*adv.*) a-thoi-in, thoi.
Ambitious, (*a.*) ṭha-hnem ngai.
Ambush, (*v.*) bun.
Amiable, (*a.*) zai-dam.
Amidst, (*prep.*) lai-a, zîng-a.
Amiss, (*adv.*) sual.
Among, (*prep.*) zîng-a.
Amount, (*v.*) tling.
Ample, (*a*). tawk-chao.
Amply, (*adv.*) tawk-chao.
Amputate, (*v.*) tan.
Amuse, (*v.*) ti lawm, ti hlim.
Amusing, (*adv.*) lawm om, hlim om.
Ancestor, (*s.*) thlah-tu.
Ancestry, (*s.*) thlah-tu-te.
Anchor, (*s.*) long chelh ding tu, long ba' din' na, thîr chak-ai.
Ancient, (*a.*) cha-tuan.
Anciently, (*adv.*) hmân-a, hmân lai.
Ancients, (*s.*) hmân lai mi.
And, (*conj.*) leh, nên.
Anecdote, (*s.*) thon-thu.
Anew, (*adv.*) thar.
Angel, (*s.*) Pathian tir-ko.
Anger, (*s.*) thin-ur.
Angle, kil, (*adv.*) (at an angle) lao.
Angler, (*s.*) sangha man-tu.
Angrily, (*adv.*) thin-ur tak-in.
Angry, (*a.*) tao, thin-ur, thin-rim, thin-lung sha, ur.
Angular, (*a.*) kil nei.
Animal, (*s.*) sa, ran-nung.

Ankle, (*s.*) ke mit, kheimit.
Anna, (*s.*) na, (four-anna piece), she ki, shi-ki, (two-anna piece) dere, (eight-anna piece), du-li.
Annihilate, (*v.*) ti bo-ral, ti chi-mit.
Anniversary, (*s.*) cham-pha-phâk.
Announce, (*v.*) hril, shoi.
Annoy, (*v.*) ti lung ni lo, ti lung-oi lo.
Annoyed, (*v.*) (to be) lung-oi-lo, lung-ni-lo.
Annoying, (*a.*) run-thlâk.
Annually, (*adv.*) kum-tin-a, kum-tin-in.
Anoint, (*v.*) thih.
Another, (*a.* and *pro.*) dang, dang-lam, hrang.
Answer, (*v.*) chhâng, chhawn, (as prayer) hlawh-tlin' tîr.
Ant, (*s.*) fang-hmîr, dâr-chong-tual-a, mong-er, nao-chaw-ṭhing-bawm, chhim-tai-vang, ṭhui-op, khuang-ruang, rai-sheh, tai-vâng, tawh-êk.
Antagonist, (*s.*) do-tu.
Ant-eater, (*s.*) (scaly) sa-phu.
Antler, (*s.*) ki.
Anus, (*s.*) mong-kua.
Anvil, (*s.*) do-lung.
Anixous, (*a.*) lung-kham, ngai-tua.
Anxiously, (*adv.*) lung-kham tak-in.
Anyone, (*pro.*) tu-pawh, tu-pôh, tu-tal, tu-tal-emaw, tu-emaw-tal.
Any, (*adj.*) eng-pawh, eng-pôh.
Anything, (*s.*) eng-pawh, eng-pôh, eng-lo.
Any time, (at) engtika-pawh, engtika-pôh, eng-hun-pawh-in.
Any time, (not at) eng-tika-ma, eng lai ma-in.
Anywhere, (*adv.*) khoi-a-pawh, khoi-a-tal.
Apart, (*adv.*) chhum, ṭhen.
Apartment, (*s.*) pin-dan, pin-dan chhûng.
Ape, (*s.*) (gibbon) hao-hûk.
Aperient, (*s.*) dai-leng-na.
Aperture, (*s.*) awng.
Apex, (*s.*) chhîp.
Apologize, (*v.*) phal, thu-pha choi.
Apostle, (*s.*) pa-lai.
Apothecary, (*s.*) dam-doi mi.
Apalling, (*a.*) hlao-om.
Apparel, (*s.*) puan, silh-fên.
Apparently, (*adv.*) a-lang-in.
Apparition, (*s.*) hmui-thla.

Appeal to, (*v.*) bei, lût, thleng.
Appear, (*v.*) (as spirit, etc.), in-lâr, lang.
Appearance, (*s.*) hmel.
Appease, (*v.*) thlêm.
Appetite, (*v.*) (to have a good) ko.
Appoint, (*v.*) ruat, shiam, tiam.
Apportion, (*v.*) chang-tîr.
Apprehend, (*v.*) hria, hre, hriat.
Approach, (*v.*) tawn, pan.
Approve, (*v.*) oih.
April, (*s.*) Lalmang-a nu hlaw roi thla.
Apron, (*s.*) fên-thuah.
Aqueduct, (*s.*) tui-zawn, tui-don.
Arbitrate, (*v.*) ro rêl.
Arbitrator, (*s.*) ro-rêl-tu, thu rem-tu.
Arduous, (*a.*) har-sha, har, khirh.
Are, (*v.*) ni, om.
Areca, (*s.*) (palm and nut) ku-va.
Argue, (*v.*) in-hnial.
Argument, (*s.*) thu hnial.
Arid, (*a.*) châr.
Aright, (*adv.*) fel, dik, ṭha.
Arise, (*v.*) tho, thawh.
Arm, (*s.*) bân.
Armed, (*v.*) hriam-shin, hriam-keng.
Armpit, (*s.*) zak, zak-hnuai.
Arms, (*s.*) hriam.
Around, (*adv.*) vêl, (*prep.*) vêl-a, vêl-in.
Arouse, (*v.*) ti-harh, kai-tho, kai-thawh.
Arrange, (*v.*) tiam, ro-rêl, shiam.
Arrayed, (against) (*a.*) ep.
Arrest, (*v.*) man.
Arrive, (*v.*) thleng, lo-thleng, ban, tong.
Arrogant, (*a.*) chal-tlai, cha-po.
Arrow, (*s.*) thal.
Artery, (*s.*) tha-zâm.
Artful, (*a.*) fing.
Article, (*s.*) thuam, thuam-hnaw, thom-hnaw.
Artificial, (*a.*) lem.
Arum, (edible) bâl, bai-bing, man-zâng, tluan-thîr, ba'kâng, ba'sai-ke, ba'pui.
As, (*a.*) tia, (*conj.*) zâr-a, zâr-in.
Ascend, (*v.*) chho, lawn.
Ascent, (*s.*) chho.

As far as, (*conj.* and *prep.*) chin, china, thleng-in.
Ashamed, (*a.*) zak, (to be ashamed of) za'pui.
Ashes, (*s.*) mei vâp, vut.
Aside, (*adv.*) hrang.
As if, ang-in, ang-chuan.
Ask, (*v.*) (for) dîl, ngên, ngiat, phût, rawn, sawm, (question) zawt, (for anything owing) ṭhîng.
Aslant, (*adv.*) awn.
Asleep, (*v.*) mut-hîl, mu-nghîl, (fast asleep) mut-hîl dêr, mu-nghîl dêr, (fall asleep sitting or standing) mut thlûk.
As long as, (*conj.*) (in time) chhûng-zong, chhûng-in.
As much as, tia.
Ass, (*s.*) sa-kor-beng-tung, sa-beng-tung.
Assail, (*v.*) bei, rûn, tawng, ṭhawng.
Assailant, (*s.*) bei-tu.
Assassin, (*s.*) phil-hmang.
Assassinate, (*v.*) phil.
Assault, (*v.*) bei, tawng.
Assemble, (*v.*) in-khawm, pung, pung-khawm, (*trans.*) pun.
Assembly, (*s.*) pung-ho-te, pung.
Assent, (*v.*) oih-pui.
Assert, (*v.*) ti tlat, shoi tlat.
Assist, (*v.*) chhom-dawl, kai, lawm, pui.
Assistant, (*s.*) pui-tu.
Associate, (*v.*) (with) in-kawm-ngeih.
Assort, (*v.*) tlei.
Assurance, (*v.*) (to have) zuam.
Assure, (*v.*) ti-zuam.
Assuredly, (*adv.*) molh.
Asthma, (*s.*) thaw chham.
As though, ang-in, ang-chuan.
Astonish, (*v.*) ti mang-ang, mak ti tîr.
Astonishing, (*a.*) mak.
Astound, (*v.*) ti-mang-ang, mak ti tîr.
Astray, (*adv.*) bo.
Astringent, (*a.*) thûr.
Asunder, (*adv.*) chhum, ṭhen.
As well, (*adv.*) kêp.
At, (affix, as in grin at, laugh at) shan.
Atmosphere, (*s.*) bo-ruak.
Attack, (*v.*) rûn, tawng, bei, ṭhawng, (suddenly) râl ṭhawn.
Attempt, (*v.*) duh-ting, tum.
Attend, (*v.*) rong bawl.
Attendant, (*s.*) kai-za-vêng, rong-bawl-tu.

Attract, (*v.*) hîp.
Augur, (*v.*) ai shân, ai en, ṭhum vawr, (*s.*) ai-shân-thiam, ai-en-thiam, ṭhum-vawr-thiam.
August, (*s.*) mi-khua mîm kût thla, Rolura thlah te mîm kût thla.
Aunt, (*s.*) (paternal) ni, (maternal) nu, (paternal uncle's wife) nu, (maternal uncle's wife) pi.
Austerity, (*v.*) (to practice) in-soi-zoi, in ti-dawng.
Authority, (one in authority) thu-nei-tu, (one under) ṭhui-hruai, (to receive) thu-hmu, thu nei, (to give) thu nei-a shiam, thu nei pê*k*.
Authoritatively, (*adv.*) thu-nei-tu ang-in.
Autumn, (*s.*) fa-vâng.
Avalanche, (of stones, used in war) (*s.*) sha-lum, sha-buak.
Avaricious, (*s.*) duh-âm.
Avenge, (*v.*) phu lâ*k*, phu-ba lâ*k*, phu lam, phu-ba lam.
Avenger, (*s.*) phu-ba lâ*k* tu.
Avoid, (*v.*) pum-pelh.
Await, (*v.*) nghâk.
Awake, (*a.*) men*g*, (to remain awake all night) (*v.*) tlai-vâr.
Awaken, (*v. int.*) men*g*.
Award, (*v.*) tham.
Away, (*adv.*) bo, ral.
Awful, (*a.*) hlaoh-om.
Awhile, (*adv.*) hrih, rih.
Axe, (*s.*) hrei, hrei-pui, hrei-tê, (small) ha-chhek.

B

Baby, (*s.*) nao-shên.
Bachelor, (*s.*) lêng-ṭûl.
Back, (*adv.*) kîr, (*s.*) hnung, hnung-zâng, zâng, (on the back) (*adv.*) zang-thal, (of head) thluk, tuk-khum.
Backbite, (*v.*) rêl.
Backbiter, (*s.*) rêl tu.
Backbone, (*s.*) zâng-ruh.
Backwards, (*adv.*) hnung, (on back) zang-thal.
Bacon, (*s.*) vok-sha.
Bad, (*a.*) chhia, chhe, ṭha-lo, huat-thla-la, sual, beng-tla-lo, (dis-positioned) nun chhia, thin-chhe, (as seed) shi.
Badger, (hog) (*s.*) sa-phi-vok.
Bag, (*s.*) ip-tê.
Baggage, (*s.*) bung-rua.
Bait, (*s.*) chah, tok-tarh, (*v.*) chah, tok-tarh.

Bake, (*v.*) rawh, hem-hmin.
Bakshîsh, (*s.*) kut-choi, dawng.
Balance, (scales) (*s.*) bûk-na, bûk-khai-na, (*v.*) pâng.
Bald, (*a.*) hmul-kawng, kolh.
Ball, (*s.*) hlum.
Balsam, (plant) hme'zial, nuai-thang, nuai-en*g*.
Bamboo, (*s.*) mao, rua, châl-tê, (edible shoots) raw-tuai, (split for tying) hnâng.
Bamboo rat, (*s.*) bui, bui-pui, bui-shen, bui-luang-pâr.
Banana, (*s.*) bal-hla.
Band, (*s.*) (endless), tluang hrui.
Bandage, (*v.*) tuam, (*s.*) tuam-na.
Band together, (*v.*) ṭang-rual, ṭang-tlâng.
Bang, (*v.*) puak.
Banish, (*v.*) hno*t*-chhua*k*.
Banjo, (*s.*) chong-pe-reng.
Bank, (of river, etc.) kam, vao-kam, râl.
Banter, (*v.*) dem, dem-fiam.
Bar, (*s.*) tlawn.
Barak river, (*s.*) Tui-ruang.
Barb, (*s.*) ki-bâr.
Barber, (*s.*) lu-mêt-tu, lu-mêt-mi.
Barbarian, (*s.*) aw zia mi, aw ze mi.
Bare, (*a.*) kolh.
Bargain, (*v.*) (with) dawr, in-don, in-dawr.
Bark, (*v.*) baoh, (to strip of bark) thel, (*s.*) hawng, pil.
Barrel, (of gun) ngul, piang-lung, pial-lung.
Barren, (*a.*) (childless) chin*g*.
Barrow, (*s.*) ta*w*-lai-lîr.
Barter, (*v.*) in-don, in-dawr, lei.
Base, (*s.*) bul, mong.
Bashful, (*a.*) zak, zak-zum.
Basin, (*s.*) mai-hun.
Bask, (*v.*) ai.
Basket, (*s.*) bawm, êm, ben-von, daw-ron, êm-pai, fong, hrai, kho, paiper, pip, thûl, reng-pui, reng-tê, tui-choi-kawng, vân-lai-fong, ba-bun-kho, bawm-râng, dân-hrai, pai-kawng, tlâm-êm.
Bastard, (*s.*) fa-lak, sawn.
Bat, (*s.*) bâk.
Bathe, (*v.*) bual, in-bual, (as with lotion) vua'fai.
Bawl, (*v.*) ao.
Bay, (*s.*) li-teng-shawl.
Bayonet, (*s.*) lai-lung-dawt, lai-fei.
Bazar, (*s.*) dawr, dawr-kai, dawr-hmun.

Be, (*s.*) ni, om, lum.
Beach, (*s.*) ṭiao-pho.
Bead, (*s.*) ṭhi.
Beak, (*s.*) hmûi.
Beam, (cross) khan-chhuk.
Bean, be, be-pui, be-pui-lei, be-pui-sa-rîl, be-tê, be-pui-shen, be-kang, be-hloi, be-hliang, (large species) fang-ra.
Bear, (*v.*) (to bring forth) hring, (to bear consequences) mawh phur, bul tum, (the strain of a weight, etc.) dawl, (fruit) rah, (*s.*) vom, sa-mang, sa-vom.
Bear, (along) (*v.*) lên'.
Beard, (*s.*) kha-be hmul.
Beast, (*s.*) sa.
Beat, (*v.*) vêl, vua*k*, (beat up) sawh-bawl, sawh.
Beat down, (*v.*) (price) nêk.
Beautiful, (*a.*) moi.
Beautifully, (*adv.*) moi.
Beautify, (*v.*) chei-moi, ti-moi.
Become, (*v.*) chang, chhua*k*.
Because, (*prep.*) vâng-in, vâng-a, ai, ai-a, ai-in, lak-a, zâr-a, zâr-in.
Beckon, (*v.*) kut-in hûi.
Become, (*v.*) om, ni, chang.
Bed, (*s.*) khum.
Bedaub, (*v.*) hnoih, bel.
Bedstead, (*s.*) khum.
Bedtime, (*s.*) mut hun, mut lai.
Bee, (*s.*) khuai, khoi.
Beef, (*s.*) se-bawng sha.
Beer, (*s.*) zu.
Beerpot, (*s.*) zu-bêl.
Bees'wax, (*s.*) khoi-hnun.
Beetle, (*s.*) (black) khao-hriang.
Befal, (*v.*) lo-thleng.
Before, hma-in, hma-a, hma-sha.
Beforehand, (*adv.*) lawk, zet.
Befriend, (*v.*) thlop.
Beg, (*v.*) hmeh-bûr-khon, kut-dawh, veh-bûr-khon, dîl.
Beget, (*v.*) hring.
Beggar, (*s.*) hmeh-bûr-khon-mi, kut-dawh-mi, veh-bûr-khon-mi.
Begin, (*v.*) bei, ṭan, ṭan-tir.
Beginning, (*s.*) (of sentence) bul.
Begonia, (*s.*) she-khup-thûr.
Behaviour, (*s.*) mit-mei, mit-meng-zia.

Behead, (*v.*) lu tan.
Behind, hnu-a, hnung-a, hnung-lama, phên-a, (a house) kom-châr-a, to get behind, (*v.*) phên.
Behold, (*v.*) en.
Belch, (*v.*) irh.
Belief, (*s.*) rin.
Believable, rim-om, oih-om.
Believe, (*v.*) oih, ring, oih-sak, ruat.
Bell, (*s.*) dâr, dâr-she-ṭhi, ṭhi, (small round) te-ngeng.
Bell metal, (*s.*) ngên.
Bellow, (*v.*) bu, kiu.
Bellows, (*s.*) pûm, (cylinders of) pûm-thei, pûm-hrûl.
Belly, (*s.*) pum, dul.
Beloved, (*a.*) duh-tak, ngai, ngai tak.
Below, (*prep.*) (house on hillside) kom-thlang-a ; thlang-lama, thlang-a.
Belt, (*s.*) kawng hrên-na, kawng-fên.
Bend, (*v. t.*) ulh, elh, ti-koi, tom, (bend back) eo, er, (droop) kûr, (leg at knee) kom.
Beneath, (*prep.*) hnuai-a, hnuai-lama.
Benefit, (by) (*v.*) sawt.
Beneficial, (*a.*) sawt, ṭha, tlâk-tlai.
Bengali, (*s.*) Kor, Kor-mi.
Benighted, (to be) (*v.*) thim.
Bent, (*a.*) koi, (crinkled) chhok-olh.
Berry, (*s.*) rah.
Beseech, (*v.*) thlêm chiam, dîl chiam vak, dîl lui, dîl tlat tlat, ngên-chiam.
Besides, (*prep.*) lo-pawh, lo-pôh.
Besiege, (*v.*) hual.
Besmear, (*v.*) tât.
Bespeak, (*v.*) hual, lei-haoh.
Best, (*a.*) ṭha-ber.
Betel, (nut and tree) (*s.*) ku-va, (creeper and leaf) pân-ruang.
Better, (*a.*) ṭha zawk, (*adv.*) ṭha deo.
Between, (*prep.*) kâr-ạ.
Bevel, (*v.*) sa-hai, sa-nghawng, (*v. t.*) ti-dap.
Beware, (*v.*) tîm.
Bewilder, (*v.*) ti-mangang, (to be bewildered) mang-ang.
Bewildering, (*a.*) mang-an'thlâk.
Bewitch, (*v.*) doi.
Beyond, liam, piah.
Bhimaraj, (*s.*) (bird) va-kul.
Bible, (*s.*) Pathian lekha-bu.

Bid, (*v.*) tîr.
Bier, (*s.*) hlâng.
Big, (*a.*) hrol, lian, pui.
Bilberry, (*s.*) cham-phai thei.
Bill, (beak) hmûi.
Billhook, (Bengali) (*s.*) fa-vah.
Bin, (*s.*) zem, pa-tê, pa-pui, pa-reng, reng-pui, reng-tê.
Bind, phuar, ṭawn, zem, (as turban) khim.
Binocular, (*s.*) en-tlang.
Birch, (tree) (*s.*) hriang, hriang-zao, hriang-fâng.
Bird, (*s.*) sa-va, va.
Bird-lime, (*s.*) hmawng-hnai, soi.
Bird's nest, (*s.*) sava bu.
Birth, (*v.*) (to give) hring.
Bison, (*s.*) shial.
Bitch, (*s.*) ui pui.
Bite, (*v.*) keih, sheh, (as snake) chu*k*, (as leech) zuk, (snap) hap, (the lips) heh pe*t*.
Bitter, (*a.*) kha.
Bitterly, (*adv.*) zoih-zoih.
Bivalve, (*s.*) kep.
Black, (*a.*) dum, vom.
Blackberry, (*s.*) thei-hmu.
Blacken, (*v.*) ti dum.
Blackguard, (*s.*) mi sual.
Blacksmith, (*s.*) thîr-dêng, thîr-chher-thiam.
Bladder, (*s.*) zung-bu, zung-bawm.
Blame, (*v.*) dem, puh, (falsely) mawh-chhia*t*, puh-khêl.
Blanket, (*s.*) puan pui.
Blast, (*v.*) (to blow up) hâl-puak, rawh-puak.
Blaze, (*v.*) alh, (with hatchet) thel.
Bleat, (*v.*) bê.
Blebby, (*a.*) ṭok.
Bleed, (*v.*) thi, (by cupping) thi lâk.
Blemish, (without) (*a.*) thiang-hlim.
Bless, (*v.*) mal-shawm sak.
Blessed, (*a.*) eng thawl.
Blighted, (*s.*) hût.
Blind, (*a.*) mit-del, (night blind) mit-mal, (as road) khêl, (as seed) shi.
Blindfold, (*v.*) mit tuam.
Blindman's buff, (*s.*) phûng-lem.
Blink, (*v.*) khap.
Blister, (*s.* and *v.*) durh:

Bloated, (*a.*) buar.
Blockhouse, (*s.*) kulh-bing, râl-vêng-buk.
Blood, (*s.*) thi, thi-shen, (to shed) thi shen chhuak.
Bloom, (*s.* and *v.*) pâr, (covered with bloom, as fruit) pawl.
Blossom, (*s.* and *v.*) pâr.
Blow, (*v.*) chhêm, (the nose) hnap hnît, (about violently) nuai, (as wind) tleh, (at one blow) fik.
Blow-gun, (*s.*) ham-hrul.
Blow-pipe, (*s.*) (for blowing fire) chhêm thei.
Blue, (*a.*) pawl.
Blunt, (*a.*) bil.
Boar, (wild) sa-nghal, nghal-rual.
Board, (*v.*) thleng.
Boast, (*v.*) in-fak, u-âng.
Boastful, (*a.*) chal-tlai.
Boat, (*s.*) long, (open boat) long-lêng.
Body, (*s.*) sak-rong, sak-ruang, tak-sa, pang, (dead) ruang.
Bog, (*s.*) chirh-dûp.
Boggy, (*a.*) chirh-dûp.
Boil, (*v.*) chhûm, (as water) sho, (galloping) nghor, (*s.*) khoi-hli.
Boisterous, (*a.*) na.
Bold, (*a.*) huai, tlâng-nêl.
Boldly, (*adv.*) huai tak-in.
Bolster, (*s.*) lu-kham.
Bolt, (*v.*) (swallow) dolh, (so that food hurts passing down gullet) helh.
Bone, (*s.*) ruh.
Bonfire, (*s.*) (inside village) om-tual, (outside) mei-pui.
Book, (*s.*) lekha-bu.
Boot, (*s.*) phei-kok, ke-kok.
Booth, (*s.*) bawk, bawk-tê, bûk.
Border, (*s.*) tlang, hmawr.
Bore, (*v.*) vit.
Born, (*v.*) (to be) piang, (prematurely) tlâk, tla-sual.
Borrow, (*v.*) hawh, pûk.
Bosom, (*s.*) hnu-tê, awm, ang.
Both, dûn, tuak, ve-ve, (both together) dûn.
Bother, (*v.*) ti buai, luh.
Bottle, (*s.*) sai-doi-um, pa-lang.
Bottom, (*s.*) mong, (false) mong-phu-hru.
Bough, (*s.*) zâr.
Boulder, (*s.*) lung.
Bounce, (*v.*) sawh-khawk.

Bound together, (*a.*) in-bel-bom.
Boundary, (*s.*) ri.
Bow, (*s.*) (for arrows) thal-ngul, (pellet bow) sai-raw-kherh (tied) suih-hlih, (of fiddle) tum-fung, naw'fung.
Bow, (down to the ground) lei shi.
Bowels, (*s.*) kua, rîl, (lower extremity of) tai; (*v.*) (to have protrusion of the bowels) tai a tla.
Bowl, (*s.*) berh-bu, sai-khûp, sâp-berh-bu.
Bow-legged, (*a.*) ke-kual.
Box, (*s.*) bawm, thing-rem, chhun-duk, sum-duk, sum-duk-bawm.
Boy, (*s.*) nao-pang, mi-pa naopang.
Boyhood, (*s.*) naopang-lai.
Boyish, (*a.*) naopang ang.
Braces, (*s.*) ke-kor a'na, ke-kor dâr-bak, dâr-bak.
Bracelet, (*s.*) bân-bun, (the name of a) ngûn.
Brag, (*v.*) uâng, in-fak.
Brain, (*s.*) thluak.
Brake fern, (*s.*) cha-kok, kât-chât.
Bran, (*s.*) vai-dip.
Branch, (*s.*) zâr, chhawl, (small) ṭang, (*a.*) pêng, (*v.*) (to branch or branch off) pêng, (road or path) kong-pêng.
Brass, (*s.*) dâr.
Brave, (*a.*) huai-shen, pasal-ṭha, huai, hrâng, hrât, ngam, (under suffering) chhel, (*v.*) (to brave a thing out) hmai thing hawng.
Bravely, (*adv.*) huai tak-in.
Brawny, (*a.*) dolh.
Brazen-faced, (*a.*) hmai-thing-hawng, tlâng-nêl.
Bread, (*s.*) chhâng.
Breadth, (*s.*) vâng.
Break, (*v.*) elh-tliak, ti-keh, ulh-tliak, (as custom or law), bawchhiat, (as rope) chat, (down) op, (through) rek-pop, (in, as horse, etc.) soi-zoi, thu-nun, (as lobe of ear, etc.), ti-peh, (wind) voih.
Breakfast, (*s.*) tuk-ṭhuan.
Breast, (*s.*) awm, eng, (breasts) hnu-tê.
Breast-bone, (*s.*) awm-ruh.
Breath, (*s.*) hu, (*v.*) (to be short of) thaw chham, thaw dang.
Breathe, (*v.*) thawk, (upon) hu.
Breathless, (*a.*) thaw chham.
Breeches, (*s.*) ke kar.
Breech-loading, (*a.*) mong thun.
Breeze, (*s.*) thli-fîm.
Brew, (*v.*) ur.
Bribe, (*v.* and *s.*) nawh-thuh, tham.

Bride, (*s.*) mo.
Bridge, (*s.*) lei, lei-lawn, (suspension) lei-pui, (curved) lei âr chang.
Brief, (*a.*) toi, tlêm.
Bright, (*a.*) êng, lâr.
Brightly, (*adv.*) êng tak-in.
Brilliant, (*a.*) êng.
Brim, (*s.*) tlâng.
Brimstone, (*s.*) kât.
Brine, (*s.*) tui al.
Bring, (*v.*) ron-thlen', keng, lâ*k*, ron-hawn, ron-shin, (bring in) lût-pui, (bring up, as child) op tlei, shiam mi-hring, (out) theh-chhuak, (round, after choloroform, etc.) ti-nung.
Bring forth, (bear) (*v.*) hring.
Brink, (*s.*) hmawr, vao-kam.
Brisk, (*a.*) ṭuan-rang.
Brittle, (*a.*) ram.
Broad, (*a.*) vâng, zao.
Broaden, (*v.*) ti zao.
Broken, (*a.*) tlia*k*.
Broken-hearted, (*a.*) lung chhiat, lung chhe.
Brood, (*v.*) (as fowl) op, tuam.
Brook, (*s.*) lui.
Brooklet, (*s.*) lui tê.
Broom, (*s.*) hmun-phiah.
Brother, (*s.*) u-nao, (a female's brother) nu-ṭa, (elder) u, (younger) nao, (own) chûl-khat kual-pui, pian'pui, (next to one's self in age) chhang-bung.
Brother-in-law, (sister's husband) mâk-pa, (husband's younger brother) nao, (husband's elder brother) u, (wife's brother) pu-zon.
Brow, (*s.*) mit ko (of hill, incline, etc.) ko.
Brown, (*a.*) hâng.
Browse, (*v.*) hnim pet.
Bruise, (*s.*) thi-tling, (*v. t.*) ti-thi-tling, (to be bruised) thi a thing.
Brush, (*v.*) nuai, (past) nûl.
Bubble, (*v.*) phûl, sho, (*s.*) phuan-puar.
Bud, (*s.*) kuh-mûm, (*v.*) kuh-mûm.
Buff coloured, (*a.*) buang.
Buffalo, (*s.*) loi, she-loi.
Bug, (*s.*) khum-fa.
Bugle, (*s.*) dâr-loi, taw-taw-rawt, loi-rawl.
Bugler, (*s.*) dâr-loi pu, dâr-loi hâm-tu, taw-taw-rawt hâm-tu, taw-taw-rawt pu, etc.

Build, (*v.*) (as nest) chhep, (house) shât.
Builder, (*s.*) sha tu, shiam tu.
Bulb, (*s.*) bul-bâl, bul-bawk.
Bulbous, (*a.*) bul-bâl nei, bul-bawk-nei.
Bulbul, (*s.*) tlai-berh.
Bulky, (*a.*) lian.
Bull, (*s.*) se-bawng-pa.
Bullet, (*s.*) si-lai mu.
Bullock, (*s.*) sebawng-pa, (driver) bawng-pu, bawng-khalh.
Bunch, (*s.*) bawr, bu, têl, thlâr.
Bunchy, (*a.*) buk.
Bundle, (*s.*) têl, ṭhe, (*v.*) (to tie up in a bundle) têl, ṭhe.
Burglar, (*s.*) ruk-ru.
Burly, (*a.*) awm-khaoh.
Burmese, (*s.*) kawl-mi.
Burn, (*v.*) hâl, kâng, urh, (as lamp, fire, etc.) alh, (out) ral.
Burning glass, (*s.*) ni-no.
Burnt, (*a.*) ût.
Burr, (*s.*) ber-bek, cha-bet.
Burrow, (*v.*) hreoh, kur-hreoh.
Burst, (*v.*) puak, shah.
Bury, (*v.*) phûm; (one end only) phun, (the face in the hands) kai-kûn, kim-ki.
Bushy, (*a.*) buk.
Busy, (*a.*) ṭûl.
But, lah, nima-she-la, shi, (except) lo-chu, lo-hi.
Butt, (*s.*) (for ridicule, etc.) chhiah, (of gun) silai mong pheng, (for pig's wash, water, etc.) tai-kuang, (*v.*) pir, shi, taoh, tai, nor.
Butterfly, (*s.*) phêng-phe-hlep, (a large species) kep-tuam.
Buttock, (*s.*) mong.
Button, (*s.*) chilh-na, kilh-na, (*v.*) chilh, kilh.
Buttonhole, (*v.*) puan-kâng-thui, (*s.*) (button-holing) puan-kâng-ṭhui.
Buy, (*v.*) lei, chawk.
Buzz, (*v.*) hrâm.
By, (*prep.*) in.
By and bye, (*adv.*) la, nakin-a, nakin-hnua, nakin-deo-a.
By chance, (*adv.*) kher, kher hlaoh.
By turns, in...chhawk.

C.

Cabbage, (*s.*) an-tam.
Cable, (*s.*) hrui-zên.
Cackle, (*v.*) dak-da-lêk, kâk.
Cage, (*s.*) rip.

Caked together, (*a.*) ruh.
Calculate, (*v.*) ngai-ruat.
Calf, (*s.*) se-bawng no, (of leg) chawn.
Call, (*v.*) ao, ko, (for) lam.
Calmly, (*a.*) tlang.
Calumniate, (*v.*) hek.
Camp, (*s.*) ria'buk.
Can, (*v.*) thei.
Cancel, (*v.*) paih.
Candle, (*s.*) khawn-vâr.
Cane, (*s.*) hrui, hrui-tung, châng-dam, sai-rîl, (split for tying) hnâng.
Cannibal, (*s.*) hring-ei.
Cannon, (*s.*) lai-pui.
Canter, (*v.*) zuang.
Cap, (*s.*) lu-khum, (percussion) dâr hlo.
Capacious, (*a.*) zao, lian.
Cape gooseberry, (*s.*) kel-a-sai-raw-phit, kel-a-sai-raw-pip, kel-a-sa-ri-phit.
Capitulate, (*v.*) thu-pha choi.
Capricious, (*a.*) lep chiah, om-eo.
Capsicum, (*s.*) hmar-cha.
Capsize, (*v.*) let.
Captive, (*s.*) (of war) sal.
Capture, (*v.*) man.
Carcase, (*s.*) ruang.
Cards, (*s.*) (playing) lekha, lekha in den'-na.
Care, (*v.*) poi ti, (to take) dîm, fîm khur.
Careful, (*a.*) dîm, fîm-khur, ngun, tîm.
Carefully, (*adv.*) ngun, dîm, ṭha-hnem-ngai-tak-in.
Careless, (to be) ngai-sam.
Carelessly, (*adv.*) duh-dah.
Caress, (*v.*) pom.
Carpenter, (*s.*) thing-rem shiam-tu.
Carpet, (*s.*) puan phah.
Carriage, (*s.*) taw-lai-lîr.
Carrier, (*s.*) puak-phur, puak-phur mi, puak-pêr phur.
Carry, (*v.*) (on head) khum, chhip-chhuang, (lamp, torch, etc.) chhi, (on back, as child) paw, pua*k*, (cock-shoulder) pung-pu-lût, (on shoulder) pu, put, (in hand, etc.) shin, (in satchel, or slung across shoulder) a*k*, (a child in front) hma-thlâ*k*, (loads on each end of pole the centre of which rests on the shoulder) kot, (on back, in a basket or as a load) phur, (on hip, or under arm) zak ze', (between two persons) zawn, (lashed to a pole between two persons) zawng-zawn.

Cart, (*s.*) taw-lai-lir.
Case, (*s.*) bawm, (judicial) thu poi.
Cast, (*v.*) (metal, etc.) chhûng, (a net, stone, etc.), dêng, (lots) ṭhum vawr.
Caste, (*s.*) chi.
Castor-oil plant, (*s.*) mu-ṭih.
Castrate, (*v.*) til re*k*, til lâ*k*.
Cat, (*s.*) zawh-tê, (wild) sa-nghar, (call for cat) chhi-tê, chhi-tê nai nai.
Catch, (*v.*) dong, dom, (in anything) ṭâng.
Caterpillar, (*s.*) pa-ngang.
Catfish, (*s.*) thai-chhawn-i nu, ngha-mi.
Cattle, (*a.*) ran.
Caul, (*s.*) ham-da.
Cause, (*s.*) bul, (*v.*) tîr, (of) phah.
Causelessly, (*adv.*) mai-mai.
Cautious, (*a.*) tîm.
Cave, (*s.*) pûk.
Cavity, (*s.*) khur, khuar, khuar-khu-rum.
Cease, (*v.*) bân*g*, hân.
Cell, (*s.*) (of prison) rip.
Censure, (*v.*) hao.
Centipede, (*s.*) tît.
Centre, (*s.*) lai, lai-tak.
Certain, (*a.* and *pro.*) tu-te-emaw, tu-emaw.
Certainly, (*adv.*) ma-thei-lo, ma-thei-lo-vin, mâk-mawh, molh, ngei, phot, êm, êm êm, (not) raih lo, riai lo.
Chaff, (*s.*) fa-vai.
Chain, (*s.*) khai-diat.
Chair, (*s.*) ṭhut-phah, ṭhut-na, ṭhut-thlêng.
Chakma, tribe (*s.*) Takam.
Chalk, (*s.*) tlak.
Chamber, (*s.*) pin-dan, pin-dan chhûng.
Chameleon, (*s.*) lai-kîng.
Chance, (*adv.*) (by) hlaoh.
Change, (*v.*) thlâk-thlen*g*, thlen*g*, (as mind or opinion) shon, (into) chang, (the mind) ril-ru shon, ril-ru lam let, thin-lung shon.
Changed, (*a.*) dang-lam.
Changsil, (*s.*) Tlong-dawr.
Channel, (*s.*) kuang, kuam.
Chapati, (*s.*) chhang-pêr.
Chapped, (*a.*) chât.

Chapter, (*s.*) bung.
Char, (*v.*) hâl.
Charcoal, (*s.*) mei-hol.
Charitable, (*a.*) thil phal.
Charm, (*v.*) ai kaih.
Chase, (*v.*) ûm.
Chastise, (*v.*) vêl, vua*k*.
Chatter, (*v.*) dang-nâl.
Chatterer, (*s.*) ţong thei.
Chattels, (*s.*) sum.
Cheap, (*a.*) to lo.
Cheaply, (*adv.*) hlawk.
Cheat, (*v.*) bum.
Cheek, (*s.*) biâng.
Cheeky, (*a.*) tlâng-nêl.
Cheer, (*v.*) thla-muan, thla-nak, (to cheer up, to be cheered) harh, thla-muang.
Cheerful, (*a.*) hlim, lawm.
Cheerfully, (*adv.*) hlim tak-in, lawm tak-in.
Cherry, (*s.*) thlai-zong.
Chest, (*s.*) awm.
Chestnut, (*s.*) (tree) thing-shia, (nut) thing-shia mîm.
Chew, (*v.*) ţhei, ţhial (as quid, etc.) hmuam.
Chicken, (*s.*) âr-tê, âr-no.
Chide, (*v.*) hao.
Chief, (*s.* and *a.*) lal.
Child, (*s.*) nao-pang, (to be with child) nao pai.
Childbirth, (*v.*) (to die in) rai-cheẹh.
Childhood, (*s.*) nao-pan*g*-lai.
Childish, (*a.*) naopang chal â.
Children, (sons and daughters collectively) fa-nao.
Chilli, (*s.*) hmar-cha.
Chilly, (*a.*) vot.
Chimney, (*s.*) mei-khu chhua'na.
Chin, (*s.*) kha-be, (double) kha-bor.
China, (*s.*) rial.
Chins, (*s.*) Poi.
Chip, (*s.*) sha-hâr, thing-hâr, (*v.*) ti-hêk, ti-bal.
Chipped, (*a.*) bal, kîng-ha.
Chirp, (*v.*) hrâm.
Chisel, (*s.*) thîr-khen.
Chittagong, (*s.*) Sitikâng.
Choke, (*v.*) hâk.

Cholera, (*s.*) tui-hri, tui-shuk.
Choose, (*v.*) ruat, ṭan, thlang.
Chop, (*v.*) shât, chek, tuk, (off) tan.
Chopper, (*s.*) chem.
Chrysalis, (*s.*) pa-ngang bawm, buh-chi-ûm, pa-ngang bu.
Chubby, (*a.*) chom, chum.
Chuckle, (*v.*) di-ri-am.
Churn, (*v.*) sawh, sawh-khal.
Cigar, (*s.*) dum-ei zial.
Cinnamon, (*s.*) thak-thîng.
Circle, (*s.*) bial.
Circuitous, (*a.*) kual.
Circular, (*a.*) val.
Circumcise, (*v.*) zang tan.
Circumstances, (*s.*) khaw-shak, khaw-shak-zia.
City, (*s.*) khua lian.
Civet cat, (*s.*) therh, sa-tlum, sa-zaw, tlum-therh, tlum-pui.
Claim, (*v.*) chuh.
Clamour, (*v.*) buai.
Clan, (*s.*) chi, hnam.
Clansman, (*s.*) (a fellow) lai-chîn.
Clap, (*v.*) bêng.
Clasp, (*v.*) hûm, (hands) kut suih.
Claw, (*s.*) tin, (of crab) ai bop, (*v.*) ham, ṭhâm.
Clay, (*s.*) bêl-lei, son-tlung-lei, son-tlung, (ready kneaded for making pots) hlum.
Clean, (*a.*) fai, thiang, thiang-hlim, (*v.*) nawt-fai, (up) thiang, thiar.
Cleanse, (*v.*) in-thian.
Clear, (*a.*) fîm, kiang, lâr, thiang, (up or away) thian-fai, (of a crime) hul, (*v.*) (jungle) sâm.
Clearly, (*a.*) fiah.
Clear-sighted, (*a.*) mit vâr.
Clerk, (*s.*) lekha-ziak-tu.
Clench, (*v.*) hûm.
Clever, (*a.*) beng-vâr, fing, them-thiam.
Cliff, (*s.*) khâm.
Climb, (*v.*) lawn, zâm-kai, zem.
Clinch, (*v.*) (the hand) kut tum.
Cling, (*v.*) bet, vuan.
Clip, (*v.*) chep.
Clock, (*s.*) sana, sana lâm thei.
Clod, (*s.*) lei-tlang, nêl-tlang.
Clog, (*s.*) phei-kok.

Close, (*v.*) chhîn, chîp, khâr, mûm, ping, (as leaf at night) mu, (hot) thaw sha, (close together) phui, zing, zîm, muk, (closed up) ping, (*prep.*) (close to) dep-a, hrual-a.
Clot, (*s.*) tlang.
Cloth, (*s.*) puan.
Clothes, (*s.*) silh-fên, (old, left off) silh-fên chhia.
Cloud, (*s.*) chhûm.
Cloudy, (*a.*) duai.
Clove, (s.) long-pâr.
Club, (*s.*) tal-tum.
Cluck, (*v.*) ṭuk.
Clump, (*s.*) hung.
Cluster, (*s.*) bu, bawr.
Coarse, (*a.*) phok.
Coast, (*s.*) kam, tui pui kam.
Coat, (*s.*) kor.
Cobra, (*s.*) chong-kor.
Coccyx, (*s.*) ngûm-fi ruh.
Cock, (*s.*) âr-pa, (*v.*) (a gun) kao, (half cock) kao-*k*hat, (full cock) kao-hnih.
Cockerel, (*s.*) âr-pa tlei-rawl.
Cockroach, (*s.*) chuk-chu, khao-hriang.
Cockscomb, (*s.*) (plant) zo âr-chhuang.
Cocoanut, (*s.*) tui-kun-luk.
Cocoon, (*s.*) pa-ngang bawm, pa-ngang bu.
Coffin, (*s.*) kuang, kuang-tuah.
Cogitate, (*v.*) ngai-tua.
Cohabit, (*v.*) in-fan, in-lu-khung.
Coil, (*s.* and *v.*) kual, vial.
Cold, (*a.*) vot, khua shik, shik, tang-thawm, (as food) ṭhing, (*s.*) (a cold) hri-tlâng. (Also to have a cold.)
Cold, (to be) khua a shik, (the cold weather) thla-shik.
Collapse, (*v.*) op, sop, chim.
Collarbone, (*s.*) khing-khang ruh.
Collect, (*v.*) chhek-khawm, khon, lawr, (*int.*) tling, (a debt) ṭhing.
Collide, (*v.*) in-chu, shu, nor, tong.
Colour, (*s.*) zia.
Coloured, (*a.*) ṭial.
Colt, (*s.*) sa-kor no.
Comb, (*s.*) (of fowl) âr-chhuang, (for hair) khuih, sam-khuih, (*v.*) khuih, khuih-hniar.
Combed out, (*a.*) hniar.
Combustible, (*a.*) kâng thei.

Come, (*v.*) lo-kal, haw, hawng, lo-haw, (come off) dawk, (come back) lo-kîr, kîr, (come to, from chloroform) nung, (come up to) pawh, (come out or off) thlon, (out) chhua*k*, (come home from work) lo sûl hawn*g*, (off, as cover, hat, etc.) phong, phok, (out, as teeth, or off, as stalk of fruit, etc.) thlon.
Comet, (*s.*) shi-mei-khu.
Comfort, (*v.*) hnêm, thla-muan, thla-hnak, thlêm.
Comfortable, (*a.*) nuam.
Comforted, (*v.*) (to be) thla-muang.
Command, (*v.* and *s.*) thu tiam, tiam, thupê*k*, tuk, (*s.*) thu thu.
Commander, (*s.*) ho-tu.
Commanding, (*a.*) ro-pui, zah-om.
Commandment, (*s.*) thu, thu pêk, thu tiam.
Commence, (*v.*) ṭan, ṭan-tîr, bei.
Commission, (*v.*) tîr, chah.
Common, (*a.*) na-mên, na-rân, na-mai, na-zong, sa-tliah, tam, (*v.*) (to have or use in common) in-ṭawm.
Commonsense, (*a.*) (without) mawl.
Companion, (*s.*) pawl te, pawl-pui, pawl-mi, ṭhian.
Company, (*s.*) ho, ho-te, ho-va-te, pawl.
Company with, (*v.*) pawl.
Compare, (*v.*) en-ton, khai-khin, teh, teh-khin, teh-khawng.
Compared with, hnê*k*-in, hnê*k*-chuan.
Compassionate, (*v.*) lai-nat.
Compel, (*v.*) lui-tîr.
Compensate, (*v.*) rûl.
Compensation, (*s.*) rûl.
Compete, (*v.*) them-thiam.
Complain, (*v.*) phun-noi.
Complaint, (*s.*) thu-poi, thu-buai.
Complete, (*a.*) chap-châr, fam-kim, kin, ko-kim, kim, peih, tlâ*k*, tlei-tla, zawh, zo, tlin*g*-tlâ*k*, ṭum-tlâ*k*.
Completely, (*adv.*) fai-rêt, shioh, shên*g*.
Complicated, (*a.*) in-vet.
Compose, (*v.*) phuah.
Composer, (*s.*) phuah-tu, ti-chhua*k*-tu.
Comprehend, (*v.*) hriat, hria, hre.
Compress, (*v.*) ti-muk.
Comrade, (*s.*) ṭhian.
Concave, (*a.*) dâm, kûm, kum.
Conceal, (*v.*) bi-ru, khuh, thu*p* ru*k*, thup, thu*k*-ru*k*, zêp.
Conceited, (*a.*) chal-tlai.
Conceitedly, (*adv.*) chal-tlai.

Conceive, (*v.*) pai.
Concerning, (*prep.*) lam-thu-zong, lam-zong, thu.
Concertina, (*s.*) phai-phu-lêng.
Conch-shell, (*s.*) kep-pum.
Conciliate, (*v.*) thlêm.
Conclude, (*v.*) tawp, ṭum-tlâ*k*.
Conclusion, (*s.*) tawp.
Concourse, (*s.*) mi pung, pung-ho.
Concubine, (*s.*) hmei.
Condemn, (*v.*) thiam lo.
Condense, (*v.*) ti khal.
Conduct, (*v.*) hruai.
Conductor, (*s.*) hruai-tu.
Confess, (*v.*) thu-pha choi, (and ask pardon) pha*l*.
Confident, (*a.*) zuam.
Confiscate, (*s.*) lâk-sak.
Confluence, (*s.*) (of rivers) in-fin-na.
Confound, (*v.*) ti-hril-hai.
Confuse, (*v.*) ti-buai.
Confused, (*a.*) buai, ham-haih, hai-haih, chi-ai.
Confusing, buai-thlâk.
Confute, (*v.*) chhâl-dang, ti-dang.
Congeal, (*v.*) dak, khal, khang.
Congregate, (*v.*) in-khawm.
Congregation, (*s.*) mi pung, pung ho.
Conjecture, (*v.*) ring.
Conjure, (*v.*) mit-doi-vai.
Conjurer, (*s.*) mit doi vai thiam.
Connect, (*v.*) zom.
Connive, (*v.*) hai-der.
Conquer, (*v.*) ngam.
Conqueror, (*s.*) ngam tu.
Conscientious, (*a.*) pui-thu.
Consecutively, (*adv.*) in-dot zêl-in, in-dot tak-in, in-dot zia-in.
Consent, (*v.*) rem-tîr, rem-châng-tîr, rem ti.
Consequence, (of) poi.
Conservative, (*a.*) pui-thu.
Consider, (*v.*) bei-shei, dawn, ngai, ngai-tua, ruat.
Considerate, (*a.*) ngil nei.
Conspire, (*v.*) phiar, thu phiar.
Constantly, (*adv.*) fo, fan.
Construct, (*v.*) shiam.
Consult, (*v.*) in-rawn, rawn.
Consume, (*v.*) ti-hek.

Consumed, (*a.*) hêk.
Consumption, (*s.*) ngor.
Contact, (in) (*v.*) in-shi.
Contemn, (*v.*) chêk-sholh.
Contented, (*v.* and *a.*) lawm, lung-oi, lung-ni.
Contiguous, (*a.*) in-shi, in-zom.
Continually, (*adv.*) ſo, ſan, ṭhîn.
Continue, (*v.*) chêng, om, om-reng.
Continuously, (*adv.*) zêl.
Contract, (*v.*) shawn*g*, thêp, tom, (disease) vei, (to make) (*v.* and *s.*) thu-thlun*g*, in-tiam.
Contradict, (*v.*) hnial, hnial-kalh, kalh, khak, lo-kalh.
Contrary, (*adv.*) (to expectation or on the contrary) thlu-hial, (to) ang-lo-vin, lo-ang-in.
Contribute, (*v.*) thawh, thawh-khawm, thawh-lawn.
Convenient, (*a.*) rem, rem-chăng.
Converse, (*v.*) thu-khawh-chăng shoi.
Convert, (*s.*) sa-phun.
Convey, (*v.*) shin.
Convict, (*s.*) mi tăng, (*v.*) thiam lo, thiam lo chan*g* tîr.
Convincing, (*a.*) oih-măk-mawh.
Convincingly, (*adv.*) oih-măk-mawh-in,
Cook, (*v.*) chhûm, ti-hmin, chhûm-hmin, (a large quantity of food for journey) fûn-pui er, (with salt) bai, (without salt) tlak.
Cooked, (*a.*) hmin.
Cool, (*a.*) dai, thlan-dai.
Coolie, (*s.*) be-kar, puak-phur, puak-phur-mi, puak-pêr phur.
Coop, (*s.*) bawm.
Copper, (*s.*) dăr-shen, (sulphate of) kah-sa-mar.
Copy, (*v.*) en-ton, zir.
Copulate, (*v.*) in-ngai, (with) lu, ngai.
Cord, (*s.*) hrui.
Cork, (*s.*) chhîn, chhîn-na, (*v.*) chhîn.
Corn, (*s.*) (Indian corn) vai-mîm, (*v.*) (to have a corn) chăt.
Cornelian bead, (*s.*) ṭhi-beh.
Corner, (*s.*) kîl.
Corpse, (*s.*) ruang.
Corpulent, (*a.*) thao.
Correct, (*a.*) chiang, fel, (*v.*) shoi-ngîl, zilh.
Correctly, (*adv.*) chiang, fel.
Corrupt, (*a.*) ṭha lo, sual, (*v.*) ti-khaw-lo.
Cost, (*s.*) man.
Costly, (*a.*) to.

Cotton, (*s.*) la (thread) la zai, (winder) la kaih-na, (spun cotton on spindle) la-tui, (rolled cotton ready for spinning) la-chawm, (wind) (*v.*) la kaih.
Cotton tree, (*s.*) pang.
Cough, (*v.*) khuh.
Council, (*s.*) pung ho, mi pung.
Count, (*v.*) chhiar, chhin-chhiah.
Countenance, (*s.*) hmel.
Counterbalance, (*v.*) in-kai-kêp.
Counterfeit, (*a.*) lem.
Country, (*s.*) khua-lam, ram.
Couple, (*s.*) tuak.
Courageous, (*a.*) huai.
Court, (*v.*) nula rîm.
Cousin, (*s.*) unao, (a paternal aunt's child) tu, (a paternal uncle's younger child) nao, (a paternal uncle's elder child) u, (a maternal aunt's younger child) nao, (a maternal aunt's elder child) u, (a maternal uncle's daughter) pi, (a maternal uncle's son) pu.
Cove, (*s.*) li-teng-shawl.
Covenant, (*s.* and *v.*) thu thlung.
Coventry, (*v.*) (to send to) kawm-sherh.
Cover, (*v.*) bawm, bawm-khat-lûk, hu*p*, khuh, khum, (*s.*) chhîn, chhîn-na, (of book) kawm.
Covet, (*v.*) ît, ot.
Cow, (*s.*) se-bawng, bawng, se-bawng-pui.
Cowdriver, (*s.*) bawng-khalh, bawng-pu.
Cowkeeper, (*s.*) se-bawng vêng-tu.
Coward, (*s.*) mi doih.
Cowardly, (*a.*) doih.
Cowry, (*s.*) pai-hol.
Cozy, (*a.*) nuam.
Crab, (*s.*) chak-ai, ai.
Crab-trap, (*a.*) ai-awt.
Crack, (*v.* and *s.*) khi, (knuckles) kut-ulh, kut-ulh-ri, (on finger nail, as flea) deh.
Cracked, (*a.*) dor, khi.
Crafty, (*a.*) ngam-thlêm hmang.
Craftily, (*v.*) (to deal) ngam-thlêm.
Craftsman, (*s.*) them-thiam.
Crafty, (*a.*) fing.
Cramp, (*v.*) (to get) tha a chat.
Cramped, (for room) (*a.*) chep, tong-khong.
Crane, (*s.*) kâng-hlai.
Crawl, (*v.*) bok-vâk.

Creak, (*v.*) nawt-kiu, nawt-chîk, nawt-ri.
Creased, (*a.*) chu-ar.
Credible, (*a.*) oih-om, oih-tlâk.
Credit, (*s.*) ba, bat.
Creek, (*s.*) li-teng-shawl.
Creep, (*v.*) vâk.
Creeper, (*s.*) hrui.
Creepy, (*v.*) (to feel) ti a za.
Crest, (*s.*) (of bird) thlik-thli-dîr.
Cricket, (*s.*) khao, (house) khuang-tîr, khuang-chi-rît.
Crier, (*s.*) (a village) tlâng-ao.
Crimson, (*a.*) shen.
Cringe, (*v.*) tom-im.
Crinkled, (*a.*) chhok-olh.
Crisp, (*a.*) ngot, ngot shiah-shiah.
Croak, (*v.*) hrâm.
Crochet, (*v.*) phan, phiar.
Crocodile, (*s.*) aw-le, sa-ri-tom.
Crook, (*s.*) koih-sa-pir.
Crooked, (*a.*) koi.
Crop, (*s.*) (of fowl, etc.) ong, chok-chaw-ong, chok-chaw-eng.
Crops, (*s.*) thlawh-hma.
Cross, (*v.*) kân, kai, tan, (to look cross) tûm, (at an angle) thler, (legs, etc.) khaw-kherh, (angry) tao, (*s.*) (roads) lam ṭhuam.
Cross-examine, (*v.*) chhâl.
Cross-eyed, (*a.*) mit kalh.
Cross-grained, (*a.*) phiar.
Crossing, (*s.*) (of river, etc.) kai.
Crosswise, (*adv.*) tan-zawng-in, thler-zawng-in.
Crouch, (*v.*) bok-phêk, tom, tom-im.
Crow, (*v.*) khuang, (*s.*) cho-âk.
Crowbar, (*s.*) thîr-tlawn.
Crowd, (*v.*) chîm, (*s.*) mi-pui.
Crowded, (*a.*) tawt, zing.
Cruel, (*a.*) beng-tla-lo, nun-chhia, rawng.
Crumble, (*v.*) ti-noi.
Crumple, (*v.*) tom.
Crunch, (between the teeth) (*v.*) vâm.
Cry, (*v.*) hrâm, (weep) ṭap, (cry out) ao, (as black ape) hual-rêo, (as elephant and monkey) khêk.
Cubit, (*s.*) tong.
Cucumber, (*s.*) fang-hma.
Cultivate, (*v.*) khoi.
Cunning, (*a.*) fing.

Cup, (*s.*) no.
Cure, (*v.*) ti dam.
Curl up, (*v.*) khawr, (as snake) vial.
Curly, (*a.*) kir.
Current, (*s.*) tui-zang.
Curse, (*v.*) ân-chhia lawh, ân-chhe lawh.
Cursed, (*a.*) ân-chhia dong.
Curtain, (*s.*) puan-zâr.
Curved, (*a.*) âr-chang-koi, koi.
Custodian, (*s.*) vêng-tu.
Custom, (*s.*) dân.
Customary, (*v.*) (to be) ngai.
Cut, (*v.*) â*t*, zai, bung, shâ*t*, tu*k*, (off) tan, hlep, (in halves) phel, (hair) mê*t*, (down) ki*t*, (*jhúm*) vâ*t*, (with scissors) chep chhum, (short) dan*g* cha*t*, (through at one blow) fik, shât fik (down weeds, trees, etc., in large quantities) sâm, (off, as edge of thatch, etc., bamboo stumps, etc.) rawt.
Cylindrical, (*a.*) mûm-shawl.
Cymbal, (*s.*) beng-thek.

D

Daily, (*adv.*) nit-tin, ni-tin-in.
Dainty, (*v.*) duh tui.
Dam, (*v.*) (as water) khua*p*, (*s.*) tui khua*p*.
Damage, (*v.*) ti-chhia*t*, ti-chhe.
Damp, (*a.*) hnawn*g*, hnom, zop.
Damsel, (*s.*) nula.
Dance, (*v.*) lâm.
Danger, (in danger of) hlaoh-om.
Dangerous, (*a.*) hlaoh-om.
Dare, (*v.*) huam, ngam.
Daring, (*a.*) ro-rum, ngam, thu-rum.
Dark, (*a.*) thin (in colour) dum, vom, duk, hâng.
Darken, (*v.*) ti thim, ti duk.
Darkness, (*s.*) thim, thim-tham, khaw-thim.
Dart, (*s.*) ham-thal, thal.
Daub, (*v.*) hnoih, bel.
Daughter, (*s.*) fa-nu.
Daughter-in-law, (*s.*) mo.
Dawdle, (*v.*) muan*g*.
Dawn, (*v.*) khua a vâr, (*s.*) (early dawn) khaw-vâr, khaw-vâr-ţian.

Day, (*s.*) ni, chhûn, (daylight, daybreak), khaw-vâr, khaw-êng, (next) a-tûk-a, (day after day) ni-zawn-in, (all day) ni-lêng, ni-lêng-in, (three days hence) nak-tiam-a.
Day after to-morrow, nak-tip a, nak-thai-a, nak-tuk tuk leh-a.
Day and night, a chhûn a zân in.
Day before yesterday, ni-min-piah.
Dazzle, (*v.*) ên-khal, mit ti-vai, (to be dazzled) mit a vai.
Dazzling, (*a.*) mi ên khal thei.
Dead, (*a.*) thi, dam lo, (as tree) ro, (*adv.*) hlum.
Deadly, (*a.*) thi-na.
Deaf, (*a.*) beng-ngon*g*, beng-chhêt.
Deafened, (*a.*) khor.
Dear, (*a.*) (not cheap) to.
Debate, (*v.*) in-hnial.
Debris, (*s.*) nawl.
Debt, (*s.*) lei, tei-ṭha, lei tlang.
Debtor, (*s.*) lei ba.
Decapitate, (*v.*) lu tan.
Decay, (*v.*) ngêt.
Deceive, (*v.*) bum, bum-thlai, ti-bum, ti-der, ti-dawn*g*.
Decide, (*v.*) ril-ru nei.
Decimate, (*v.*) suat.
Declare, (*v.*) hril.
Decompose, (*v.*) ṭoih.
Decrease, (*v.*) kâm, kang.
Deeds, (*s.*) chê*t*-zia, thil ti.
Deep, (*a.*) thûk, (as sound) thûm.
Deer, (barking) sa-khi, (sambar) sa-zuk.
Defeat, (*v.*) ngam.
Defæcate, (*v.*) dai-lên*g*, ê*k*.
Defence, (*v.*) (to make a) thiam-na thu shoi.
Defend, (*v.*) hum.
Defer, (*v.*) dah, khêk.
Deformed, (*a.*) pian*g*-sual, shil-ong.
Defraud, (*v.*) ti dawng.
Defrauded, (to be) dawng, dawng-thlawn.
Degrade, (*v.*) ti-chhiat, ti-chhe, ti-kiam, (degraded) chhiat, chhe, kiam.
Delaswari river, (*s.*) Tlong.
Delay, (*s.* and *a.*) rei, (without) rei lo vin, rei rial lo vin, rei om lo vin.
Delayed, (to be) tâp.
Deliberate, (*v.*) dawn, ngai-tua.
Delicate, (*a.*) chhia-ṭha.
Delicious, (*a.*) tui.

Delight, (*v.*) lawm.
Delightful, (*a.*) lawm-om.
Deliver, (*v.*) man-tîr.
Demagree, (*s.*) Tla-bung.
Demand, (*v.*) phût.
Demolish, (*v.*) ti chhia*t*, ṭhiat.
Demon, (*s.*) huai, ram huai.
Demoralized, (*v.*) (to be) zâm.
Den, (*s.*) pûk.
Dense, (*a.*) hrêng, (with undergrowth) bon.
Deny, (*v.*) ṭan*g*, phaṭ.
Depart, (*v.*) kal, kal bo.
Depend upon, (*v.*) bêl, nghêng.
Dependant, (*s.*) ṭhui hruai.
Depose, (*v.*) ti tlawm.
Deposed, (*a.*) tlawm.
Depressing, (*a.*) thaw-pik-thlâk, uap.
Deprive, (*v.*) ti-dawn*g*, (to be deprived of) dawng, dawng thlawn.
Depth, (*s.*) pil.
Deride, (*v.*) dem, nui-shan.
Descend, (*v.*) chhuk.
Descendant, (*s.*) chi thlah, hnah-thlâk, thlah.
Descent, (*s.*) chhuk.
Desert, (*v.*) kal-bo-shan, (in order to go over another party) pa-kai shan, (*s.*) thla-ler ram, thla-ler.
Deserted, (*a.*) ram.
Desirable, (*a.*) duh-om, ît-om.
Desire, (*v.*) duh, ît, (*s.*) duh-thu sâm, (to express one's desires) duh-thu sâm.
Desist, (*v.*) in-shûm.
Desolate, (*a.*) thla-ler.
Despair, (*v.*) lung-ngai.
Despise, (*v.*) hmu-shit, tlawh-bet.
Despond, (*v.*) lung-ngai.
Destitute, (*v.*) pa-chhia.
Destroy, (*v.*) ti-chhiat, ti-chhe, (wilfully) ngai-sha.
Destructive, (*a.*) rawng.
Desultory, (*a.*) om-eo, lep-chiah.
Detached, (*a.*) fâl.
Detain, (*v.*) châr, châr-chilh, chelh, khuah-khirh, hrên*g*.
Deter, (*v.*) ṭhulh-tîr.
Determine, (*v.*) tum-tlat, tum-lui, tum-lui-hrâm, tum-hrâm, tum-ruh, tum-sa-ruh, ruh tak-in tum.

Detest, (*v.*) lung-ten, ten.
Detestable, (*a.*) ten-om.
Develop, (*v.*) (as breasts) um.
Devil, (*s.*) ram huai, huai.
Devise, (*v.*) rem-ruat.
Dew, (*s.*) dai.
Dewlap, (*s.*) or-fual.
Diaphragm, (*s.*) hâm.
Diarrhœa, (*s.*) kaw-chhia, von-a-shor, kaw-khawh, (*v.*) (to have) kua a chhia, von a shor, kua a khawh, kua a ṭha lo, kua-in zût.
Die, (*v.*) thi, hnuk a chhat, (to lie dying) thi chhawng-in lum, (to be in a dying state) thi chhawng-in om, [a natural death (used of domestic animals), to die and not have usual sacrifice offered, to die from exposure] thi-sawn, (die out) chi-mit, mang, (an unnatural death) sâr-in thi, sâr-thi, (suddenly, in sleep) zachham-in a la.
Difference, (*s.*) lêm, lêm-chuang.
Different, (*a.*) hrang, dang, dang-lam, lêm, lêm-chuang.
Difficult, (*a.*) har, har-sha, rit, khirh, ril.
Difficulty, (with), (*adv.*) hrâm.
Diffident, (*a.*) zak-zum.
Dig, (*v.*) lai.
Digest, (*v.*) pai.
Diligent, (*a.*) tai-ma, tha-tho.
Dim, (*a.*) (as sight) vâr lo.
Dimple, (*s.*) biang-chhu, biang-khuar.
Din, (*s.*) beng-chheng.
Dine, (*v.*) chaw ei.
Dip, (*v.*) hnim, chiah, hnim-lût, (up) thâl.
Direction, (*s.*) lam, zawng.
Directly, (*adv.*) ve-leh.
Dirt, (*s.*) bol-hlawh.
Dirty, (*a.*) bâl, bol-hlawh, ṭom, uk, ung.
Disable, (*v.*) ti-sil.
Disabled, (*a.*) sil.
Disagree, (*v.*) in-hal.
Disagreeable, (*a.*) tao.
Disallow, (*v.*) oih lo.
Disappear, (*v.*) liam, ral.
Disappointed, (*a.*) nuar.
Disapprove, (*v.*) hnual-shuat.
Disbelieve, (*v.*) hnar-thla, hnar-kîr, oih lo, sa-thla, zawm lo.
Disciple, (*s.*) zir.
Discolour, (*v.*) uk, ung.

Discontented, (*v.* and *a.*) lung-ni-lo, lung-oi-lo.
Discontinue, (*v.*) bâng.
Discouraged, (*a.*) lung-ngai.
Discover, (*v.*) hmu.
Discuss, (*v.*) in-hnial.
Disdain, (*v.*) hmu-shit.
Disease, (*s.*) na, hri.
Disembark, (*v.*) chhuak, khaw-mual chhuak.
Disgrace, (*v.*) hming ti chhiat.
Disgraced, (to be) hming chhiat, hming hliao.
Disgraceful, (*a.*) zah-thlâk.
Disgusting, (*a.*) ten-om.
Dish, (*s.*) thlêng.
Disheartened, (*a.*) lung-ngai.
Dishevelled, (*a.*) buk, hreo, thêo.
Dishonest, (*a.*) dep-dê, awk-hrawl.
Dish up, (*v.*) khorh.
Dislike, (*v.*) duh-lo, hreh, lung-ten, ten, huat, haw.
Dislocate, (*v.*) ti-pelh-solh.
Dislocated, (*a.*) pelh-solh.
Dismantle, (*v.*) (house, etc.) ṭhiat.
Dismiss, (*v.*) ṭîn-tîr.
Disobey, (*v.*) oih lo.
Disobedient, (*a.*) kawh-mawh, luh-lul, ti-mawh, ngol-tawt.
Disown, (*v.*) lung-ten.
Dispatch, (*v.*) tîr, kal-tîr, thon.
Disperse, (*v.*) darh, kiang, ṭeh, ṭiao, ṭîn.
Displease, (*v.*) ti lung ni lo, (displeased,) (*v.* and. *a.*) lung-oi-lo, lung-ni-lo, tao.
Disposition, (*s.*) ṭong-ka, ṭong-kam, nung-chang.
Dispute, (*v.*) in-hnial.
Disregard, (*v.*) ngai-tlawm, poi-sha-lo.
Disrespect, (*v.*) poi-sha-lo, (the rights of) nêk.
Dissension, (*s.*) thu-buai.
Dissimilar, (*a.*) in-ang-lo, ang lo.
Dissolve, (*v.*) ti-tui.
Dissuade, (*v.*) ui, ui-bâng.
Distance, (at or from a) (*prep.*) râl-a.
Distant, (*a.*) hla.
Distil, (*v.*) chhûm, ur.
Distinct, (*a.*) fiah.
Distinction, (*v.*) (to make), thlei.
Distinctly, (*adv.*) fiah.
Distinguish, between, (*v.*) thlei.

Distrain, (*v.*) kar-nân hrêng.
Distribute, (*v.*) shem.
Distrust, (*v.*) hlao-thawng.
Disturb, (*v.*) ti-buai.
Disturbance, (*s.*) beng-chheng, (*v.*) (to make a) chok-hnok, chok buai, beng chheng.
Ditch, (*s.*) tui-hawr.
Dive, (*v.*) li-luh.
Diverge, (*v.*) ar.
Divert, (*v.*) (stream, etc.) thliar.
Divide, (*v.*) in-shem, shem, hlîr, ṭhen.
Divorce, (*v.*) mâ*k*.
Divulge, (*v.*) kam-tam.
Dizzy, (*a.*) hai, lu a hai.
Do, (*v.*) ti, lum, thaw*k* bei, chêt.
Doctor, (*s.*) dam doi mi, (*v.*) thoi.
Dog, (*s.*) ui, (wild) ching-hnia, ching-hne, (call for) chi-u, chi-u-hiah.
Doings, (*s.*) thil ti.
Dolphin, (*s.*) zawng-dûli nu.
Domestic animals, poultry, etc., (*s.*) ran.
Domesticate, (*v.*) khoi.
Donkey, (*s.*) sa-beng-tung, sakor-beng-tung.
Door, (*s.*) kong-khâr.
Door-post, (*s.*) kong-ka biâng, kong-khâr biâng.
Door-way, (*s.*) kong, kong-ka.
Double, (*a.*) thuah hnih, in-thuah, thuah, phîr, (*v.*) (up) (as leaf, etc.) khawr.
Double-faced, (*a.*) ver-vêk, ver-ther.
Doubt, (*v.*) ring-hlel.
Doubtless, (*adv.*) ma-thei lo-vin, hlel lo.
Dove, (*s.*) ṭhu-ro.
Down, (*adv.*) bet, chhuk, (verbal prefix) zuk.
Down-hearted, (*a.*) kim-ki, ngui, nguai.
Downhill, (*adv.*) chhuk.
Down stream, (*adv.*) lui mong lam-a.
Downward, (*a.*) thlang lam, chhuk lam.
Downwards, (*adv.*) chhuk, chhuk-zawng-in.
Drag, (*v.*) hnûk.
Dragon fly, (*s.*) dai, tui-the.
Drake, (*s.*) va-rak pa.
Draught, (*s.*) thli.
Draw (water), (*v.*) choi, (breath) hîp, hûp, (in, as stomach) îp, (as water from well) khai, (with syphon) shiak, (in, as head) tlum.

Drawn together, (*a.*) tom.
Dread, (*v.*) hlao.
Dream, (*s.*) mang, mu-mang, (*v.*) mu-mang-a mang, mu-mang nei.
Dregs, (*s.*) noi.
Dress, (*s.*) silh-fên, puan.
Drift, (*s.*) nawl.
Drill, (*v.*) lâm, (a hole) verh, verh-awng.
Drink, (*v.*) in, (through a tube) khawn, (*s.*) in-tûr.
Drinkable, (*a.*) in-tlâk.
Drip, (*v.*) far.
Drive, (*v.*) khalh, (away) kno*t*, hno*t*-daih, (out) hno*t*-chhua*k*.
Drizzle, (*s.* and *v.*) ruah-phing-phi-shiao.
Droop, (*v.*) kûr.
Drooping, (*a.*) kuai.
Drop, (*s.*) far, fang, mal, (*v.*) thlaoh, (down) thlâk-thla.
Drown, (*v.*) tui-a tla hlum.
Drowsy, (*a.*) mit-men'sak.
Drudge, (*s.*) tir-chhiah.
Drug, (*s.*) hlo.
Drum, (*s.*) khuang.
Drum-stick, (*s.*) tum-fung.
Drunk, (*v.*) (to be) rui, zu rui.
Drunkard (boisterous), (*s.*) zu-ngol-vei.
Dry, (*a.*) rêp, ṭhe, ro, hram, hul, khêng, shâng, ṭan*g*, (*v.*) hem, hem ro, (up) kang, (in sunshine) pho, (over fire) rêp.
Dry season, (*s.*) (the) ṭhâl.
Duck, (*s.*) va-rak, (wild) tui-va-rak.
Ducks and drakes, (*v.*) (to make) lai lên tui pal.
Duckling, (*s.*) va rak no.
Due, (*v.*) ṭûl.
Dull, (*a.*) (intellect) tlok-tlaw, ngong, chut, (in colour) mûk, duk (weather) duai.
Dumb, (*a.*) ṭong thei lo.
Dung, (*s.*) êk.
Dung beetle, (*s.*) pawng-êk-lîr.
Dunghill, (*s.*) êk-dûr.
Durable, (*a.*) chhe-har, tlo.
During, (*prep.*) chung-in, hlân-in.
Dust, (*s.*) vai-vut, vut, phut, (*v.*) hrûk-fai, (to make dust) vai-vut ti-khu, (suspended in the air) vai vut khu.
Dwell, (*v.*) om.
Dysentery, (*s.*) san-tên, (*v.*) (to have) san-tên.
Dyspepsia, (*s.*) kaw chhia.

E

Each, (*pro.*) ṭheoh, (of two) ve ve, (other) in.
Eager, (*v.*) nghâk hlel.
Ear, (*s.*) beng, (of grain) vui, (of maize in the cob) kawm, (*v.*) vui.
Early, (*adv.*) hma.
Earn, (*v.*) hlawh.
Earnest, (*a.*) ṭha hnem-ngai.
Ear-ring, (*s.*) (woman's) beng-beh, (man's) ṭhi beh.
Earwig, (*s.*) mong-chep.
Earth, (*s.*) lei, (to earth up) vûr.
Earthen, (*a.*) lei.
Earthquake, (*s.*) lîr nghîng, (*v.*) lîr a nghîng.
Earthworks, (*s.*) lei-kulh.
Easily, (*adv.*) ol, sham.
East, (*s.*) chhak-lam, khaw-chhak, chhak.
Eastward, chhak lam-a.
Easy, (*a.*) ol, sham.
Easy going, (*a.*) thin-nel.
Eat, (*v.*) ei, (to eat and drink) ei in bâr, (with spoon) hawp.
Eatable, (*a.*) thei, ei thei, ei rual.
Eaves, (*s.*) ba-thlâr.
Eavesdropper, (*v.*) (to listen as an) ngai-thlâ*k*.
Echo, (*s.* and *v.*) thang-khawk.
Eclipse, (*s.*) awk lêm, (*v.*) (to be eclipsed) awk-in a lem, lân, hlia.
Economise, (*v.*) ren.
Edge, (*s.*) hma, hmawr, tlâng, ha, vao-kam, (*v.*) (to be on edge) ziao, (to set on edge) ti-ziao, (on edge through eating acid fruit) tîm.
Eel, (*s.*) ngha-rûl.
Effervesce, (*v.*) sho.
Egg, (*s.*) tui, (to lay an egg) tui.
Egg-fruit, (*s.*) bok-bawn.
Eight, (*a.*) pa-riat, riat.
Eighteenth, (*a.*) shom leh pa-riat-na.
Eighth, (*a.*) pa-riat-na.
Eightieth, (*a.*) shom-riat-na.
Eighty, (*a.*) shom-riat.
Either, (*pro.*) a-zeng-pawh, a-eng-pawh.
Eject, (*v.*) chhua*k*-tîr, ti-chhua*k*.
Eke out, (*v.*) ren.
Ekra, (*s.*) luang.
Elastic, (*a.*) fân.

Elated, (*v.*) (to be) thin lung a hlim.
Elbow, (*s.*) kiu.
Elder, (*s.*) kawn-bawl, u-pa.
Elephant, (*s.*) sai.
Elephant trap, (*s.*) sai hum.
Elevated, (*a.*) (as country) zo.
Eleven, (*a.*) shom leh pa-khat.
Elfin lock, (*s.*) bak.
Else, (*conj.*) ani-lo-leh, ani-lo-vêk-leh.
Elsewhere, (*adv.*) dang lama.
Embank, (*v.*) chhûng-kha*t*,
Embankment, (*s.*) chhûng-kha*t*.
Embark, (*v.*) lawn.
Embarrassed, (*a.*) thaw-pik.
Embarrassing, (*adv.*) thaw-pik-thlâk.
Ember, (*s.*) mei-ling, mei-vân, thuk-duk.
Embrace, (*v.*) ir leh ir chuk-tuah, pom.
Eminent, (*a.*) lian.
Emissary, (*s.*) pa-lai.
Emphasize, (*v.*) uar.
Emphatically, (*adv.*) tlat.
Employ, (*v.*) ruai, ṭan*g*-tîr.
Employé, (*s.*) roih.
Employer, (*s.*) ruai-tu.
Empty, (*a.*) ruak, ram, (out) bun.
Emulate, (*v.*) el.
Enable, (*v.*) tîr.
Encamp, (for the night) ria*k*.
Encircle, (*v.*) bun, vial.
Enclose, (*v.*) fûn, hung.
Enclosure, (*s.*) huang, huang-chhûng.
Encourage, (*v.*) fuih, muan, (to be encouraged) muang.
Encumbered, (*a.*) hnok, (with a family) chhang-chhe, chhang-chia*t*.
End, (*s.*) tawp, hmawr, hmûr, (of sentence) lêr.
Endure, (*v.*) ngai, tuar, ngai-thei, (patiently) tlawm-ngai, chhel.
Enemy, (*s.*) râl, hmêl-ma.
Energetic, (*a.*) tai-ma.
Engage, (*v.*) ṭan*g*-tîr, (one's self) ṭan*g*.
Engrave, (*v.*) ziak.
Engraving, (*s.*) zia.
Enjoyable, (*a.*) lawm-om.
Enlarge, (*v.*) ti-zao, horh-zao.
Enlighten, (*v.*) ti-harh.
Enlightened, (*a.*) beng-vâr.

Enmity, (*v.*) (to be at) in-do, in-nghir-ngho, in-tai.
Enormous, (*a.*) lian pui.
Enough, (*adv.*) khop, tawk, (*v.*) (to be) kim, tawk, (it is enough) khai-le, khai-tawh-le, khai-tawh.
Enquire, (*v.*) rawn, zawt.
Enrage, (*v.*) ti-thin-ur.
Entangle, (*v.*) ti-phiar, ti-pheng.
Entangled, (*a.*) phiar, pheng, phek, (not entangled) hniar.
Enter, (*v.*) lût, len*g*.
Entertain, (*v.*) chên' pui, om-pui.
Entice, (*v.*) thlêm.
Entire, (*a.*) kim.
Entirely, (*adv.*) vek, var, viah, vua, vur-var, fam-kim.
Entrails, (*s.*) rîl.
Entrance, (*s.*) (to a village) kot-chhuah.
Entreat, (*v.*) ṭa'awh.
Entrenchment, (*s.*) lei-kulh.
Entrust with, (*v.*) kol-tîr.
Envelope, (*v.*) bawm.
Enviable, (*a.*) ît-shîk-om.
Environs, (*s.*) dai-vel.
Envoy, (*s.*) pa-lai.
Envy, (*v.*) ît-shîk, ot.
Epidemic, (*s.*) hri-pui.
Epileptic, (*s.*) khaw-pal, (*v.*) (to have an epileptic fit) khua-in pal.
Equal, (*a.*) in-chen, in-hen, in-tluk, thu-hmun, tluk.
Equally, (*adv.*) zât leh zât-in.
Equivalent, (*a.*) thu-hmun.
Erase, (*v.*) paih.
Erect, (*a.*) fuk.
Erroneous, (*a.*) sual.
Eructate, (*v.*) irh.
Escape, (*v.*) pum-pelh, relh, relh-ru, tlân-chhua*k*, tlân-bo.
Escort, (*v.*) thlen*g*, hruai.
Especially, (*adv.*) molh.
Estimate, (*v.*) ngai-ruat.
Eternal, (*a.*) cha-tuan.
Eternally, (*adv.*) cha-tuan-a.
Etcetera, chuti khati, eng-kim.
Evaporate, (*v.*) kang, (salt water) ten*g*-khal.
Even, (*adv.*) mah, tal, pawh, pôh, (*a.*) mar, mâm-rem, rual, rual-rem, (not odd) kop kim.
Evening, (*s.*) khaw-thim, tlai-lam, (star) chong-moi-i.
Ever, (*adv.*) ngai, (for ever) cha-tuan-a, chatuan-in, kum-khua-in.

Every, (*a.*) tin.
Everyone, (*pro.*) ṭheoh.
Everything, (*s.*) eng-kim.
Everywhere, (*adv.*) khaw-tin-a, ram-tin-a, ṭheoh.
Evil, (*a.*) sual.
Evil eye, (*v.*) (to be affected with) khaw-ring, khaw-ring-in ei, (one having), (to ward off) khaw-ring thiar, (*s.*) khaw-ring-nei, khaw-ring-nei tu.
Ewe, (*s.*) berâm-pui.
Exact, (*a.*) tak tak, tak.
Exactly, (*adv.*) tak, thên, ti-tak-in, zia, tê.
Exaggerate, (*v.*) uar.
Exalt, (*v.*) choi-moi, (one's self) in ngai-hlu, in-ngai-na.
Exalted, (*a.*) moi.
Examine, (*v.*) (by questioning) chhuah-chhâl.
Example, (*v.*) (to set) kulh-a ṭang, tu-pa-a ṭang, ti-hmu.
Exasperate, (*v.*) run-râl, run.
Exasperating, (*a.*) run-thlâk.
Exceeding, or exceedingly, (*adv.*) êm, êm êm, viao, zet, na-sh a na, hle.
Excel, (*v.*) lân, (to strive to) el.
Excellent, (*a.*) ṭha, tui.
Except, (*prep.*) lo-chu, lo-hi, etc.
Excepting, (*prep.*) lo-chu, lo-chuan.
Exchange, (*v.*) in-thleng, thlâk-thleng.
Excite, (*v.*) ti-hai-haih, ti-chi-ai, ti-ham-haih.
Excited, (*a.*) hai-haih, chi-ai, ham-haih.
Excommunicate, (*v.*) hnong-tîr, (to be excommunicated) hnong.
Excrement, (*s.*) êk.
Excrescence, (*s.*) bawk.
Excuse, (*s.*) chhuan-lam, (*v.*) (to make) chhuan-lam, chhuan-lam nei, hnial.
Exercise, (*v.*) soi-zoi, (to take) in-soi-zoi.
Exert, (*v.*) ṭang.
Exhausted, (*v.*) (to be) chao.
Exhaustless, (*a.*) hek-thei-lo.
Exhibit, (*v.*) en-tîr.
Exhort, (*v.*) zilh.
Exhume, (*v.*) phorh.
Exist, (*v.*) om, tla.
Exorcise, (*v.*) thoi.
Exorcist, (*s.*) pui-thiam.
Expect, (*v.*) bei-shei, ngai-bei-shei.
Expel, (*v.*) hnot-chhuak.

Expend, (*v.*) hral.
Expensive, (*a.*) man, to.
Expert, (*a.*) them-thiam.
Expire, (*v.*) thi.
Explain, (*s.*) hril-fiah, hriat-tîr, shoi-ngîl, (thoroughly) khun-tak-in hril.
Explode, (*v.*) puak.
Expose, (*v.*) puang.
Expound, (*v.*) hril-fiah.
Extensive, (*a.*) zao, o.
Exterior, (*s.*) pawn, pawn-lam.
Exterminate, (*v.*) ti-chi-mit, ti-mang.
Extinct, (*a.*) mang, chi-mit.
Extinguish, (*v.*) ṭhelh, ti-chi-mit, ti-thi, ti-hlum, ti-mit.
Extol, (*v.*) fak.
Extort, (*v.*) hlêp-ru.
Extract, (*v.*) phoi.
Extraordinary, (*a.*) duai lo, duai-dîm lo, na-mên lo.
Exude, (*v.*) chhua*k*.
Eye, (*s.*) mit, (of needle) beng, (to have something in the eye) mit a mîm.
Eyeball, (*s.*) mit-mu.
Eyebrows, (*s.*) mit-ko, mit-ko-tlâng.
Eye-glasses, (*s.*) tar mit.
Eyelashes, (*s.*) mit hmul.
Eye-lid, (*s.*) mit-vun.
Eye-witness, (*s.*) hmu-tu.

F

Fable, (*s.*) thon-thu.
Face, (*v.*) hma-chhon, chhon*g*, ep, hma-ton, (to be face to face) in hma-ton, in hoi-ton, (*s.*) hmai, hmel.
Facing, (*prep.*) ep-a.
Fade, (*v.*) reh, chuai, da.
Fail, (without) (*adv.*) hlel lo, ma-thei-lo-vin, ma-thei-lo, mâ*k*-mawh.
Faint, (*v.*) thi-dang.
Fair, (*a.*) ngo, (*s.*) dawr pui.
Fairly, (*adv.*) fe, ngial.
Faith, (*s.*) rin.
Fall, (*v.*) tla, tlâk, (not from a height) tlu, tlûk, (collapse) chim, (upon) delh, (out) thlon, (off, as hair, etc.) ṭîl, (through) pût thla.

False, (*a.*) dawt, der.
False alarm, (*s.*) khêl (also to be falsely alarmed).
Falsehood, (*s.*) dawt thu.
Falsely, (*adv.*) der.
Familiar, (*v.*) (with) ngam-pao, ngam-pah, nêl.
Family, (*s.*) chhûng, chhûng-te.
Famine, (*v.*) (to suffer) ṭâm.
Famous, (*a.*) hming thang, hrât-khaw khêng.
Fan, (*s.*) hmai zah, (*v.*) zâ*p*.
Fang, (*s.*) (of tooth) ha-bul.
Fan palm, (*s.*) buar-pui, she-lu, shial-lu.
Far, (*a.*) hla, thui, (apart) khât.
Farewell, (*v.*) (to say) ṭong ṭha-in thlah.
Farther, (*adv.*) hla deo, (*a.*) hla zawk.
Farthest, (*a.*) hla ber.
Fascinate, (*v.*) ai kaih.
Fast, (*adv.* and *a.*) chak, tlat, (*v.*) nghei.
Fasten, (*v.*) chilh, zam.
Fastidious, (*a.*) duh-tui.
Fat, (*a.*) chom, thao, chum.
Father, (*s.*) pa.
Father-in-law, (*s.*) (husband's father) pa, (wife's father) pu-zon.
Fatigue, (*v.*) ti-hah.
Fatigued, (*v.*) (to be) hah.
Fatiguing, (*a.*) nin-om, hah-thlâk.
Fault, (*s.*) sual, (*v.*) (to find) chip-chiar, dem, phun-chiar, phun, shoi-shêl.
Faultless, (*a.*) ṭhat-fam-kim.
Favour, (*v.*) vôh, (one more than another) duh-sak bîk, vôh-bîk, (by favour of) zâr-a, zâr-in.
Fear, (*v.*) hlao, hlao-thawng, ṭi, ṭih.
Fearful, (*a.*) hlao-om, râp-thlâk.
Fearless, (*a.*) thu-rum.
Fearlessly, (*adv.*) chang.
Feast, (*v.*) (to make) ruai theh, (partake of) ruai dong, (to prepare) ruai ṭuan, (*s.*) (one who presides at feast) fa-tu, (a public feast and to give the same) khuang choi.
Feather, (*s.*) hmul, sava-hmul.
Featherstitch, (*v.*) puan pui zûng ṭhui. (Also feather-stitching.)
Feeble, (*a.*) chak-lo.
Feed, (*v.*) ei-tîr, chawm, hrai, fah.
Feel, (*v.*) hria*t*, hre, (*tr.*) dek, hme*t*, (sick, etc.), chhuak, (after) dap, (sorry for another) lung chhiat pui.
Fell, (*v.*) ki*t*.

Fellow, (*s.*) kop-pui, khing-pui, (villager) tual, (term of contempt) nek, (traveller) hnung-zui, (*a.*) pui.
Female, (*s.*) nu, hmeichhia, pui.
Fence, (*s.*) huang, pal, dai, hung, (*v.*) (to fence in) hung.
Fern, (*s.*) (brake) cha-kok.
Ferocious, (*a.*) kolh.
Ferry, (*s.*) pûm-hrût.
Fetch, (*v.*) lâ*k*, va-la.
Fetter, (*s.*) kol, (*v.*) kol-bun.
Fever, (*s.*) khaw shik, shik-sherh, (*v.*) (to have) khua a shik.
Few, (*adv.*) tlêm, tlêm-te.
Fiddle, (*s.*) ṭing-ṭang.
Fidget, (*v.*) nin-hlei.
Fidgetty, (*a.*) nin-hlei.
Field-glasses, (*s.*) en-tlang.
Fierce, (*a.*) kolh.
Fifteen, (*a.*) shom leh pa-nga.
Fifth, (*a.*) pa-nga-na, nga-na.
Fiftieth, (*a.*) shom-nga-na.
Fifty, (*a.*) shom-nga.
Fig, (*s.*) thei-pui, sa-zu thei-pui, thei-ba'tê, thei-bâl, thei-thît.
Fig, (*s.*) (Indian) bûng, hmawng, hnah-hlun, ri-hmîm, zai-hri.
Fight, (*v.*) in-kâ*p*, in-sual, tawng.
Figure, (*s.*) (form) tlawn-tlai.
File, (*s.*) su-rai, (*v.*) surai-in nawt.
Fill, (*v.*) ti-khat, (in or up) hnawh, phu-hru*k*, vûr.
Fillip, (*v.*) pen.
Filth, (*s.*) bol-hlawh.
Filthy, (*a.*) hnawm, bol-hlawh.
Fin, (*s.*) pâng-parh.
Find, (*v.*) chhar, hmu, hmu leh.
Fine, (*v.*) choi-tîr, (to pay) choi, (*s.*) lei, lei-chhia, lei-ba, (*a.*) (in texture) nem, shîn.
Finger, (*s.*) kut-zung, (first) kut-zung chal (middle) kut-zung lai, (third) kut-zung tê-u, kut-zung u, (little) kut-zung tê, (fingers and thumb collectively) kut-zung ṭang.
Finger-ring, (*s.*) zung-bun.
Finish, (*v.*) tawp, tiak, ti-kin, tlei-tla, tling-tlâ*k*, ṭum-tla, zawh, zo.
Finished, (*a.*) kin.
Fir, (*s.*) fâr.
Fire, (*s.*) mei, thuk-duk, (*v.*) kâ*p*, (shovel) vut luah, vut lawh.
Firebrand, (*s.*) mei-chher.
Fireirons, (*s.*) thuk-thai.

Fireplace, (*s.*) tap, thuk.
Firefly, (*s.*) dum-dê.
Firewood, (*s.*) thing fâk.
Fireworks, (*s.*) mei-thal-lawn.
Firm, (*a.*) nghet, (as muscle) ruh.
Firmly, (*adv.*) nghet, phui-tak-in, tlat.
First, (*adv.*) hma-sha, hma-sha ber, zet, (at first or first of all) a-tîr-in, tîr-in, (first met with) ton'tîr.
Fish, (*s.*) sa-ngha, ngha, (Bengali dried fish) ngha thu.
Fisher or fisherman, (*s.*) sa-ngha man-tu.
Fish-hook, (*s.*) ngha-kuai, ngha-koi.
Fishing-rod, (*s.*) ngha-kuai ngul, ngha-koi ngul.
Fish trap, (*s.*) ngoi.
Fist, (*s.*) kut tum.
Fit, (*a.*) tlâk, rual, moi, tui, (to have a fit) phûng zawl.
Five, (*a.*) pa-nga, nga.
Fix, (*v.*) (to be in a) ngai-na rêng hre lo, (to put in a) ngai-na rêng hre lo vin shiam, ti-mang-ang.
Flabby, (*a.*) bui.
Flame, (*s.*) alh, mei-alh.
Flannel, (*s.*) bu-tu puan.
Flap, (*v.*) zâp.
Flare, (*v.*) alh.
Flash, (*v.*) êng phut.
Flat, (*a.*) per, phei, phêng, cham, (flat and thin) per, phêk.
Flatter, (*v.*) fak.
Flawless, (*a.*) him.
Flay, (*v.*) hlai, lip.
Flea, (*s.*) uihli.
Flee, (*v.*) tlân bo.
Flesh, (*s.*) sha, ti, ti-sha.
Flexible, (*a.*) nel, zoi.
Fling, (*v.*) paih, vom, deng.
Flint, (*s.*) mei-lung, zeh-lung, (flint, steel and tinder) mei-talh.
Float, (*v.*) lêng, lên'lâng, lâng, (on the back) zang-thal tui hleoh.
Flock, (*s.*) ho, pawl, rual.
Flog, (*v.*) vuak vêl.
Flood, (*s.*) tui lêt.
Floor, (*s.*) chhuat.
Flour, (*s.*) chhang-phut, (*a.*) (floury) phut.
Flow, (*v.*) luang.
Flower, (*s.*) pâr, pang-pâr, (to flower) pâr.
Fluent, (*a.*) ṭong thei.
Fluffy, (*a.*) por, por nei.

Fluid, (*s.*) tui.
Flute, (*s.*) phêng-long.
Flutter, (*v.*) zâ*p*.
Fly, (*v.*) thlaw*k*, (fly about) lên*g*, (*s.*) to.
Fly-blown, (*a.*) ṭâ têk.
Flying creatures, (*s.*) chung-lêng.
Foal, (*s.*) sakor-no.
Foam, (*s.*) (at mouth) chil phuan, phuan, (*v.*) phuan, (at mouth) chil a phuan, chil phuan a tla, chil phuan a chhua*k*.
Foe, (*s.*) do-tu, hmel-ma.
Fog, (*s.*) chhûm.
Foggy, (*v.*) (to be) chhûm a zîng.
Fold, (*s.*) huang, huang-chhûng, (*v.*) (to fold up) thle*p*.
Follow, (*v.*) zui.
Follower, (*s.*) hnung-zui, ṭhui-hruai.
Fond of, (*v.*) hma-ngai, ngai-na, (especially of eatables) châk.
Fontanel, (*s.*) lu-dîp.
Food, (*s.*) chaw, ei-tûr, (left over after eating) ei-bâng.
Fool, (*s.*) mi-â, â.
Foolhardy, (*a.*) thu-rum.
Foolish, (*a.*) â, mawl.
Foot, (*s.*) ke, ke-phah, phei, (of tree, pole, etc.) bul.
Footfall, (*s.*) ke-per-ri, ke-chheh-ri, ra*p*-ri.
Footprint, (*s.*) hnu, hniak, (*v.*) (to make footprint) hniak.
Footstool, (*s.*) ke-ngha' chhan, tlawh-chhan.
For, (*prep.*) chung-a, sak, shi, tân, ta-tûr.
Forage, (*v.*) tla.
Forbear, (*v.*) dawh-thei, dawh.
Forbearing, (*a.*) dawh-thei, dawh, en-thei.
Forbid, (*v.*) hnar, ui, khap.
Force, (with) hrep, nek, (*v.*) lui tîr.
Ford, (*s.*) lui kai, shuar.
Fore, (*a.*) hma.
Forefather, (*s.*) chi-thlah-tu, thlah-tu.
Forefinger, kut-zung chal.
Forehead, (*s.*) chal.
Foreign, (*a.*) vai.
Foreigner, (*s.*) aw-zia, aw-zia-mi, aw-ze-mi, vai.
Foreknow, (*v.*) hre lawk.
Foremost, (*a.*) hma-sha-ber.
Forenoon, (*s.*) chaw-hma.
Forerunner, (*s.*) hna-hruai-tu.
Foresee, (*v.*) hre-lawk.
Forest, (*s.*) ram, ram-hnuai.

Foretell, (*v.*) hril-lawk, shoi-lawk.
Forever, (*adv.*) cha-tuan-a.
Forewarn, (*v.*) hril-lawk.
Forge, (*v.*) chher.
Forget, (*v.*) theih-nghil, hai, hmaih, hmaih-ṭhelh.
Forgetful, (*a.*) hai-hot.
Forgive, (*v.*) ngai-dam, ngai-hna thiam.
Fork, (of tree, etc.) kâk, (of leg) kap.
Forked, (*a.*) kâk, phîr.
Form, (*s.*), hmel, pang-ti tlawn-tlai, ti.
Former, (*a.*) hmâna.
Formerly, (*adv.*) hmân-a, hman-lai.
Fornication, (*v.*) (to commit, with) zen.
Fornicatress, (*s.*) chhu hur.
Forsake, (*v.*) en-shan, thlao, thlao-thla, thlah-thlam.
Fort, (*s.*) kulh.
Forth, (*adv.*) chhuak.
Forthwith, (*adv.*) nghâl.
Fortieth, (*a.*) shom-li-na.
Fortunate, (*a.*) ham-ṭha, ni-hlaw, vân-nei, (in war) chem-kal.
Forty, (*a.*) shom-li.
Forward, (*adv.*) bok-khup-in.
Foundation, (*s.*) (of house, etc.) lei-phum.
Founder, (*s.*) ti-chhuak-tu.
Four, (*a.*) pa-li, li.
Fourfold, (*a.*) thuah-li.
Fourteen, (*a.*) shom leh pa-li.
Fourth, (*a.*) pa-li-na, li-na.
Four times, voi-li.
Fowl, (*s.*) âr, (jungle) ram-âr, (call for fowls) chîr chîr, chiri chiri.
Fowl-house, (*s.*) âr in, (under eaves) âr chhiar, chhiar.
Fragile, (*a.*) sop-rop.
Fragment, (*s.*) shi.
Fragrant, (*a.*) tui.
Framework, (*s.*) ruh.
Frayed, (*a.*) por.
Free, (*v.*) chhuak, thlah.
Freely, (*adv.*) chang.
Frequently, (*adv.*) fan, fo, zîm, ṭhîn, zing.
Fresh, (*a.* and *adv.*) hlim, (as fruit, etc., not dried) hring.
Fret, (*v.*) lung-ngai.
Friend, (*s.*) lai-na, ṭhian, phung-chhâng, tual, zung-zâm, (bosom friends) ṭhian kom ngeih, (*v.*) (to make friends) in-ṭhian.
Friendly, (*v.*) (to be) in-phung-châng, in-ṭhian, zawl.

Fright, (*v.*) (to receive a great) thla-bâr, (to die of fright) thla-bâr-in thi.
Frighten, (*v.*) râp, ti-ṭhaih, ti-zâm.
Fringe, (*s.*) fêm.
Frisk, (*v.*) tual-chai.
Frivolous, (*a.*) lep-chiah.
Frog, (*s.*) chung-u, dawng-thlek.
From, (*prep.*) a, ata, a-ṭang-in, hnêna, hnêna-ta, sak, ṭang-in, lak-a.
Front, (*a.*) hma, (*v.*) (to get in front of) leh-khalh.
Frost, (*s.*) (hoar) vûr.
Froth, (*v.*) phul, phuan, (*s.*) phuan.
Frown, (*v.*) mit-vun chuar.
Fruit, (*s.*) rah, (edible) thei, thei rah.
Fry, (*v.*) kang.
Fulfil, (*v.*) hlen.
Fulfilled, (*v.*) (to be) lo-thleng.
Full, (*a.*) khat.
Fullgrown, (*a.*) ṭhan' kin.
Fungus, (*s.*) pa.
Funny, (*a.*) fiam, nui-za-thlâk.
Funny-bone, (*s.*) kiu-hit, kiu-hik.
Fur, (*s.*) hmul, sa-hmul,
Furlong, (*s.*) fîng.
Furniture, (*s.*) sum, (wooden) thing-rem.
Furthermost, } (*a.*) hla ber, tawp ber.
Furthest, }
Fuss, (*v.*) (to make) i-he.
Fussily, (*adv.*) dîm-dêm.
Fussy, (*v.*) (to be) ti dîm-dêm, ti kher-kher, ti shi-she.

G

Gabble, (*v.*) pawng hrâm.
Gable, (*s.*) hul-hliap.
Gag, (*s.*) kap-na, (*v.*) kap.
Gain, (*v.*) hlêp, hlawk.
Gainsay, (*v.*) i-he, hnial.
Gale, (*s.*) thli pui.
Gallop, (*v.*) zuang.
Gamble, (*v.*) buh vorh.
Gambol, (*v.*) tual-chai.
Gape, (*v.*) ham.

Garden, (*s.*) huan, (kitchen garden at a distance from house) lei-pui.
Gardener, (*s.*) huan vêng-tu, huan-pu.
Garland, (*s.*) pâr-ṭhi-hrui.
Garment, (*s.*) puan, silh-fên.
Gate, (*s.*) kong-khâr.
Gather, (*v.*) (together) fuan-khawm, khawm, (in or up) sheng, (sticks, etc.) fom, (up) rût, (harvest) buh lâk, buh sheng, (rice, etc., here and there) lawr.
Gayal, (*s.*) (domesticated) shi-al, she, (wild) kawl-fung, ram-shial, she-lê, tum-pang, (call for) hûi hûi.
Gecko, (*s.*) chaw-kê.
Generally, (*a.*) chawk.
Generation, (*s.*) chhuan.
Generous, (*a.*) thil phal.
Genial, (*a.*) zai-dam.
Gently, (*adv.*) zoi-in, zoi-zoi-in.
Genuine, (*a.*) tak.
Get, (*v.*) nei, hmu, (at the same time) kêm, (up) tho, thawh.
Ghost, (*s.*) phûng, hmui-thla.
Giddy, (*a.*) hai, (*v.*) lu a hai.
Gigantic, (*a.*) lian-pui.
Giggle, (*v.*) nui.
Gill, (of fish) kep.
Gin, (*v.*) (cotton) her, (*s.*) her-awt.
Ginger, (*s.*) sawh-thing.
Gird, (*v.*) veng.
Girdle, (*s.*) kawng-chilh, kawng-hrên-na, kawng-fên, suk-sawn, (brass) chum-chi, rang-kha.
Girl, (*s.*) hmei-chhia, naopang.
Give, (*v.*) pe, pêk, ṭheh, hlân, (back) pêk kir, (up) thlao thla, mâk, (as evil ways) shim, (away, when leaving) hnut-chhiat.
Gizzard, (*s.*) thial.
Gladly, (*adv.*) lawm tak-in.
Glass, (*s.*) dâr-thla-lang, rial, (tumbler) rial no.
Glib, (*a.*) dang-nâl.
Glisten, (*v.*) mom.
Glory, (*s.*) ro-pui-na.
Glorify, (*v.*) choi-moi, ti-ro-pui.
Glorified, (*v.*) (to be) moi.
Glossy, (*a.*) tliang, tlor.
Glove, (*s.*) kut kor, kut-phah kor.
Glowing, (*a.*) dûr.
Glow-worm, (*s.*) pa-ngang dum-dê.

Glue, (*s.*) char-na.
Gnash teeth, (*v.*) kha-khawng.
Gnat, (*s.*) tho-shi.
Gnaw, (*v.*) sheh.
Go, (*v.*) kal, vâk, (to and fro) vei, (through and come out other side, or go anywhere and return the same day) leh-lâng, (before) hma-hruai, (over) hlên, (in) lût, leng, (down) chhuk, zuk kal, (up) chho, han kal, (round) hel, vêl, (away) kal-bo, (let) *k*al-tîr, chhua*k*-tîr, chhuak, (out) chhua*k*, (on water in boat, etc., or to go along) zawh.
Goat, (*s.*) kêl, (call for goats) me, (wild) sa-thar, sa-za.
Goblin, (*s.*) phûng.
God, (*s.*) Pathian.
Goitre, (*s.*) hrok-puar, nghawng-puar, ong-puar, or-puar.
Gold and golden, (*s.* and *a.*) rang-ka-chak.
Gong, (*s.*) dâr-mang, dâr, dâr-khuang, dâr-ngiao, dâr-bu.
Good, (*a.*) ṭha, ti-zia, (good-looking) hmel ṭha, (tempered) zai-dam, thin nel, thluak nem, nun nem, (natured) thin-lung ṭha, thluak-nem, zai dam, (as child that does not cry) tlei, (for good) (*adv.*) hlen.
Goods, (*s.*) bung-rua, thuam, thuam-hnaw, thom-hnaw, sum.
Goose, (*s.*) va-tawk.
Goose skin, (to have the appearance of) mûr.
Gossip, (*v.*) kam-tam, thu-khawh-chång shoi.
Gourd, (*s.*) bûr.
Govern, (*v.*) ro rêl, op.
Governor, (*s.*) ro-rêl-tu, op-tu.
Gradually, (*adv.*) telh telh, tlêm-tlêm-in, deo-deo, zoi-zoi-in, zoi-in.
Grain, (*s.*) fang, mal.
Granary, (*s.*) chhiar, chhiar-in, chhêk-in.
Grand, (*a.*) ro-pui.
Grandchild, (*s.*) tu.
Granddaughter, (*s.*) tu-nu.
Grandfather, (*s.*) pu.
Grandmother, (*s.*) pi.
Grandson, (*s.*) tu-pa.
Grant, (*v.*) phal, oih.
Grasp, (*v.*) chelh, hûm, man, vuan.
Grass, (*s.*) hlo-bet, hnim.
Grasshopper, (*s.*) khao.
Grate, (*s.*) thuk, (*v.*) (teeth) ṭhial.
Grateful, (*a.*) lawm, lawm-na chang hre, lawm-na chang hria.
Gratuitously, (*adv.*) mai-mai, tlawn, tlawn-in.
Grave, (*s.*) thlân, (vault) tian'hrâng thlân.

Gravel, (*s.*) lung-ṭhil.
Gray, (*a.*) ṭuak.
Graze, (*v.*) hnawl, ti-khok, (pasture) tla, (to be grazed) khok.
Grease, (*s.*) sa-hriak, thao.
Greasy, (*a.*) thang, thu, mom, tlor.
Great, (*a.*) lian, lian-pui, pui, lal.
Great Bear, (*s.*) Zang-khua.
Great grandfather, (*s.*) pu.
Great grandmother, (*s.*) pi.
Greedy, (*a.*) duh-âm, huam-haoh, huam-hap, ṭha-hnem ngai.
Green, (*a.*) hring.
Greens, (*s.*) (generic name for all) an.
Grieve, (*v.*) lung-ngai, lung chhe, lung chhiat, run, run-râl.
Grievous, (*a.*) run-thlâk, lung-chhiat-thlâk.
Grimaces, (*v.*) (to make) ṭhen, (at) chhiat shan, ṭhen shan.
Grin, (*v.*) ṭhen, (to grin at) ṭhen shan.
Grind, (*v.*) rawt-som.
Grindstone, (*s.*) lung-tât.
Grip, (*v.*) vuan, chelh.
Gritty, (*a.*) ngap.
Groan, (*v.*) rûm.
Groin, (*s.*) ṭhâl, (the gland in the groin) ṭhâl bê.
Groove, (*s.*) kuang, kuam.
Ground, (*s.*) lei.
Group, (*s.*) pawl, ho.
Grow, (*v.*) ṭhang, ṭo, (up) shei lian.
Growl, (*v.*) ngur, rûm.
Grub, (*s.*) vual.
Grudge, (*v.*) ui.
Gruff, (*a.*) thûm.
Grumble, (*v.*) chip-chiar, i-he, phun, phun-chiar.
Grunt, (*v.*) ngûk.
Guard, (*v.*) vêng.
Guess, (*v.*) rin shoi, ngai-ruat.
Guest, (*s.*) chên'pui.
Guesthouse, (*s.*) khual-bûk, zawl-bûk.
Guide, (*v.*) hruai.
Guilt, (*v.*) (to be cleared of) thiam chang, thiam hawn, (to clear of) (*v.*) thiam chang-tîr, thiam hon-tîr.
Guilty, (*a.*) thiam lo, (to pronounce guilty) thiam lo.
Guitar, (*s.*) chong-pe-reng.
Gullet, (*s.*) hrok.
Gum, (*s.*) châr-na, be-raw.
Gumboil, (*s.*) ha-hni-puam, (to have) ha-hni a puam.

Gums, (*s.*) ha-hni.
Gun, (*s.*) si-lai, (double barrelled) lai phîr, (spring) perh-khet, (muzzle-loader with cap) tu-ki-li, ti-ki-li, tu-ku-li, (breech-loader) ulh thliak silai, (muzzle-loader) mong-thun silai.
Gunny bag, (*s.*) kawl-la-ip, sai-ip.
Gunpowder, (*s.*) silai hlo, zên.
Gun stock, (*s.*) silai kawm.
Gutter, (*s.*) tui-hawr, kawm.
Gutur River, (*s.*) Tut.

H

Habit, (*s.*) dân, nun*g*-chan*g*.
Habitable, (*a.*) om-na-zia, om-na-tlâk, om-na-tui.
Hades, (*s.*) Mi-thi khua.
Hail, (*v.*) rial a tla.
Hailstone, (*s.*) rial.
Hair, (*s.*) hmul, (of head) sam, (a hair) sam zai, (knot of hair) sam zial, tuk, (Poi's knot) hrûm.
Hair-pin, (*s.*) dawh-kilh, (brass) ṭhim-kual, ṭhing-kual.
Hairy, (*a.*) hmul.
Half, (*s*) chan-vê, tia-ve, tum-bung, zât-ve.
Halo, (round the moon) thla hual, [used thus—'a in-in thla ahual'= there is a halo round the moon (literally, the moon is encircled by its house).]
Halt, (*v.*) ding.
Halve, (*v.*) phel.
Hamlet, (*s.*) khua tê, khua per, khaw-tê, khaw-per.
Hammer, (*s.*) tu-bôh, tu-baoh, (of gun) silai ai-bop, (*v.*) dên*g*, (in) khên*g*.
Hand, (*s.*) kut, (with one hand) khing khat-in, (with both hands) khing hnih-in, (shake hands) kut in-man, (to clasp the hands) kut suih.
Handcuff, (*s.*) kol, (*v.*) kol bun-tîr.
Handkerchief, (*s.*) hnap-hnît-na puan.
Handle, (*s.*) fong, beng, ha, liang, (*v.*) khâl, nghai-sha, soi-sha.
Handsome, (*a.*) hmel-ṭha.
Hang, (up) târ, khai, bân*g*, (by neck or leg) awk, (as cloth on line, etc.) zâr, (to kill by hanging) awk-hlum, (the head) kài-kûn, kai-ki.
Hangnail, (*s.*) ai hni, tin hna ai hni.
Hank, (*s.*) duang.
Haply, (*adv.*) hlaoh, kher, kher-phei-in, vaih.

Happy, (*a.*) lawm, hlim, (to feel) thin-lung a hlim.
Hard, (*adv.*) chiam, vak, na-sha-tak-in, hrep, hrot, rim, (*a.*) khirh, shak, chang, fîp, ruh.
Hardly, (*adv.*) hrâm, lo-deo.
Hare, (*s.*) sa-zu pui.
Hark, (*v.*) ngai, ngai-thlâ*k*.
Harlot, (*s.*) naw-chi-zuar, naw-ti-zuar.
Harm, (*v.*) poi khoih.
Harvest, (*v.*) buh lâ*k*, buh-sheng.
Hasten, (*v.*) hman-hmaw.
Hat, (*s.*) lu-khum, khum-beo.
Hatchet, (*s.*) hrei-pui.
Hate, (*v.*) hua*t*, haw, hal, hmêl-mâ*k*, tai.
Have, (*v.*) nei, om.
Hawk, (*s.*) mu, mu-âr-la, mu-chhia, mu-vân-lai, shial-shîr.
Haze, (*s.*) ro-mei.
He, (*pro.*) a, ama, ani.
Head, (*s.*) lu, (*adv.*) (head over heels) bing-bi-let, (of a family or company) ho-tu.
Headache, (*s.*) lu na, (*v.*) (to have) lu a na.
Heal, (*v. t.*) ti dam, (*v.*) dam.
Healthy, (*a.*) dam, hri-shêl, (looking) shâr.
Heap, (*s.*) vûng, vûm.
Hear, (*v.*) hria*t*, hre, beng-in hria*t* (or hre).
Heart, (*s.*) lung, thin-lung, (of tree, etc.) ril.
Heart-breaking, (*a.*) lung chhiat thlâk.
Heart-broken, (*a.*) lung chhe, lung chhiat.
Hearth, (*s.*) tap, rap chhak.
Heat, (*v.*) rawh, ti-lum.
Heaven, (*s.*) vân.
Heavy, (*a.*) rit, (as bread) khal.
Heed, (*v.*) ngai-thlâ*k*, oih, ngai-sak.
Heedless, (*a.*) ngai sam.
Heel, (*s.*) ke-âr-tui.
Heir, (*s.*) khawm-tu-tûr, ro-khawm-tu, ro-luah-tu.
Help, (*v.*) chhan, pui, chhom-dawl, kam-ki, ṭan-pui, (to rise) kai-tho, kai-thawh.
Hen, (*s.*) âr-pui.
Hence, (*conj.*) chuv-âng-in.
Henceforth or henceforward, (*adv.*) tûn-china, tûna-china, tûn-hnua.
Her, (*pro.*) a, ama, ani.
Herald, (*s.*) tlâng-ao, (*v.*) tlâng-ao.
Herd, (*s.*) ho, pawl, rual.

Here, (*adv.*) heta-hian, ta-hian, he-ta.
Hereafter, (*adv.*) tûn hnua.
Here and there, (*adv.*) lawr.
Hermaphrodite, (*s.*) pa-dawp.
Heron, (*s.*) va-cha.
Herself, (*pro.*) ama-in, ani-in, (reflex-prefix) in.
Hew, (*v.*) ki*t*, shât, ek.
Hiccough, (*v.*) irh-fiak.
Hide, (*s.*) sa-vun, (*v.*) thuk, thu*k*-ru*k*, thu*p*, thu*p*-ru*k*.
Hidden, (*a.*) in-thup.
High, (*a.*) shân*g*, zo, (as voice) shîn, fiak, (*adv.*) thui, (as voice) fiak, (smelling) nam, uih.
Higher up, chak-a, chak-lama.
Hill, (*s.*) mual, tlâng.
Him, (*pro.*) ama, ani.
Himself, (*pro.*) ama-in, ani-in, (reflexive prefix) in.
Hind, (*s.*) zuk-pui.
Hinder, (*v.*) bum-ro, khuah-khirh, kuah-khirh, ti-khol-kham.
Hint, (*v.*) dîp, phût.
Hip, (*s.*) khel.
Hire, (*v.*) ṭan*g*-tîr.
Hireling, (*s.*) hlawh-fa.
His, (*pro.*) a, ama, ani, ama-a-ta, ama-ta.
History, (*s.*) ti-ti.
Hit, (*v.*) vêl, vua*k*, hêm.
Hither, (*adv.*) heta, han.
Hitherto, (*adv.*) tûn-thleng-in.
Hoard, (*v.*) khêk.
Hoarse, (*v.*) (to be) aw a chhâng.
Hoary, (*a.*) ṭuak.
Hoe, (*s.*) (large) bawng-tuh-thlawh, tuh-dâl, (small) tuh-thlawh, (*v.*) lai, chê*k*.
Hog-badger, (*s.*) sa-phi-vok.
Hog-plum, (*s.*) toi-taw.
Hold, (*v.*) chelh, dom, shin, keng, man, vuan, lek, (up or wave) lek, (out, *i.e.*, to last) daih, (out, as hand) dawh, (out, as arm, etc.) phar, (up) kai.
Hole, (*s.*) horh, pop, khur, khuar, khuar-khu-rum, (to have a hole in) horh, pop, etc., kua.
Holiday, (*s.*) om ni.
Hollow, (*s.*) kaw-rong, khuar-khu-rum, (*a.*) kaw-rong, ruak (*v.*) ker-kua.
Holy, (*a.*) thiang-hlim, ṭhat-fam-kim.
Homage, (to pay), do-vân kai.

Home, (*s.*) om-na, in.
Homeless, (*v.*) (to be) vâk-vai. (Also a homeless person.)
Homesick, (*v.*) (to feel) lung a lêng.
Hone, (*s.*) lung-tât.
Honest, (*a.*) rin-om.
Honey, (*s.*) khoi-zu.
Honeycomb, (*s.*) khoi-thlâr, khuai-thlâr.
Honourable, (*a.*) zah-om.
Honoured, (to be) moi.
Hoof, (*s.*) tin.
Hooked, (*v.*) (to be) bât.
Hook-stick, (*s.*) khoih-sa-pir.
Hookah, (*s.*) tui-kun-luk.
Hop, (*v.*) (as locust, etc.) kat, (on one leg) ti-khong-khaw-bai, bai-ba-hlâng; per.
Hope, (*v.*) bei-shei.
Horizon, (*s.*) kawl, kawl-kil.
Horizontal, (*a.*) kham-phei, phei.
Horizontally, (*adv.*) kham-phei-in, phei, kham-phei.
Horn, (*s.*) ki, (powder) fung-ki, pai-tung.
Hornbill, (*s.*) va-pual, va-hai.
Horrible, (*a.*) hreh-om, hmu a hreh-om.
Horse, (*s.*) sa-kor.
Horsefly, (*s.*) tlip, tlip-phâr.
Hospital, (*s.*) dam-lo in.
Hostage, (*v.*) (to keep as) hrêng.
Hot, (*a.*) lum, sha, shat, thaw-sha, uap, (as pepper) thak.
Household, (*v.*) chhûng-te, chhûng, ho te, ho-va te.
House, (*s.*) in.
How, (*adv.*) eng-tin-nge ? (exclamatory) va !
Howbeit, (*conj.*) eng-pawh-ni-shela, eng-pawh-ni-roh-se, eng-pawh-ti-la.
However, (*conj.*) ni-ma-she-la, ama-eraw-chu.
How far ? eng ang hla nge ? eng-tia-hla-nge ? eng-chen-hla-nge ?
How long ? (time) eng-ti-nge ?
How long ? } (time or length) eng-chen-nge ?
How much ? }
How many ? } eng-zât ? eng-zât-nge ? eng-ti-nge ?
How much ? }
Hum, (*v.*) rûm.
Humble, (*a.*) thu hnuai rolh.
Humbled, (to be) in-ngai-tlawm.
Humour, (*v.*) duat.
Hunchbacked, (*a.*) zâng-bawk, zâng-kûl.

Hundred, (*a.*) za, (hundred and fifty) za nu fa.
Hundred thousand, (*a.*) nuai.
Hunger, (*s.*) ril ṭâm.
Hungry, (*v.*) ril a ṭâm, ṭâm.
Hunt, (*v.*) ûm, ram-chhua*k*, sa pêl.
Hurl, (*v.*) vom.
Hurriedly, (*adv.*) hman-hmaw.
Hurry, (*v.*) hman-hmaw.
Hurt, (*v.*) ti-na, (*int.*) na, (one's feelings) (*v. t.*) ti-vui.
Husband, (*s.*) pa-sal, (husband and wife) nu pa.
Hush, (*v.*) oi, (hush to sleep) oi-mu.
Hut, (*s.*) bûk, bawk, bawk-tê.
Hymn, (*s.*) hla, zai.
Hypochondriac, (*s.*) khaw-tlâng-lung-lên'.
Hypocrite, (*s.*) mi ver-vêk, mi ver-ther.
Hypocritical, (*a.*) awk-hrawl, ver-vêk, ver-ther.

I

Ice, (*s.*) vûr, tui-khal.
Idiot, (*s.*) mi-â, â-baw-raw.
Idiotic, (*a.*) â, â-baw-raw.
Idle, (*a.*) dawng-dah, tha-dah, tha-thla.
Idol, (*s.*) mi-lem, mi-lim.
If, (*conj.*) chuan, leh.
Ignite, (*v.*) hâl.
Ignorant, (*a.*) â, fing-lo.
Ill, (*a.*) dam-lo, na, nat.
Ill-behaved, (*a.*) huang tao, nghal.
Ill-tempered, (*a.*) vîn, thin-chhia*t*, thin-chhe.
Ill-treat, (*v.*) nghai-sha, ti-duh-dah.
Image, (*s.*) mi-lem, mi-lim, lim, lem.
Imagination, (*s.*) mit-thla.
Imagine, (*v.*) mit thla-in hmu.
Imitate, (*v.*) zir, zir-sak.
Imitation, (*a.*) lem.
Immediately, (*adv.*) chop-le-chil-in, nghâl, ve-leh.
Immense, (*a.*) lian-pui, na-sha.
Immerse, (*v.*) chiah-pil.
Immortelle, (*s.*) (a species of) chuai-lo.
Impatient, (*a.*) nghâk-hlel, (to be impatient for) khua hâr, (in sickness) zuao.
Impede, (*v.*) dâl.
Impenitent, (*a.*) in-chhîr lo.

Imperfect, (*a.*) him lo.
Implicate, (*v.*) kaih-hnoih.
Implement, (*s.*) hriam.
Important, (*a.*) ril, thu-pui, poi-mawh.
Importune (*v.*), luh.
Impossible, rual ani lo.
Impotent, (*s.*) ching.
Impress, (*v.*) nem-in ziak.
Impression, (*s.*) hnu.
Imprison, (*v.*) khung, lung-in-a khung.
Imprisoned, (*a.*) tâng.
Improper, (*a.*) dik-lo.
Improvident, (*a.* and *v.*) pok.
Impulsive, (*a.*) ho.
In, (*prep.*) a, chhûng-a.
Inattentive, (*a.*) hawk-dâk.
Inaccurate, (*a.*) dik-lo.
Incompatible, (to be) (*v.*) in-hal.
Inconsiderate, (*a.*) ngil nei lo.
Inconsiderately, (*adv.*) thu-dawn-lo-vin.
Inconvenient, (*a.*) rem lo.
Incorrect, (*a.*) dik lo.
Increase, (*v.*) pung, (as money, etc.) sawt, (as bulbs, potatoes, etc.) tak.
Incredible, (*a.*) oih-om lo.
Indeed, (*adv.*) bok.
India-rubber, (*s.*) ṭhial-rêt, ṭhel-rêt.
Indigestion, (*s.*) kaw-chhiat, kaw-chhe.
Indignant, (*v.*) thin ur.
Indigo, (*s.*) chi-cha, ṭing.
Indolent, (*a.*) that-chhia, that-chhe, tha-dah, tha-thla, dawng-dah.
Indulgence, (*v.*) (to treat with) duat.
Indulgent, (*a.*) thiam.
Inexpert, (*a.*) tlok-tlaw.
Infant, (*s.*) nao-shên.
Inflate, (*v.*) ham-puar, hâm-puar.
Inflexible, (*a.*) khaoh.
Inform, (*v.*) hril, hrilh, zai.
Inhabit, (*v.*) luah.
Inherit, (*v.*) (property) ro khawm.
Injure, (*v.*) ti-sil.
Injured, (*a.*) sil.
Ink, (*s.*) lekha tui, lekha ziak-na tui.
Ink-pot, (*s.*) lekha tui bawm, lekha tui bûr.

Inmost, (*a.*) chhûng nung ber.
Inner, (*a.*) chûng-nung.
Innermost, (*a.*) chûng-nung-ber.
Innocent, (*a.*) thiam.
Inquire, (*v.*) zawt.
Inquisitive, (*a.*) dîl-shût, dîl-chhût, hawk-dâk.
Insane, (*a.*) â.
Insect, (*s.*) ran-nung.
Insert, (*v.*) hnawh, phu-bru*k*.
Inside, (*s.*) chhûng, (of animal) kaw-chhûng, (*prep.*) chhûng-a.
Inside out, (*adv.* and *a.*) let-ling.
Insist, (*v.*) lui.
Inspect, (*v.*) fang.
Instant, (*s.*) mit khap (in an instant) mit khap kâr lo vin.
Instantaneously, (*adv.*) mit-khap-kâr-lo-vin.
Instantly, (*adv.*) nghâl, chop le chil-in.
Instead of, (*prep.*) ai, ai-a, ai-in, chhang-in, chhang.
Institute, (*v.*) ti-chhua*k*.
Institutor, (*s.*) ti-chhuak-tu.
Instruct, (*v.*) zilh, hril, zir-tîr.
Insult, (*v.*) ti-vui.
Intemperate, (*a.*) in-shûm kâr nei lo.
Intend, (*v.*) tum, ril-rû*k*.
Intense, (*a.*) na, na-sha (also intensely).
Intentionally, (*adv.*) lui.
Intercept, (*v.*) dang.
Interest, (*v.*) (to take interest) ngai shâng.
Interesting, (*a.*) beng-lût, beng-lût-zawng, ngai-shân'-tlâk.
Intermittently, (*adv.*) (as fever) nat ni nei-in.
Interrupt, (*v.*) chîl-bual, ṭong-chhilh.
Intervals, (*adv.*) (at long) khât, (at short) zîm.
Intestine, (*s.*) ril.
Into, (*prep.*) a, chhûnga.
Intoxicate, (*v.*) rui tîr, ti-rui.
Intoxicated, (*a.*) rui.
Introduce, (*v.*) khaw' hmu.
Intrust, (*v.*) kol-tîr.
Inured, (*a.*) chhel.
Invisible, (*a.*) lang lo.
Invite, (*v.*) sawm.
Iris, (*s.*) le-len.
Iron (*s.*) thîr.
Irritable, (*a.*) vîn, thin-chhe, thin-chhia*t*.
Irritating, (*a.*) (as flannel) me.

Is, (*v.*) ni, e, ni e.
Island, (*s.*) thliar-kâr.
Isolated, (*a.*) bing, fâl.
It, (*pro.*) a, ama, ani.
Itch, (*v.*) thak, (*s.*) vai-hrên-hri, ui-thak.
Itinerate, (*v.*) fang, khua khua fang, khua fang.
Its, (*pro.*) a, ama, ani.
Itself, (reflex prefix) in, (*pro.*) ama-in, ani-in.
Ivory, (*s.*) sai-ngho.

J

Jack, (tree and fruit) tât-kawng.
Jackal, (*s.*) shi-hal.
Jacket, (*s.*) kor.
Jagged, (*a.*) ther, (*s.*) (a jagged edge) ther.
Jail, (*s.*) lung in.
Jailor, (*s.*) lung in vêng tu mi tâng vêng tu.
Jam, (*v.*) chilh.
Japanning (juices used for), (*s.*) chhim-hruk, hrui-thui, kawh-tê-bêl, mei-thui, vai-phaw-hlo, vom-bâl.
Jaw, (*s.*) (lower) kha, kha-be.
Jealous, (*v.*) thîk, (of) hu-phurh, ît-shîk.
Jeopardy, (*v.*) (to be in) hlao thawn'om tak-in om.
Jerk, (*v.*) phih.
Jest, (*s.*) fiam thu, (*v.*) fiam thushoi, (at) dem-chiat, (jesting stock) dem chhiat.
Jhûm, (*s.*) lo, thlawh-hma, (a disused *jhûm*) thlawh-bua, (a cut *jhûm*) chap-châr, (between burning and springing of first seed) kâng-vâr, (this year's *jhûm*) ring thar, (*jhûm*-house) thlâm, (*v.*) (to go to *jhûm*) feh, (to cut) vât.
Job's tears, (*s.*) mîm.
Join, (*v.*) chuk-tuah, in-fin, zom, zawm, (in with) hnim-lût.
Joint, (*s.*) châng, chuk-tuah-na, in-chuk-tuah-na, in-zom-na, tuah.
Joke, (*s.*) fiam thu, (*v.*) fiam thu shoi.
Journey, (*v.*) (to go on a) zin.
Joyful, (*a.*) hlim, hlim-om, thin-lung hlîm.
Joyfully, (*a.*) hlim tak-in.
Judge, (*s.*) ro-rêl-tu, thu-rem-tu, (*v.*) ro rêl.
Jug, (*s.*) no.
Juice, (*s.*) tui, hnai.
Jump, (*v.*) zuang, ṭum, (down) zuang thla, tum thla, (with surprise) phut zok.
Jumper, (*s.*) (iron) thîr tu'lung, thîr tu'ṭhulh.

June, (*s.*) chong-fang thla, fûr-chon thla, vok-hnia-zon thla.
Jungle, (*s.*) ram.
Jungly, (*a.*) ṭûl.
Just, (*a.*) fel, (*adv.*) (time), hlol, hlim.
Justified, (*v.*) (to be) thiam, thiam chang, thiam hawn.
Justify, (*v.*) thiam.
Jut, (*v.*) lor.
Jute, (*s.*) zi-za.

K

Kassalong, (*s.*) (river) Samat, (bazar) Samat dawr.
Keen, (*a.*) (of sight, hearing, etc.) vâr, (keen-sighted) mit vâr, mit fîm.
Keep, (*v.*) von*g*, kol, khuah-khirh, chên'-pui, om-pui, von*g*-reng, châr, châr-chilh, (to keep hold of), châr, châr-chilh, (holiday or rest day) hrilh, sherh, (keep guard over) ngai ven', (to one's self) pai, (as animals, poultry, etc.), vulh, (as command) zawh.
Keeper, (*v.*) om-pui-tu, vêng-tu.
Kernel, (*s.*) chhûng-mu, mu.
Key, (*s.*) kilh-na, (of concertina, organ, flute, etc.) bi.
Kick, (*v.*) chhir, chhuih, (against) in-chhir, (*v.*) (out behind) khêng, (out or about) leng, (with bottom of foot) tlawh.
Kid, (*s.*) kêl no, kêl doi.
Kidney, (*s.*) kal.
Kill, (*v.*) ti-hlum, tal, ti-thi, tha*t*, (off) suat, (by poisoning food) hrai-hlum.
Kind, (*s.*) hmun, pawl, (*a.*) khaw-ngai thei, ngil-nei.
Kindle, (*v.*) chhêm.
Kindly, (*adv.*) khaw-ngai-tak-in.
Kindred, (*s.*) lai-chîn, unao.
King, (*s.*) lal, lal-pa.
Kingdom, (*s.*) ram, khua leh tui.
Kinsfolk, kinsman, (*s.*) lai-chîn, unao.
Kiss, (*v.*) faw*p*.
Kite, (*s.*) (bird) mu.
Kitten, (*s.*) zawh-tê no.
Knead, (*v.*) hmeṭ, hlawn.
Knee, (*s.*) khûp, (cap) khûp koi.
Kneel, (*v.*) ṭhing-ṭhi.
Knickerbockers, (*s.*) ke-kor.
Knife, (*s.*) chem-tê.
Knit, (*v.*) phan, phiar.
Knobby, (*a.*) lok.

Knock, (*v.*) (rap) kik, (top of head against) ton*g*, (down or over) ti-tlû*k*, (the head against) taoh, (together) in-shu, (as heads) in-taoh, (against) nam, shu, chu*k*, ton*g*, (*a.*) (knock-kneed) khûp-tuah.
Knot, (*s.*) bawk, bil-baw-lawk, suih-bawk, suih, (of hair) sam-zial, tuk, (Poi's knot of hair) hrûm.
Know, (*v.*) hria*t*, hre, thiam, (how) thiam, ngai-na hre, ngai-na hria*t*,
Knuckle, (*s.*) kut châng.
Kodali, (*s.*) bawng-tuh-thlawh, tuh-dâl.

L

Labour, (*v.*) thawk-rim, (with child) (*v.*) nao vei.
Lac, (*s.*) thal-hrit.
Lack, (*v.*) chham, ro.
Ladder, (*s.*) hlân, (leading to Lushai house) kai-ṭên.
Ladle, (*v.*) shua*k*, (*s.*) hai-tê.
Lake, (*s.*) dîl.
Lamb, (*s.*) berâm no.
Lame, (*a.*) ke bai, bai.
Lament, (*v.*) ṭa*p*.
Lamp, (*s.*) khawn-vâr, (glass) khawn-vâr bûr.
Lance, (*v.*) fei.
Land, (*s.*) lei, khaw-mual, (*v.*) khaw-mual-a chhua*k*.
Landmark, (*s.*) pho-lêng, (to make) pho-lêng târ.
Landslip, (*s.*) lei min.
Language, (*s.*) ṭong.
Languid, (*a.*) thîm.
Lantern, (*s.*) khawn-vâr.
Lap, (*v.*) lia*k*, (*s.*) mal-chung, âng.
Lard, (*s.*) vok sa-hriak.
Large, (*a.*) lian, pui, hrol, hlai, zao.
Larynx, (*s.*) hrok-hrawl.
Lasso, (*v.*) hlîng.
Last, (*adv.* and *a.*) hnu-hnung-ber, tawp, tawp-ber, (*v.*) daih.
Last night, ni-zân-a.
Last year, ni-kum-a.
Late, (*adv.*) har, tlai.
Lather, (*s.* and *v.*) phuan.
Lattice, (*s.*) zawng-dai-kalh, zawng-bilh-tah.
Laugh, (*v.*) nui, (to feel like laughing) nui za, (at) nui-shan.
Laughable, (*a.*) nui-za-thlâk.
Laughing stock, (*s.*) nui-chhiah.

Law, (*s.*) dân.
Lawful, (*a.*) thian*g*.
Lawsuit, (*s.*) thu-poi.
Lay, (*v.*) (egg) tui, (up in store) khawl, khawl-khawm (hands upon) kut thlâ*k*, (to lay out a dead body or lay a dead body in the grave), zalh.
Layer, (*s.*) thuah.
Lazy, (*a.*) that-chhia, dawng-dah, zom-thaw.
Lead, (*s.*) shuan.
Lead, (*v.*) hruai, kai, (lead the way or take lead in work, etc.) hma-hruai, hma-tawng, (to take the lead) kulh-a ṭang, tupa-a ṭan*g*.
Leader, (*s.*) hma-hruai-tu, hma-tawng.
Leaf, (*s.*) hnah.
Leaf insect, (*s.*) kât-chât.
Leak, (*v.*) far, horh, pût.
Lean, (*v.*) (upon) bawh, delh, ngheng, (the head or body on one side) thlê, (back) eo, (against) nghen' chhan, rin' chhan, (*a.*) chêr, (*s.*) ti.
Leap, (*v.*) zuan*g*, (down) zuan*g*-thla, ṭum-thla.
Learn, (*v.*) zir.
Least, (*a.*) tê ber, tlêm ber.
Leather, (*s.*) sa-vun.
Leave, (*v.*) hnut-chhia*t*, kal-shan, kal-bo-shan, thlah-thlam, zuah, (affix) shan, (to one's own devices) en-shan, (to one's own devices or in the lurch) thlah-thlam.
Leavings, (*s.*) chaw ei bâng.
Lee, (*prep.*) (under the lee of) phên-a.
Leech, (*s.*) (land) vang-vat, (water) hlît, sai-hlît.
Left, (*a.*) bâng, bâk, (hand side) vei lam.
Leg, (*s.*) ke, bop, fu-ke, phei, (hind leg) bop, (fore leg) dâr.
Leisure, (*v.*) (to have) hman.
Leisurely, (*adv.*) muan*g*, (*a.*) muan*g*, muan*g*-chang.
Lemon, (*s.*) sêr, sêr-ṭok.
Lemon grass, (*s.*) thal-thîng.
Lemur, (*s.*) (the slow-paced) sa-huai.
Lend, (*v.*) pûk-tîr, hawh-tîr.
Length, (*s.*) dung.
Lengthwise, (*adv.*) dung-zawng, dung-lam.
Leopard, (*s.*) kei tê.
Leper, (*s.*) phâr, mi phâr.
Leprosy, (*s.*) phâr.
Less, (*a.*) tlêm zawk, (*adv.*) tlêm deo.
Lessen, (*v.*) ti-kiam, (*int.*) kiam.

Lest, (*conj.*) chu-ti-lo-chuan, dah-law-maw, dah-ang-e, (not) dah-ne-maw.
Let, (*v.*) tîr, phal, oih, (down) thlâ*k*, thlâk-thla, (go) thlah, (alone) thlah-thlam.
Letter, (*s.*) lekha.
Level, (*a.*) zawl, cham, rual, phei, rual-rem, (*v.*) chok-rual, chûl-cham, chûl-rual.
Lever, (*v.*) kar.
Levy, (*v.*) (tax) choi-tîr.
Liar, (*s.*) daw' thei, mi-daw' thei.
Liberal, (*a.*) thil-phal.
Liberties, (to take) huang tao.
Lick, (*v.*) lia*k*, hliao.
Lid, (*s.*) chhîn, chhîn-na, (of woman's pipe) chhîn-khai, khai-chhîn.
Lie, (*s.*) dawt-thu, (*v.*) daw'thei, dawt thu shoi, dawt shoi, (down) mu*t*, bok, (in ambush or in wait) châng, bun.
Lifetime, (*s.*) dam chhûng, dam lai.
Lift, (*v.*) khai, choi, (head) dâk, (across, over, up, or down) hlâng, (up, as cloth) hlîm.
Light, (*s.*) êng, ên-na, vâr, (in colour) ngo, (*a.*) (not dark) êng, vâr, (not heavy) zâng, (spongy) thawp.
Lighten, (*v.*) kawl a phe.
Lightning, (*s.*) kawl phe.
Like, (*a.*) ang, tia, tiang, (*v.*) duh, châk, hma-ngai, tlâk-tlum-tîr, ngai-na.
Liken, (*v.*) teh, teh-khin.
Likewise, (*adv.*) pawh, bok, ve.
Lime, (*s.*) chi-nai, hol-ri-vâp, (fruit) sêr, (bird) soi.
Limestone, (*s.*) chi-nai lung, hol-ri-vâp lung.
Limp, (*a.*) zoi, (*v.*) bai.
Line, (*s.*) rîn, (*v.*) (to draw) rîn, (*a.*) (in a straight line) in-zawn.
Lining, (*s.*) chhûng-phûm.
Linked together, (*a.*) in-ba*t*.
Lip, (*s.*) (upper) hmui, (lower) heh.
Listen, (*v.*) ngai, ngai-thlâ*k*, zawm, ngai ven'.
Listless, (*a.*) ngui, nguai.
Litter, (*s.*) ṭom, (littered) (*a.*) ṭom.
Little, (*a.*) tê, tlêm, tlêm-tê, (*adv.*) chang-chang, (little by little) deo deo, tlêm-tlêm-in.
Live, (*v.*) nun*g*, om.
Lively, (*a.*) phok.
Liver, (*s.*) thin.
Lizard, (*s.*) chaw-kê, dai-dêp, lai-tel, (large) tang-kawng, tang-keo, (flying) u-leoh.

Load, (*s.*) phur, puak-phur, puak-pêr-phur, (*v.*) (a gun) hlo thun, (boat, etc.) thiar lût.
Loaf, (*s.*) chhang-pêr.
Lock, (*s.*) kilh-na, (of a gun) cheng, (*v.*) kilh.
Lockjaw, (*s.*) kha chîp.
Locust, (*s.*) khao.
Lodge, (*v.*) hron, thleng, (and provide one's own food) in-kulh.
Lodging, (*s.*) (temporary) thlen' in.
Loft, (*s.*) ṭhe-hlân.
Log, (*s.*) thing.
Loin, (*s.*) kawng, (cloth) hrên.
Loggerheads, (*v.*) (to be at) in-ńghir-ngho.
Loiter, (*v.*) muang.
Lonely, (*a.*) khaw-hâr, khaw-hâr thlâk.
Long, (*a.*) shei, fual, (time) rei, (*v.*) (to long for) ngai, châk.
Look, (*v.*) en, thlîr, chu-ân, (for) zong, lam, (out for) in-ring, (at or in) bih, (in on sly) bih thla, (out, about or upwards) dâk, (after) en-kil, ngai ven', (down upon) en-tleo, (steadfastly at) melh.
Looking-glass, (*s.*) dâr-thla-lang.
Loom, (for weaving) them-bu.
Loop, (*s.*) hrui-valh, valh.
Loose, (*a.*) nghet-lo, fual, (fitting) thawl.
Loosen, (*v.*) phelh, phelh-dul, ti-dul.
Loot, (*v.*) rûn, rû*k*.
Lopsided, (*a.*) awn, thlê.
Lose, (*v.*) hloh, chân, ti-bo-râl.
Loss, (*v.*) (to be a) ui-om, (to be at a) ngai-na rêng hre lo.
Lost, (*a.*) bo.
Lot, (*s.*) chang.
Loud, (*a.*) ring.
Loudly, (*adv.*) ring.
Louse, (*s.*) âr-hrik, hrik.
Love, (*v.*) hma-ngai, khaw-ngai, ngai, (to be in love with) hmel duh.
Low, (*v.*) bu, (*adv.* and *a.*) hniam, phai.
Lower, (*v.*) thlâ*k*, thlâk-thla, ti-hniam, (*adv.*) thlang.
Luck, (*s.*) chan.
Lucky, (*a.*) ham-ṭha, vân-nei, ni-hlawh.
Luggage, (*s.*) bung-rua.
Lumbago, (*s.*) kawng na.
Luminary, (*s.*) ên-na, ên-tu.
Lump, (*s.*) tlang.
Lunatic, (*s.*) mi-â, â baw-raw.
Lung, (*s.*) chuap.
Lure, (*v.*) ngam-thlêm.

Lushai, (*s.*) Lushei, (general name for Lushais and surrounding hill tribes) Zo, Mi-zo.
Lust, (*v.*) hur.
Luxurious, (*a.*) nuam.
Lye, (*s.*) ching-al.

M

Mad, (*a.*) â.
Madman, (*s.*) mi-â.
Maggot, (*s.*) lung.
Maggotty, (*a.*) lung.
Magh, (*s.*) Mi-rang.
Magic, (*s.*) doi.
Magician, (*s.*) doi-thiam, mit-doi-vai thiam.
Magistrate, (*s.*) thu rem tu.
Magnificent, (*a.*) ro-pui.
Magnify, (*v.*) ti-lian, shoi-lian.
Magnifying glass, (*s.*) ni-no.
Maiden, (*s.*) nu-la.
Maiden-hair fern, (*s.*) lung-sam.
Maim, (*v.*) ti-sil.
Maimed, (*a.*) pian*g*-sual, sil.
Maize, (*s.*) vai-mîm.
Make, (*v.*) shiam, (into) chan, chhuah, (saltpetre or lye) thlor, (lattice) ṭheo, kalh, (net) shâ*l*, (blanket) puah, (road) shial, (any thing raised above the ground, as table, bed, bridge, etc.), dawh.
Make for, (*v.*) pan.
Make known, (*v.*) puan*g*.
Make up, (*v.*) (after quarrel) in-kawm-ngeih, in-ngeih.
Maker, (*s.*) shiam-tu.
Male, (*s.*) mi-pa, pa.
Mallet, (*s.*) tal-tum.
Man, (*s.*) mi, mi-hring, (young) rol-thar, tlang-vâl.
Manacle, (*s.*) kol.
Manage, (*v.*) khua sha*k*, ro rêl, khaw-sha.
Mane, (*s.*) bak.
Mango, (*s.*) thei-hai, hai-favâng, hai-dai.
Manipuri, (*s.*) Mei-tei.
Mankind, (*s.*) mi-hring.
Manly, (*a.*) pasal ṭha.
Manner, (*s.*) dân, mit mei, mit-meng zia.
Mantis, (*s.*) ṭêk-râl, (praying) ui-fawm.
Manure, (*s.*) êk, (*v.*) êk-in vûr.
Many, (*a.*) tam, zo-zai, hnem, kaû, (how) eng-zât ? eng-zâ*t*-nge ?
Mar, (*v.*) ti-poi.

Marigold, (*s.*) der-ken.
Mark, (*v.*) chhin-chhiah, (out) rua hman, (*s.*) chhin-chhiah, chhin-chhiah-na.
Market, (*s.*) dawr.
Market place, (*s.*) dawr-hmun.
Marrow, (*s.*) thling.
Marry, (*v.*) (a wife) nu-pui nei, (husband) pa-sal nei, (without parents' consent) in-fan.
Mars, (*s.*) (planet) shi kei shen.
Martin, (*s.*) va-mûr.
Marvel, (*v.*) mak ti.
Marvellous, (*a.*) mak, ro-pui.
Mahseer fish, (*s.*) ngha-phu.
Mass, (in a) hlawm.
Massacre, (*v.*) sâm, rawt.
Master, (*s.*) ho-tu, om-pui-tu, pu.
Masticate, (*v.*) ṭhei, ṭhial.
Mat, (fine woven) zâm-pher.
Match, (lucifer) (*s.*) mei-talh, naw' alh.
Match, (*v.*) in-phu.
Mate, (*s.*) kop-pui, khing-pui.
Materials, (*s.*) hman-rua.
Matted together, (*a.*) hlawm.
Matter, (*v.*) poi.
Matting, (*s.*) (coarse bamboo) dâp.
Mattress, (*s.*) awng-phah.
Mature, (*a.*) chang, hmin.
May, (*s.*) (the month of) thla phur, (*v.*) thei, awm.
Me, (*pro.*) mi*n*, keima mi*n* (also for me, and to me).
Meal, (*s.*) (of food) chhuan.
Mean, (*a.*) fir, kom, ver-vêk, ver-ther.
Meaning, (*s.*) om-zia, ti-na, ti-na-zia.
Means (of or for), phah, (by means of) (*prep.*) in.
Measure, (*v.*) teh, (*s.*) teh-na, (for measuring charge of gun-powder) zen-chong.
Meat, (*s.*) sha.
Medal, (*s.*) tang-ka pui.
Medicine, (*s.*) dam-doi, hlo.
Meditate, (*v.*) ngai-tua.
Medium, (*a.*) vâng-tlâng.
Medlar, (*s.*) thei-she-chal, vul.
Meek, (*a.*) thu hnuai rolh.
Meet, (*v.*) hmua*k*, tawk, ton*g*, nan*g*.
Mela, (*s.*) dawr-pui.

Melancholic, (*v.*) (to be) khaw-tlâng lung len'.
Melon, (*s.*) hma-zil, (water) don-fawh.
Melt, (*v. t.*) er, ti-tui, (*v.*) tui.
Membrane, (*s.*) dal, ham-da.
Men and women, (collectively) (*s.*) a-hmei-a-pa.
Mend, (*v.*) shiam-ṭha.
Menses, (*s.*) thi, (to have) (*v.*) thi nei.
Mention, (*v.*) lam.
Mercenary, (*a.*) dong-rawl duh.
Merciful, (*a.*) zah-ngai thei tak.
Mercy, (*v.*) (to have or show) zah-ngai.
Merely, (*adv.*) mai, mai-mai.
Merry, (*a.*) hlim.
Message, (*v.*) (to bear) zual-ko.
Messenger, (*s.*) tir-ko, zual-ko.
Meteor, (*s.*) chhoih-fa, chhoih-fa thlawk.
Meteorite, (*s.*) ṭêk.
Mew, (*v.*) hrâm.
Mica, (*s.*) long-barh.
Midday, (*s.*) chaw-fâk-hun (or lai), (meal) chaw-fâk. (Also to eat the midday meal.)
Middle, (*s.*) lai.
Midnight, (*s.*) zân-lai.
Midst, (in the) (*prep.*) lai-a, zînga.
Mighty, (*a.*) ro-pui, tha-hrui nei.
Migrate, (*v.*) pêm.
Mildew, (*s.*) hmuar.
Mildewed, (*a.*) ap, hmuar.
Milk, (*s.*) hnu-tê, hnu-tê tui, (*v.*) hnu-tê sawr.
Milky-way, (*s.*) thla-shik kong.
Millet, (*s.*) buh-tun.
Millipede, (*s.*) ke-tam-i nu.
Mimosa, (*s.*) hling-khang, vok-pui ruang ruh.
Minah, (bird) (*s.*) vai-va.
Mind, (*s.*) thin-lung, ril-ru.
Mine, (*pro.*) kei-ma-ta, ka-ta.
Minister, (*s.*) rong-bawl-tu, (*v.*) rong bawl.
Mire, (*s.*) bol-hlawh, chirh-diak, diak.
Miry, (*a.*) chirh-diak, diak, bol-hlawh.
Miscarriage, (*v.*) (to have a) fa a tla-sual, fa a chhia*t*, nao a chhia*t*, nao a tla sual, no a tla sual, no a chhiat.
Mischief, (to do) poi khoih, (to make) poi shoi.
Miser, (*s.*) mi-fîr.
Miserly, (*a.*) fîr, kom.

Miserable, (*a.*) hreh-om, ngui, nguai, re-thei.
Misrepresent, (*v.*) lei-ko, thu vei-vir, zual-ko.
Miss, (*v.*) ṭhelh, (fire, as gun) tlolh.
Missing, (*v.*) (to be) tâp.
Mist, (*s.*) chhûm, ṭiao-chhûm.
Mistake, (*v.*) hai, (*adv.*) (by mistake) sual.
Mix, (*v.*) polh, ti-polh, ti-pawm, (*int.*) pawl, sawh.
Moan, (*v.*) rûm.
Mock, (*v.*) nui-shan, zir-sak.
Mode, (*s.*) dân.
Model, (*s.*) lim, lem, mi-lim, mi-lem.
Moderate, (*a.*) vâng-tlâng.
Moderately, (*adv.*) tawk-fang-in.
Modest, (*a.*) zak.
Moist, (*a.*) hnawng.
Molar, (*s.*) ha-pui.
Molasses, (*s.*) kûr-tai.
Mole, (*s.*) bui-ke-lek, (spot) khua-vâng chhin-chhiah.
Mollusc, (*s.*) (bivalved) kep.
Moment, (*s.*) mit khap, (*adv.*) (in a moment) mit khap kâr lo vin.
Money, (*s.*) tang-ka, tang-ka sum.
Monkey, (*s.*) zawng, (grey) ngao.
Monotonous, (*a.*) nin-om.
Month, (*s.*) thla, (next) thla leh, (last) thla hlui, thla hmasha, (this) tûn thla.
Monthly, (*adv.*) thla tin.
Moon, (*s.*) thla, (the night of full moon) âr kai zân, hlei-nga zân, (half) chi-khawn-phel, (full) hlei-nga, (first quarter) she-pui ki tia, (new) thla thar, (to be new) thla a de, (last quarter) thla noi, (when there is no moon) thla mong lai (or hun), (when only three quarters is visible) vom-lu.
Moonbeam, (*s.*) thla êng.
More, (*adv.*) deo, zawk, leh-zual, zual, (*a.*) dang, (more likely) zawk, (than others) lêm, lêm chuang, chuang, bîk, (than) liam, liam-a.
Morning, (*s.*) chaw-hma, (this) tûk-in-a, (early) zîng-a, (every) tuk-tin.
Morose, (*a.*) ngoi-choi.
Morsel, (*s.*) hmol.
Mortar, (*s.*) (for pounding rice, etc.) sum.
Mosquito, (*s.*) tho-shi.
Mosquito curtain, (*s.*) tho-shi lên.
Moss, (*s.*) pât.
Most, (*adv.*) ber.

Moth, (*s.*) phêng-phe-hlep.
Mother, (*s.*) nu, (mother and child) nu fa.
Mother-in-law, (wife's mother) pi-zon, (husband's mother) nu.
Motionlessly, (*adv.*) che-lo-vin.
Mottled, (*a.*) râng.
Mould, (*s.*) hmuar.
Mouldy, (*a.*) ap, hmuar, (smelling) ung.
Mound, (*s.*) mual, vûn*g*, ko.
Mount, (*v.*) chuang.
Mountain, (*s.*) tlâng.
Mountainous country, (*s.*) thing-tlâng.
Mourn or go into mourning, (*v.*) lu shûn, sam hram pu.
Mourn, (*v.*) mi-thi ngai.
Mouse, (*s.*) chai-chîm.
Mouth, (*s.*) ka, kam, (of bottle or jar) rong, tlâng, (of river) mong.
Move, (*v.*) che, shon, in-shon, phe phe, (along) tol, (*trans.*) dah-shon, (as ears, nostrils, etc.) phût, (the head or body on one side) thlê.
Much, (*adv.*) êm êm, êm, mang, tam, zo-zai, feng, hle, hnem, kaû, ngot, ṭha hnem, (how) eng zât ? eng zâ*t*-nge ? eng-chen-nge ?
Mucus, (*s.*) thao, (of nose) hnap.
Mud, (*s.*) chirh-diak, diak, lei diak.
Muddle, (*s.*) buai, (*v.*) ti-buai.
Muddled, (*a.*) buai.
Muddling, buai-thlâk.
Muddy, (*a.*) chirh diak, diak, (as water) nu.
Mug, (*s.*) no.
Mule, (*s.*) sakor beng-tung, sa-beng-tung.
Multitude, (*s.*) mi-pui.
Mumps, (*s.*) biang-bôh.
Murder, (*v.*) tual-tha*t*, (secretly) phil.
Murmur, (*v.*) phun, phun-noi, phun-ru.
Muscle, (*s.*) ti, (of upper arm) bân-puam.
Mushroom, (*s.*) pa, (*v.*) (to mushroom out) ner.
Musket, (*s.*) silai.
Mustache, (*s.*) hmûi-hmul.
Mustard plant, (*s.*) an-ṭam.
Mutilate, (*v.*) nghai-sha.
Mutter, (*v.*) phun, phun-ru.
Mutton, (*s.*) he-râm sha.
Muzzle, (*s.*) silai kua.
My, (*pro.*) kei-ma, ka.
Myself, (*pro.*) keima-in, kei-in, (reflex prefix) in.
Mystery, (*s.*) thu-rîl.

N

Nag, (*v.*) âng, hrâm.
Naga, (*s.*) Mi-rong.
Nail, (*s.*) tin, kilh-na, (*v.*) khêng, kilh, (to, up or down) khêng bet.
Naked, (*a.*) ruak, sa-ruak.
Name, (*s.*) hming, (in the name of) hming-a, hming-in, (*v.*) (to take the name of another or call one's self by another's name) hming chhâl, (to name) vuah, hming sha (falsely in the name of) hming chhâl-in.
Nape, (*s.*) thluk, tuk-khum-khur, tuk-khum.
Narrate, (*v.*) hril.
Narrow, (*a.*) zîm, (as mouth of pot, etc.) kum.
Nasty, (*a.*) tui-lo, chhiat, chhe.
Nation, (*s.*) hnam.
Nature, (*s.*) nung-chang.
Naught, (*pro.*) eng-ma.
Navel, (*s.*) lai.
Near, (*prep.*) dep-a, kiang-a, hrual-a, (*a.*) hnai.
Nearest, (*a.*) ton'tîr.
Nearly, (*adv.*) dawn-ta, thaw, ṭhelh.
Necessary, (*v.*) (to be) ngai, (imperatively) ma-mawh.
Neck, (*s.*) nghawng, ring.
Necklace, (*s.*) ṭhi-hrui.
Need, (*v.*) duh, ṭûl, (imperatively) ma-mawh.
Needle, (*s.*) hriao.
Neglect, (*v.*) thlah-thlam.
Neigh, (*v.*) ao ur ur.
Neighbour, (*s.*) ṭhen-om, vêng, vêng-te.
Neighbourhood, (*s.*) vêng.
Neither, hek-lo.
Nephew, (*s.*) (a man's brother's son, and a husband's brother's son) fa-pa, (a sister's son, a husband's sister's son) tu-pa, (a woman's brother's son) vah-pa.
Nerve, (*s.*) tha-zâm.
Nervous, (*a.*) ṭi, ṭih.
Nest, (*s.*) bu.
Net, (*s.*) lên.
Nettle, (stinging) kang-ṭhai, la-pui, ṭai-ṭêm, ṭai-ṭêng, thak-pui, zawng-kâng-ṭhai.
Neuter, (*s.*) pa dawp.
Never, (*adv.*) ngai lo, top lo, tawh lo.
Nevertheless, (*conj.*) ama-e-raw-chu, ani-na-a, eng-pawh ni-shela, eng-pawh-ti-la, eng-pawh-ni-roh-se.

New, (*a.*) thar, hlim.
Newlaid, (*a.*) tui hlim.
Newly, (*adv.*) hlim, thar.
News, (*s.*) chan-chin, thu, ti-ti.
Next (*a.* and *adv.*) dot, leh-pek, (to each other) in-dot, (*s.*) dot-tu.
Nibble, (*v.*) sheh.
Nice, (*a.*) nuam, tui.
Nickname, (*s.*) hming-der, hming chhia, hming lem.
Nicotine water, (*s.*) tui-bûr.
Niece, (*s.*) (a man's brother's daughter, and a husband's brother's daughter) fa-nu, (a sister's daughter, a husband's sister's daughter) tu-nu, (a woman's brother's daughter) vah-nu.
Niggard, (*s.*) mi fîr.
Nigh, (*adv.*) hnai.
Night, (*s.*) zân, khaw-thim, (fall) khaw-thim, (night blind, to be) mit mal, (night after night) zân-zawn-in, (all) zân-khua-in, zân khua, (night before last) nimin zân-a, (three nights ago) nimin-piah zân-a.
Nightjar, (*s.*) va-bak.
Nightly, (*adv.*) zân-tin, zân-tin-a, zân-tin-in.
Nine, (*a.*) pa-kua, kua.
Nineteen, (*a.*) shom leh pah-kua.
Nineteenth, (*a.*) shom leh pa-kua-na.
Ninetieth, (*a.*) shom-kua-na.
Ninety, (*s.*) shom-kua.
Ninth, (*a.*) pa-kua-na, kua-na.
Nip, (*v.*) che*p*, shik.
Nippers, (*s.*) (of a gun, which hold the flint) silai kep tê.
Nipple, (*s.*) hnu-tê hmûr.
No, (*adv.*) ni-lo, hnai-lo, ni-shu-e.
Nobody, (*v.*) (*pro.*) tu-ma, tu-ma...lo.
Nod, (*v.*) bu*k*.
Nohow, eng-tin-ma...lo.
Noise, (*s.*) beng-chheng, (*v.*) (to make) beng-chheng.
Noisy, (*a.*) beng-chheng.
None, (*pro.*) eng-ma, tu-ma.
Noon, (*s.*) chaw-fâk.
No one, (*pro.*) tu-ma, tuma...lo.
Noose, (*s.*) valh, (*v.*) hlîng.
Nor, (*conj.*) hek lo.
North, (*s.*) hmâr lam, khaw-hmâr, hmâr.
North-east, hmâr-chhak.
Northern, (*a.*) hmâr.

Northward, (*adv.*) hmâr lam-a.
North-west, (*s.*) hmâr-thlang.
Nose, (*s.*) hnâr, (flat) hnâr per, (turned up) hnâr kem, (aquiline) hnâr kûl, (indentation above nose) hnâr kawn, (flaps of nose) hnâr te-ngeng.
Nostril, (*s.*) hnâr-kua.
Not, (*adv.*) lo, nêm, (at all) dêr-lo, hek-lo.
Notch, (*v.*) chhu, shât-rek rah-bi, re*k*.
Notched, (*a.*) re*k*.
Note, (*v.*) chhin-chhia.
Nothing, (*s.*) engma, engma...lo.
Notwithstanding, (*conj.*) pawh-in, pôh-in.
November, (*s.*) sa hmul phah thla, sawm hmul phah thla.
Now, (*adv.*) tûn-a, tûn-a-hian, tûn-a zong, (now already) tûna-pang-in, (now at once) tûna-pang-a, (by now) tûna, tûna zong, (now, at this moment) tûn-la-la-a, tûn-law-law-a, tûna tei.
Nowadays, (*adv.*) tûn-lai.
Nowhere, (*adv.*) khoi-a-ma...lo, khoi-a-ma.
Nowise, (*adv.*) top lo.
Nude, (*a.*) ruak, sa-ruak.
Nuisance, (*a.*) chim-om, hreh-om.
Nurse, (*v.*) choi, enkol,

O

Oak, (*s.*) sa-shua, hlai, khaw-thli, ṭhîl,
Oar, (*s.*) vai-cha,
Oath, (*v.*) (to take) chhia chham, chhe-chham.
Obedient, (*a.*) ti-nuam, tirh-nuam, tirh-oih.
Obey, (*v.*) oih, pom, ngai, thu-thu-in om, zawm, zawh.
Object, (*v.*) hreh, (*s.*) (of or for) chhan, phah,
Objectionable, (*a.*) huat-thla-la.
Objections, (*v.*) (to raise) shoi-shêl.
Obliquely, (*adv.*) awn, lao.
Oblong, (*a.*) shawl.
Obscure, (*v.*) hlia, (obscurely) (*adv.*) fiah lo tak-in, fiah le, a thoi-in.
Observe, (*v.*) hmu, zawh (as a rest day, etc.), sherh, hrilh.
Obstacle, (*s.*) dâl-na.
Obstinate, (*a.*) luh-lul, ti-mawh, ngol-tawt.
Obstruct, (*v.*) dâl.
Obstructed, (*a.*) hnok.
Obstructive, (*a.*) hnok-sak.
Obtain, (*v.*) nei.

Occasionally, (*adv.*) a chång-chång-in, khåt.
Occupy, (*v.*) awh, luah.
October, (*s.*) khuang-choi thla.
Odd, (*a.*) (not even) kop kim lo.
Odour, (*s.*) rim.
Of, (*prep.*) in, a.
Off, (*adv.*) bûl, bal, chhum, tan.
Offend, (*v.*) run, run-râl, ti-lung ni lo, ti-vui.
Offended, (to be) vui, lung ni lo, run, run-râl.
Offer, (*v.*) hlân, pê*k*, theh, (for sale) zuar.
Offering, (to make an offering to spirit of departed) mi-thị chhiah.
Officer, (*s.*) ho-tu.
Offspring, (*s.*) fa, chhuan.
Often, (*adv.*) fo, fan.
Oil, (*s.*) sa-hriak, (lamp) khawn-vâr tui, tui alh.
Old, (*a.*) hlui, tar, un, (man) pu-tar, (woman) pi-tar, (old and young) a puia pang.
Omit, (*v.*) tlolh, thulh.
On, (*prep.*) chung-a, a, in.
Once, (*a.*) voi-khat.
One, (*a.*) pa-khat, khat, (with one another, one another) in, (one at a time) mal-zêl-in, mal-ṭheo-vin, mal-mal-in, (one after another) zêl, chhawk-zêl.
Onion, (*s.*) pu-rûn.
Only, (*a.*) hlir, mai, fâl, fang, ngût, (*adv.*) chaoh, chaoh-vin.
Open, (*v.*) hong, (as flower, hand, etc.), ar, parh, pharh, (as umbrella) kap-parh, kap-pharh, (as mouth) âng, (as legs, cut, earth, etc., also to pull or force open) kao, (the legs) kam ka, (to force an opening through, or force open) keo, (as eyes) meng.
Openly, (*adv.*) a-lang-in.
Opportune, (*a.*) rem-chång, ti-zia.
Opportunely, (*adv.*) fuh.
Opportunity, (*s.*) rem-chång.
Oppose, (*v.*) kalh, lo-kalh.
Opposite, (*prep.*) zawn, hma-zawh-a, hma-zawn-a.
Oppress, (*v.*) hneh-chhia*t*, hneh-sawh, ra*p*-be*t*, ti duh-dah, tlawh-bet.
Or, (*conj.*) nge, leh, emaw.
Orange, (*s.*) sêr-thlum.
Orchid, (*s.*) nao-bân.
Ordain, (*v.*) ruat.
Order, (*v.*) thu thiam, tuk, (about) tir-chhiah.
Ordinary, (*a.*) na-men, na-rân, na-mai, na-zong, sa-tliah.
Originate, (*v.*) chhua*k*, ti-chhua*k*.

Originator, (*s.*) ti-chhuak tu.
Orion, (*s.*) chho-hrei-vûng.
Ornament, (*s.*) chei-moi-na.
Ornamental, (*a.*) moi.
Orphan, (*s.*) fa-hrah.
Oscillate, (*v.*) (as water) fawn.
Other, (*a.*) dang, dang-lam.
Otherwise, (*conj.*) chuti-lo-chuan, ani-lo-leh.
Otorrhœa, (*s.*) beng kherh.
Otter, (*s.*) sa-hram.
Our, (*pro.*) kema-ni, kan.
Ours, (*pro.*) keima-ni-ta, kan-ta,
Ourselves, (reflexive prefix) in.
Out, (*adv.*) chhua*k*.
Outer, (*a.*) pawn-ta.
Outermost, (*a.*) pawn-ta-ber.
Outlet, (*s.*) chua*k*-na.
Outlive, (*v.*) shûn.
Outside, (*s.*) pawn, (of bamboos) na, (*prep.*) pawn-a, pawn-lama.
Outskirts, (*s.*) dai.
Outstrip, (*v.*) leh khalh.
Outwardly, (*a.*) a-lang-in.
Over, (left) chuang, (*adv.*) hlên.
Over and over again, (*adv.*) non, (over again) vêk.
Overcome, (*v.*) hneh.
Overflow, (*v.*) liam.
Overgrow, (*a.*) hnim.
Overlap, (*v.*) sul-pêl.
Overlook, (*v.*) hmaih, hmaih-ṭhelh, (intentionally) hai der.
Overseer, (*s.*) en-kil-tu, ho-tu.
Overshadow, (*v.*) hlia.
Overtake, (*v.*) nan*g*, phâ*k*.
Overturn, (*v.*) let.
Overworked, (*a.*) rim tong.
Owe, (*v.*) ba, bat.
Owl, (*s.*) chhim-buk, (horned) chhim-buk shial ki, (large) ching-piri-nu.
Owner, (*s.*) nei-tu, om-pui-tu.
Ox, (*s.*) se-bawng til rek, se-bawng til ret.

P

Pace, (*v.*) kâr, pên, (*s.*) pên.
Pacify, (*v.*) thlêm.

Paddle, (*s.*) vai-cha, (*v.*) vai, kar.
Page, (*s.*) (as of book) phêk.
Pain, (*s.*) na, nat.
Painful, (*a.*) na.
Pair, (*s.*) tuak, pawl.
Palate, (*s.*) dang.
Pale, (*a.*) dâng.
Palisade, (*s.*) pal, kulh.
Palm, (*s.*) (of hand) kut-phah.
Palmistry, (*s.*) (one skilled in) **kut zia en thiam, kut ze en thiam.**
Pamper, (*v.*) duat.
Pan, (*s.*) thlêng, (of gun) silai-beng-thlêng.
Pancake, (*s.*) chhang-pêr.
Pangolin, (*s.*) sa-phu.
Panic-stricken, (*v.*) (to be) zâm.
Pant, (*v.*) thaw hlop hlop.
Papaw, (*s.*) nu-hnûn, thing-fang-hma.
Paper, (*s.*) lai-shuih, le-kha.
Parable, (*s.*) thon-thu.
Parasitical insects, (*s.*) hrik.
Paradise, (*s.*) Pial-râl.
Paralysed, (*a.*) (as limb) zeng.
Parasol, (*s.*) ni-hliap.
Parched, (*a.*) châr.
Pardon, (*v.*) ngai-dam, ngai-hna thiam.
Pare, (*v.*) hlep.
Parents, (*s.*) nu leh pa.
Parrot, (*s.*) va-ki.
Part, (*s.*) ṭhen, bung, hmun, (the hair) (*v.*) ba-rî ṭhen.
Particular, (*a.*) kher-mei, ti-kher-kher, ti-shi-she, ti-dîm-dêm.
Particularly, (*adv.*) dîm-dêm, kher-mei, (not) hlei lo, hlel deo.
Parting, (of hair) (*s.*) ba-rî.
Partition, (*s.*) pin-dan.
Partly, (*adv.*) lak-lawh.
Partridge, (*s.*) va-rung, (hill) va-hla.
Party, (*s.*) pawl, ho.
Pass, (*v.*) kal-pêl, pêl, hêl, (away) ral, (through a village without putting up for the night) chhûn-pelh, (over) hlên, (on, from one to another) in-hlân, (time) ni lên', (pass time quickly) ni tum toi, (by or through or out) pêl, (to allow to pass) pêl.
Paste, (*s.*) char-na.
Pastime, (*s.*) ni tum toi-na.
Pasture, (*v.*) tla.
Pat, (*v.*) bêng.

Patch, (*v.*) bel.
Patella, (*s.*) khûp-koi.
Path, (*s.*) kong, kal-kong.
Patient, (*a.*) en-thei, dawh-thei, (under suffering) chhel.
Patiently, (*adv.*) tlawm-ngai-tak-in.
Pause, (*v.*) ngoi.
Pay, (*v.*) rêl, man pê*k*.
Peace (to be at) in-rem, rem, (to have peace of mind) tla muang, lung muang.
Peaceably, (*adv.*) tlang.
Peach, (*s.*) thei-tê.
Peacock, (*s.*) âr awn-rang-ka-chak.
Peak, (*s.*) tlâng-chhîp.
Pebble, (*s.*) lung.
Peck, (*v.*) chu*k*, (up) chu*k*.
Peel, (*v.*) khok, pil-khok.
Peep in, (*v.*) bih.
Peevish, (*a.*) pang-chang.
Pellet, (*s.*) sai-hlum, hlum, (bow) sai-raw-kherh.
Pelt, (*v.*) in-tawng.
Pen, (*s.*) (fold) huang, huang-chhûng, (for writing) lekha-ziak-na.
Pencil, (*s.*) lekha-ziak-na.
Penetrate, (*v.*) len*g*.
Penis, (*s.*) zang.
Penitent, (*v.*) in-chhîr.
People, (*s.*) vân*g*-tlân*g*-mi, mi, tlâng, (the common people) hnam-chom.
Pepper-corn, (*s.*) thing hmar-cha.
Perceive, (*v.*) hmu, hria*t*, hre.
Perch, (*v.*) fu.
Perfect, (*a.*) ṭhat-fam-kim.
Perfectly, (*adv.*) dêr, var, viah, vua, vur-var.
Perform, (*v.*) ti, chê*t*, thawk.
Perfume, (*s.*) rim tui.
Perhaps, (*adv.*) ani-ang-e, awm, dah-law-maw, dah ang-e, mah-na, (not) dah-ne-maw.
Peril, (to be in) hlao thawn' om tak-in om.
Perilous, (*a.*) hlao-thawn' om.
Perish, (*v.*) bo-ral.
Perishable, (*a.*) bo-ral-thei.
Permission, (*adv.*) (without) rok, (*v.*) (to give) thu pê*k*.
Permit, (*v.*) phal, rem ti, rem tîr, rem-châng-tîr, tîr.
Perpendicular, (*a.*) bir.
Perpendicularly, (*adv.*) bir.

Perplex, (*v.*) ti-mang-ang, (perplexed, to be) mang-ang.
Perplexing, (*adv.*) mang an' thlâk.
Perquisite, (to receive) zâr zo.
Persecute, (*v.*) ti-duh-dah.
Persevere, (*v.*) lui-hrâm, tlawm ngai.
Persevering, (*a.*) hrât.
Perseveringly, (*adv.*) lui-hrâm, tlawm-ngai-tak-in.
Persist, (*v.*) lui-hrâm.
Persistently, (*adv.*) lui-hrâm, lui.
Person, (*s.*) mi, mi-hring.
Personate, (*v.*) in-chhal.
Perspiration, (*s.*) thlan.
Perspire, (*v.*) thlan a sha.
Persuade, (*v.*) thlêm, thlêm-thlu, luh-thluk, ṭa'awh.
Perverse, (*a.*) luh-lul.
Pervert, (*v.*) ti khaw lo.
Perverted, (*a.*) khaw-lo.
Pestilence, (*s.*) hri pui, (to die of) pûl.
Pestle, (*s.*) suk.
Petticoat, (*s.*) puan-fên.
Pettish, (*a.*) pang-chang.
Pewter, (*a.*) hâr.
Pheasant, (*s.*) va-vu, (black) va-hrit, (peacock) va-ri-haw.
Philtre, (*s.*) zawl-ai-di.
Phlegm, (*s.*) khâk.
Phlegmatic, (*a.*) chut.
Phosphorescent, (*a.* and *v.*) thla-vâr.
Photograph, (*s.*) hlim, hlim lâk, (*v.*) hlim lâk, (camera) hlim lâk-na.
Pice, (*s.*) pai-sha, poi-sha.
Pick, (*v.*) (as a sore) kheoh, (out) khei, (out or over) thiar.
Pickaxe, (*s.*) lung râl, lung tu'hrât, lung-tuk-na.
Pick up, (*v.*) chhar.
Picnic, (*v.* and *s.*) in khual te lem.
Picture, (*s.*) hlim, lem, lim, mi-lem, mi-lim.
Pie, (*s.*) (money) pai-sha dere, pai-sha khing phel.
Piebald, (*a.*) râng.
Piece, (*s.*) hmol, hrang, ṭhem, (*adv.*) (in pieces) bung, chip, noi, som, (small piece) kem, noi.
Pierce, (*v.*) bûr, chhun, vit.
Pig, (domestic) vok, (call for pigs) ri ri.
Pigeon, (*s.*) pâr-va, thu-mi.
Pile, (*s.*) (to support a house), ṭhom-mawl, (of wood) ai, (*v.*) (up) chhep, tiang, vûm.
Piled up, (*a.*) in-tiang, (as measure, etc.) vûm.

Pillow, (*s.*) lu-kham.
Pimple, (*s.*) ar-ngeng, bol.
Pin, (*s.*) hriao hmawr bawk.
Pincers, (*s.*) chai-che'.
Pinch, (*v.*) chilh, hme*t*, pei, shik.
Pine, (*s.*) fâr.
Pineapple, (*s.*) la-khuih-thei, thei-la-khuih, la-hui.
Pioneer, (*v.*) hma-hruai, (*s.*) hma-hruai-tu.
Pipe, (*s.*) (tube,) dawt, (woman's) tui-bûr-lai, (man's) vai-bêl.
Pit, (*v.*) chik, (*s.*) hum.
Pitted, (*a.*) chik.
Piteous, (*a.*) khaw-ngai-thlak.
Pitfall, (*s.*) hum.
Pithy, (as radishes, etc.) thawp.
Pitiful, (*a.*) (compassionate) khaw-ngai-thei.
Pity, (*v.*) khaw-ngai, (to be a pity) poi, ui-om.
Place, (*v.*) dah, (*s.*) hmun, lam, lai, om-na.
Plague, (*s.*) hri pui, (to die of) pûl.
Plain, (*a.*) fiah, (unadorned) mawl, (*s.*) phai.
Plainly, (*adv.*) fiah.
Plains, (the) phai-tual.
Plait, (*v.*) phiar, (matting) tah.
Plan, (*v.*) phiar, rem ruat, rêl, rua hman, (*s.*) thu-phiar.
Plane, (*s.*) thing mâm-na.
Planet, (*s.*) hrâng-chhuan-a.
Plant, (*v.*) chîng, phun, lîn*g*, tuh, (*s.*) kûng, hnim.
Plantain, (*s.*) bal-hla, ban-ria, ban-pui, ban-pawl, (edible bud) tumbu, (wild) chang-êl, (fruit of wild) chang-kêl.
Plaster, (*v.*) bel.
Plastic, (*a.*) khal.
Plate, (*s.*) thlêng, sai-phah.
Plateau, (*s.*) tlâng-zawl.
Platform, (outside Lushai house) lei-ka, lei-ka-pui, lu-ka, lu-ka-pui, (erected in memory of the dead) lung-dawh.
Play, (*v.*) chai, in-om-lem, (musical instrument) tum, (about with) fiam, khâl.
Plead, (*v.*) ngên-chiam.
Pleasant, (*a.*) nuam.
Please, (*v.*) ti lawm, ti lung-oi, (to be pleased) lawm, lung-oi, lungni, (with) chhuang.
Pleasing, (*a.*) lawm-om, hlim-om.
Pleasure, (to take pleasure in) hlut, hlut-sak.
Pleasurable, (*a.*) hlim-om, lawm-om.
Pleat, (*v.*) phuah-khawm.

Pleiades (*s.*) shi ruh.
Plentiful, (*a.*) tam.
Plot, (*v*) phiar, (*s.*) thu phiar.
Plough, (*s.*) lei hrût-na, (*v.*) lei hrût.
Plover, (*s.*) mang-khai râl-vêng.
Pluck, (*v.*) lawh, lo.
Plum, (*s.*) lum-lêr, (hog plum) toi-taw.
Plume, (worn by those who have slain men in raid) lên-chhawn, (worn by those who have given public feast) thlan-thla-chang.
Plump, (*a.*) chom, chum.
Plunder, (*v.*) ram.
Plunge, (*v.*) li luh.
Pocket, (*s.*) ip-tê.
Pod, (*s.*) kawm.
Poet, (*s.*) hla phuah-thiam.
Poetry, (*s.*) hla, (*v.*) (to compose poetry or songs) hla phuah.
Point, (*s.*) hmûr, hmawr, (*v.*) kawk, (point at in contempt) eo.
Pointed, (*a.*) zum.
Point out, (*v.*) kaw'hmu.
Poison, (*v.*) hrai-hlum, (fish) vua*k*, (*s.*) thi-na hlo, tûr, (for poisoning fish) ru.
Poisonous, (*a.*) thi-na, tûr nei, (very poisonous, as snake) tûr a ṭha.
Poke, (*v.*) holh.
Poker, (*s.*) thuk-thai.
Polish, (*v.*) nawt-tle, (polished) mom, tle, tliang.
Pond, (*s.*) dîl-tê.
Ponder, (*v.*) ngai-tua, ril-rû*k*.
Pony, (*s.*) sa-kor.
Pool, (*s.*) tui-hawk, dîl-tê, (deep pool in river) li.
Poor, (*a.*) pa-chhia, re-thei, riang-vai.
Pop, (*a.*) pok.
Popgun, (*s.*) ka'pup.
Popular, (*a.*) chal-lang.
Porcupine, (*s.*) sa-kuh.
Pork, (*s.*) vok-sha.
Porpoise, (*s.*) zawng-dûli nu.
Portion, (*v.*) (out) in-shem, (*s.*) bung, chan, chan-ai, chan-vo, chan-hrang.
Position, (*s.*) zawng.
Possess, (*v.*) (as spirit) chelh, (to have) nei, (to be possessed, as by spirit) zawl, (much of) ngah.
Possession, (*v.*) (to take or enter into) luah, ro-chung.

Possible, (*v.*) rual.
Possibly, (*adv.*) mah-na.
Post, (*s.*) (of house) ban, (post upon which gayals' heads are placed) she-lu phan, (inside a house supporting ridge pole) shût.
Posterior, (*s.*) mong.
Posterity, (*s.*) chi-thlah, ṭhâl-be a mi.
Pot, (*s.*) bêl, (water) kawl-a bêl.
Potash, (*s.*) ching-al.
Potato, (*s.*) (sweet) ba-hra-thlum, kawl-ba-hra.
Potter, (*s.*) bêl-vua-tu, bêl-vua*k*-thiam, bêl-vaw-tu.
Pounce upon, (*v.*) bawh, zuan.
Pound, (*v.*) dên*g*, (*s.*) (for stray animals, etc.) hrên'na in.
Pour, (*v.*) (in or out) chhûn*g*, (out) bua*k*, bun, leih.
Powder, (*v.*) (to powder), chip, dip, (*a.*) (finely powdered) dip, (*s.*) phut, (powder measure) hah-teh, (powder horn) pai-tung, fung-ki, (gun) silai hlo.
Power, (*s.*) thil ti thei-na.
Powerful, (*a.*) chak.
Practise, (*v.*) them-thiam.
Praise, (*v.*) fak.
Prawn, (*s.*) kai-kuang.
Pray, (*v.*) dîl chiam-vak, dîl lui, dîl tlat-tlat, (to God) ṭong-ṭai, bia*k* be, chham-phual.
Precipice, (*s.*) khâm.
Predicament, (to be in) mang-an*g*.
Predict, (*v.*) shoi-lawk, hril-lawk.
Prefer, (*v.*) duh zawk.
Pregnant, (*a.*) rai, ruak-lo, (great with young) rai-ṭeoh.
Premises, (on the) hmun-a.
Prepare, (*v.*) buat-saih, shiam, (beforehand or make preparation for) in-ring.
Presence of mind, (*v.*) (to lose) chi-ai, ham-haih, hai-haih.
Present, (for the *or* at) hrih, rih, (*v.*) om, tel.
Presently, (*adv.*) nak-in-a, nak-in-deo-va, la, nak-in-hnua.
Preserve, (*v.*) dah-ṭha, von*g*, von*g*-reng.
Press, (in) bên*g*, nem, (closely together) ti-muk.
Prestige, (*v.*) (to lose) tlawm.
Presumptuously, (*adv.*) vei.
Pretend, (*v.*) der, ti-der.
Pretty, (*a.*) moi.
Prevail, (*v.*) ngam.
Prevaricate, (*v.*) zêp.
Prevalent, (*v.*) (as disease) lên*g*.

Prevent, (*v.*) dâl, ṭhulh-tîr, ti-khol-kham, ti-tlolh.
Prevented, (*v.*) (to be) ṭhulh, tlolh.
Previously, (*adv.*) zet.
Price, (*s.*) man, (*v.*) (to ask a price) chhiar.
Prick, (*v.*) chhun, chiu, khei, (as ears) tun*g*.
Prickle, (*s.*) hlîng.
Priest, (*s.*) pui-thiam.
Prim, (*a.*) u-luk.
Prime, (*v.*) (a gun), beng-chah, hma-theh.
Priming, (*s.*) (of gun) beng-chah, hma-theh.
Print, (*v.*) nem-in ziak.
Prison, (*s.*) lung in.
Prisoner, (*s.*) mi-tâng.
Prize, (*v.*) ro.
Probe, (*v.*) holh, rolh.
Proclaim, (*v.*) tlâng-ao.
Procure, (*v.*) hmu, nei.
Produce, (*v.*) de*k*-chhua*k*.
Profit, (*v.*) (to make) hlêp, (by) sawt.
Profitable, (*a.*) kong awh, sawt.
Profound, (*a.*) rit, ril.
Progenitor, (*s.*) thlah-tu.
Prohibit, (*v.*) khap.
Project and projecting, tôh-lawt, lor.
Prolix, (*v.*) (to be) shoi shei.
Promise, (*v.*) tiam, tuk, thu tiam.
Promote, (*v.*) choi-moi.
Pronounce, (*v.*) lam.
Proof, (*s.*) hriat-na, hriat-fiah-na.
Prop, (*v.*) chhun-kal, do.
Proper, (*a.*) chiang, dik, tlâk, fel, moi.
Properly, (*adv.*) chiang.
Property, (*s.*) ro, thuam-hnaw, thom-hnaw.
Prophesy, (*v.*) hril-lawk, shoi-lawk.
Prophet, (*s.*) zawl-nei.
Proportion, (*a.*) (in right) in-phu.
Propose, (*v.*) rot, (for marriage) bia*k*.
Proselyte, (*s.*) sa-phun.
Prosper, (*v.*) ni-khua, thaw-ven*g*, vân-ni chang.
Prosperous, (*a.*) muk, nghet, eng-thawl.
Protect, (*v.*) hum.
Protrude, (*v.*) lor.
Proud, (*a.*) cha-po, (of) chhuang.
Prove, (*v.*) fiah.

Proverb, (*s.*) teh-khin-thu.
Provident, (*a.*) kom deo.
Provoke, (*v.*) run, run-râl.
Prow, (*s.*) (of boat) hmûr.
Prudent, (*a.*) rem hria*t*, rem-hre.
Prudently, (*adv.*) rem-hre-tak-in.
Pseudo, (*a.*) shuak.
Public, (*s.*) tlâng, vân*g*-tlân*g*-mi.
Publicly, (*adv.*) vân*g*tlâng zîng-a, vân*g*tlâng hriat-in, vân*g*-tlâng hmu-in, a-lang-in.
Publish, (*v.*) puan*g*.
Puckered, (*a.*) chuar.
Puddle, (*s.*) tui-hawk, tui-hawk-tling.
Puff, (*v.*) (out the stomach) san*g*.
Pull, (*v.*) hnûk, kai, po*t*, (up) po*t*, (out) phoi, (off) khok, (out, as teeth) thlon, (towards one, as bough, etc.) kuai kûr, kuai.
Pullet, (*s.*) âr-la.
Pulse, (*s.*) mar, (*v.*) (to feel) mar dek.
Pulverize, (*v.*) ti-noi.
Pumpkin, (*s.*) mai, mai-pawl, ûm.
Punch, (*v.*) chûm, (with knuckles) chûm lok, lok.
Pungent, (*a.*) ru, thak, thîp.
Punish, (*v.*) hrem, soi.
Pup, (*s.*) ui no.
Purchase, (*v.*) lei.
Purify, (*v.*) in-thian.
Purpose, (*v.*) châk-khai, ril-rû*k*, ti, tum, rêl.
Purposely, (*adv.*) lui.
Purr, (*v.*) rûm.
Pursue, (*v.*) ûm, (for long distance) thlûr.
Pus, (*s.*) hnai.
Push, (*v.*) nam, hnawl, nor, pir, (on one side) tawn, (in) holh, rolh, (over the edge) nam-liam, (over) ti-thlû*k*, nam-tlû*k*, (*s.*) ar-ngeng.
Put, (*v.*) dah, (down, as load) nghat, (out) chhuak-tîr, (by or off) dah, khêk, (on, as coat) hâ*k*, (in) khung, thun, (on top or one on top of another) tian*g*, chher-chhuan, chhuan*g*, (together in one place) chhek-khawm, dah-khawm, (away or in order) dah-ṭha, (on the fire-shelf) hâ*k*, (into mouth) hmom, (up for the night) ria*k*.
Putrefy, (*v.*) ṭoih.
Putrid, (*a.*) ṭoih.
Python, (*s.*) sa-phai.

Q

Quadruped, (*s.*) fu-li-a-fa.
Quail, (*s.*) va-hmîm.
Quarrel, (*v.*) in-hao, in-sual.
Quarter, (*s.*) zâł-ve khing phel.
Queen, (*s.*) Lal-nu, (Lushai name for Queen Victoria, lit. 'The Company's mother') = Kumpi-nu.
Quell, (*v.*) ṭhelh.
Question, (*s.*) zawt-thu, thu-buai, (*v.*) chhuah chhâl, chhâl, (to ask a) zawt.
Quick, (*a.*) chak, ṭuan-rang, (scented) hnâr fing, (of understanding) beng-vâr, (*s.*) (of nail) tin-hna.
Quickly, (*adv.*) thuai, rang, thuai-thuai, saoh-saoh, sawt, hman-hmaw.
Quick-tempered, (*a.*) thin ram.
Quiet, (*a.*) chut, ngoi, ngoi-choi, nguai, ngui, (*v.*) dai, ti-ngoi.
Quietly, (*adv.*) thlang, muang.
Quits, (*v.*) (to be) in-hen.
Quite, (*adv.*) dêr, var, viah, vua, vur-var, hle, (not quite) deo lo.
Quiver, (*v.*) khûr.

R

Rabbit, (*s.*) sa-zu-pui.
Race, (*v.*) in-tlân-shiak.
Radish, (*s.*) an-ṭam bul bâl.
Raft, (*s.*) pûm.
Rafters, (of roof) in-chun.
Rag, (*s.*) puan chhia.
Raid, (*v.*) rûn.
Rail, Railing, } (*s.*) khuah-hrolh, pal-za.
Rain, (*s.*) ruah, (*v.*) ruah a shûr, (to go or be out in rain) do.
Rainless, (as weather) shâng.
Rainwater, (*s.*) ruah tui, (caught from roof) kawn-tui.
Rainbow, (*s.*) chhim-bâl.
Rain-coat, (used by Chins) hnaw-kal.
Raindrop, (*s.*) ruah mal.
Rainy weather, (*s.*) khaw cheng.
Rainy season, (*s.*) fûr.
Raise, (*v.*) phok, ti-kâng, choi, (head) dâk, (to a sitting posture) tung-tho, tung-thawh.
Rake, (*v.*) huih, (*s.*) huih-na.
Ram, (*s.*) be-râm pa, (*v.*) holh-khâk, sawh-mûk, sawh-khâk.
Rammer, (*s.*) tu-lung.
Ramrod, (*s.*) holh-fung, silai holh-fung.

Range, (*s.*) (of hills) tlâng-dung.
Rank, (*a.*) ṭûl.
Rankle, (in the mind) eng-to-a nei.
Ransom, (*v.*) tlan.
Rap, (*v.*) kik, lok.
Rapid, (*s.*) shuar.
Rare, (*a.*) vâng.
Rascal, (*s.*) mi sual.
Rashly, (*adv.*) thu dawn lo-vin.
Raspberry, (*s.*) thei-hmu, chul-thei-hmu.
Rat, (*s.*) sa-zu, (musk) chhim-tîr, (large species) zu-hrei, (water) tui-zu.
Rather, (*adv.*) deo, fe, zawk.
Ravage, (*v.*) ram.
Ravenous, (*a.*) ko.
Ravine, (*s.*) kor, kor-dung.
Raw, (*a.*) hel.
Razor, (*s.*) bak me'na, bak me'chem.
Reach, (*v.*) ban, pawh, phâ*k*, tlin*g*.
Read, (*v.*) chhiar.
Readiness, (*v.*) (to be in) lo in-ring, lo beng vâr.
Reading and writing, (*s.*) lekha, lai-shuih.
Ready, (*a.*) in-shiam, peih, tiam, (affix, as in ready-made, etc.) sha, (*v.*) (to be or get ready) in-shiam, buat-saih, (to get or make ready) lo ring, shiam.
Real, (*a.*) tak.
Really, (*adv.*) ngei, tak, tak-zet, tak-meoh, tak-tak, zet, ngût.
Reap, (*v.*) â*t*.
Reaping-hook, (*s.*) fa-vah.
Rear, (*v.*) (as animals) vulh.
Reason, (*s.*) châk-khai, (of or for) chhan, phah, (*v.*) (together) in-rawn.
Rebound, (*v.*) sawh-khawk.
Rebuke, (*v.*) hao, kam-khat.
Receive, (*v.*) hmu, von*g*, von*g*-reng, chang.
Recipient, (*s.*) nei-tu, bûr.
Reckless, (*a.*) ro-rum, thu-rum.
Reckon, (*v.*) chhiar, ngai-ruat.
Recline, (*v.*) mu*t*, bok.
Recognize, (*v.*) hmel hria*t*.
Recollect, (*v.*) hre chhuak, hre leh, hre chhuak leh, hria*t*-leh.
Recompense, (*s.*) rûl, man.
Recompense, (*v.*) rûl.
Red, (*a.*) shen.

Reduce, (*v.*) ti-kiam, (reduced) kiam.
Redeem, (*v.*) tlan.
Red hot, (*a.*) ling, vâm.
Reduce, (*v.*) ti-kiam.
Reed, (*s.*) phai, phai-pheng.
Reel, (*s.*) (for cotton) la hlûm-na, (of cotton) la hlûm.
Reflect, (*v.*) ngai-tua.
Reform, (*v.*) shim.
Refrain, (*v.*) in-shûm.
Refresh, (*v.*) ti-harh.
Refreshed, (*v.*) (to be) harh.
Refreshment, (*s.*) hmom-som.
Refuse, (*s.*) hnep-hnol.
Refuse, (*v.*) hnial.
Refute, (*v.*) chhâl-dang, le*t*-thlâ*k*, ti-dang.
Regard, (*v.*) ngai-shâng, ngai-sak, poi-sha, poi-ti, (with favour) khaw-ngai.
Regent, (*s.*) thui-hruai, kai-hruai, (*v.*) (to act as regent for) thui-hruai, kai-hruai.
Regret, (*v.*) in-chhîr.
Reject, (*v.*) duh lo.
Rejoice, (*v.*) lawm, (at another's misfortune) di-riam, di-chim.
Rejoiceful, (*a.*) di-riam, diriam-om, di-chim-om, di-chim-tlâk, diriam-tlâk.
Relate, (*v.*) hril, shoi.
Relation, (*s.*) u-nao, lai-chîn.
Release, (*v.*) chhua*k*, thlah.
Reliable, (*a.*) rin'tlâk, rin'om.
Relieve, (*v.*) thlâ*k*.
Religion, (*s.*) sa, sa-khua.
Religious, (rights and customs) sa, sa-khua.
Rely, (*v.*) ring.
Remain, (*v.*) om, om reng, chêng.
Remaining, (*a.*) bâng, bâk.
Remains, (*s.*) bâng.
Remedy, (*s.*) dam-na.
Remember, (*v.*) ril-rû*k*, hre-reng, hria*t*-reng, hria*t*, hre, ngai-tua-reng.
Remind, (*v.*) hriat-pui.
Remove, (*v.*) kal-pui.
Renounce, (upon oath) mal-mâk.
Renowned, (*a.*) hming-thang, (for bravery) hrât-khaw-khêng.
Repair, (*v.*) chei, sham ṭha.
Repay, (*v.*) rêl.

Repeat, (*v.*) hril-leh-chhawng, shoi leh.
Repent, (*v.*) in-chhîr, shim.
Reply, (*v.*) chhâng, chhawn.
Report, (*s.*) thu-thang.
Reproach, (*v.*) hao.
Reprove, (*v.*) zilh.
Request, (*v.*) dîl.
Require, (*v.*) duh.
Requisite, (*s.*) châk-khai.
Resemble, (*v.*) ang, (parents) chhûn.
Rescue, (*v.*) chhan, chhan-dam, chhan-chhuak, chhan-him, hum-him.
Resolutely, (*adv.*) heh pe'in.
Resolve, (*v.*) tum-tlat, tum-lui-hrâm, tum ruh, tum-sa-ruh, tum-hrâm.
Respect, (*v.*) poi-sha, (in other respects) thil-dang-a.
Respectable, (*a.*) zah-om.
Rest, (*v.*) awl, om, chawl, (the forehead on) shi, (against or upon) nghat, ngha'chhan, (*s.*) (of any kind, for arms, feet, etc.) ngha'-chhan.
Restrain, (*v.*) chelh, ka-in chelh, khap, (one's self) in-shûm.
Retain, (*v.*) (as urine, etc.) îp.
Retainer, (*s.*) boih.
Retch, (*v.*) uak.
Return, (*v.*) kîr, lêt, lo-kîr, pêk-kîr, (to one's home or village) hawng.
Reveal, (*v.*) puang.
Revere, (*v.*) zah.
Reverse, (*v.*) let, ti-let-ling.
Revive, (*v.*) harh, (*tr.*) ti-harh.
Revolt, (*v.*) hel-leh.
Revolve, (*v.*) her, vir.
Revolver, (*s.*) puak-tam-silai.
Reward, (*s.*) man, tham, (*v.*) tham.
Rheumatism, (*s.*) ruh sheh, (*v.*) (to have) ruh sheh vei.
Rhinoceros, (*s.*) sa-mak, chal-ki-khât.
Rhododendron, (*s.*) chhok-hlei, (Indian) bui-lu-kham.
Rib, (*s.*) nâk ruh.
Rice, (*s.*) buh, (cleaned) buh-fai, (unhusked) buh-hûm, (cooked) chaw, (parched) vai.
Rich, (*a.*) hao-sak.
Riches, (*s.*) sum.
Ride, (*v.*) chuang.
Ridge-pole, (*s.*) tlûng.
Ridicule, (*v.*) ti-el.

Ridiculous, (*a.*) nui-za-thlâk.
Rifle, (*s.*) (repeating) puak-tam silai, (Martini-Henri) chung-đûp silai, kaih-dêp silai, (Snider) ben'hon silai.
Right, (*a.*) dik, thiang, (hand side) ding-lam, (right on) (*adv.*) zêl.
Righteous, (*a.*) dik.
Rigid, (*a.*) nghet.
Rim, (*s.*) hmawr.
Ring, (*s.*) zung-bun, (*v.*) vua*k*.
Ringleader, (*s.*) tupa ber.
Ripe, (*a.*) hmin, chang, tai, (fully) hmin ṭuah.
Ripen, (*v.*) hmin, (*tr.*) ti-hmin.
Rip up, (*v.*) thlêr.
Rise, (*v.*) tho, thawh.
Risk, (*v.*) (one's life) thi dawn lo.
River, (*s.*) lui, lui pui.
Road, (*s.*) kong, kal-kong, lam-lian, (*v.*) (to make) hong shial.
Roast, (*s.*) hem, hem-hmin, rawh.
Rob, (*v.*) rûk sak.
Robber, (*s.*) englo rûk hmang, rûk-ru.
Robust, (*a.*) pheng, phek.
Rock, (*s.*) lung, lung chhia, lung pui.
Roll, (*v.*) lîr, lum, (about, as tongue, etc.) tîl, (up, bedding, paper, etc.) zial, (up in hand) hrual, (as ship) fawn, (up) lep, lep-she.
Romp, (*v.*) chai.
Roof, (*v.*) (to put on roof, thatch, etc.) chih, (*s.*) chung, in-chung, (the edge of a roof) di-thla-far-fêm, di-thli-far-fêm.
Room, (*s.*) pin-dan, pin-dan-chhûng.
Roost, (*v.*) fu.
Root, (*s.*) zung.
Rope, (*s.*) hrui, hrui-zên, hrui-hrual.
Rosy, (*a.*) tai.
Rot, (*v.*) moih, rop, ṭoih.
Rotate, (*a.*) vir.
Rotten, (*a.*) moi, ṭoih, (as cloth) rop.
Rough, (*a.*) bum-bôh, buk, thap, thur, por, (to taste) phak.
Round, (*a.*) bial, mûm, mûm-pal, (*prep.*) vêl-a, vêl-in, (*adv.*) vêl, (round about) kual.
Rouse, (*v.*) kai-tho, ti-harh.
Row, (*s.*) tlar, (*adv.*) (in a row) tlar, (*v.*) (as boat), dâr-vai, vai, kar.
Row, (*s.*) (noise) beng-chheng.
Rub, (*v.*) hrû*k*, naw*t*, tât, nuai, (on) hnoih, (against) nûl.
Rubbish, (*s.*) hnep-hnol, ṭom, (heap) bol-hlawh dûr.
Ruck up, (*v.*) tom.
Rude, (*a.*) huaf-thla-la, nghal.

Rudder, (*s.*) kar-her-na.
Ruddy, (*a.*) tai.
Rugged, (*a.*) bum-bôh, lok.
Ruin, (*v.*) ti-bo-ral.
Ruined, (*v.*) (to be) bo-ral.
Rule, (*v.*) op.
Ruler, (*s.*) op-tu.
Rumour, (*s.*) thu-thang, (*v.*) (to be rumoured) thang.
Run, (*v.*) tlân, (out as water) pût, (up against) tawn, (to run short of anything) chham.
Runner, (*s.*) (with mail) lekha-tlân-pui.
Rupee, (*s.*) cheng, tang-ka.
Rust, (*s.* and *v.*) tui-êk.
Rusty, (*a.*) tui-êk.

S

Sack, (*s.*) ip, kawl-la-ip, sai-ip.
Sackcloth, (*s.*) kawl-la puan.
Sacrifice, (*v.*) ran-in bia*k* (or be), ran-in luh, in-thoi, (outside village) bawl, (an animal to accompany departed to *Mithikhua*) thlai-chhiah.
Sacrum, (*s.*) ngûm ruh.
Sad, (*a.*) ngui, nguai, lung-ngai, lung chhe, lung chhia*t*, (*v.*) lung-ngai, lung a lêng.
Saddle, (*s.*) (of hill) kawn, (joining two ridges) khan-kawn.
Safe, (*a.*) him.
Safely, (*adv.*) him-tak-in, him.
Sag, (*v.*) dul, fual.
Sago, (*s.*) (palm), tûm, (cake) tûm chhang.
Sahib, (*s.*) sâp.
Sale, (*v.*) (offer for), zuar.
Saliva, (*s.*) chil.
Salt, (*s.*) chi, (salt spring) chi khûr, (cake of salt), chi khawn, (*a.*) al.
Saltpetre, (*s.*) silai-hlo.
Salute, (*v.* and *s.*) chi-bai bûk.
Same, (*a.*) ngai, pa-ngai, pa-ngai-in, thu-hmun, hmun-khat.
Sand, (*s.*) ṭiao-vut, ṭiao-vai-vut.
Sandbank, (*s.*) ṭiao-pho.
Sandfly, (*s.*) vai-hmi-tê.
Sandy, (*s.*) (shingle) ṭiao.
Sap, (*s.*) hnai.
Sarcastically, (*v.*) (to speak) ti-el.

Satchel, (*s.*) ip-tê, (netted) sa-hmîm, (the skin cover for same) sa-hmîm khuh.
Savage, (*a.*) kolh.
Save, (*v.*)kti-dam, chhan-him, chhan-dam, hum-him, ti-nung, (for future) khêk, up, tuak, tuak-khawm.
Saved, (*a.*) dam, him.
Saviour, (*s.*) ti-dam-tu, chhan-dam-tu, chhan-him-tu, ti-nung-tu.
Savour, (*v.*) (to close) da, (*a.*) (savoury smelling) hmui.
Saw, (*s.*) thing zai-na.
Sawdust, (*s.*) thing zai-noi.
Say, (*v.*) shoi, ti.
Saying, (*s.*) thu.
Scab, (*s.*) khir.
Scabbard, (*s.*) pai.
Scald, (*v.*) tui sho-in leih.
Scales, (*s.*) (for weighing) bûk-na, bûk-khai-na, (of fish, etc.) phu-hlip.
Scanty, (*a.*) vâng.
Scapula, (*s.*) dâr-ruh.
Scar, (*v.* and *s.*) sher.
Scarce, (*a.*) vâng.
Scarcely, (*adv.*) hrâm.
Scare, (*v.*) râp.
Scarecrow, (*s.*) mi-lem, mi-lim.
Scatter, (*v.*) vorh.
School, (*s.*) lekha zir-na in.
Scissors, (*s.*) sa-kor bak-che'.
Scoff, (*v.*) ti-el, nui-shan.
Scold, (*v.*) zilh-hao.
Scoop, (*v.*) law*k*.
Scorch, (*v.*) em, hem, hem-ût, hem-ung, hem-ul.
Scorched, (*a.*) ul.
Scorn, (*v.*) hmu-shit.
Scorpion, (*s.*) khaw-mual kai-kuang, (pseudo) khaw-mual kai-kuang shuak.
Scatter, (*v.*) varh, ti-darh.
Scattered, (*a.*) darh.
Scour, (*v.*) hrû*k*-fai, naw*t*, nawt-fai.
Scout, (*v.*) en-thla, (*s.*) en-thla, en-thla-tu.
Scramble, (*v.*) in-chuh.
Scrape, (*v.*) huih, mê*t*, shui, zia*t*, (with hoe) rî*t*, (up) thai.
Scratch, (*v.*) hiat, rîn, (up) hai, thai, (*s.*) rîm.
Scream, (*v.*) ao.
Screen, (*v.*) hlia.

Screw, (*v.*) her, (*s.*) kilh-na ṭial, ṭial.
Screw pine, (*s.*) buar-pui, la-khuih, ngai.
Scribe, (*s.*) lekha ziak tu.
Sculpture, (*v.*) chher.
Scum, (*s.*) phuan.
Scurf, (*s.*) lu-phut, (*a.*) (scurfy) phut.
Sea, (*s.*) tui-pui, tui-al, tui-fin-riat.
Sealing-wax, (*s.*) thal-hrit.
Seam, (*s.*) ṭhui.
Search, (*v.*) (for) zong, lam, vai.
Season, (*s.*) hun, lai.
Seat, (*s.*) ṭhut-thlêng, ṭhut-phah, ṭhut-na.
Second, (*a.*) pa-hnih na, hnih-na.
Secret, (*s.*) thu-rûk, thu-zêp-in.
Secretly, (*adv.*) a-rûk-in, rû*k*.
Security, (*v.*) (to give as) dah kham, hrên*g* tîr, hrên*g* a pê*k*, (to keep as) hrên*g*, (to take as) hrên' a lâ*k*, hrên' tûr in lâ*k*.
See, (*v.*) hmu, (off) thlah.
Seed, (*s.*) chi, mu.
Seek, (*v.*) zong.
Seer, (*s.*) bûk, khîn.
Seize, (*v.*) man, chelh, vuan, (as spirit) awh, (stealthily) veh.
Select, (*v.*) thlang.
Self, mani, ngei, meoh.
Self-collected, (*v.*) (to be) muan*g*, muan*g*-chang, (self-collectedly) muan*g*.
Selfish, (*a.*) ngil nei lo.
Self-sown, (*a.*) hli.
Self-willed, (*a.*) kawh-mawh, luh-lul, ngol-tawt, ti-mawh.
Sell, (*v.*) hral, de*k*-ral, zuar, khawh-ral.
Semen, (*s.*) baw.
Send, (*v.*) kal-tîr, tîr, thon, (away) kal-tîr, kal-bo-tîr, (for) ko-tîr, chah.
Sensitive plant, (*s.*) hlo-zak-thei, mei-tei ruk-ru.
Sentry, (*s.*) râl-vên*g*.
Separate, (*a.*) hran*g*, in-ṭhen, hlîr, (*v.*) ṭhen, thlei, (as hair, cotton threads, etc.) kê*k*.
Separately, (*adv.*) dang-dang-a, hran*g*, ṭhen.
Sepoy, (*s.*) si-pai.
September, (*s.*) savunga mîm kût thla, thla sherh.
Serpent, (*s.*) rûl.
Servant, (*s.*) be-kar, chhia-hlawh, rong-bawl-tu.
Serve, (*v.*) rong-bawl, (for a wife) lu-khung, fan, (out) khorh, (with food) hlui.

Serviceable, (*a.*) tlâk-tlai.
Sesamum, (*s.*) chhawh-chhi.
Set, (*v.*) (trap) kam, (on, as dog) fuih, (the heart or mind upon) hma khua ngai, hma khaw ngai.
Settle, (*v.*) ti-tlu, (alight) fu, (as water) tling.
Settled, (*v.*) (to be) tlu.
Seven, (*a.*) pa-sari, sari.
Seventeen, (*a.*) shom leh pa-sari.
Seventh, (*a.*) pa-sari-na, sari-na.
Seventieth, (*a.*) shom-sari-na.
Seventy, (*a.*) shom-sari.
Sever, (*v.*) ti-chhum, ti-bung.
Severed, (*v.*) (to be) chhum.
Several, (*a.*) tam.
Sew, (*v.*) ṭhui.
Shade, (*s.*) hlim.
Shadow, (*s.*) hlim.
Shake, (*v.*) nghîng, nghor, sor, thing, (hands) kut in-man, (out) thing parh, thing pharh.
Shallow, (*a.*) pawn, (*s.*) (in river) shuar.
Sham, (*a.*) der.
Sham fight, (*v.*) (to have) râl lem a chang.
Shame, (*v.*) (to be put to) mual-pho, (to put to) ti-mual-pho, ti hril-hai, ti-zak.
Shameful, (*a.*) zah-thlâk.
Shape, (*a.*) hmel, om-zia.
Share, (*v.*) in-khing, in-ṭawm, (*s.*) chan, chan-ai, chan-vo, chan-hrang.
Sharp, (*a.*) (quick) beng-vâr, hriam.
Sharpen, (*v.*) tât hriam, (to a point) zum.
Shatter, (*v.*) ti-keh.
Shave, (*v.*) mê*t*.
Shavings, (*s.*) phuai, thing thel-na ṭom.
She, (*pro.*) a, ana ani.
Sheaf, (*s.*) phal.
Sheath, (*s.*) pai, (at joints of bamboos) khâng.
Sheep, (*s.*) be-râm.
Sheepfold, (*s.*) berâm huang.
Shelf, (*s.*) chhuar, kham-tluan, ṭhe-hlân, chhûng-pui, (over fire) rap.
Shell, (*s.*) hawng, kawm, kom-kaw-raw.
Shelter, (*v.*) (from wind) ti-ûp, (in shelter of) phên-a.
Sheltered, (from wind) thli ûp.
Shepherd, (*s.*) berâm pu, berâm vêng-tu.
Shield, (*s.*) phaw.

Shift, (*v.*) (with) tla-lam, tla.
Shin, (*s.*) ngal, ngal-chȃr.
Shine, (*v.*) mom, êng, (upon) em, hem, (upon, into) chhun.
Shingle, (*s.*) ṭiao lung, ṭiao, (a shingle beach) ṭiao-pho.
Ship, (*s.*) long, long-lian.
Shirt, (*s.*) kor-pum.
Shiver, (*v.*) khȗr.
Shock, (*v.*) (to die as the result of a shock) thla-bȃr-in thi, (to receive) thin a ṭhawn*g*, thla-bȃr.
Shoe, (*s.*) ke-kok, phei-kok.
Shoot, (*s.*) zîk, chor.
Shoot, (*v.*) kȃ*p*, (and hit) kȃ*p*-fuh, (and miss) kȃ*p* thelh, (dead) (kȃ*p*) hlum, (with pellet bow) perh.
Shop, (*s.*) dawr, dawr-kai, dawr-in.
Shopkeeper, (*s.*) dawr-kai ho-tu.
Shore, (*s.*) kam.
Short, (*a.*) toi, chhîng, hniam, (crisp) ngot, ngot shiah shiah.
Short cut, (*s.*) pum-pelh.
Shot, (*s.*) silai-mu, (small) mu-shep.
Shoulder, (*s.*) ko-ki, dȃr.
Shout, (*v.*) ao.
Shovel, (*v.*) lawk.
Show, (*v.*) en-tîr, hmu-tîr, hriat-tîr, (*s.*) en-nom, hmu-nom.
Shower, (*s.*) ruah mual liam, ruah vȃr pui, ruah bing.
Shriek, (*v.*) kȗk.
Shrink, (*v.*) tom, (from) tîm.
Shrivel, (*v.*) shawn*g*.
Shudder, (*v.*) khȗr.
Shut, (*v.*) khȃr, chhîn, chhîng, chîp, (as umbrella) ti-dul, phelh-dul, (the eyes) mai mit chhin*g*, (one eye) mit shiai, mit khing shiai.
Shy, (*a.*) zak, zak-zum.
Sick, (*a.*) dam lo, na, (*v.*) (vomit) lua*k*, law, (to feel) luak a chhuak.
Sickly, (*a.*) fem.
Sickness, (*s.*) na*t*, hri-tlȃng.
Side, (*s.*) nȃk, pang, rȃl, shîr, (other or opposite side) leh lam, (on both sides) leh lam leh lam.
Side by side, (*adv.*) ṭhiang.
Sideways, (*adv.*) sai-shîr.
Side with, (*v.*) ṭan, ṭan-pui.
Sieve, (*s.*) chhih-hri, thlang-ra.
Sift, (*v.*) hri, thlei, (in a *thlang-ra*) ṭhȃp.
Sigh, (*v.*) in-hîp, thaw*k*.
Sight (of gun), silai tho-chuan.

Sign, (*s.*) chhin-chhiah, chhin-chhiah-na, (*v.*) (to make) zai-zir.
Silence, (*v.*) dang-chhat, dang-thla.
Silent, (*a.*) ngoi, reh.
Silk, (*s.*) mai maw, (yellow) kawl-eng.
Silly, (*a.*) â.
Silver, (*a.*) tang-ka, (*s.*) tang-ka rua.
Silversmith, (*s.*) tang-ka rua chher-tu.
Similar, (*a.*) in-ang.
Simply, (*adv.*) mai-mai.
Sin, (*s.*) sual.
Since, (*conj.*) zâr-a, zâr-in, a-chin, a-hnu-in, chin, chin-a, (*adv.*) ani-tawh, ani-ta.
Sinew, (*s.*) tha.
Sinful, (*a.*) sual.
Sing, (*v.*) sha, hla sha, zai.
Single, (*a.*) fang, (unmarried) hnah khat.
Sink, (*v.*) lût, pil, (contract) thêp, (as foot in mud, etc.) tlum.
Sinner, (*s.*) mi-sual.
Sip, (*v.*) hûp.
Sir, ka pu.
Sister, (*s.*) u-nao, (a man's sister) far-nu, (a woman's sister) lai-zawn, lai-zawn-nu, (own) pian-pui, (elder) u, (younger) nao, (next to one's self in age) chhang-bung.
Sister-in-law, (*s.*) (brother's wife) mo, (younger brother's wife) nao, (elder brother's wife) u, (husband's younger sister) nao, (husband's elder sister) u, (wife's sister) pi-zon.
Sit, (*v.*) ṭhut, (down to food) kîl, (upon) chuang, (cross-legged) bop-khaw-kherh-in ṭhu, (as fowl) op, (right down) ṭhut sop, (on haunches) ṭhut tung, (up, upright) ṭhut chhuak, ṭhut ngîl.
Six, (*a.*) pa-ruk, ruk.
Sixteen, (*a.*) shom leh pa-ruk.
Sixteenth, (*a.*) shom leh pa-ruk-na.
Sixtieth, (*a.*) shom-ruk-na.
Sixty, (*a.*) shom-ruk.
Skein, (*s.*) mit.
Skeleton, (*s.*) tlaw.
Skewer, (*v.*) thil, (*s.*) tûl.
Skilful, (*a.*) them thiam.
Skin, (*s.*) vun, dal, hamda, (*v.*) hîk, hlai.
Skip, (*v.*) tual-chai.
Skirt, (*s.*) puan-fên.
Skull, (*s.*) lu ruh.
Sky, (*s.*) vân.
Slack, (*a.*) dul.

Slacken, (*a.*) ti-dul.
Slander, (*v.*) hek.
Slant, (*v.*) ti-awn, lao, (slanting) (*a.* and *adv.*) awn, lao, sa-nghawng, sa-hai.
Slap, (*v.*) bêng, (with open hand) fa-hrah ben'in bêng, nu hron ben' in bêng, (with hollowed hand) nu tak ben'in bêng.
Slate, (for writing) lung lai-shuih, (pencil) lung lai-shuih ziak-na.
Slaughter, (*v.*) sâm, ti-hlum.
Slave, (*s.*) boih, (of war) sal.
Slay, (*v.*) ti-hlum, that.
Sleek, (*a.*) tlor.
Sleep, (*v.*) mut, mut-hîl, mu-nghîl, (lightly) harh-vâng, (fast) mut-hîl dêr, mu-nghîl dêr.
Sleepy, (*a.*) mut a chhuak.
Slender, (*a.*) ria, fêk.
Slice, (*v.*) chan, (*s.*) chan, phêk, hrang.
Slide, (*v.*) tleng.
Slight, (*v.*) hleih nei, thliar, thliar-thla, (*a.*) ria, fêk.
Slightly, (*adv.*) chang-chang, deo.
Slip, (*v.*) tleo, (off or through) dûk, (as land) min.
Slip-knot, (*s.*) valh.
Slippery, (*a.*) nâl.
Slip-rail, (*s.*) she-kot-rolh.
Slop over, (*v.*) fawn buak.
Slovenly, (*a.*) in-thlah-dah.
Slow, (*a.*) muang, muang-chang, ṭuan-fûm, zoi.
Slowly, (*adv.*) chak-lo, muang, rei, zoi-in, zoi-zoi-in, zoi-te-in, zoi.
Slug, (*s.*) hnap-khawn, (for gun) mu-shao.
Sly, (*adv.*) (on the) a-rûk-in, rûk.
Small, (*a.*) tê, zîm, chep, noi, (as mouth of bottle, pot, etc.) kum.
Small-pox, (*s.*) zawng-hri, phurh, phurh-hri.
Smart, (*v.*) thîp.
Smear, (*v.*) hnoih.
Smell, (*v.*) hnim, rim hriat, (*s.*) rim, (to smell of, to give forth a smell, or to be strong-smelling) nam.
Smile, (*v.*) ṭhen.
Smithy, (*s.*) pûm.
Smoke, (*s.*) mei-khu, (*v.*) zuk, mei zuk, khu.
Smooth, (*a.*) mân, mâm-rem, nâl, thluam.
Snail, (*s.*) (water) chêng-kol, (large) kawng-kaw-roi, (land) pi-ring.
Snake, (*s.*) rûl.
Snake gourd, (*s.*) be-rûl.
Snap, (*v.*) (break) elh-tliak, ulh-tliak, thliak, (the fingers) hmet ri, (the fingers by shaking hand) kut thingri.

Snapped, (*a.*) thlia*k*.
Snare, (*s.*) thang.
Snatch, (*v.*) (away) chhuh, chhuh-sak, (up) chuh.
Sneeze, (*v.*) ha-chhiao.
Sniff, (*v.*) hnap shut.
Snipe, (*s.*) chirh-dawt, va-chirh-dawt.
Snipped, (*s.*) ki-reo, ki-riu.
Snivel, (*v.*) in-hîp, in-hnîp.
Snore, (*v.*) hnâr.
Snow, (*s.*) vûr.
Snuff, (*v.*) (candle, torch, etc.) mei êk thiar.
So, (*adv.*) chu-ti-fa-hran-chuan, he-tia, he-ti-ang, chu-ti êm êm chuan, (so and so) chu-ti kha-ti.
Soak, (*v.*) chiah.
Soap-nut tree, (*s.*) hlîng-shi.
Sob, (*v.*) in-hîp, in-hnîp.
Sodomy, (*s.*) (one who practises) mong-hur, mong-kaw-hor.
Soft, (*a.*) dûp, dûr, nêm, hnip, nêl, no.
Sojourn, (*v.*) thang.
Solder, (*s.*) hâr.
Soldier, (*s.*) si-pai, râl.
Sole, (of foot), ke-phah hnuai.
Solid, (*a.*) fîp.
Some, (*a.*) eng-e-maw, (some others) ṭhen, ṭhen-khat (some kind of), zeng-emaw.
Somebody, (*pro.*) tu-e-maw, tu-e-maw-zong, tu-e-maw tal.
Somehow, (*adv.*) fan fan, hrâm hrâm.
Someone, (*pro.*) tu-e-maw, tu-e-maw-zong, tuemaw-tal.
Somersault, (*v.*) (to turn) bing-bi-let, (on a bar) ui sa le' lin'.
Something, (*s.*) eng-lo, eng-e-maw, eng-e-maw-zong.
Sometime, rei ngial, (ago) rei ta ngial, (at some time) (future) eng huna emaw, (past) eng lai in emaw.
Sometimes, (*adv.*) chãng chãng-in.
Somewhat, (*adv.*) deo.
Somewhere, (*adv.*) khoi-a-emaw, khoi-a-tal.
Son, (*s.*) fa, fa-pa, (adopted) fa-hron.
Sonai, (*s.*) (river) tui-rial.
Son-in-law, (*s.*) mak-pa.
Song, (*s.*) hla, zai.
Soon, (*adv.*) hma, lok, pang.
Soot, (*s.*) in-ṭing, bel-mang.
Sorcerer, (*s.*) doi-thiam.
Sore, (*s.*) pân.
Sorrel, (*s.*) shiak-thûr, an-bong.

Sorrowful, (*a.*) lung-ngai.
Sorry, (*v.*) lung-ngai.
Sort, (*s.*) ang, chi, hmun.
Soul, (*s.*) thla-rao.
Sound, (*v.*) rîk (as to one's opinions, etc.) dîp, (*s.*) rîk, thawm.
Soundly, (*adv.*) dêr.
Sour, (*a.*) hîng, thûr, tok.
Source, (*s.*) (of stream), hnâr, hna.
South, (*s.*) chhim, khaw-chhim, chhim-lam.
South-east, (*s.*) chim-chhak.
Southwards, (*adv.*) chhim-lama.
South-west, (*s.*) chhim-thlang.
Sow, (*s.*) vok-pui.
Sow, (*v.*) tuh, ching.
Sowbug, (*s.*) pu-vân-a sai-hlum.
Spade, (*s.*) bawng-tuh-thlawh.
Span, (*v.* and *s.*) khâp, sai-pir-khâp.
Spare, (*v.*) zuah, zah-ngai.
Spark, (*s.*) mei shi, (*v.*) (to throw out sparks) ṭêk.
Sparrow, (*s.*) chong-zong.
Speak, (*v.*) thu shoi, ṭong, (to) biak, be, (away from the point) shoi-koi, (depreciatingly of) shoi-hnawm, (to the point) shoi-ngîl, (of) lam, (against) shoi-chhia, shoi-shêl.
Spear, (*s.*) fei, (*v.*) chhun, khawh.
Special, (*a.*) bîk.
Specially, (*adv.*) bîk, molh.
Spectacle, (*s.*) en-nom, hmu-nom.
Spectacles, (*s.*) tar-mit.
Speech, (*s.*) ṭong.
Speechless, (*a.*) dang, (with pain) hnang.
Speedily, (*adv.*) thuai, lok.
Spend, (*v.*) dek-ral, hral, khawh-ral, shêng, (time) ni lên'.
Spherical, (*a.*) bial.
Spider, (*s.*) mai-mom, (thread) mai-mom rîl, (web) mai-mom in, (large black) ching-chip, (edible) ṭâng-ṭial, (long-legged) pi-buh-dêng.
Spike, (*s.*) (on end of spear) fei-chhor, (for concealing in paths in war time) fung.
Spill, (*v. t.*) ti-bua, ti-buak, ti-baw, (*intrans.*) buak, baw.
Spin, (*v.*) kai.
Spinal cord, (*s.*) zâng-ruh tling.
Spine, (*s.*) zâng-ruh.
Spindle, (*s.*) hmui-thlûr, hmui-thal.
Spinster, (*s.*) (living alone) hmei-thai.

Spiral, (*s.*) ngûn-kual.
Spirit, (*s.*) thla, thla-rao, (evil) ram-huai, huai, (drink) rak-zu.
Spit, (*v.*) chhâk, chil chhâk, (through teeth) chil chik, (through fingers) chil pik.
Spittle, (*s.*) chil.
Splash, (*v.*) theh.
Spleen, (*s.*) la, (*v.*) (to have enlarged spleen), la a tla.
Splendid, (*a.*) moi, ṭha.
Splinter, (*s.*) ther.
Splints, (*s.*) ṭhem-dawh-na, (*v.*) (to put in splints) ṭhem dawh.
Split, (*v.*) thlêr, hlai, phel.
Spoil, (*v.*) ti-chhia*t*, ti-chhe, ti-khaw-lo, ti-poi, (as child) duat.
Spoiled, (*a.*) chhia*t*, chhe, khaw-lo.
Spongy, (*a.*) thawp.
Spoon, (*s.*) fian.
Spotted, (*a.*) chik, ṭial.
Spout, (*s.*) zang.
Sprain, (*v.*) bilh, ulh, (wrist) kut ulh.
Spread, (*v.*) thang, puang, phar, ar, phah, pherh, pharh, (as creeper) zâm.
Spring, (*v.*) per, zuan, (*s.*) (of water) shih, hna, (of steel, etc.) li, (salt spring) chi-khûr.
Springless, (*a.*) rul.
Springy, (*a.*) tîng.
Sprinkle, (*v.*) phul, theh.
Sprout, (*s.* and *v.*) chor, ṭiak.
Spud, (*s.*) tuh-ṭhulh.
Spur, (*s.*) (of hill) mual, muai-dung, (of cock, etc.) shiak.
Spurious, (*a.*) shuak.
Spurt, (*v.*) chik.
Spy, (*v.*) en-thla, bih, (*s.*) en-thla, en-thla, en-thla tu.
Square, (*s.*) kil-li, bial.
Squabble, (*v.*) in-el.
Squeak, (*v.*) chîk.
Squeal, (*v.*) ngêk.
Squeeze, (*v.*) chilh, hme*t*, hmer, nem, sawr, nem-sawr, (through) pût.
Squint-eye, (*a.*) mit-kalh.
Squirrel, (*s.*) ṭhe-hlei, che-pa, chhang-khei, (flying) va-hluk, biang, (black) or-râng.
Squirt, (*v.*) chik.
Stab, (*v.*) chhun, chiu.
Stack, (*s.*) ai, (*v.*) chhep.
Staff, (*s.*) tiang.

Stag, (*s.*) sa-khi-chal, zuk-chal.
Stagger, (*v.*) pai.
Stag moss, (*s.*) chang kor.
Stair, (*s.*) rah-ka.
Stale, (*a.*) ṭhing, ṭhe.
Stalk, (*s.*) hnûn.
Stammer, (*v.*) dang-awk.
Stamp, (*v.*) per, (upon) chîl.
Stand, (*v.*) ding, lo-ding, (on head) rûl pui lu din', (on tip-toe) ding-di-hlîp.
Star, (*s.*) âr-shi, (shooting) âr-shi thlawk, (morning) vâr-parh.
Stare, (*v.*) melh.
Start, (*v.*) ṭan, ṭan-tîr.
Startle, (*v.*) phawk, phu-tîr-zok, ti-phu-zok.
Startled, (*v.*) (to be) phu*l*-zok.
Starve, (*v.*) ṭâm.
Staunch, (*v.*) ti-bâng, ti-reh, (blood by charming) thi kîr.
Stay, (*v.*) om, thang, (over a day and night) ni chuang, (the night) ria*k*.
Steadily, (*adv.*) muang.
Steal, (*v.*) rû*k*.
Stealthily, (*adv.*) a rûk-in, ruk.
Steam, (*s.*) tui-hu.
Steam-boat, (*s.*) mei-long, mei-khu-long.
Steel, (*s.*) kah-pa-thîr, (of gun) silai-ui-lei.
Steep, (*a.*) oih, (upwards) chho, chho tung-tu-rût, (downwards) chhuk.
Steer, (*v.*) (for) pan.
Stem, (*s.*) hnûn, kung, dawn.
Step, (*v.*) kâr, pên, (*s.*) pên, (stairs) rah-ka, (over) kân.
Stepfather, (*s.*) pa-hron.
Stepmother, (*s.*) nu-hron.
Stern, (of boat) mei.
Sternum, (*s.*) ir ruh.
Stew, (*v.*) mung, mung-koi.
Stick, (*v.*) kai, bei, bet, châr, bel, (in) bûr, thiat, (as in throat, etc.) tâng, (on a pole) târ, (*s.*) tiang, fung, (insect) âr-mong-holh.
Sticky, (*a.*) ban.
Stiff, (*a.*) khaoh, khong, (with work or being in one position) kham, rol.
Still, (*conj.*) ama-e-raw-chu, ni-ma-shela, shi, (*adv.*) hle hle, la, tûna-pawh, tûn thleng pawh-in.
Still-born, (*a.*) hring hlum.

Stilt, (*s.*) kal-chhet.
Sting, (*v.*) sheh, (*s.*) zang.
Stinging, (*a.*) (to tongue) hiar.
Stingy, (*a.*) fîr, kom.
Stink, (*v.*) uih.
Stir, (*v.*) chok, hot, sawh-bawl, (up) chok-hnok, chok-buai.
Stock, (*s.*) (of gun) kawm.
Stockade, (*s.*) kulh, dai-pui.
Stocks, (*s.*) kol.
Stomach, (*s.*) pum-pui, (of ruminating animal) bîng.
Stone, (*s.*) lung, (in bladder) zun-im-pui, (*v.*) dèn*g*, lung-in dên
Stool, (*s.*) ṭhut-thlêng, ṭhut-na, ṭhut-phah.
Stoop, (*v.*) kûn.
Stop, (*v.*) bân*g*, dâl, dang, din*g*, lo-din*g*, om, reh, ngoi, (stop crying) khui.
Stopper, (*s.*) chhîn, chhîn-na, (*v.*) chhîn.
Store up, (*v.*) khawl-khawm, khawl.
Storm wind, (*s.*) thli-pui.
Stormy looking, (*a.*) khaw dur, khaw duai.
Story (tale), (*s.*) thon-thu, (of house) chhawng.
Stove, (*s.*) thuk.
Straight, (*a.*) ngîl, mar, (*adv.*) ngîl, fuh.
Straighten, (*v.*) (the arm, etc.) phar, char, (leg) thluan*g*, ti-ngîl.
Straightway, nghâl.
Strain, (*v.*) thli*t*, (tenesmus) san*g*.
Strainer, (*s.*) chhih-bri.
Stranger, (*s.*) hmel hriat lo mi, mi-khual.
Strangle, (*v.*) rêk-hlum.
Stratagem, (*v.*) (to use) ngam-thlêm.
Straw, (*s.*) pawl.
Stray, (*v.*) kal-bo, bo.
Stream, (*s.*) lui.
Streamlet, (*s.*) lui tê.
Street, (*s.*) kot-thlêr, kot-lai, kot-lai-thlêr, thlêr.
Strength, (*s.*) tha.
Strengthen, (*v.*) ti-harh.
Stretch, (*v.*) fân, (one's self) vân, zi.
Stretcher, (*s.*) hlâng, taw-lai.
Strict, (*a.*) } kher-mei.
Strictly, (*adv.*) }
Stride, (*v.*) kâr, pên, (*s.*) pên.
Strike, (*v.*) vêl, vua*k*, vaw, khawng, kut thlâ*k*, (together) talh.
String, (*s.*) hrui, hrui-zên, hrui-hrual.
Stringy, (*a.*) (as beans, etc.) na nei.

Strip, (*v.*) (off, as leaves) hloi, (off) hîk.
Striped, (*a.*) ṭial.
Strive, (*v.*) phe phe, tum lui-hrâm, tum hrâm.
Stroke, (*v.*) chûl, zût.
Stroll, (*v.*) lêng.
Strong, (*a.*) tûr, tha-hrui nei, chak, (as rope) fei; khaoh, (as beer, tobacco, etc.) ru, (as beer) thlum, (durable) tlo.
Struggle, (*v.*) tâl.
Stubble, (*s.*) kûng-hmui, pawl-bul.
Stubborn, (*a.*) luh-lul, ngol-tawt, ti-mawh.
Stuck together, (*a.*) in-bel-bom.
Stumble, (*v.*) kat, pe-tek.
Stump, (*s.*) bul, (short stumps of bamboo, rice, etc.) kûng-hmui.
Stupid, (*a.*) beng-tla-lo, ngong.
Stutter, (*v.*) dang-awk.
Subdue, (*v.*) ti-hmin, hmin.
Subjects, (of a chief) khua leh tui.
Subjugate, (*v.*) hmin, ti-hmin, (to be subjugated) hmin.
Submerge, (*v.*) chîm.
Subscription, (to get up a) thawh-khawm, thawh-lawm.
Substance, (*s.*) pang-ti, ti.
Substitute, (*s.*) ṭai-awh-tu, thlâk-tu, (to take as) kai, (*v.*) (to become a) ai-awh.
Succeed, (*v.*) hlawh-tling, pui-tlin', (to a chieftainship) ṭhut.
Suck, (*v.*) fawp, fêp, hnê*k*, zu*k*, (in mouth) hnuam, (up) dawt, dût, hîp, hûp.
Suckle, (*v.*) hne-tîr.
Suddenly, (*adv.*) phut, rum, thawk-khat-a, thut, voi-khat-a*n*.
Suffer, (*v.*) ngai-thei.
Suffice, (*v.*) daih.
Sufficient, (*a.*) khaile, khai tawh le, khai tawh, kim, tawk.
Sufficiently, (*adv.*) khop, tawk.
Suffocate, (*v.*) hu*p*-hlum.
Sugar, (*s.*) chi-thlum.
Sugarcane, (*s.*) fu.
Suggest, (*v.*) rot.
Suit, (*v.*) phu.
Suitable, (*a.*) phu.
Sulk, (*v.*) ngoi-tao.
Sulky, (*a.*) ngoi-tao.
Sulphur, (*s.*) kât.
Sultry, (*a.*) uap.
Summer, (*s.*) ni pui hun, ni pui lai.
Summit, (*s.*) chhîp, chung.

Summon, (*v.*) lam.
Sun, (*s.*) ni.
Sunbeam, (*s.*) ni êng.
Sunrise, (*s.*) ni chhua*k*.
Sunset, (*s.*) ni tlâ*k*.
Sunshade, (*s.*) ni hliap.
Sunshine, (*s.*) ni sha, ni lum.
Superfluous, (*a.*) chuang.
Superintend, (*v.*) en-kil, kil-koi.
Superintendent, (*s.*) en-kil-tu.
Supersede, (*v.*) lân.
Supper, (*s.*) zân-riah.
Supple, (*a.*) nel.
Support, (*v.*) dawm, kam, ṭâng-kham, thlop, (to feed) chawm.
Supporter, (*s.*) kai-za vêng, chawm-tu.
Suppose, (*v.*) ring, (supposing if) phei chuan, phei-in.
Suppress, (*v.*) zêp.
Sure, (*a.*) zuam.
Surely, (*adv.*) mathei-lo-vin, phot.
Surge, (*v.*) fawn.
Surly, (*a.*) thin chhe, thin chhiat.
Surmise, (*v.*) hria*t*, ring.
Surprise, (*v.*) phu-tîr-zok, ti-phu-zok, (surprised, to be) phu*t*-zok.
Surround, (*v.*) baw*m*, hual, kîl, vêl, (animal, when hunting) zîm.
Suspense, (*v.*) (to be in) tui lai râp ang-in om, ngai-na rêng hre lo, (to hold in) tui lai râp ang-in shiam, ngai-na reng hre lo vin shiam.
Suspend, (*v.*) khai, zam.
Swallow, (*v.*) lem, dolh, (*s.*) va-mûr, (the wrong way) hâk.
Swarm, (*s.* and *v.*) rao.
Swear, (*v.*) chhe-chham, chhia-chham, vân-ni-chhâl, (not to) sherh.
Sweat, (*s.*) tlan, (*v.*) tlan a sha.
Sweep, (*v.*) hmun phiat, phiat.
Sweet, (*a.*) thlum.
Sweet-potato, (*s.*) ba-hra thlum, kawl-ba-hra.
Swell, (*v.*) puam, vûn*g*, bawk.
Swelling, (*s.*) bawk, vûn*g*, puam.
Swift, (*a.*) chak.
Swiftly, (*adv.*) chak.
Swim, (*v.*) tui hleoh, (or float catching hold of knees) bûr chhe lân, (with face under water) hmai phûm tui hleoh, (like a dog) ui tui hleoh, (upright, carrying net and catching fish) lên fung choi, (on side) ngha-tun-bek-bor-tleng-in hleoh, (with hands behind the back) sal tui hleoh, (to walk water) tui-dung chhir.

Swindle, (*v.*) ti-bum, ti-dawn*g*.
Swindled, (*v.*) (to be) dawn*g*.
Swing, (*v.*) uai, (to and fro) thên, (*s.*) pi-pu.
Swollen, (*a.*) pawng, puam, vûn*g*.
Swoop down, (*v.*) thlawk-bir.
Sword, (*s.*) khan-dai, ngûm-hnâm, chem-shei.
Syphilis, (*s.*) sai-hri.
Syphon, (*s.*) don-kawn, (*v.*) shiak.
Syringe, (*s.*) ka'chik.

T

Table, (*s.*) dawh-kân.
Tadpole, (*s.*) u-long.
Tail, (*s.*) mei.
Tailor, (*s.*) puan ṭhui-tu, kor ṭhui-tu.
Tailor bird, (*s.*) dai-kat, hnah-khawr, hnah-fun.
Take, (*v.*) lâ*k*, keng, pom, (away) kal-bo-pui, kal-pui, (off, as coat) hlîp, (away from) lâk-sak, chhuh, chhuh-sak, (out) phorh, (to pieces) ṭhiat, (up spinning top) dong, (part in) tel, (heed) fîm-khur, (out from eye) thian*g*, thiar, (to one's home or with one) hawn*g*, (on one side) hruai hrang, (with one) hruai, (off, as hat, cover, etc.) phong, phok, (off the fire) shuan.
Tale, (*s.*) thon-thu.
Talk, (*v.*) ṭong, thu shoi, (in sleep or delirium) ṭong-â, ṭong-vai, (to one's self), phun, phun ru.
Talkative, (*a.*) dang-nâl, kam-tam.
Tall, (*a.*) shân*g*.
Talon, (*s.*) tin.
Tamarind, (*s.*) chhim-kel-lêk.
Tame, (*v.* and *a.*) khoi, ngam.
Tamp, (*v.*) hnawh, phu-hru*k*.
Tan, (*v.*) (as sun) hem-hâng, hem-dum.
Tang, (*s.*) (of knife, etc.) zang.
Taper, (*v.*) zuih (also tapering).
Tarry, (*v.*) om.
Task, (*s.*) (special or allotted) tum, (*v.*) (to do task) tum.
Tassel, (*s.*) peh-buk.
Taste, (*v.*) tem, hria*t*, hre.
Tattoo, (*v.*) ṭial, (*s.*) (a tattoo) ṭial.
Taut, (*a.*) chhîng.
Tawny, (*a.*) vom.
Tax, (*v.*) choi-tîr, (*s.*) lei-ba, lei-ṭha, lei-tlang, chhiah.

Tax-collector, (*s.*) chhiah-khon-tu.
Tea, (*s.*) thing-pui.
Teach, (*v.*) hrilh.
Tear, (*v.*) ṭet, thlêr.
Tears, (*s.*) mit-tui.
Tease, (*v.*) chhaih.
Teat, (*s.*) hnu-tê hmûr.
Teeth, (*s.*) ha, (milk) ha-hlam, (permanent) ha-ṭha, ha-thar, (molars) ha-pui, (incisors) ha-hmai, (canine) ha ui ngho.
Telescope, (*s.*) dâr-chhem-thei, en-tlang.
Tell, (*v.*) hril, hrilh, zai.
Temper, (*v.*) (as steel) tuai.
Temperate, (*v.*) (to be) in-shûm, (*a.*) in-shûm-thei.
Tempered, (*a.*) (as steel) tuai-om, (bad tempered), vîn.
Temples, (*s.*) (the) ṭhial-pawn.
Tempt, (*v.*) ṭhlêm.
Ten, (*a.*) shom.
Tenacious of life, (*v.*) hnuk a fei.
Tend, (*v.*) chawm, en-kol, (fire) tuah, (with care) duat.
Tender, (*s.*) no.
Tendon, (*s.*) tha.
Tendril, (*s.*) ba.
Tent, (*s.*) puan in.
Tenth, (*a.*) shom-na.
Tepid, (*a.*) lum deo.
Terrible, (*a.*) hlao-om.
Terrify, (*v.*) râp.
Terrified, (*v.*) (to be) zâm.
Terrifying, (*a.*) râp-thlâk.
Test, (*v.*) fiah.
Testicle, (*s.*) til, til-mu.
Than, (*conj.*) ai, ai-a, ai-in, hnê*k*-in, hnê*k*-chuan, ai-chuan.
Thank, (*v.*) lawm thu shoi.
Thankful, (*a.*) lawm-na chang hria, lawm-na chang hre, lawm.
That, (*conj.*) lam, tih, (*pro.* and *a.*) chu, kha, chu-chu, chûng-chu, saw, saw-saw, kha-kha, (up there) khi khi, (down there) khu khu.
Thatch, (*v.*) di chih, chih, (*s.*) (thatching grass) di.
Thee, (*pro.*) che, (also to thee, from thee, and for thee).
Their, (*pro.*) an, an-ma-ni, an-ni.
Theirs, (*pro.*) an-ta, anmani-ta, an-ni-ta.
Them, (*pro.*) an-ma-ni, an-ni.
Themselves, (reflex prefix) in; an-mani-in, an-ni-in.
Then, (*conj.*) ani-lo-leh, chu-ti-chuan, chiat, tal, (*adv.*) leh.

Thence, (*adv.*) chuta-chu-an, chuta-ṭang-chuan.
There, (*adv.*) chu-ta-chuan, kha-ta, kha-ta-khân, saw-ta, saw-ta-sawn, saw-lama, (up) khi-ta, khi-ta-khian, (down) khu-ta, khu-ta-khuan.
Therefore, (*conj.*) chu-vâng-in, chu-ti-vâng-in, chu-ti-chuan.
These, (*a.* and *pro.*) chûng-chu, chûng-te-chu, chûng-ho-chu, hêng-hi, hêng-te-hi, hêng-ho-hi.
They, (*pro.*) an, an-ma-ni.
Thick, (*a.*) chhah, phok, khal, ban, (as bamboo) var-lo, (as liquid) hnang, (set, in build), sa-vok-len-lon.
Thief, (*s.*) mi ruk-ru, mi ruk-ru-hmang, kut kem nei, ruk-ru.
Thigh, (*s.*) mal-pui.
Thin, (*a.*) chêr, (thin out) (as paper, etc.) pan, (as liquid) chiao, (as bamboo) var, (*v.*) hrâm, suat.
Thine, (*pro.*) nangma-ta, nang-a-ta, i-ta.
Thing, (*s.*) thil, mi.
Things, (*s.*) bung-rua, sum, thuam thuam-hnaw, thom-hnaw.
Think, (*v.*) ring, ngai-tua, bei-shei, dawn, ril-ru*k*.
Thirst, (*v.*) tui hâl.
Thirsty, (*a.*) tui hâl.
Thirteen, (*a.*) shom leh pa-thum.
Thirty, (*a.*) shom thum.
This, (*pro.* and *a.*) he, he-hi, hei-hi, chu, chu-chu,
Thistle, (*s.*) buar.
Thorn, (*s.*) hlîng.
Thorough, (*a.*) ṭha-hnem-ngai.
Thoroughly, (*adv.*) kip-a-koi-in, phui-tak-in, ṭha-hnem-ngai-tak-in, ṭha.
Those, (*a.* and *pro.*) chûng-chu, chûng-te-chu, chûng-ho-chu, khâng-kha, sawng-saw, (down there) khûng-khu, (up there) khîng-khi.
Thou, (*pro.*) nang-ma, nang, i.
Though, (*conj.*) ma-shela.
Thoughtful, (*a.*) ngil nei.
Thousand, (*a.*) shang, (ten thousand) shîng, (one hundred thousand) nuai.
Thrash, (*v.*) vêl, vuak.
Thread, (*s.*) zai, (of screw) ṭial.
Threaten, (*v.*) thu tiam, tiam, vo, (by gesture) tin.
Three, (*s.*) pa-thum, thum.
Thresh, (*s.*) vua*k*.
Threshing-floor, (*s.*) fa-suar, hrui.
Thrice, (*adv.*) voi-thum.
Thrifty, (*a.*) kom-deo.

Thrive, (*v.*) ni-khua.
Throat, (*s.*) hrok, or.
Throng, (*v.*) nêk.
Throttle, (*v.*) rêk-hlum.
Through, (*adv.*) tlang.
Throughout, (*prep.*) vêl-a, vêl-in.
Throw, (*v.*) dêng, vom, (up) vorh, (away) paih, (down from the back, as a load of wood) keoh, (as spear, etc.) khawh, (down) thlâk, (into the air) vân vorh.
Thrust, (*v.*) (from one) hnar kîr, hnar-thla, (the arm in) zen.
Thumb, (*s.*) kut-zung pui.
Thunder, (*s.* and *v.*) khaw-pui ri, puvâna thlêng pui hnu' rîk.
Thunderbolt, (*s.*) ṭêk.
Thus, (*adv.*) chu-ti-chuan.
Thy, (*pro.*) nang-ma, nang-a, i.
Tick, (*s.*) sa-phi-hrik.
Tickle, (*v.*) dêk, ti-za, zar.
Tidy, (*v.*) chei, (*a.*) u-luk, in-chei.
Tie, (*v.*) tawn, chilh, (in a weaver's knot) suih, (in a knot) suih tung-tu-rut, (a knot in a single piece of string, etc.) suih bawk, (in a bow) suih-hlih, (together) suih-fin, (in corner of cloth) bawk, (hands behind back) hnung-khirh, (up, as animal) thlung.
Tier, (*s.*) chhawng.
Tiger, (*s.*) sa-kei, phai sa-pui.
Tight, (*a.*) (taut, stretched tightly) mar.
Till, (*conj.*) thleng-in, chin-a, hma lo chuan.
Time, (*s.*) (future) hun, (past) lai, (*v.*) (to be high time) ṭûl.
Timid, (*a.*) ṭi, ṭih.
Tin, (*s.*) rang-va.
Tinder, (*s.*) mei-bu, (box) mei-talh bawm.
Tingle, (as with cold) (*v.*) hit, hik.
Tip, (*s.*) hmawr, hmûr, tlâng.
Tipperah, (*s.*) Tui-kuk.
Tip up, (*v.*) bûk.
Tire, (*v. tr.*) hah-tîr, (*v.*) (to be tired) re-thei, hah, kham.
Tired of, (*v.*) ning.
Tiresome, (*a.*) hah-thlâk, nin-om.
Tiring, (*a.*) hah-thlâk.
To, (*prep.*) hnên-a.
Toad, (*s.*) u-ṭok, u-phâr.
Toadstool, (*s.*) pa-chhia.
Toast, (*v.*) hem-ro, (*s.*) chhang hem-ro.
Tobacco, (*s.*) dum-ei, vai-hlo.
Tobacco box, (*s.*) dum bawm, dum bûr.

To-day, (*s.*) voi-in, voi-in-a.
Toe, (*s.*) ke-zung, (big) ke-zung-pui, (second) ke-zung chal, (middle) ke-zung lai, (fourth) ke-zung u, ke-zung tê u, (little) ke-zung tê, (toes, collectively) ke-zung ṭang.
Together, (*adv.*) fin, khawm, ron, rual, in, (with) chop-in.
Toil, (*v.*) thawk rim.
Toilsomely, (*adv.*) rim.
Toilworn, (*a.*) rim.
Tomato, (*s.*) sâp-bok-bawn.
Tomb, (*s.*) thlân.
Tomorrow, nak-tûk-a, (tomorrow night) nak-tûk-zân-a.
Tone, (*s.*) zai.
Tongs, (*s.*) chai-che', (for lifting pot from fire) shuan-kual.
Tongue, (*s.*) lei, (of reed in musical instrument) zang.
To-night, (*s.*) nak-zân-a, zân-in-a.
Too, (*adv.*) law-tuk, lu-tuk, lua, lua-tuk, (as well) ve, kêp, fawm.
Tool, (*s.*) hriam.
Tooth, (*s.*) ha, ngho.
Toothache, (*s.*) ha na.
Top, (*s.*) chung, chhîp, (of tree, etc.) ler, (spinning) kaih-bu.
Torch, (*adv.*) mei-chher.
Torrent, (*s.*) (rainy season) tui-tai.
Tortoise, (*s.*) sa-tel, tel-khaw-mual, tel-pui, (small) tel-râng.
Torture, (*v.*) nghai-sha.
Toss, (*v.*) vorh, (from a sieve) chhok.
Touch, (*v.*) dek, khoih, dep, nghêng, kut thlâ*k*.
Touch-hole, (of gun), (*s.*) silai beng-kua.
Touchy, (*a.*) thin ram.
Tough, (*a.*) pheng.
Toward, (*prep.*) lam-a.
Towel, (*s.*) in-hrûk-na puan.
Town, (*s.*) khua, khaw.
Trace, (*v.*) chhui.
Track, (*v.*) chhui, hnu chhui, hnu zui.
Trade, (*v.*) sum dawng.
Trample, (*v.*) chîl, ra*p*-bet, tlawh-bet.
Trance, (*v.*) (to put into a) zêl.
Transform, (*v.*) lêt, chan*g*-tîr.
Transparent, (*a.*) dang-da, en-tlang-thei, fim.
Trap, (*s.*) thang, fal, khawng-pui, mang-khawng (wild fowl) bê-ai-thang, (tiger) fal-pui, (which spears) kar, (for fish) ngoi, (bear) vom-tlâk, (monkey) zawng tlâk, zawng-khâr-khep.

Tread, (*v.*) ra*p*, (out or upon) chîl.
Treasure, (*v.* and *s.*) ro.
Treat, (*v.*) (badly) chhe-tak-in ti, hneh-chhiat, hneh-sawh, (well) ṭha-tak-in ti, (with unfairness) nêk, (to anything) ti-tlai.
Tree, (*s.*) kûng, thing.
Tree fern, (*s.*) kok-pui.
Tremble, (*v.*) khûr.
Triangular, (*a.*) kil ṭhum.
Tribe, (*s.*) chi.
Tributary, (*a.*) (as village or state) chhiah.
Tribute, (*s.*) lei-ba, lei-ṭha, lei-tlang.
Trickle, (*v.*) pût, far.
Trigger, (*s.*) hme'per-na, silai hme'per-na.
Trip, (*v.*) (against) pal.
Trivet, (*s.*) lung-thu.
Trouble, (*v.*) ti-buai, chîl-bual.
Troubled, (*a.*) lung-kham.
Troublesome, (*a.*) hah-thlâk, hreh-om.
Trough, (*s.*) kuang, thlêng.
Trousers, (*s.*) ke-kor.
True, (*a.*) dik.
Truly, (*adv.*) ti-tak-in, ti-tak-a, tak, dik.
Trunk, (*s.*) (of tree) kûng, (of elephant, etc.) non.
Trust, (*v.*) ring.
Trustworthy, (*a.*) rin' thlâk, rin' om.
Truth, (*s.*) thu tak, thu dik.
Try, (*v.*) chhin, tin, hrâm.
Tub, (*s.*) tai-kuang.
Tube, (*s.*) dawn, dawt.
Tuber, (*s.*) bul-bâl, bul-bawk, (young tubers) nê.
Tuck in, (*v.*) ze*p*.
Tumbler, (*s.*) rial-no.
Tune, (*s.*) hla kai-zia
Turban, (*s.*) diâr.
Turbid, (*a.*) nu.
Turkey, (*s.*) sai-âr.
Turmeric, (*s.*) ai-eng.
Turn, (*v.*) her, hoi, (down, as lamp) herh-lut, (up, as lamp) herh chhuak, (over, upside down or round) let, ti-let, (up or inside out) lep, lep-she, (towards) chhon*g*, (to right or left when walking) pên*g*, (up) hlîm, (to take turns) in-chhawk, (over, as page of book, stone, etc.) phok, (*adv.*) (in turns) chhawk.
Turtle, (*s.*) tui-sa-tel.
Tusk, (*s.*) ngho.

Tweezers, (*s.*) chai-che'.
Twelve, (*s.*) shom leh pahnih.
Twenty, (*a.*) shom-hnih.
Twice, (*adv.*) voi-hnih.
Twig, (*s.*) ṭang.
Twilight, (*s.*) thim-hmul, thim-hlim.
Twin, (*a.*) phîr, (twins) fa phîr.
Twist, (*v.*) tei, ṭhuei-chhum, (round and round) zem, (round) herh, (as rope) hrual.
Twisted together, (*a.*) in-kherh, lek.
Two, (*a.*) pa-hnih, hnih, (two together) dûn.

U

Udder, (*s.*) hnu-tê.
Ugly, (*a.*) hmel chhia*t*, hmel chhe.
Ulcer, (*s.*) khoi-hli.
Umbrella, (*s.*) ni-hliap, (Lushai), shik-shîl.
Unable, (*v.*) thei lo, mawh.
Unadorned, (*a.*) mawl.
Unanimous, (*v.*) (to be) thu-rual, thu khat vua*k*.
Unanimously, (*adv.*) thu-rual-in, thu khat vua-in, tlâng.
Unavenged, (*v.*) (to be) phu tâp.
Uncle, (*s.*) (paternal) pa, (maternal aunt's husband) pa, (maternal) pu.
Unclean, (*a.*) thian lo, bol-hlawh, (because of a death) sam hram pu.
Uncock, (gun) (*v.*) khung.
Uncomfortable, (*a.*) nuam lo, hreh-om.
Uncommon, (*a.*) duai lo, duai-dîm lo, na-mên lo, vâng.
Uncover, (*v.*) phok, hong.
Undecided, (*a.*) ril-ru nei lo.
Undemonstrative, (*a.*) chut.
Under, (*prep.*) hnuai-a, hnuai lam-a.
Undergrowth, (*s.*) hnim.
Undermost, (*adv.*) hnuai ber.
Underneath, (*adv.* and *prep.*) thuai-a, hnuai-a.
Understand, (*v.*) hria*t*, hre.
Undeservedly, (*adv.*) mai-mai.
Undetermined, (*a.*) ril-ru nei lo.
Undo, (*v.*) phelh, ṭhiat.
Unearth, (*s.*) (by scratching) hai.
Unencumbered, (*a.*) (with children) hul-hâr.

Uneven, (*a.*) bum-bôh, rual-lo.
Unfasten, (*v.*) phelh.
Unfledged, (*a.*) hmul-kawng.
Ungrateful, (*adv.*) lawm-na chang hre lo.
Unfortunate, (*a.*) ham-chhia, re-thei, van-duai, dawng, dawng-thlawn.
Unharmed, (*a.*) him.
Unhealthy, (*a.*) bor-shom.
Uninhabited, (*a.*) ram, thla-ler.
Unintentionally, (*adv.*) palh.
Unite, (*v.*) zom.
Unkind, (*a.*) ngil nei lo.
Unlawful, (*a.*) thiang lo.
Unless, (*conj.*) lo chuan.
Unlike, (*a.*) ang lo.
Unload, (*v.*) (boat, etc.) thiar-chhuak.
Unlucky, (*a.*) vân-duai.
Unmarried, (*a.*) hnah-khat.
Unprincipled, (*a.*) ver-vêk, ver-ther.
Unreliable, (*a.*) hlem-hlê, awk-hrawl, dep-dê, ong-rop.
Unreservedly, (*adv.*) sheoh.
Unripe, (*a.*) hel, hmin lo.
Unroof, (*v.*) hawk.
Unruly, (*a.*) huang-tao.
Unselfish, (*a.*) ngil nei.
Unsheath, (*v.*) phoi.
Unskilful, (*a.*) them-thiam lo.
Unsubstantial, (*a.*) ong-rop.
Unsuccessful, (*a.*) hlawh-chham.
Unsuitable, (*a.*) phu lo.
Untempered, (*a.*) (as steel) hnual.
Unthankful, (*a.* and *v.*) lawm-na chang hre lo.
Untidy, (*a.*) in-chei lo, ṭom, in-thlah-dah, por.
Untie, (*v.*) phelh.
Until, (*conj.*) hma-lo-zong, hma-lo-chuan.
Untrue, (*a.*) dawt, dik lo.
Untrustworthy, (*a.*) dep-dê, hlem-hlê.
Unwell, (*a.*) dam lo, hri-tlâng (also to be unwell).
Up, (*adv.*) chho, kâng, han, (to) chin-a, thleng-in, (there) khi-ta, khi-ta-khian.
Upbraid, (*v.*) hao.
Uphill, (*adv.* and *a.*) chho.
Upon, (*prep.*) a, chung-a.
Upper, (*a.*) chung-nung.

Uppermost, (*a.*) chung-nung ber.
Upright, (*a.*) ding, tung, ding ngîl.
Upset, (*v.*) ti-bua.
Upside down, (*v.*) (to turn) let, (*a.*) le*t*-lin*g*.
Unstop, (*v.*) horh.
Upstream, (*adv.*) lui hnâr lama.
Urge, (*v.*) fuih.
Urinate, (*v.*) zung.
Urine, (*s.*) zun, zun-tui, (*a.*) (stoppage of) zun in, zun im.
Unruly, (*a.*) nghal.
Us, (*pro.*) mi*n* (also 'for us' and 'to us').
Use, (*v.*) hman*g*, chhor, (*s.*) châk-khai, (up) shên*g*.
Used to, (*v.*) (to be) nêl, ṭhang.
Used up, hêk.
Useful, (*a.*) hman*g*-tlâk, hman-rua, hman-zia, ṭang-kai, kong awh, ṭha-hnem, tlâk-tlai.
Useless, (*a.*) hman*g*-tlâk lo, hnai-shai lo.
Uselessly, (*adv.*) chuang-in, mai-mai, thlawn, a thlawn-in.
Usually, (*adv.*) fo.
Utensil, (*s.*) bêl.
Uvula, (*s.*) dang-mawn.

V

Vaccinate, (*v.*) bân zai.
Vagabond, (*s.*) vâk-vai.
Vain, (in) a thlawn-in, thlawn.
Valiant, (*a.*) huai, huai-shen.
Valley, (*s.*) lui-dung, (small) kor, kor-dung.
Valuable, (*a.*) hlu.
Value, (*s.*) man.
Vanish, (*v.*) ral.
Vapour, (*s.*) hu.
Variegated, (*a.*) zia.
Vase, (*s.*) no.
Vast, (*a.*) zao, lian-pui.
Vault, (*s.*) tian'hrâng thlân.
Vegetable, (*s.*) thlai.
Vehemently, (*adv.*) chiam, vak, nek.
Vein, (*s.*) tha-zâm.
Venom, (*s.*) tûr.
Venomous, (*a.*) tûr a ṭha, tûr nei.
Verandah, (*s.*) sum-hmun, hul-hliap, (enclosed back verandah) bah-zâr.
Verdict, (*v.*) (to give) thu ti-tlu.

Verse, (*s.*) châng.
Vertical, (*a.*) bir.
Vertically, (*adv.*) bir.
Very, (*adv.*) êm, êm êm, tak, viao, zet, ber, hle, mang.
Vessel, (*s.*) bawm.
Vest (sleeveless), (*s.*) kor bân bul.
Vex, (*v.*) ti lung-ni lo, ti lung-oi lo.
Vexed, (*a.*) lung-ni lo, lung-oi lo.
Vibrate, (*v.*) khûr.
Vicinity, (*s.*) vêng.
Vicious, (*a.*) beng-tla-lo, nun'-chhia, rawng.
Victorious, (*a.*) huai.
View, (*v.*) thlîr.
Vie with, (*v.*) el.
Village, (*s.*) khua, khaw, vêng, (a small outlying or tributary village) khaw-per, khua-per.
Violence, (without) (*adv.*) tlâng.
Violently, (*adv.*) sok, vak.
Violin, (*s.*) ṭing-ṭang.
Virgin, (*s.*) nu-la.
Virgin forest, (*s.*) ngaw.
Visible, (to be) lan*g*.
Vision, (*s.*) thlarao in-lâr.
Visit, (*v.*) kan, tlawh, zin.
Voice, (*s.*) aw, aw-ka, thawm.
Volley, (to fire) ron, (when returning from a hunt) tlâng-tlir.
Vomit, (*v.*) lua*k*.
Vulture, (*s.*) mu-lu-kolh, mu-beng-nei.
Vulva, (*s.*) chhu.

W

Wad, (*s.*) silai mu hnawh.
Wade, (*v.*) dai.
Wag, (*v.*) hêm.
Wagtail, (*s.*) (bird) lai-lên.
Wages, (*v.*) hlawh, man, (to receive as wages) hlawh.
Wail, (*v.*) ṭa*p*.
Waist, (*s.*) tai.
Waistband, (*s.*) kawng-chilh, kawng-fên.
Waistcoat, (*s.*) kor bân bul.
Wait, (*v.*) nghâk, lo-nghâk, om, khua hâr, ngai, (about) thep.
Wake, (*v.*) meng, harh, (to hold a wake) mi-thi râl.
Waken, (*v. t.*) kai-tho, kai-harh, kai-thawh, ṭhang-harh, ti-harh.

Wale, (*s.*) vual.
Walk, (*v.*) kal, ke-in kal, lên*g*, vâk, (on hands) âr kal, let-ling kal, (backwards) hnung tolh, (on hands and feet with stomach upwards), ai-fiar kal, (along) zawh.
Wall, (*s.*) bang.
Wallow, (*v.*) in-bual, (*s.*) sa-bual.
Wall-plate, (*s.*) liang.
Walnut, (tree) hnûm, khaw-kherh, (nut) hnûm rah, khaw-kherh rah.
Wander, (*v.*) vâk, vâk-vai.
Wanderer, (*s.*) vâk-vai.
Want, (*v.*) duh, nuam, tum, châk, ît, ngiat.
War, (*v.*) râl.
Warm, (*v.*) ti-lum, (one's self), ai, (*a.*) lum.
Warp, (*s.*) puan-tung, (*v.*) châng, er.
Warrior, (*s.*) râl, râl-hrât.
Wary, (*a.* and *v.*) fîm-khur, tîm.
Wash, (*v.*) (face), phih, (clothes) shu*k*, (hands, plates, etc.), sil, (by pouring water over) tlên*g*.
Wasp, (*s.*) khoi-dâng.
Waste, (*v. t.*) ti-hek, (time) ti-khaw-tlai, (away, as with illness) rawp.
Watch, (*v.*) vên*g*, en-thla, ngai-ven', (for) châng, (stealthily) veh, (*s.*) (timepiece) sana, sana-lâm-thei.
Watcher, (*s.*) vêng-tu.
Water, (*s.*) tui, (*v.*) (plants, etc.) leih, tui leih.
Water bottle, (*s.*) tui-thawl.
Waterfall, (*s.*) tui-khawh-thla, tui-thlâr.
Water-newt, (*s.*) tui-pui tang-kawng.
Water plants and weeds, (*s.*) tui hnah.
Waterproof, (*s.*) ṭhel-ret kor.
Watershed, (*s.*) lui in-khan.
Water spider, (*s.*) tui-hna shiam-tu.
Water supply, (*s.*) tui-tlân.
Watertight, (*a.*) hul.
Watery, (*a.*) chiao.
Wave, (*v.*) vai, hêm, nghîng, (about) lên, (*s.*) tui fawn.
Wax, (bees') khoi-hnun.
Waxy, (*a.*) (as potato) khal.
Way, (*s.*) dân, lam, kong, (all the way to) thleng-in, thleng-thleng-in, (to get out of way) dang om, dang, (to get or be in the way) dîp, (*a.*) (in the way) hnok-sak, (*v.*) hnok, (*adv.*) (on the way) kal pah-in, (to block up way or be in the way) kong awh.
Waylay, (*v.*) châng.

We, (*pro.*) kei-ma-ni, kei-ni, kan.
Weak, (*a.*) chak-lo, (as beer) nem, thlum a pawn.
Wealthy, (*a.*) tangka ngah.
Weapon, (*s.*) hriam.
Wear, (*v.*) (loin cloth) kaih, (as hat) khum, (round neck) or, (as cloth, etc.) shin, silh, (in hair) ton, (in ear) beh, (boots, ring, etc.) bun.
Weary, (*a.*) hah.
Weather, (*s.*) khua, khaw.
Weave, (*v.*) tah.
Weaving machine, (*s.*) them-bu, (with partly woven cloth) puan-bu.
Wedge, (*s.*) kap-na, hêm, (*v.*) (to split with) hêm, kap.
Weed, (*s.*) hlo, (*v.*) thloh.
Week, (*s.*) ni sari.
Weep, (*v.*) ṭa*p*, (over or about) ṭa'chhan, (cause of weeping) ṭa' chhan.
Weigh, (*v.*) bûk, khîn.
Weir, (*s.*) (for fishing) sangha dan'na, tui-hna paih-na.
Welcome, (*v.*) lawm.
Well, (*s.*) tui khur, tui-chhun-chhuah, (*a.*) dam, (*adv.*) ṭha, ṭha hnem-ngai tak-in.
Well-to-do, (*a.*) ṭha.
West, (*s.*) khaw-thlang, thlang, thlang-lam.
Westward, thlang-lam-a.
Wet, (*a.*) huh, (*v.*) nan, ti-huh.
What, (*pro.*) eng-nge ? eng-maw ? eng-nga ? eng-tin-nge ?
Whatever, (*pro.*) a-piang, eng-pawh-apiang, na-zong, na-rân.
Wheedle, (*v.*) hak, pâk.
Wheel, (*s.*) taw-lai-lir.
When, (*conj.*) lai-khân, lai-khân-in, ve-leh, lai-a, lai-in, hun-a, hun-in, nâk-a-lai-in, pawh-in, chuan, khân, khân-in, tik-a, chuan-in, hun-chuan, hun-chuan-in, (*adv.*) eng-ti-ka-nge ? eng-tik-a ?
Whence, (*adv.*) khoi-a-nge ? khoi-a-ta-nge ? khoi-a-mi-nge ? khoi-a-lama-nge ? khoi-a-lama-ta-nge ? na-chin.
Whenever, (*adv.*) a-piang-in, a-piang-a, na-zong-in na-rân-in.
Where, (*adv.*) khoi-a-nge ? khaw-nge ? khoi-a ? khoi-nge ? na-chin.
Whereabouts, (*s.*) om-na chin.
Wherefore, (*adv.*) eng-a-nge ? eng-a-ti-nge ? eng-a-tân-nge ?
Wherever, (*adv.*) khoi-a-pawh...na-a-piang-a, khoi-lama-pawh... na-apiang-a, na-apiang-a, na-zong-in, na-rân-in.
Whether, (*conj.*) emaw, emaw chu. (Also whether or not.)
Whetstone, (*s.*) lung-tât.

Which, (*pro.*) khoi-i-nge ? a-eng-ber-nge ? a-eng-nge ? a-zeng-nge? kha, chu.
While, (*conj.*) chung-in, hlân-in.
Whine, (*v.*) u.
Whirlwind, (*s.*) ṭhawng-a-lei-vir.
Whisper, (*v.*) be-ru, phun-ru.
Whistle, (*v.*) fai-fûk, hui, (with knuckles) chang tum, (through teeth) sai-shîk.
White, (*a.*) vâr, ngo, (as hair) ṭuak.
White-ant, (*s.*) tlung-pi, lei-ṭha, lei-kha, (winged) phing-phi-hlîp, (white-ant mound) son-tlung.
Who, (*pro.*) chu, kha, tu ? tu-nge ?
Whoever, (*pro.*) a-piang, tu-pawh-a-piang, na-zong, na-rân.
Whole, (*a.*) pum, pum-hlûm.
Whom, (*pro.*) tu-nge ? (Also ' to whom ' ?)
Whomever, (*pro.*) a-piang, na-rân, na-zong.
Whooping-cough, (*s.*) khuh-hîp.
Whose, (*pro.*) tu...nge ? tu-ta-nge ? tu-ta.
Why, (*adv.*) eng-a-nge ? eng-a-ti-nge ? eng-a-tân-nge ?
Wicked, (*a.*) sual.
Wide, (*a.*) vâng, zao.
Widow, (*s.*) hmei-thai, (young) hring-kîr, leng-leh, nu-thloi.
Widower, (*s.*) pa-rol, (young) leng-leh.
Width, (*s.*) vâng.
Wife, (*s.*) nu-pui.
Wilderness, (*s.*) thla-ler, thla-ler ram.
Willing, (*v.*) tiam, (*adv.*) (willingly) tlâng.
Willow, (*s.*) tui-pui-shut-hlah, tui-pui-shul-hlah.
Wilt, (*v.*) thîm, uai, vuai.
Win, (*v.*) hneh.
Wind, (*v.*) (round and round) zem, vir-vêt, (cotton) la kaih.
Wind, (*s.*) thli.
Winder, (*s.*) (cotton) la kaih-na.
Winding, (*a.*) kual.
Window, (*s.*) tuk-verh.
Windpipe, (*s.*) hrok-hrawl.
Wind-tie, (*s.*) kaih-kulh, kol-tuk. (Also to secure a roof by wind-ties.)
Wing, (*s.*) thla.
Wink, (*v.*) mit shiai, mit khing shiai.
Winnow, (*v.*) zâ*p*, thli*t*-fai.
Winnowing fan, (*s.*) shi-shêp.
Winter, (*s.*) thla-shik.
Wipe, (*v.*) hrû*k*.

Wire, (*s.*) thîr hrui, (thin brass) dar-zai.
Wise, (*a.*) fing, beng-vâr, rem-hriat.
Wisely, (*adv.*) rem hre tak-in.
Wish, (*v.*) duh, nuam, tum, lung-kham, ngiat, (*s.*) thu thu, duh-zawng.
Witch, (*s.*) doi thiam.
Witchcraft, (*s.*) doi.
With, (*prep.*) hnên-a, lak-a, nên, zîng-a, chung-a, in.
Withal, (*adv.*) vei-nên.
Wither, (*v.*) thîm, uai, vuai, rawp.
Within, (*prep.*) chhûng-a.
Without, (*prep.*) pawna, lo-vin.
Withstand, (*v.*) do-dâl.
Witness, (*s.*) hre-tu, thu-hre-tu.
Wizard, (*s.*) doi thiam.
Wizened, (*a.*) zûr.
Woman, (*s.*) hmei-chhia.
Womb, (*s.*) chhûl.
Wonder, (*v.*) mak ti.
Wonderful, (*a.*) mak.
Wood, (*s.*) thing, (wooden) thing.
Wood-louse, (*s.*) pu-vân-a sai-hlum.
Woodpecker, (*s.*) thloh, tuk-lo, va-lîm-chho.
Wood-pigeon, (*s.*) va-hûi, ram-pârva.
Wood-sorrel, (*s.*) shiak-thûr, thûr-shiak.
Woof, (*s.*) puan phei.
Wool, (*s.*) be-râm hmul, hmul, kawl-la.
Word, (*s.*) thu.
Work, (*s.*) hna, hna-thaw*k*, thil ti, (*v.*) thaw*k*, ti, chê*t*, hna thaw*k*, phe phe, (for wages) hlawh fa, hlawh, (at) nghai-sha, soi-sha, (hard) thawk rim, (special or allotted work) tum, (to do the same) tum.
Workman, (*s.*) be-kar, hna-thawk, hna-thawk-tu.
Works, (*s.*) thil ti, chêt-zia.
World, (*s.*) khaw-vêl, lei.
Worm, (*s.*) chang-pât.
Worms (*s.*) (disease), hût, rûl-hût, (*v.*) (to have worms) hût pai, rûl-hût pai.
Wormwood, (*s.*) sai.
Worried, (*a*.) lung-kham, mang-an*g*.
Worry, (*v. t.*) ti-buai, ti-mang-ang.
Worse, (*a.*) ṭha lo zawk, chhe zawk, (*adv.*) ṭha lo deo, chhe deo.
Worship, (*v.*) biak.
Worth, (*v.*) (to be) hu.

Worthless, (*a.*) hnai-shai-lo, engma ṭang-kai lo.
Worthy, (*a.*) rual, tlâk, tui.
Wound, (*v.*) hliam, ti-sil, ti-pem, (*s.*) pân, (fresh) pem.
Wounded, (*a.*) in-hliam, pem, sil.
Wraith, (*s.*) hmui-thla.
Wrap, (*v.*) fûn, (round) tuam.
Wrapper, (*s.*) fûn-na.
Wrench, (*v.*) ṭhuei-chhum.
Wrestle, (*v.*) in-buan.
Wretched, (*a.*) hreh-om.
Wriggle, (*v. t.*) kar, (*int.*) tâl.
Wring, (*v.*) sawr.
Wrinkle, (*v.*) chuar, vuai, zûr.
Wrist, (*s.*) bân-rêk.
Write, (*v.*) ziak.
Wrong, (*a.*) dik lo, sual, thiang lo.
Wrong way about, (*a.* and *adv.*) let-ling.

X

Nil.

Y

Yam, (*s.*) ba-hra.
Yard, (*s.*) huang, huang-chhûng.
Yarn, (*s.*) la, (red) shen-te-lêk, ṭing shen, (blue) ṭing, ṭing dum.
Year, (*s.*) kum, (this) kumin-a, (next) nak-kum-a, (last) ni-kum-a.
Yearly, (*adv.*) kum-tin.
Yearn, (*v.*) ngai, duh, châk.
Yeast, (*s.*) chol, doi-dim.
Yellow, (*a.*) eng, (as fruit) tai.
Yelp, (*v.*) be-leoh.
Yes, (*adv.*) aw, a-ni, ni-e, ani-e.
Yesterday, ni-min-a.
Yet, (*adv.*) la, tûn-thleng-in, (*conj.*) ni-ma-shela, shi, tûna-pawh, tûn-thleng-pawh-in.
Yoke, (*s.*) nghawng-kol.
Yolk, (*s.*) tui chhûng mu.
You, (*pro.*) nang-ma-ni, nang-ni, in, (*obj.*) che u. (Also from you, for you, and to you.)

Young, (*a.*) naopang, shên, no, rol-thar, (*s.*) (of animals, birds, etc.) no.
Your, (*pro.*) nang-ma-ni, nang-ni, in.
Yours, (*pro.*) nangmani-ta, nangni-ta, in-ta.
Youth, (*a.*) rol-thar, tlang-vâl.

Z

Zealous, (*a.*) ṭha-hnem-ngai.
Zealously, (*adv.*) tha-hnem-ngai-tak-in.
Zenith, (*s.*) vân lai zawl.
Zig-zag, (*a.*) ki-kiao.
Zinc, (*s.*) rang-va tui thei.
Zinnia, (*s.*) vai der-ken.